Stadium City

STUDIES IN SPORTS MEDIA

Edited by Victoria E. Johnson and Travis Vogan

For a list of books in the series, please see our website at www.press.uillinois.edu.

Stadium City

Sports and Media Infrastructure in the United States

HELEN MORGAN PARMETT

© 2025 by the Board of Trustees
of the University of Illinois
All rights reserved
1 2 3 4 5 C P 5 4 3 2 1
♾ This book is printed on acid-free paper.

Cataloging data available from the Library of Congress
LCCN 2025008193
ISBN 978-0-252-04673-5 (cloth : alk.)
ISBN 978-0-252-08883-4 (paper : alk.)
ISBN 978-0-252-04825-8 (ebook)

For Nakobe and Justin

Contents

Acknowledgments   ix

Introduction   1

PART I   ATLANTA: MEDIATIZATION, GOVERNANCE, AND CITIZENSHIP

1. Going Major League, Going Global   27
2. Governing the Fan-Advocate-Citizen in the Interactive Stadium   57
3. Entrepreneurialism through Abandonment: The Making of a Stadium District   85

PART II   SEATTLE: PLACE-IDENTITY AND BRANDING

4. Boosting the Northwest   103
5. Place-Branding the Local   131

PART III   MINNEAPOLIS: STADIUMS AS WHITE SPACE

6. White Flight: To the Suburbs and Downtown Again   165
7. Surveillance and the Datafied Stadium   190

Conclusion 221

Notes 235

Index 285

Acknowledgments

First and foremost, I want to acknowledge how central Kate Ranachan has been to this project. Without her, this book would never have been written. So many of the insights within can be attributed to Kate's unbelievably vast knowledge of sporting culture and fandom. Much of the work here originated as conference presentations and short articles we collectively conceived and wrote, and her spirit remains in the text here. Though we didn't make it to the finish line together, I remain eternally grateful for her contributions to this book, for how I think about sports, and, more importantly, for her friendship.

I am also indebted to the insights provided by the stakeholders I interviewed for this book from Mercedes-Benz Stadium, the Minnesota Twins, the Twins Community Fund, the Pohlad Foundation, Historic South Downtown, the SoDo Business Improvement Area, the Pioneer Square Business Improvement Association, the Pioneer Square Residents Council, NuLoop Partners, the Seattle Office of Planning and Community Development, the Washington State Ballpark Public Facilities District, and the Minnesota Ballpark Authority. Although much of this book is critical of the role of stadiums in our cities, I remain struck by the genuine commitment and concern these stakeholders displayed in our interviews, including those whose role is to support the stadium, for their effects on neighborhoods and communities. I am grateful for how they showed me that the sportification of place is not easily parsed out into a simplistic analysis of power between dominant elites and the dominated but, rather, is site-specific, complicated, and complex as stakeholders negotiate the dynamic hyper- and intra-local cultural and spatial politics within their cities.

The book is enriched as well by the archival materials provided by the Kenan Research Center at the Atlanta History Center, Atlanta University Center Robert W. Woodruff Library, King County Archives, Seattle Municipal Archives, Hennepin County Library, and the Gale Family Library at the Minnesota Historical Society. I'm grateful to their archivists for their thoughtful guidance and assistance in gathering the primary materials to support my research. Thanks also go to Routledge and the Taylor & Francis group for their permission to publish small and revised portions of previously published material, which appears in the introduction, chapters 2 and 7, and the conclusion. This material was originally published as Helen Morgan Parmett, "The Sportification of Place: Governance, Mediatization, and Place-Branding through the Stadium," in *The Routledge Companion to Media and the City*, ed. Erica Stein, Germaine R. Halegoua, and Brendan Kredell (London: Routledge, 2023), and Helen Morgan Parmett, "'Keep It Off the Field': The Mediatized Sports Stadium as White Space," in *White Supremacy and the American Media*, ed. Sarah D. Nilsen and Sarah E. Turner, Routledge Studies in Media, Communication and Politics (New York: Routledge, 2022).

Research for this book was supported by a Small Grant provided by the Dean's Office in the College of Arts and Sciences and a subvention grant from the Humanities Center at the University of Vermont, and I am thankful for their support in helping me to complete site visit research and offset the costs of publication. My colleagues and students in Film and TV Studies; English; and Gender, Sexuality, and Women's Studies at the University of Vermont have provided a supportive academic home for my scholarly research. I am especially thankful to Katie Gough—her friendship and commiseration are everything. Sarah Nilsen and Sarah Turner, whose edited collection, *White Supremacy and the American Media*, helped me rethink this project at a time when I thought I might abandon it, are to be thanked as well. The debaters and coaches of the Lawrence Debate Union keep my thinking sharp and are endlessly supportive. Mia Fischer was central to helping me get to the finish line and provided helpful comments and critique along the way. Thanks also go to the academic community provided by the SCMS Urbanism, Geography, and Architecture Scholarly Interest Group. Special thanks go to my writing group members from the SIG—Noelle Griffis, İpek Azime Çelik Rappas, Elizabeth Patton, Anna Sborgi, and Erica Stein. Your work inspires me, and your comments and support throughout the various iterations of this book have been invaluable. I'm indebted as well to the University of Illinois Studies in Sports Media editors, Vicky Johnson and Travis

Vogan, along with Danny Nasset and the team at Illinois and the anonymous reviewers of the book proposal and manuscript. They each provided central questions, critiques, and suggestions that have made this a much better book.

Finally, thank you to all the people who kept pushing me to complete this project. My grandparents, Walter J. and Jane Hebert, never gave up on me, continually asking how the project was coming along with genuine love and belief in me that I could write something meaningful. I never would have finished without Uncle Lew texting me throughout my sabbatical to ask if I'd been writing. And most of all, I am grateful beyond words for Justin and Nakobe for their love, patience, and belief in me. You are my forever favorites, and this book is for you.

Introduction

I was living in Minnesota's Twin Cities in 2010 when Target Field, home of the city's Major League Baseball (MLB) team, the Minnesota Twins, opened in the city of Minneapolis to much fanfare. There was palpable excitement for the return of outdoor baseball. Freed from the shackles of the multipurpose monstrosity that was the Hubert H. Humphrey Metrodome (commonly referred to as the Metrodome), the Twins finally found a place to call "home." Having grown up in New England, the excitement about the "Minnesotaness" of the stadium did not necessarily resonate. Yet it was clear the Twin Cities had, even before the first pitch, developed an affective bond with this new stadium. Built in the retro-modern tradition of the Baltimore Orioles' Camden Yards, opened in 1992, Target Field evokes nostalgia in its design (its footprint and size are roughly the same as Fenway Park) and a sense of localism in its construction (using limestone from northern Minnesota) along with a cosmopolitan sensibility via its advanced integration of media and digital technology. Given the success of Target Field, it was no surprise that the Minnesota Vikings, the city's National Football League (NFL) team, soon demanded a new stadium of their own.

Target Field embodies a new mood in stadium building, stitching stadiums to their unique environment by making them both a city destination *and* a neighborhood fixture. The stadium is positioned as both spectacular and ordinary.[1] Today's stadiums need to be spectacular enough to draw people into urban neighborhoods. They are no longer simply about the building itself, and, indeed, perhaps they never were. Rather, stadiums are involved in remaking the city as a whole, and even the people, as well as the neighborhoods around the stadium, projecting a spectacular image of a city brand. Yet stadiums also need to be ordinary enough to become part of the fabric of the neighborhood and a community gathering place.

Stadiums thus play an important role in which a sense of city and regional identity is established and struggled over through the production of affective fan experiences both inside and outside the stadium. The threat of teams leaving cities is often met with horror and generous state and local incentives to keep teams "at home." As a result, at the time of this writing, the last thirty years has seen an intensive period of stadium building in the United States. Since 1992, twenty-one Major League Baseball teams and twenty-seven National Football League teams built new stadiums. It is no coincidence that this period coincides with an increasingly competitive and expansive sports media market. In an uncertain media environment, sports represents (at least for the time being) a relatively safe media investment. While media companies are still investing heavily in sports, teams themselves are creating their own media by entering into ownership agreements with media or telecommunication companies (e.g., Atlanta Braves and Comcast), developing their own media entities (e.g., New York Yankees' YES network), and going all-in on digital media capabilities.[2]

The stadium is a central component of these broader media strategies. Whether it's the increased incorporation of media elements into the stadium itself (e.g., screens and fiber optics), the development and promotion of ancillary services (e.g., restaurants and bars in the area), or the simple fact that the stadium makes televising/screening the game possible, stadiums are sites of media production. The stadium is a central material manifestation of a team's, and often a city's, brand identity. It is the mediated version of the stadium (and the fans within it) broadcast and streamed around the world, announcing its team, city, and even the neighborhood, to a national and, at times, global audience. Screens within the stadium are ubiquitous, ensuring fans do not risk missing the action while they are enjoying their consumptive practices. Jumbotrons have grown exponentially, promising fans that their view of the game will not be compromised by their decision to go to the stadium. Cameras panning the crowd might pick up a fan enthusiastically waving to their friends and family. Thus, the stadium has embraced the one value it has over television—the social capital that comes from "being there"; the idea of physical proximity to games as they unfold still holds more cachet than any claim to merely watching the game on television.[3] Today, stadiums are both media production studios and key components of a broader entertainment "experience economy."[4]

Access to social media through the smart phone heightens this desire to demonstrate our attendance, our ability to "be there." We are no longer beholden to broadcast media, hoping their camera might catch a glimpse of us; instead, we can produce our own media content for our social networks. These technologies both increase and alter the stadium's importance as a site of media production. David Rowe maintains that sport's networked age is marked by fan performativity, where fans feel an imperative not just to be there but "to share."[5] They perform for the television and share their experiences with those watching at home in real time through participatory and interactive social media. Stadiums and the teams they house thus no longer invite fans to simply watch the game, but, rather, through the proliferation of screens and increased emphasis on concessions, ancillary services, and social media, fans are enjoined to *experience* and *share* in the overall production of the game.[6]

It is not just the stadium and team owners who aim to capitalize on this experience; city governments collaborate to broaden that experience to include the wider city as well, often in exchange for public financing and generous tax incentives. All the while, the integration of media technology and mediated practices into the stadium guarantees the frenzy of new stadium building, and, likely, the demand for more public expenditures, will continue ad infinitum, as technological and cultural shifts inevitably mean the newest, most mediated, and technologically advanced stadiums will be out of date in the next twenty to thirty years. Perhaps that is why it seems like such an achievement, and oddity, to US Americans when European stadiums mark their one-hundred-year anniversaries.[7]

This coming together of sporting industries, media culture, stadiums, and urban governance constitutes what I call the *sportification of place*. Appropriating "sportification" from sports sociology, *Stadium City* proposes that sport, as a convergent media industry *and* a social and cultural practice, produces and governs urban space in and through the stadium. By producing and drawing on affective connections between teams and place via stadium location siting, architecture, design, and mediatization, the "sportification of place" describes the unique ways in which the concomitant forces of sport, media, and the stadium are put to work to constitute new urban landscapes and forms of governing citizenship.

Sportification consists of "processes distinctive to the development, modernisation, production, reproduction and consumption of sport [that] have now been reappropriated across a wider spectrum of social institutions."[8] Sportification conceptualizes how non-sporting practices are transformed through the "performative, interpretive and superficial elements of sporting phenomenon."[9]

Sportification is also tied to a longer history of what Norbert Elias and Eric Dunning refer to as "sportization," a term they use to describe how English pastimes were transformed into modern sport through codification and formalization.[10] Beginning in the seventeenth and eighteenth centuries, rural pastimes, such as cricket, boxing, and fox hunting, were made into more formal and organized activities, defined by a particular set of rules and governing bodies. Sportization stemmed from modern industrialization and urbanization as power shifted from rural landowners to urban centers. Turning rural activities into formalized sport was part of a civilizing mission, where sport served as a vector for producing and governing liberal forms of citizenship. Likewise, sport became a way of expressing national identity and spreading British imperialism.[11]

Sportification stems from this history of sportization, describing not only how activities come to be defined as sport, but also how the logic of sport constitutes sociality in a more everyday sense. Ivo Jirásek and Geoffrey Kohe write, "Such theatrification is characterised . . . by overt symbolism in social interaction, a quest for sensationalism and dramatics in the mediated performances of everyday life, and, seemingly insatiable cravings by the public for transcendental, hyper-realistic, affective experiences in and through forms of popular culture."[12] In this sense, sport plays a constitutive role in governing contemporary social life, as it constructs a biopolitical imperative to maintain the "health" and "life" of the populous (through its discourses and practices of healthy bodies) as well as in a broader sense of defining the kinds of entrepreneurial and self-reliant individualism on which contemporary, neoliberal society depends.

Sportification is inextricably intertwined with mediatization.[13] The mediatization of sport and its imbrication as a key part of visual and popular culture plays a significant role in the sportification of culture more generally, where sport is a nexus by which bodies are produced and governed. Jirásek and Kohe suggest:

> Through an emphasis on visual culture and spectatorship, media sport, popular culture and postmodernity . . . sportification has . . . consolidated a close relationship between sport, leisure and health practices and the social world; and in particular, popularised and populated meanings we ascribe to active and inactive bodies (in and beyond sporting contexts). The quest within sportification for ever-increasing heights of theatricality has . . . continued to blur the lines . . . regarding athletes' private bodies and public ownership, sporting "reality" and mediated sport experiences, and embodiment and social symbolism.[14]

The ongoing convergence of sports teams, media culture and practices, and the transformation of sports leagues into media industries themselves further enables the connection between mediatization and sportification as teams increasingly produce and distribute their own media content or are owned by or have an ownership stake in larger media conglomerates. These partnerships are imagined to help both sports teams and legacy media industries (who have long been dependent on sports) to capitalize on the interactive and participatory fan practices indicative of the social media era.

These convergences manifest in the built environment and landscape of the stadium. Stadiums are sites of enacting experiences for both those within and outside the stadium. In these endeavors, sports franchises and cities increasingly blur the lines between stadium, team, city, and fan. The stadiums are indicative of media convergence. Convergence culture refers to "the flow of content across multiple media platforms, the cooperation between multiple media industries, and the migratory behavior of media audiences."[15] Stadiums are key parts of this synergistic flow, especially within the television industry, as live sports constitute a significant portion of legacy TV revenue. As these companies try to branch out from analog media to ensure their competitiveness in the digital era, sport—as an experience in place that can be both lived (through attending the game or mediated synchronous viewing) and transcend that liveness (through digital interactivity)—has been a central site for enacting these strategic priorities. These logics are built into the very stadium itself, not only to broadcast and stream events on television, satellite, or online but also to integrate lived and online lives into a combined stadium and urban "experience" that folds retail, leisure, residential, and commercial development together. The stadium aims to capitalize on the interactive participation of players and fans alike—building online interactivity into the stadium, the game, and the experience to create lifeworlds and communities—as well as to extend that participation outside the stadium into the city. The convergence of media and sport in and through the stadium is thus imagined to both draw on and produce newly engaged and interactive fans and community members. So, too, the mediatization of the stadium enables the constant monitoring and datafication of stadium practices and the surrounding city.

Despite research on sportification extending the cultural logic of sport into a variety of domains, surprisingly little research takes up how the convergence of sport and media fuels the production of space and place. By bringing sportification to bear on place, this book contends that an ontology of mediasport—as performative and interpretive, mediated and participatory—pervades the stadium and its architecture, design, and practices in ways that produce and govern urban space and place. I focus particularly on baseball and football stadiums in the United States.

Though sportification of place resonates on a global scale, it has unique ties and dimensions specific to the US context. Undoubtedly, the increasing mediatization of sports venues across the world implicates, and is implicated by, the spaces and places in which they operate. However, I've chosen to focus on the US context here because of the unique qualities of US sporting, urban, and media cultures. The tension between the public interest and profit orientation of corporate media (and how this plays out in governing and citizenship practices) creates a unique dynamic in the United States. In many other national settings, such as a number of European countries, planning, legislative, and institutional sporting frameworks are arguably more aligned with public service media and regulated state planning processes, at least historically. Other sporting cultures, such as those emerging in the Middle East, similarly derive from quite different cultural contexts, thus rendering the infrastructural role and meaning of sports stadiums distinct in their own nation-building and globalization projects, often in ways that play out long-standing tensions between East and West. Thus, while all national cultures debatably construct infrastructural and affective relationships among sports teams, venues, and their places, the particular cultural context in which those relationships emerge matter.

Further, while basketball, hockey, tennis, and other sports are popular in the United States, baseball and US American football remain the two most popular sports nationally. They each play a significant role in the US cultural imaginary. Although baseball helped constitute a national identity in a critical period when the nation's demographics were changing because of the influx of immigrants during industrialization, football is now America's favorite pastime, as the sport most associated with ideals of contemporary US citizenship.[16] The NFL's ties to the military, forged after the 9/11 attacks on the World Trade Center in New York City, further solidify its role in nation building.[17] Although football outstrips baseball in terms of sheer numbers of fans, baseball remains important to US culture, particularly in terms of its evocation of nostalgia for a less complicated, "better" America. *Stadium City* thus focuses on baseball and football stadiums to illustrate how sporting spaces are constitutive of a struggle over US American identity with distinct characteristics based on the cities, neighborhoods, and regions in which the stadiums are located.

To this end, I've selected three cities in different regions across the United States that serve as case studies—Atlanta (South), Seattle (West/Northwest), and Minneapolis (Midwest). None are generally considered "first-tier" cities—in other words, they are not global financial centers like New York, Los Angeles, or Chicago. They are cities that compete to enter the first tier in the hierarchy of cities to seize the supposed benefits—economically, socially, politically, and culturally—that go to those major cities. For each as well, sports, both historically and today, plays a crucial role in their efforts to move up the ladder, where stadiums mark crucial turning points in that quest.[18]

In analyzing stadium infrastructure across these three cities, *Stadium City* emphasizes the prevailing role media plays not only in sporting culture but in sporting spaces as well. Toward these ends, this book theorizes sports stadiums not only as sites of media production or sites represented by media but, rather, *as* media and, in particular, as media infrastructure.

Media, Sport, and the Urban

In the chapters that follow, I explore how the stadium works as an *urban media infrastructure*, at once *mediatized* (integrated and enmeshed with media practices, institutions, and technology), *mediatizing* (a space for making things into media content), and *mediating* (it stands between, as a signifier that makes meaning) in ways that are bound up with the constitution of US American citizenship ideals and the remaking of contemporary cities. Building on scholarship across media and cultural studies, communication, geography, architecture, urban studies, and sociology that considers how the stadium works to produce hierarchical power relations and cultural identities, *Stadium City* explores the central roles media and the built urban environment play in the production of and struggle over cultural identities and space.

While sports teams have long been dependent on media and are innovating to adapt to and capitalize on changes in media, cities (which have also long relied on sports) are poised to get in on the game as well. Cities today work to synergize the collaborative partnerships between media industries and sports teams to facilitate new urban regeneration, branding, and governing strategies. Thus, the sportification of place adds the stadium as a new dimension to studies of "mediasport," a term used by Lawrence Wenner to denote the interrelationship between media and sport.[19]

Mediasport research theorizes media and sport as inextricably connected. Sut Jhally calls this connection a "sports/media complex," which he suggests developed out of the production of fans as a commodity for advertisers. Jhally addresses the economics that intertwined media industries and sports institutions from newspapers to television, tracing their increasing interdependence. Sports, he says, "has been fundamentally altered by their relations with the media."[20] Building on Jhally's work, David Rowe coined the term "media sport cultural complex" to demonstrate "both the primacy of symbols in contemporary sport and the two-way relationship between sports media and the great cultural formation of which it is a part."[21] Rowe emphasizes the cultural dimensions of mediasport, focusing on the media studies trifecta of sports media production, texts, and audiences. Expanding on this articulation of sports and media as culturally co-constitutive, Victoria Johnson argues that media influences sport but that sport also influences media through its connection to media industries and its role in technological advancements, as well as through its formal, aesthetic, and viewing practices.[22] While Johnson attends to the relationship between sport and television, Brett Hutchins and David Rowe chart the influential relationship between digital media and sports in what they refer to as "networked mediasport."[23] Collectively, mediasport scholarship emphasizes how the interrelationship between media and sport is significant not just in terms of economics but also for how it speaks to broader cultural formations. As such, Johnson asserts that mediasport is a site of cultural struggle, a "field of deeply affective cultural and political resonance," as a "shared venue for working through questions of community ideals, struggles over national and regional mythologies, and questions of representation and citizenship."[24]

Stadium City extends this insight to the stadium, viewing stadiums as a particular kind of media-sport-space and infrastructure that intervenes in cultural struggles over representation, identity, community, and citizenship.[25] Sports, particularly in the US context, are often idealized by teams, fans, politicians, media, and sporting institutions as "apolitical," as a place where everyone can come together, regardless of identity, background, and political affiliation, to escape. In this escape world, there is no room for politics, only the purity of the game. Yet, the idea that sports are apolitical is a myth—itself political and connected to the desire to see sport as a unifying force.[26] This myth, although always a latent part of US sports culture, surges in times of societal upheaval, when political elites espouse sports to quell unrest, often counterposing idealized, conservative American values against those agitating for social change. In these efforts, sports very much become tied to a political agenda, albeit one that is often conservative and reactionary.[27]

Thus, while athletes, and sometimes teams, have long used their platform to participate in activism and advocate for justice, they are frequently depicted in negative terms, chastised for politicizing sports, reverberating the refrain "Shut up and play."[28] Other critics suggest players might have a right to protest—as long as they do it off the field. This refrain to "keep it off the field," counterpart to "shut up and play," is ubiquitous when it comes to politics in sports. The directive to keep politics off the field upholds the mythology of sport as apolitical, reifying the value of sport as a "unifying" force, and makes the space of play—that is, the stadium—the primary site of the myth's production and, ultimately, in constituting ideals of US American citizenship.

Stadium City focuses especially on how stadium politics participate in the cultural politics of race and its intersections with other identities (especially class) and the urban. Sports are central sites of political struggle over race.[29] Sports have long cultivated biological theories of race, where Black athletes, for example, are represented as having natural athletic ability while lacking the more "mental" and intellectual components of the game. Yet, sports are also imagined to demonstrate the potential for racial harmony through promoting ideologies of meritocracy, fueling the mythology of post-racialism.[30] Likewise, racial struggles also play out in and over the "urban," particularly in the post–World War II context when racial and class divisions drastically widened between affluent suburbs and impoverished inner cities. Steve Macek explains that these divisions were principally influenced by three key forces: (1) the so-called white flight of residents, businesses, and, subsequently, their tax dollars and political investment, to the suburbs; (2) the "Great Migration" of Black citizens from the South to the North and their subsequent ghettoization in the urban core; and, (3) neoliberal economic restructuring and the waning of the social welfare state.[31] Macek notes that the geographical segregation of white and Black citizens fostered an "escalating climate of fear surrounding the postindustrial city," propagated by elites and media who constructed a discourse of urban decline and crisis that "blamed the urban minority poor for the deprivation and social isolation they were forced to endure and inflated the danger they posed to the rest of American society."[32] The discourses of urban decline and crisis associating Blackness, the urban core, crime, and poverty are not reflections of reality; they are produced by always-already imagined representations that are undergirded by racist and classist ideologies. Those associations and the ideologies underpinning them are structurally enabled and reinforced through social and economic policies and practices like redlining, "slum" and "blight" designations, and educational disinvestment.

Sports, too, have long fostered associations between the Black sporting body and urbanism. While discourses of urban decline marked earlier eras of stadiums, in the neoliberal city it is a discourse of "authenticity" that draws on racially coded signifiers of Blackness and multiculturalism to figure the urban as a "cool" and "hip" place. The stadium tends to package "authenticity" for middle-class, white consumers, often commodifying Blackness and multiculturalism and evacuating them of their relationship to histories of political struggle. Promoting players through a "ghettocentric" aesthetic, the NFL, for example, is complicit in "fetishizing and essentializing . . . black sporting bodies for their perceived, and indeed conjoined, athletic ability and urban authenticity: they are unproblematically assumed to be the products, and/or progeny of the mythologized (equally romanticized as demonized) American ghetto."[33] Black sporting bodies become signifiers of urban "authenticity," wherein their "racial-spatial difference" becomes linked to "authenticating and advancing the symbolic value, and hence the exchange value, of particular branded commodities," including city and neighborhood brands.[34]

Thus, sports, sporting bodies, sporting spaces, and the urban are mutually constitutive and implicated in racial formation, or "the process by which social, economic and political forces determine the content and importance of racial categories, and by which they are in turn shaped by racial meanings."[35] Media is a powerful vector through which these racial ideologies and discourses are transmitted, both in bringing to the forefront, as well as working to conceal, racial tensions. And, so too, I argue, is the mediatized, mediatizing, and mediating stadium—stadiums govern spaces and manage flows and bodies in ways that draw from always-already imagined social constructs of race as they intersect with discourses of the urban while also producing new discourses and forms of racialization.

While much of the existing research on mediasport focuses on textual representation, audience consumption, and industrial/institutional political economics, *Stadium City* instead takes a non-media-centric media studies approach. David Morley suggests that non-media-centric media studies widen the scope of what is considered media by placing it within the contexts in which it is produced and used, as a practice, and analyzing the interconnections between media's symbolic and material dimensions.[36] Drawing on this approach, I theorize the stadium as an urban media infrastructure.

The study of media infrastructures is part of the shift toward a non-media-centric approach to theorizing and researching media's material and practical capacities. Lisa Parks defines media infrastructures as "the material sites and objects involved in the local, national, and/or global distribution of audiovisual signals and data."[37] When studying media infrastructures, scholars generally turn to the kinds of material objects we typically associate with media—for instance, satellites, telephone poles, and undersea fiber optics.[38] Stadiums are not ordinarily thought of as part of the media system, even though the sports they house are central components of that system and, for television at least, are perhaps its paramount production.

Stadiums are media production studios, but they are enmeshed in media systems, institutions, and practices in other ways, too, as products of conglomerated media/sport companies and as architectures composed of media (from closed-circuit television [CCTV] surveillance systems to computer systems, from digitized turnstiles to toilets). Steve Secular, in his analysis of the National Basketball Association (NBA), suggests that this mediatization, along with marketization, turns sports into media platforms. Tracing changes in the NBA through various spatial nodes (e.g., wires, venue, couch), he argues that the NBA transformed from "primarily administrative organizations into multibillion-dollar media enterprises."[39] Secular suggests that the league partnered with Silicon Valley to integrate sophisticated digital technology into arenas. Like Ted Turner (the American television owner who used his ownership of the Atlanta Braves to connect his varied and dispersed media entities), then, Silicon Valley companies view sport and sporting spaces as places where they can market and distribute their technologies. Secular argues that the mediatization of the arena turns the venue into an "immersive real-world video platform" designed to "maximize fan engagement and augment the physical experience of sporting spectatorship" and merge the live and at-home experience.[40]

This mediatization and platformization also makes stadiums into spectacular infrastructures in an urban visual economy, influencing the distribution of bodies, goods, resources, information, and images within and outside the stadium. They are often screens themselves; as monumental and iconic buildings in their cities, stadiums are what Dave Colangelo refers to as "massive media," increasingly "screen-like" architectures "entwined with other media and screens."[41] The stadium is thus a multilayered and layering media infrastructure, constituting both what Shannon Mattern refers to as "hard," or stuff you can kick, and "soft," or cultural/informational, infrastructure.[42] It is a physical component of the built urban environment, but the stadium is also a signifier and communicative symbol within that environment, and its internal physical infrastructure communicates, creates, and distributes.

Stadium City figures the stadium as a particularly *urban* form of media infrastructure. Naomi Schiller suggests, "The study of urban infrastructure—a category that includes communications media—allows us to think about how particular urban sites, materials, and peoples are connected and disconnected across 'interpenetrating scales of relationality'."[43] Schiller further notes that infrastructures are bound up with practices of governance and struggles over power as "pathways through which goods, ideas, energy, water, and people move. As central 'terrain of power and contestation,' all infrastructure is deeply social and political, not simply technical," as they connect and disconnect, distributing resources and the flow of bodies, capital, and information.[44] It is these questions of power—of how stadiums' imbrication in media industries, cultures, and practices serve to connect and disconnect, make place and displace, and distribute and block the flow of resources—that animate the central concerns of this book.

In this sense, stadiums, as urban media infrastructures at once mediatized, mediatizing, and mediating, are components of the "media city," a term Scott McQuire suggests describes how the "modern city has become a media-architecture complex in which the *mediatised production of urban space* has become a constitutive frame for a new mode of social experience."[45] McQuire explains that this is not new. He traces the media city through histories of electrification, television, and the digital.[46] According to Myria Georgiou and Jun Yu, the media city "is recognized through its powerful representations in the media . . . [and] deeply connected internally and externally through communication infrastructures mediating interactions among individuals and between institutions and individuals."[47] The city is thus related to representational, aesthetic, industrial, and material practices of media and media culture. Theories of the media city suggest that the connection between the urban and media is constitutive. Referring to this constitutive relationship as a shift from thinking of "media and the city" as a separate but intertwined phenomenon and toward "media urbanism" instead, Erica Stein and Germaine R. Halegoua write, "The social production of urban space is enacted through mediation and the social production of mediation is imbricated with urbanism and urban environments. Media architectures and infrastructures are inseparable from the social lives and economies of cities; they produce one another through ongoing interactions."[48]

While aesthetic and representational analysis remains a prevalent way of theorizing and approaching the media city, scholars increasingly attend to how media is imbricated in the production and practice of city space in more material ways.[49] Nanna Verhoeff and Germaine Halegoua, for example, draw attention to how media technology, including screens, digital, and smart technology are integrated into cities in ways that fundamentally alter how the city is produced, used, and practiced.[50] Further, other research demonstrates how the media city is produced through practices of media production and labor as well as through tourism spurred by intertwining images and production practices.[51] For example, in my previous book, *Down in Treme: Race, Place, and New Orleans on Television*, I argued that the city harnessed film and TV production in New Orleans to help rebuild following Hurricane Katrina, where production practices meant media were not just representing the city's rebuilding but, through on-location shooting, local hiring, and media-induced tourism, the show was actually participating in that rebuilding in ways that fundamentally altered the city's spatiality and neighborhoods.

What I found in my research on sports stadiums is that they were working not so differently from film and TV production in New Orleans—that is, stadiums are also film, TV, and digital media production studios, harnessed to rebuild struggling neighborhoods in cities across the country, attracting fans (residents and tourists alike) to cities and particular neighborhoods. And that harnessing has meant integrating media technologies, practices, and logics not only into the stadium but into the very city itself. The sportification of place demonstrates how sport and sporting spaces, like other forms of media, influence and are influenced by contemporary practices of urbanization, as sport serves as a primary vehicle of visual culture and practice that implicates our daily lives and how we navigate, experience, and conceive of city space.

Stadium City thus demonstrates how stadiums are urban media infrastructures and central components of the contemporary media city. As Brian Larkin notes, "The act of defining an infrastructure is a categorizing moment. . . . It comprises a cultural analytic that highlights the epistemological and political commitments involved in selecting what one sees as infrastructural (and thus causal) and what one leaves out."[52] Thus, defining sports stadiums as media infrastructure opens up thinking about them in new ways beyond existing analyses of their semiotic, architectural, or political economic implications. One of those ways is in considering how sports stadiums as urban media infrastructure work as technologies of governance and governmentality. Michel Foucault defines governmentality as "the conduct of conduct."[53] It is the diffusion of a governing rationality—the historically specific aims of dispersed institutions involved in governing a population—into sites and practices that orchestrate the conduct of citizens in ways that adhere to that rationale. Larkin contends that theorizing media infrastructure as technologies of governance reveals "forms of political rationality that underlie technological projects and which give rise to an 'apparatus of governmentality.'"[54] In thinking of stadiums as urban media infrastructures reliant on technologies of governing, then, I consider how stadiums "form us as subjects not just on a technopolitical level but also through this mobilization of affect and the senses of desire, pride, and frustration" tied to stadiums and their relationship to sport, team, and city.[55]

Because stadiums are spaces defined by highly charged emotions and affective intensities, affect is central to understanding how stadiums perform cultural governance. Drawing on the seventeenth-century philosopher Baruch Spinoza and contemporary philosophers Gilles Deleuze and Félix Guattari, Nigel Thrift defines "affect" as "the way in which each thing, in acting, living, and striving to preserve its own being, is 'nothing but the actual essence of the thing.'"[56] Affect can thus be understood as a kind of potentiality, or as

Deleuze and Guattari put it, "the capacity to affect and to be affected."[57] It thus assumes an immanent ontology in which there is no stable subject or subject/object division but, rather, wherein all matter is in a state of collective and relational potential and becoming. This makes affect a connector; it has capacity to connect our bodies to other bodies and to other forms of matter, spaces, and times. Affect theorist Brian Massumi uses soccer to describe how affect works as potentiality, suggesting sport exemplifies the collective potentiality of bodies and objects moving, acting, being together in relation. Massumi suggests that the field activates this potentiality, creating a surge in affective intensity: "The field of play is an in-between of charged movement. It is more fundamentally a field of potential than a substantial thing, or object. . . . It is a tensile force-field activated by the presence of bodies within the signed limits."[58]

Affect scholarship aims to study "how things feel, for whom, and with what potential."[59] The turn to affect is part of a broader influence of non-representational, materialist, and performance theory in media and communication scholarship, including non-media-centric media studies, as scholars work to think outside of representation and meaning (what happens inside our heads) and instead focus on what we do (what happens in and between our bodies and the world around us), or, as Melissa Gregg and Greg Seigworth put it, what "drive[s] us toward movement."[60] Still, studying affect generally requires focusing on the traces that affect leaves, often in terms of how it is communicated and represented through discourse.[61] This tension relates to one of the most pronounced debates in affect scholarship: the relationship between affect and emotion. Some affect scholars distinguish strongly between emotion and affect, where the former is the cognitive expression that comes after one is affected.[62] Others, however, push back on this distinction. Sara Ahmed, for example, believes that this strong distinction is not helpful and that it furthers the mind/body dualism while minimizing feminist, Indigenous, and queer scholars who have long theorized emotion.[63] I agree; throughout this book I refer to affect and emotion in terms of what I understand to be an inextricable interrelationship.

The stadium is a key site for orchestrating affect, where its architecture and infrastructure are designed to arouse emotion and affective intensities. Through enclosure, the co-presence of the crowd, the architectural design to accentuate noise, and the ritualistic production of fandom through symbolic unification, synchronization, and emotional prompters (such as the jumbotron encouraging emotional outbursts), Michael S. Schaefer and Jochen Roose suggest, the stadium enjoins players and fans alike to express emotion within particular boundaries of intensity. Likewise, through practices of crowd control, refereeing, and policing, the stadium prevents the expression of emotions and affective intensities considered outside those boundaries.[64] As Massumi argues, sporting practice predates its codification and formalization; codification captures affective intensities produced through sporting bodies and practices to convert it into market-based value.[65] But therein lies the rub—that potentiality remains as trace and specter, always threatening to emerge in excess of subsumptive capture. As such, the stadium embodies this central tension between collective potentiality inherent in the affective intensities produced in and through sport and the powerful forces that seek to contain and capture that potentiality.

Thus, like other urban media infrastructures in the media city, whether screens or smart technology, the sportification of place is implicated in struggles over power. Those struggles are geographically and historically contextual, bound up with affects produced among sport, team, and place over time. Stadiums are often constitutive of an inequitable production of space, creating spaces in the city that include some so as to exclude and discipline Others, habitually along intersecting lines of race, class, and gender. A central concern explored in this book is therefore how city residents, especially those subject to and most affected by stadiums, respond to, participate in, and resist those projects in ways that imagine and create more equitable and just distributions of city space and its mediatizations. Contending with these questions requires a consideration of place in its mediated and sportified context.

Space, Place, and Site

Sports stadiums are enshrined in what John Bale calls, drawing on Yi-Fu Tuan, "*topophilia*," or love of place.[66] Stadiums act as the physical embodiment of the town or community they represent. This book builds on Bale's important work exploring the relationship between sport, space, and place by also contending with media and its relationship to urbanism. As I detail in the following chapters, stadium builders and designers increasingly emphasize the specificity of place and location. While place has always been important to stadiums, earlier generations were often criticized for their placelessness; they were seemingly indistinguishable from one another, following a cookie-cutter model of design, making one city and team just like any other.[67] In the most recent generation, however, that logic has been replaced with a hyper-focus on place and location and a desire for the stadium to both reflect and contribute to placemaking.

Geographers distinguish between space and place: space denotes an abstract location prior to meaning, whereas place is space realized in the particular and given meaning through connection to culture. Yi-Fu Tuan notes, "Place incarnates the experiences and aspirations of a people, . . . a reality to be clarified and understood from the perspectives of people who have given it meaning."[68] According to Tuan, "Monuments, artworks, buildings, and cities are places because they can organize space into centres of meaning," as they are often put to work to create a sense of pride or cohere identity formations.[69] This understanding of place is central to *Stadium City*, which considers the stadium as a specific location constituted through its connection to culture and the social. In Doreen Massey's view, place is constituted through a double articulation with the social, where place works to constitute social relations, but those social relations in turn implicate the material production of place as well.[70] Place is, thus, inextricably intertwined with identity, as places are constituted through identity formations and uses of space and those places, in turn, influence the production of identity.

Stadiums, and the neighborhoods, cities, and regions that house them, are particular kinds of places. Though stadiums share broader characteristics because of the larger social, political, economic, and cultural forces that constitute them, so too does each differ based on the specific conditions into which they enter and intervene. *Stadium City* therefore draws on a series of case studies in the interest of a site-specific analysis of stadiums, cities, and the cultures and identities they co-constitute. "Site-specificity" is a term used across disciplines of geography, landscape architecture, and art. Anita Berrizbeitia writes, "Unlike place . . . site-specificity did not seem to claim to be all-inclusive, historically bound, or totalizing about a place. . . . It only engaged one, or sometimes a few, aspects of it. . . . Site was open-ended, whereas place was singular."[71] Site-specific art is designed for specific places, engaging as Berrizbeitia suggests, not necessarily the totality of the place but some aspects of it. Berrizbeitia notes that art theorists Craig Owens and Miwon Kwon expanded site-specificity to conceptually refer to "the site itself (as highly specific readings of a physical location), to the institutional frame (as cultural and political site of a work's production) to discursive site (that is, gender, nature, or sexuality as sites themselves)."[72]

In conceptualizing stadiums in site-specific terms, I consider how they intervene into a specific locale along with their institutional and discursive specificities. Like the television sets in public places analyzed by media studies scholar Anna McCarthy, I am interested in how the stadium "not only adapts to the conventional spatial or sensorial arrangements of its location, but [how] it also enters into, and takes up a position within, the immaterial networks of power" that constitute the urban.[73] Like the TV, where the stadium is located matters; the specific cities and their concomitant histories, geographies, politics, and cultures implicate how the stadium is designed and built as well as how it mediates the urban.

As such, I argue the contemporary stadium is more than spectacle, tourist bubble, mallpark (a combination of shopping mall and theme park), or commodification of place, arguments put forth by other scholars contending with stadium building practices and their relationships to cities and media culture.[74] Instead, I suggest that stadiums draw on affective connections people create to place through sport, team, and fandom as a form of cultural governance. Although this serves to connect some in more meaningful ways to the spaces and places of sport, *Stadium City* is also a story of disconnection and displacement, where some residents' attachments to place is treated as a problem to be solved via stadium construction. Usually, this occurs in the case of working-class and racialized Others who are seen as threats to the revaluation of place by way of the stadium and whose attachments are themselves problematized to build new kinds of attachments to place. This book takes both attachments and detachments seriously; that is, I do not suggest stadiums are merely a ruse or a simulation of place-based attachments. Rather, I look at how the production of "authenticity" itself is constituted and contested through these practices of attachment and detachment.

Toward these ends, I've drawn extensively on research at state and city archives to historicize stadium building in each of the cities, tracing their site-specific debates about stadium building, location, architecture, design, and mediatization. In addition, my primary research included observation and participant observation through site visits and game/event attendance; stadium tours; analysis of urban planning and design documents; intertextual and paratextual sources, including news and commentary; and interviews with stadium executives, designers, and individuals involved in neighborhood organizations and stadium activism.[75] I have approached these primary materials through Foucault's theory of discourse, contending with "what was being said in what was said?"[76] I am thus not looking for the "truth" hidden behind the ideology of stadium building but, rather, how these sources themselves produce a particular truth to the stadium. In other words, a discursive approach looks at the formation of authorized knowledge, or how power produces ways of talking, speaking, writing, and thinking about phenomena that become accepted as truth, forming what Foucault called a "regime of truth," and realized in the material production of social reality. Foucault's approach to discourse is historical; discourses produce truths within a given historical context. Following this, I trace the continuities and discontinuities of discourses surrounding stadium building in these cities at differing historical periods, showing how discourses of the urban, media, sport, and the stadium are constructed in response to historically and site-specific exigencies.

In addition to historicization, a discursive approach is also invested in the material, as it assumes that language and the material are co-constitutive. In this vein, my approach, while drawing on cultural geographical theories of place and site-specificity, considers how discourses around stadium building manifest in what Henri Lefebvre refers to as "the production of space." Lefebvre says, "(Social) space is a (social) product."[77] Social space incorporates social action, and the production of space can hence be interpreted as an act/process of creation. That act is tied to power; for Lefebvre, power was bound up with capital, transforming space into a product to be produced and through which profit and value can be extracted. As I aim to show in my analysis of stadium building, the production of space is also bound up with other intersectional forms of power, especially race.

To trace the power dynamics involved in how stadium building produces space, and struggles over space and place, I draw on Lefebvre's spatial triad theory. Lefebvre contends with the competing forces in how space is produced, which he parses out into three central forces: *perceived space* (how we engage with space in the everyday, through routines and rhythms); *conceived space* (dominant space, produced through the imagination of those in positions of power—the cartographer, city planner, government official); and *lived space* ("space as directly lived through its associated images and symbols . . . the space of 'inhabitants' and 'users'").[78] The primary materials I've gathered address these competing productions of space as they contend with the visions of urban planners, stadium owners and designers, and governing officials; media and visual culture's representations of cities and stadiums; and the competing uses of space in which fans, residents, activists, and organizations representing citizens most affected by stadiums produce lived spaces. I am interested in the tensions, contradictions, and possibilities opened by the juxtaposition of stadium plans and visions to how space is practiced, used, and appropriated in the everyday.

Drawing on this approach, each of the case studies in the following chapters attends to the site-specific articulations of the sportification of place. To address their site-specificity, I consider not only contemporary, or what I refer to as "third-generation," stadiums, but I also delve into the longer history of sports and stadiums in these cities and bring this historical perspective to bear on the present. The following chapters of the book detail these histories in terms of the individual cities at the center of the study, but to contextualize these specifics, I next provide a brief history of stadiums in the United States.

Three Generations of Stadium Building

John Bale contends that sports order the spaces where they are located, remaking the landscapes around them and constituting the subjects within through the political rationalities of sporting culture.[79] Sports are fundamentally about space, since what distinguishes sports from other activities, like recreation and play, is that they take place within a prescribed area according to an explicit and codified set of rules. Bale uses the notion of the "sportscape" to describe how sports remake landscapes by shaping how people and cultures interact with and understand space. Sports have long been a site of struggle for defining what it means to be a US American, as well as displaying regional differences that constitute this contested identity.[80]

The study of sports stadiums and their history is thus a study of power. The building of stadiums is the business of a few wealthy elites whose "broader agendas are yoked to sport and sport architecture."[81] These agendas change over time, responding to historically contextual shifts in sport and culture. Stadiums' involvement in power relations dates to ancient stadiums, which were built to communicate power and provide the masses with diversions elites believed would keep them pacified and prevent uprisings (i.e., "bread and circuses"). Thus, while ancient stadiums provided the possibility of assembling the public, they were more importantly used for "the presentation of power."[82] Stadium design thus constitutes what Foucault refers to as a "technology of power," or the investment and exercise of power in and through the body, as ancient stadiums were designed to assemble the masses and create a sense of belonging and escape from the outside world by structuring clear demarcations between inside and outside. Once inside the stadium, seating and spatial structure communicated varying degrees of social power, enabling elites to be seen by the masses while also reinforcing the sense that other elites were watching them. Stadiums provided a space where power was performed and learned.

In the medieval era, the grand stadiums built by the Greeks and Romans fell into disrepair as "religion became more important, and architectural effort was turned to the building of churches rather than places of recreation and entertainment."[83] It was not until the nineteenth century, amid modern industrialization and urbanization, that renewed stadium efforts took hold. As sporting rules became codified, folk games that were formed by the localized spatial limitations of players' surroundings transitioned into "spatially confined and increasingly artificial" enclosures.[84] Stadiums emerged once elites realized that sporting could be commodified by charging spectators.

US stadium history can be divided into three generations. Here, I've adapted Rod Sheard, Robert Powell, and Patrick Bingham-Hall's five generations of stadium building to denote three major shifts in stadium building as they relate to cultural shifts in media and urban spatiality.[85] Notably, stadium history typology is contested.[86] However, the goal of this book is not to intervene into this debate about typology but, rather, to chart how shifts in stadium building are related to broader cultural changes in media and the urban. I suggest that a triadic typology represents three distinct logics of architectural development in stadium building while also connecting these logics to uses of stadiums in the production of and contestation over urban space and their relationship to shifts in media culture, institutions and industries, technology, and practices. Nevertheless, as for any typology, exceptions are inevitable and, I contend, demonstrate the importance of site-specificity.

First-generation stadiums (roughly 1870s–1950s) made possible the extraction of value from the production of leisure of the new industrialized working class through codifying, containing, and enclosing sport for paying fans. Built primarily for baseball and American football, they were typically large bowl-like structures with few amenities, accommodating as many fans as possible, and placing a premium on affordable, working-class entertainment. The best example of a first-generation stadium still standing today is Boston's Fenway Park, where its dense urban location largely blends in with its surroundings, making it seem like another part of the neighborhood rather than a stand-out architectural feature. First-generation stadiums served the role of governing from a distance, as technologies for instructing citizens on how to appropriately practice liberal ideals of citizenship. Fans were allowed to display rowdy behavior that was not permitted in other sites of citizenship training of this era, such as museums.

First-generation stadiums were thus sites for orchestrating forms of white, working-class masculinity responsive to struggles over changing norms around citizenship, gender, race, and class at the time. Modern stadium building in the United States took shape during a time of tremendous change, including the influx of new immigrants and renewed emphasis on building national identity. Sports, alongside media (especially radio, cinema, and newspapers), influenced these efforts, as they were collectively put to work to shape shared identities.[87] Sporting rivalries were imagined to replace ethnic antagonisms, and sport was promoted as a vehicle to nation building.[88] While stadiums were sites of constituting citizens and creating shared identities, some were perceived as more assimilable than others. Stadiums, and the sports contained within them, for example, were marked by segregationist policies that treated Black citizens as unassimilable and explicitly excluded them from, and treated them as a threat to, the national imaginary. And although women attended games, the first-generation stadium was not built for them; it was masculine-coded space. The stadium was viewed as dangerous and not appropriate for respectable women.[89] Thus, early stadiums helped to constitute forms of citizenship connected to hierarchies of race, class, and gender. These hierarchies remain as traces in subsequent stadium designs and policies.

Post–World War II suburbanization and the interstate highway system fundamentally changed practices of the urban and sport, bringing in a second generation of stadium building between the 1950s and the 1990s to accommodate automobility, suburbanizing fans, and television. This was also a period in which professional sports was expanding to the south and west to cities seeking national recognition. Houston's Astrodome, built in 1965 and a model for many subsequent stadiums, best exemplifies this period. The Astrodome was a study in innovation, featuring a domed roof, the first artificial turf (Astroturf), air-conditioning, and a large bank of luxury seating areas, or boxes. In contrast to the earlier generation, these stadiums depended on public financing, which influenced a push toward multipurpose and often multisport structures. Ticket prices rose and increasingly catered to a middle-class, rather than working-class, fan, with an emphasis on "family fun," including restaurants, merchandising, boxes, and other amenities inviting spectators to participate in new forms of consumer citizenship.[90] Thus, while earlier stadiums were associated with a contained working-class masculinity engaged in citizenship training by providing a place where more "rowdy," but not too rowdy, behavior could be contained, the second generation was more explicitly aimed at containing rowdy behavior in order to make the stadium a safe space for families to consume. Assigned individual seating and greater emphasis on safety within the stadium through security guards and CCTV surveillance systems were key design features of the period.

Whereas newspapers, cinema, and radio were the media forces developing alongside first-generation stadiums, it was primarily television, and the suburbanized lifestyles that it both idealized and helped to make possible, that influenced the production of second-generation stadium building. Television, for the first time, could bring sporting events directly into the homes of sports fans and consumers both visually and sonically. Yet, the stadium and television have also had an uncomfortable, and at times tense, relationship. Team owners were reluctant to allow games to be televised, as they feared it would make fans less likely to come to the stadium and thus cut into their profits. But by the 1960s, teams and stadium owners adapted to the perceived challenges of television by building stadiums that incorporated television broadcasting, with designs aimed to capture the event on live TV and to invite the imagined television audience into the stadium. With many new stadiums built in this period specifically with the aim to accommodate broadcasting, efforts were made to make the stadium more "telegenic, with increased control of the internal environment satisfying a perceived need for predictable playing conditions."[91]

To accommodate suburban fans—whose "white flight" from the city was made possible through racist housing policies, such as redlining and zoning—stadiums were built to facilitate easy on/off access from the new interstate highways, whether in the city's downtown, edge, or suburbia.[92] Building stadiums adjacent to the highway ensured not only that suburban fans could access the game easily but also that they could feel safe doing so. This discourse of safety was undergirded by racial resentments that problematized the city center and imagined it as a space containing Black criminality and valorized the suburbs as a space of whiteness to flee to. Ensuring that fans could remain separate from the city while still attending a game was thus a primary motivator for the design and construction of these second-generation stadiums. Stadiums themselves, along with the highway, were often part of larger urban planning efforts in the name of "slum clearance."[93] Stadiums of this era constituted the white, middle-class family while constructing and producing urban Blackness as a problem to be disciplined and controlled.

Like the second generation, geographical and media shifts also influenced the third generation (from around the 1990s to today). Satellite television and the internet meant teams became invested in not only regional and national fandoms but also global ones. Further, to compete with the proliferation of entertainment and interactive capacities of the web, stadiums have themselves been redesigned to enmesh with and enhance a converged media experience and vice versa. Likewise, post-industrial reinvestment and the return of white bodies and capital to the urban center influenced a renewed era of stadium building within the downtown core.[94] In contrast to second-generation buildings, these stadiums are built to explicitly draw people into the city and to create a specific sense of place. In baseball, the third-generation stadium is especially marked by nostalgic designs that hark back to first-generation stadiums. While second-generation urban renewal often resulted in bulldozing entire neighborhood blocks, third-generation stadiums, in contrast, are conceived instead as components of broader neighborhood regeneration and "placemaking" projects. The rhetorical framing of the stadium's relationship to urban renewal/regeneration today largely eschews the second generation's discourses of demonization and fear of impoverished Black neighborhoods in favor of a post-racial discourse that seeks to use stadiums as sites of neighborhood "empowerment" while frequently resulting in gentrification and displacement in ways not so different from earlier generations.[95]

A distinct shift toward third-generation stadium building can be dated to the 1992 opening of the Baltimore Orioles' Camden Yards. Camden Yards is notable for its return to the downtown urban core and nostalgic "retro-modern" design, which is tied to urban site-specificity. Camden Yards continues to promote the claims of urban renewal (now termed "regeneration") and economic promise of the second generation to extract financial concessions from state and local government while using the site-specificity of first-generation stadiums to evoke nostalgia for a city of a seemingly simpler time. These stadiums seek to capture the fan experience of first-generation stadiums, focusing on unobstructed views for all fans and a return to sport-specific urban stadiums. Unlike their second-generation counterparts, they make an explicit link to place-based materialities and affects of the city, and they are called upon to articulate the city's place brand.

Stadium designers encourage city governments to see stadiums not as individual sites but, rather, as "an essential ingredient of the urban matrix that binds our cities together."[96] They "play a role in creating a multi-functional urban environment around themselves."[97] This language used by stadium designers demonstrates how those invested in stadium building see stadiums as part of a wider urban infrastructure. Contemporary stadiums are now frequently connected to shopping centers, hotels, housing, conference centers, museums, restaurants, and even schools, which create a whole urban center where the stadium becomes a city hub—a communicative infrastructure through which the larger city connects, and, in turn, connects the city to regional, national, and global infrastructures of tourism, investment, and fandoms. These entertainment hubs reconfigure the spatiality of the city itself as the stadium becomes a site for stimulating cultural, social, and material development based on sporting logics.

This history shows how stadiums have always been connected to media and the urban as well as the production of and struggle over power. Although each generation responds to historically specific conditions, the stadium remains a continuous force in governing from a distance and producing and struggling over US American ideals of citizenship and identity. The following chapters provide case studies that throw this more general history of stadium building and the third-generation's sportification of place into focus at a more granular and site-specific level.

The sportification of place is marked by three distinct but interrelated practices that work as organizing structures for the case studies of this book: (1) sportified governance and mediatization, (2) place-branding, and (3) a white spatial imaginary. The remainder of the book focuses on how these characteristics of the sportification of place play out, respectively, in stadiums in three cities across the country—Atlanta, Seattle, and Minneapolis. The case studies show how the sportification of place works in site-specific ways that respond to the unique histories, cultural geographies, and sporting cultures of each city while also connecting to broader forces at work in media, sport, and urbanism that transverse these sites. Given the interconnectedness between these characteristics, all the case studies address these elements at some level, but each case study foregrounds and emphasizes a particular characteristic. *Stadium City* concludes with a reflection on the broader and future implications of the sportification of place on media, sport, and culture.

PART I

Atlanta

Mediatization, Governance, and Citizenship

CHAPTER 1

Going Major League, Going Global

Atlanta plays an important role in the US cultural imaginary. City elites have long promoted it as a shining city of progress, one of national and global significance. Race is a central antagonism through which that image is refracted. On the one hand, promoters market the city as a space of racial harmony and tolerance, as a birthplace of the civil rights movement and Martin Luther King Jr. In this image, Atlanta is "the city too busy to hate," as Mayor William Hartsfield famously quipped in the 1960s in an effort to attract business investment to Atlanta, including Major League Baseball, and distinguish the city as more progressive than its Southern counterparts. That image reemerged in the 1980s as city leaders bid for Atlanta to host the 1996 Olympic Games. Promoters foregrounded Atlanta as a global leader in human rights in their quest to position the city as one of international import. During this time, Atlanta was on the rise and experienced a kind of "reverse migration" of African Americans moving in from the Northeast and Rust Belt cities, creating a burgeoning Black upper and middle class that impacted not only the urban core but also the city's sprawling suburbs.[1] In these figurations, Atlanta is imagined as a Black Mecca that celebrates the possibility of Black economic success and an embodiment of the American Dream.[2]

On the other hand, however, Atlanta is marked by massive wealth disparities and deep racial inequities. According to US Census data, the city has the highest income inequality in the nation.[3] While Atlanta is a site of Black wealth, its Black residents also make up a disproportionate percentage of those living in poverty, and the intersection between race and class plays out geographically. These disparities, coupled with the image of Atlanta as a bastion of Black economic success, constitutes what David Sjoquist refers to as the "Atlanta Paradox": a city of "abject poverty in a region of tremendous wealth, of a poor and economically declining city population in the face of dramatic economic growth, and of a Black mecca... confronting a highly racially segregated population and the substantial problems associated with racism and poverty that pervade the city."[4]

The Atlanta Paradox marks the cultural geography of the city and renders those inequities and disparities in the built environment. Atlanta's racial, class, and spatial landscapes stand out from its counterparts, especially in the South, in how they reflect a range of economic classes within racial groups as well as by how the city is implicated by immigration from the Southern, Midwestern, and Northeastern United States.[5] Moreover, it is a city with some of the most flagrant displays of urban sprawl, exposing intersecting class and racial tensions between the urban core, which is predominantly Black and where the city's most impoverished residents live, and its suburbs, which are largely segregated but have a large proportion of middle- and upper-class Black and white residents alike along with other residents of color. Larry Keating argues that Atlanta's urban development is the result of a biracial coalition between middle- and upper-class white and Black elites with an urban growth agenda.[6] That coalition traces back to the post–Civil War era, in which white elites cultivated ties to middle- and upper-class Black elites as a compromise to prevent a coalition of Black Atlantans from gaining political power. The coalition drove a wedge between Black Atlantans along class lines that continues to resonate today. While not unique per se, the Atlanta Paradox makes evident the wealth disparities within racial categories and throws focus onto how Blackness in Atlanta, as elsewhere, is itself a site of dialogue and struggle.

The Atlanta Paradox plays out in numerous industries and investments throughout the city but is glaringly evident in Atlanta's cultural industries, of which Atlanta is a key player. Atlanta is a leader in music, fashion, film and TV, sports, and other highly profitable cultural industries, where much of its prowess is rooted in Black labor and culture. On the one hand, Atlanta's cultural industries are key sites for both representing and generating Black wealth, joy, and power. On the other hand, the industries are bound up with the city's urban growth machine and reproduce racial and class inequities by, for example, contributing to gentrification.

Atlanta's film and TV industries—Atlanta's film mogul Tyler Perry, in particular—exemplify this paradox. Driven by aggressive tax incentives to lure film and TV production to the state, Georgia is now one of the industry's top production locations.[7] Undeniably, Tyler Perry has played an outsized role in Atlanta's production culture. He was born and raised in New Orleans, and his move to and rise in Atlanta embodies the promise of the Black Mecca. As the first Black person to own their own film studio, Perry, with his decision to locate his studio to Atlanta, has been credited with helping to foster a vibrant Black filmmaking culture in the city.[8] The production infrastructure in Atlanta has led to a proliferation of on-location filming there. While elites tout these productions as evidence of Atlanta's promise, the representations within those films and TV series often render a more complex image of Atlanta and its racial, class, and spatial politics, especially productions created by Black writers, directors, and producers. For example, Donald Glover's TV series, *Atlanta* (FX, 2016–2022), represents the city's vibrant hip-hop scene in ways that lay bare Atlanta's complicated racial and class fractures and struggles, including in its cultural geography. However, despite these kinds of complex representations, Atlanta's production industry, especially as it is based in the city's infrastructure and the role of the biracial coalition between white and Black elites in promoting a growth agenda, has also contributed to those very same fractures and struggles. While Tyler Perry stands in for Black Mecca, his "fame and wealth have not trick[l]ed down to working-class and poor black people in his home city of Atlanta."[9] Perry claims to have built his sprawling 330-acre studio "in a neighborhood that's one of the poorest black neighborhoods in Atlanta, so that young black kids can see that a black man did that and they can do that, too."[10] Meanwhile, critics suggest that the "sweetheart" tax deal he received from the city for purchasing the land, which included a discount on the market price for the land and an exemption from paying taxes on it from 2015 to 2022, subsidized Perry at the expense of putting taxpayer money into those very same neighborhoods. As symbols of the Atlanta Paradox, Perry and his studio stand out as a shining example of Black wealth and potential while being surrounded by neighborhoods and southwestern suburbs that "remain among the most poverty stricken" in Atlanta.[11]

The raced and classed spaces of Atlanta reflect more than a century's worth of city planning, development, and political struggle, including the building of sports infrastructure. Keating argues that the urban growth coalition privileges "business-driven public policy," which overwhelmingly serves and benefits "non-Atlantans: conventioneers, tourists, national and international sports fans, and new middle- and upper-class residents" at the expense of impoverished residents in the urban core.[12] Numerous sites exemplify Keating's claim— from the Georgia World Congress Center, Underground Atlanta, and World of

Coke to the city's many sports stadiums and arenas. Charles Rutheiser likens the urban growth coalition framework of Atlanta's downtown development to a Disney-esque form of "Imagineering"—an intensive boosterism that markets and remarkets a shifting image of "phantasmagorical" Atlanta.[13] Atlanta's downtown was turned into a "tourist bubble," with "hardened citadels closed off from the street to create little outposts of suburbia downtown."[14] That material fortification was driven by discursive constructions of urban decline and crisis that imagined Atlanta's urban core as dangerous and criminal because of its associations with Blackness and impoverishment.

Historically, sports stadiums figure centrally in this development strategy, playing a massive role in Atlanta's development. Sports are one of Atlanta's most recognizable assets. The Atlanta Braves were one of the first teams that were broadcast nationally on media mogul Ted Turner's WTBS cable superstation. Consequently, they are often referred to as "America's team." Despite boosters continually promoting Atlanta, its image is amorphous and has shifted to suit the needs of the moment. The city is figured as a phoenix rising from the ashes, signifying the "Atlanta Spirit" as capable of becoming something new and different, in an ode to the city's history of rebuilding after it nearly burned to the ground during the Civil War. But that amorphousness means Atlanta struggles to lay claim to a sense of "authentic" place and locality. Thus, city boosters and elites have long turned to sports to fill that gap in order to constitute an image connected to place and history. In a Southern, majority-Black city, sports enable city elites to capitalize on the fact that both white and Black Atlantans have affective connections to the city's sports teams, thus enabling the promise of the city as a progressive Black Mecca. However, as this and the following two chapters make clear, those affective connections also trouble that image, laying bare the paradoxes at its core and the ways in which sports and sporting infrastructure serve as sites of struggle both between and within racial groups.

Atlanta Goes Major League: Atlanta–Fulton County Stadium

Atlanta–Fulton County Stadium, largely referred to as Fulton County Stadium (FCS), opened in 1965 as part of the second-generation stadium building in the United States as teams migrated from the "rustbelt to the sunbelt."[15] Atlanta's then-mayor, Ivan Allen Jr., and urban elites built a new stadium to lure Major League Baseball's (MLB's) Milwaukee Braves to Atlanta in 1966. In addition to the Braves, the stadium helped Atlanta gain a National Football League team, the Falcons, as part of the league's expansion in 1965. Upon the stadium's opening,

Allen congratulated himself and his partners for bringing in the team, saying, "We built a stadium on ground we didn't own, with money we didn't have, for a team we hadn't signed," suggesting this reflected the Atlanta Spirit.[16]

The effort to bring an MLB team to Atlanta was part of Allen's and city elites' desire to transition Atlanta from a regional hub into a city of national importance—a "major league city." At that time, sports and sporting infrastructure played a key role in putting a city on the map, demonstrating it was open for business. But for Atlanta this was also racialized; attracting a major league team also served to divide the city from its Jim Crow past and its Southern counterparts in the wake of the rising civil rights movement. It showed the nation it had evolved and stood out from its regional competitors, ready to participate as a serious contender in the newly emerging postwar national consumer economy, of which both sports and media culture (especially lucrative broadcasting deals) were key components. Yet, Atlanta elites had to maintain a careful balance, showing they were distinct and progressive while also not angering white elites, who were increasingly fleeing for the suburbs. Likewise, the city's fragile biracial coalition depended on not angering Black elites.

News surrounding hopes for a new stadium at the time reflected these aims and tensions. As a 1964 *New York Times* article noted, "Today, Atlanta is struggling to become a 'national city.' In a typically aggressive fashion, the city is building an $18 million sports stadium in an effort to obtain the baseball franchise of the Milwaukee Braves," desiring to be regarded as "the Wall Street of the South."[17] An advertisement from the *Times* the following day demonstrated precisely what boosters thought it meant for Atlanta to be "major league," listing Atlanta as "Major League in Population . . . Manufacturing and business . . . Transportation and distribution . . . Newspapers . . . Opportunity," where the latter was characterized in terms of opportunity for businesses looking to relocate.[18] Building the stadium was imagined to demonstrate that Atlanta could attract businesses and build major infrastructure to support them. The advertisement was part of an aggressive marketing campaign undertaken by Forward Atlanta, a program initiated by Allen's father in the 1920s and reignited in the 1960s. Publicly subsidized by the city and overseen by the chamber of commerce, Forward Atlanta promoted Atlanta to businesses outside the region in newspapers and magazines marketed to wealthy elites, making the city "one of the best advertised metro areas in the country."[19]

The Forward Atlanta advertising campaign demonstrates the significant relationship between sports, urbanism, and media at the time, as sports stadium infrastructure would enable the city to gain national media attention on a regular basis. In turn, boosters hoped that attention would bring more private investment to the city, which would contribute to more infrastructure in order to facilitate the distribution of goods and capital. City boosters like the chamber of commerce were intent on using the stadium opening to maximize media coverage and promote Atlanta as a national city. In an operations manual for the Braves' stadium's opening day, they urged the mayor to "appoint a broadcasting committee to meet as soon as possible" so that they could use the event "as the possible news peg which could lead to significant national TV and radio attention to the city of Atlanta."[20] They hoped the networks would cover not just the opening but Atlanta as a whole—"What kind of town is this Atlanta where Big League baseball is making its debut? That is the story underlying the big event itself."[21]

The Atlanta–Fulton County Recreation Authority's (AFCRA) dedication booklet published for FCS's opening reveals the image that boosters hoped to project. They imagined that the stadium transformed Atlanta from provincial regional hub to the "Big Leagues":

> Atlanta Stadium was built on the daring of a handful of men who set their sights on making Atlanta truly a major league city.... And with it came the transformation of an image. In pre-stadium days, Atlanta was recognized as a great city, capital of the southeast, one of the world's major transportation hubs, regional office to the nation's commerce. But she wasn't Big League. Then the stadium rose, in all its grandeur, sitting against the backdrop of an ever-changing skyline, Exhibit A for a growing city. Before the first pitch was thrown, before the first kickoff, Atlanta gained a new image, a new sheen. The stadium had become, Mayor Allen stated, "one of the greatest stimulants, one of the greatest inspirations, that this city have [sic] ever had. It has been a catalyst. It has changed our thinking, and the thinking of others around us. There's no provincial small town attitude here anymore. We're Big League."[22]

Boosters thus imagined that the stadium not only symbolized a new city. It was also a catalyst, creating a new Atlanta—from the connections and cooperation between government, corporations, and contractors needed to build the stadium; to the private investment that boosters hoped would follow; to the ways the stadium would change how residents and visitors alike would materially occupy and navigate the city. Like the railroad interchange that serves as the origin story mythologizing Atlanta's beginnings, boosters imagined the stadium as an infrastructure that would once again make Atlanta the center of capital exchange and distribution but on a national scale. "The future is Atlanta," the AFCRA declared, "golden, bright, exciting. History is Milwaukee and Boston."[23]

The stadium thus meant Atlanta was a city of the future, not only distinct and competitive with its Midwestern and Northeastern counterparts but ahead

Fig. 1.1: Atlanta–Fulton County Stadium, 1974. (Kenan Research Center)

of them as well, with what was at the time a technologically sophisticated and innovative piece of urban infrastructure. From the outset, the stadium incorporated a mediatized logic, not just in how the city hoped it would attract media representation through covering games but also through the integration of mediatization into the stadium and surrounding urban infrastructure. In addition to television broadcasting capacities, FCS integrated computer processing, a technology in its infancy at the time. The construction team used the Critical Path Method (CPM), which involves entering major actions into a computer and projecting each major action to be taken in which order over a twelve-month timeline, thus streamlining construction tasks.[24] This short timeline, imposed by the city to ensure the Braves would come to the city, spurred the use of CPM. Its use aligned with the stadium's simple architectural design—a circular structure with an upper-level built in eighty identical sections of "box steel bents."[25] The design facilitated a speedy build, but it also enabled the stadium to be used for both baseball and football, which were, as AFCRA conceded, "actually incompatible sports."[26] The stadium design tried to make them compatible by creating a flexible and versatile structure, but the Braves would later claim their incompatibility in order to demand a new stadium. At the time, though, the multipurpose stadium was ubiquitous in new stadiums across the nation.

Today, critics of second-generation stadiums like FCS chastise these structures as placeless, cookie-cutter "concrete donuts." But at the time, they were technological innovations, and their placelessness was precisely the point. FCS was literally cookie-cutter, as it was built out of identical sections (see fig. 1.1). Put together, the sections created a placeless architecture that signified to the nation that Atlanta was just like any other major city. And that was the point: Atlanta elites wanted the stadium to position the city as competitive and ahead of other cities, but essentially it wanted to demonstrate it was just like them. In an ironic twist, it created a new kind of emplacement of Atlanta as a "national city" by erasing what distinguished it.

Although much of the discourse surrounding FCS emphasized how it attracted outsiders to Atlanta and projected a national image, boosters also promoted the value of the stadium to Atlantans. In a letter from Eric Hill Associates (the planning firm contracted by AFCRA to conduct a stadium feasibility study), associate Leon S. Eplan wrote, "We would like to emphasize the impact which such a facility would have on the entire Atlanta area," suggesting there would be "far reaching economic and intangible effects of such a venture."[27] The report extols the stadium as a future "landmark for Atlanta" that will "not only give the area a national focus, it will also stimulate a local awareness that is important to producing a progressive community and which so represents this modern and unusual city. All Georgians, in fact, will be able to claim a public building of exciting beauty and grace, a modern facility of unusual efficiency, and a source of considerable enjoyment and personal pride."[28] In other words, the stadium was imagined as transforming not only the city but the citizens as well into national ones, capable of producing and participating in the "progressive" and "modern" city.

The term "progressive" is a veiled reference to the city's stance on civil rights in contrast to other Southern cities at the time. But the Atlanta Stadium dedication book, from which the Eric Hill Associates report quotes are drawn, makes no direct reference to race or to Atlanta's Black citizens. This absence expresses how much of the city's Black population was treated and understood in relation to the stadium. On the one hand, they, and especially Black elites, were essential to the image Atlanta wanted to project as progressive and modern. On the other hand, however, poor Black Atlantans represented a threat to that image, as their living conditions belied the promised progressiveness of what elites imagined a modern Atlanta should look like. Despite the fact that there were many Black baseball fans and a storied history of the city's Negro Leagues baseball team, the Atlanta Black Crackers, FCS boosters made little effort to connect with Atlanta's Black population as fans.[29] Instead, boosters constructed impoverished Black neighborhoods and their residents through discourses of urban decline that treated them as problems to be solved rather than as fans to be entertained.

The stadium dedication book describes FCS's neighborhood as "barren, an open scar of slum clearance."[30] Notably, the professed barrenness of the neighborhood was a result of the city's demolition of much of the area, displacing tens of thousands of people, businesses, and disrupting the lives of remaining residents. The stadium was just one of many urban renewal programs at the time that led to new city infrastructure through the displacement of Atlanta's poor, including the interstate highway system and the Atlanta Civic Center (later replaced by the Georgia World Congress Center). FCS is a typical second-generation stadium, as described in the introduction, in that it played a key role in these urban renewal and "slum clearance" practices, particularly in the neighborhoods bordering the stadium: Summerhill, Peoplestown, and Mechanicsville (see map 1.1). These neighborhoods were deeply affected by the highway, which cut through predominantly Black neighborhoods. In the name of slum clearance, urban renewal destroyed whole blocks and, in some instances, whole neighborhoods, such as the historically Black neighborhood Buttermilk Bottom, decimated to build the civic center. In addition to removing and displacing neighborhoods, the highway system reinforced segregation between white and Black neighborhoods by creating a buffer.[31] The highways made accessing the central city easier for residents traveling from predominantly white neighborhoods and suburbs while isolating predominantly Black neighborhoods.[32] The I-75/85 and I-20 interchange, completed in the 1960s, built on Summerhill's northwest corner, led to the demolition of several neighborhood blocks, cutting the neighborhood off from downtown and the west side of the city.[33]

The highway interchange was one of the primary reasons cited for the location of the stadium. It enabled easy access for fans from across the region as well as Atlantans who fled the city for the suburbs. The land for the stadium was part of the Rawson-Washington urban renewal/slum clearance project on either side of the expressway in Mechanicsville and Peoplestown.[34] According to Ronald Bayor, Mayor Allen decided to locate the stadium in Summerhill in response to debates over public housing. Allen faced pressure to comply with the Federal Housing Act of 1954, which required the city to provide public housing to replace housing demolished for urban renewal. But Allen also feared pressure from white elites. He originally planned to comply with federal policy and appease these white elites by building public housing for whites only, but Black

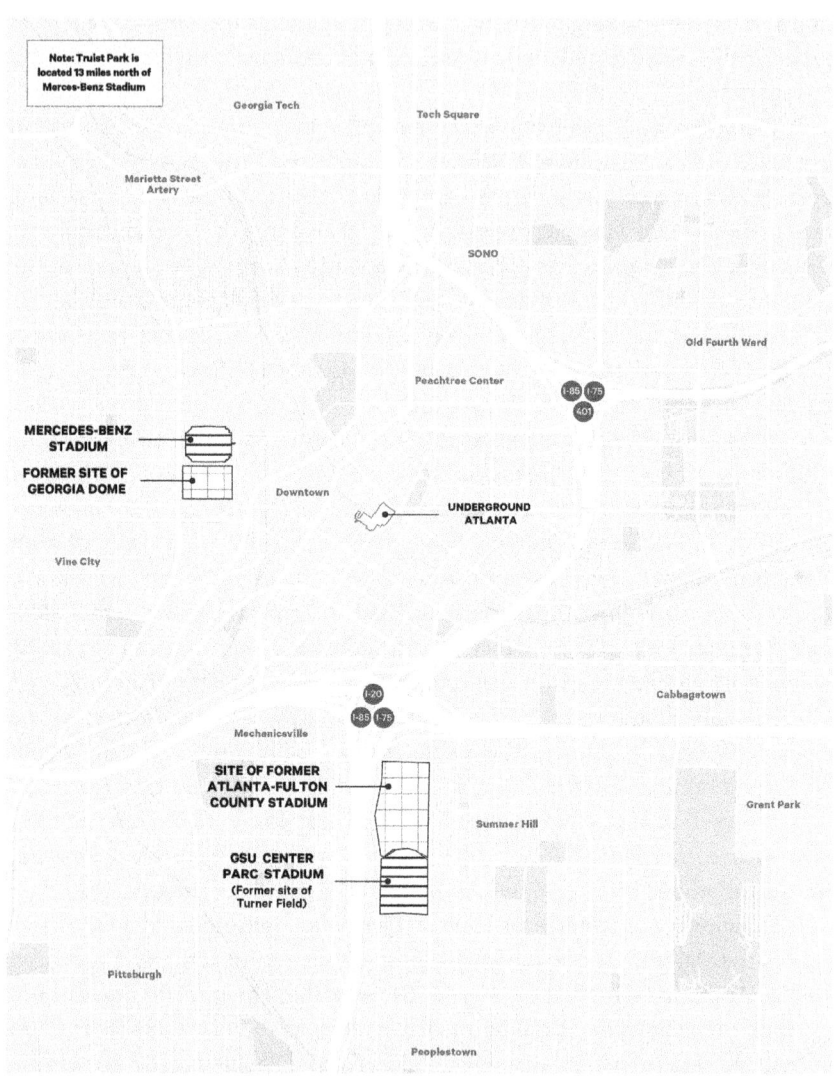

Map 1.1: Atlanta's second-generation stadiums ensured easy on/off access to the new highway system, connecting the city to the outer suburbs but also cutting off impoverished and primarily Black neighborhoods from downtown. The Georgia Dome was located in downtown Atlanta's Westside. (Credit: Gillian Tiley, used with permission)

leaders pushed back, insisting on the urgent need for housing displaced Black communities. Instead, Allen opted to build the stadium on the site to mollify the business community and avoid having to answer to Black leaders.[35] The stadium exacerbated displacement, ejecting thousands of mostly Black residents from one of the city's oldest neighborhoods, established as a community of freed slaves and Jewish immigrants in the late 1800s, with a long and rich cultural history.[36] While the 1949 and 1954 Federal Housing Acts required replacement housing, there was no mechanism for enforcement, and the federal government didn't make funding available for relocation until 1971.[37] Black residents, restricted by discriminatory housing practices, were forced into the city's already overcrowded neighborhoods or were forced to flee Atlanta altogether.

For the parts of the neighborhoods not cleared and now bordering a stadium, residents had to endure major disturbances to daily life that changed the culture of the neighborhood. Traffic and parking proved to be major issues, as all streets leading to the stadium were converted to one way before and after games. Likewise, the team put on fireworks displays after winning games, and they refused to stop the practice when neighbors complained about the noise and even after one of the displays caused a fire.[38] Essentially, FCS changed who and what the neighborhood was for, shifting it from a space laid claim to by residents, who were already forced to the margins of the city, to a place that served "fans," defined largely as those outside the neighborhood who would travel to game day via interstate highways.

But the city's urban renewal programs and the building of FCS did not go uncontested. Rutheiser says displaced residents referred to urban renewal as "negro removal," making it clear they understood it was an expressed effort to remove and disappear Black residents from the city.[39] While the Allen administration and other white business leaders pushed programs to "restore property values, sales, and the tax base in the city's central business district," Black political leaders and residents demanded improvement in Black neighborhoods, especially more housing, better services, and basic infrastructure.[40] Resistance reached an apex in September 1966 after an unarmed Black man named Harold Prather was killed by police. Approximately one thousand residents from the Summerhill area organized in protest, not only to this event and inequitable policing but also to the overarching injustices the community faced, including the effects of the stadium. The protesters were met with staunch police resistance. The newspapers portrayed the unrest as a "riot," leaning on long-standing depictions of Black resistance to injustice in criminal terms. Nevertheless, residents continued to push back against the Allen administration and demand the city invest in the neighborhood and repair the harms created by the stadium.

Going Global: The 1996 Atlanta Olympics

While boosters used FCS to position Atlanta as a national, major-league city, they used the infrastructure built in the lead-up to the 1996 Olympic Games, including new baseball and football stadiums, to take the city to the next level—as a global city. Boosters drew on the image of Atlanta as a diverse city and leader in civil rights to brandish a global image. The organizations tasked with preparing for the Olympics—the Atlanta Department of Planning and Development (ADPD) and the Corporation for Olympic Development in Atlanta—evoked this image in their 1993 master planning document:

> In preparing itself as a 21st Century City Atlanta intends to reach out into two directions: to an expanding Atlanta region so as to serve as its central place for coalescing the different cultures, peoples, ideas and lifestyles of an increasingly diverse community; and to a network of cities scattered throughout the world as Atlanta assumes the global responsibilities now being placed upon it.[41]

Prior to the Olympics, since the 1970s Atlanta's governing and business elites had been courting foreign capital, much of it invested in downtown development projects such as Omni International (which became CNN Center) and the Atlanta Center.[42] The city's Olympic bid aimed to capitalize on this nascent investment to propel the city to a new height of global competitiveness.

Atlanta's international aspirations reflected changing dynamics of the postindustrial economy as it shifted toward the global and transnational flow of capital and information starting in the late 1970s. Saskia Sassen maintains that economic globalization increased the significance of the subnational sphere, especially the city, by creating "global cities," such as London, New York, and Tokyo.[43] Global cities serve as command centers for servicing and financing the global economy, radically altering city space by constituting places to facilitate the flow of capital, information, and labor. Sassen emphasizes that global cities create new claims on place, thus precipitating intense struggles over who and what the city is for.

The increasing significance of the subnational sphere also coincided with waning federal support for state and local governments in the 1980s and 1990s, an era Neil Brenner and Nikolas Theodore refer to as "roll-back neoliberalism." During this period, federal funding and institutions were severely damaged, and cities were increasingly expected to be self-reliant in order to generate income for city governance, urban revitalization, and social welfare.[44] Kevin Fox Gotham and Jeannie Haubert note that the rollback of federal assistance for urban revitalization put "increased pressure on state governments and local municipalities to adopt more market-centered measures to attract investment."⁴⁵ This subsequent "roll-out neoliberalism" established new institutions and governing practices geared toward constituting self-maximizing and entrepreneurial citizens and neighborhoods.

As cities like Atlanta endeavored to reach this new echelon of global importance and respond to disinvestment, they invested significant resources in downtown development, real estate, housing, and telecommunications while often further cutting and diverting resources from low-income areas. Such practices exacerbated existing social inequities. The international aspirations of Atlanta's city government and business elites were thus about more than economics; they were a strategy of governing citizenship. The city's globalization made new demands on citizen behavior to be counted as valuable; they were expected to engage in consumer-oriented performances of citizenship, demonstrating entrepreneurial and self-responsible subjectivity to gain access to goods, including housing and basic services. Whereas FCS produced national subjects, Atlanta's Olympic infrastructures mark a shift to the neoliberal city, aiming to produce self-responsible individuals of capacity, able to compete and bring Atlanta into the global fold. Nikolas Rose contends that the shift from national citizenship to self-responsible individuals, neighborhoods, and communities is a hallmark of advanced liberalism (neoliberalism). Under neoliberal logics of the social, Rose says:

> The human beings who were to be governed ... were now conceived as individuals who are to be active in their own government. And their responsibility was no longer to be understood as a relation of obligation between citizen and society enacted and regulated through the mediating party of the State; rather, it was to be a relation of allegiance and responsibility to those one cared about the most and to whom one's destiny was linked ... oneself, one's family, one's neighbourhood, one's community, one's workplace.⁴⁶

This shift in governing toward the individual, community, and neighborhood is evident in Atlanta's Olympic-driven urban revitalization projects, including new stadium infrastructure as it intertwined with media culture and practices.

Organizers sought to use the Olympics as a catalyst for creating a coherent Atlanta design that would better reflect the city's identity and contracted the Regional/Urban Design Assistance Team (R/UDAT) in 1992 to help articulate that identity. The team's report suggested that Atlanta's urban design should be used to project its aspirations as a global city and center of civil and human rights and tolerance, as a Black intellectual center, and as a regional hub. The authors wrote, "We see the Olympic venues as pieces of a much larger order of connections at the city-wide scale," in which lasting infrastructure, especially sporting venues, would be the city's legacy of the Games.[47] That infrastructure, then, was viewed as central to constituting this new sense of place to symbolize Atlanta as an international leader.

Four new venues were constructed for the Games, along with a housing complex for the Olympic Village and a new park.[48] The city paid at least $250 million alone to build two sports stadiums, with some estimates of overall government expenditures on Games infrastructure approximating $1 billion.[49] Government officials justified the expenditures because they intended to use each new stadium for the home sports teams after the Games—one for the Falcons in the Westside area, and one for the Braves adjacent to FCS in Summerhill, with a plan to demolish FCS after the Games.

Race and the image of Atlanta as a Black Mecca, including because of the perceived diversity of its sports industries and being home to sporting greats like the boxer Muhammad Ali, helped them win the Olympic bid. The organizing committee characterized the city as "a place where people of color were thriving," and the International Olympic Committee (IOC) claimed Atlanta's leadership in civil and human rights was the foremost reason they were chosen over competing bids.[50]

But the conditions of the neighborhoods that would become the center of Olympic events and these new sporting infrastructures suggested otherwise; deprived of resources as the city diverted money to corporate developments instead, Atlanta's downtown core painted a picture that was vastly different from the thriving, diverse city it aimed to project. Thus, to conform to the Atlanta imagined in the bid, the city embarked on a major program to revitalize downtown neighborhoods where Olympic events would be held, a three-mile area of the downtown core referred to as the "Olympic Ring" (see figs. 1.2 and 1.3).

Mediatization was key to the city's Olympic revitalization, as "the increasing profile and media coverage of the Games meant growing attention was directed to the impact on not just local business and the urban landscape, but host city residents as well."[51] In keeping with their efforts to present Atlanta as a global and interconnected city, organizers promised the Olympic Centennial Games would debut "state-of-the art telecommunications . . . in operation on a 24-hour basis. The host broadcaster alone will produce 3,000 hours of live radio and television coverage. In addition, some 40 television mobile units, 400 cameras and 275 video tape machines will be used, and will make Atlanta, for about a month, the worldwide hub of global communications."[52] Organizers endeavored to present an image of a world-class and inclusive city in which people of color were thriving to millions of viewers on their TV screens and

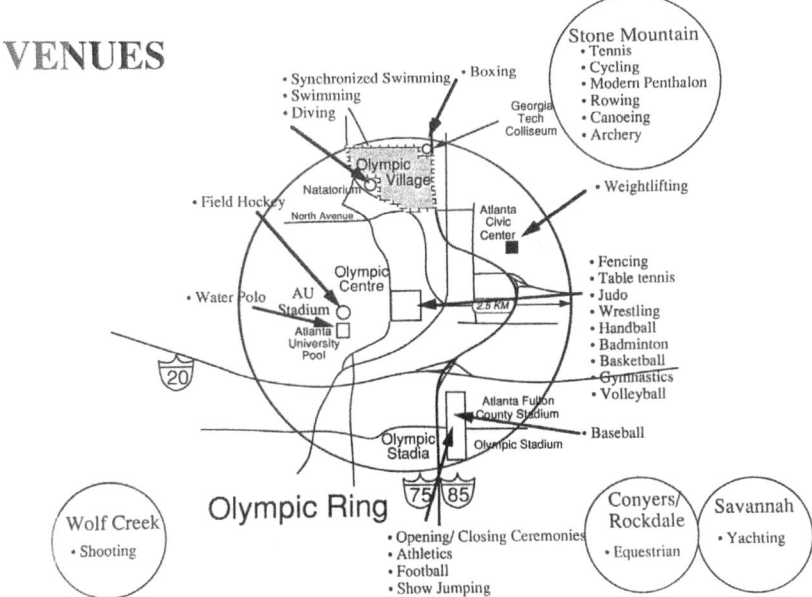

Fig. 1.2: The Olympic Ring created a new spatialization of Atlanta's downtown neighborhoods. (Atlanta University Center Robert W. Woodruff Library)

the newly emerging World Wide Web. Thus, what was most important about revitalizing neighborhoods was getting them to *look* like the desired image on screen. Neighborhoods long neglected by government—targeted either for segregation from the city's white economic and cultural centers or demolished as part of slum clearance—were now newly included in efforts to bring them into alignment with the city's image as a civil rights leader and an international, cosmopolitan sporting city.

Revitalizing the Olympic Ring neighborhoods was a significant component of the city's transformation. The whole of the Olympic Ring became a kind of stadium, constituted as a site of sporting culture spectacle through the gaze of the TV camera. Envisioning these neighborhoods as part of the Olympic Ring created a new sportified spatial rationale. Some critics argue that Olympic revitalization of neighborhoods was merely a ruse with no real intent on actual revitalization.[53] Yet, on my read, there was real intent to transform these neighborhoods into the sportified Olympic image, and various agencies engaged in material practices to transform not only city space but that of residents as well. However, those practices were never intended to resolve structural issues un-

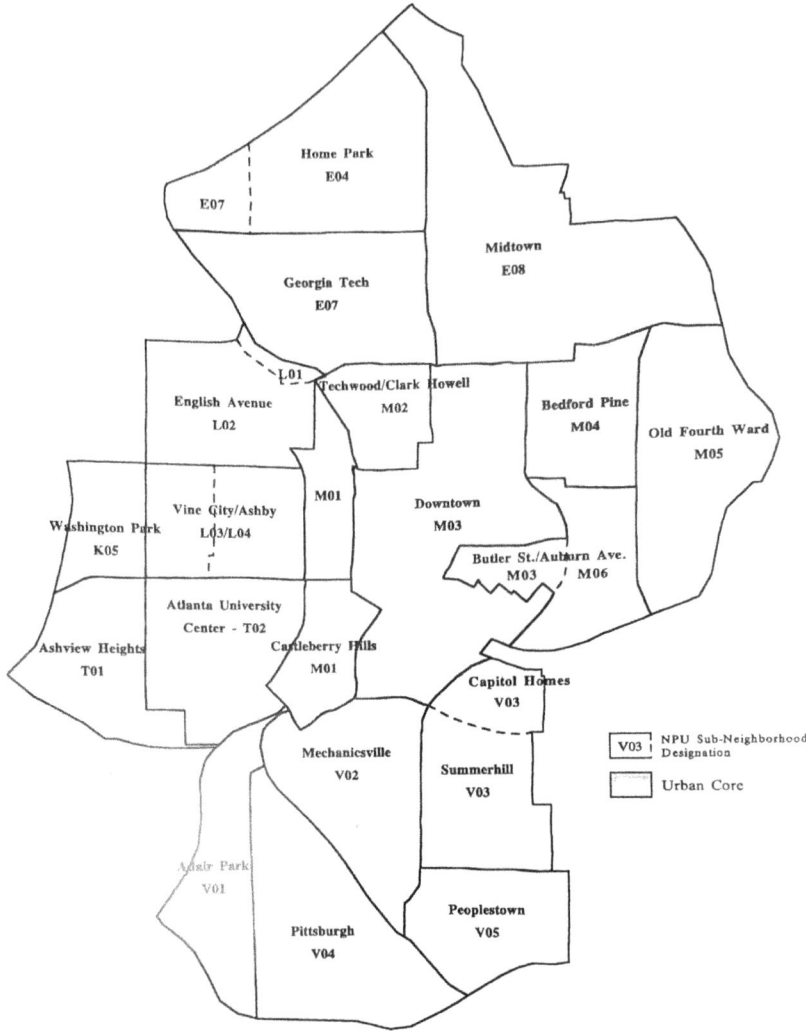

OLYMPIC RING NEIGHBORHOODS

Fig. 1.3: The Olympic Ring created a new spatialization of Atlanta's downtown neighborhoods. (Atlanta University Center Robert W. Woodruff Library)

derlying the neighborhood conditions, because city government and business elites did not see the structural issues—that is, economic disenfranchisement and the siphoning and diversion of resources and basic services—as the problem; they saw the people and their culture as the problem. That perception was rooted in the always-already imagined representation that connected the urban with Blackness, and Blackness with criminality. Olympic-era neighborhood revitalization was primarily a matter of constituting new forms of sportified citizenship practices to transform citizens into self-responsible and active residents invested in the projection of image and spectacle inherent in the visual culture of sport and Olympified Atlanta.

Though the Olympic Ring defined the venue area, it also created new cultural geographies, connecting disparate parts of the city and subjecting them to sportified development frameworks and strategies of governing. Through this new spatial rationale of the Olympic Ring, Games organizers disconnected those neighborhoods from their histories and identities, problematized by business elites and government agencies as spaces of poverty, crime, and despair, to create a new sense of place articulated to the city's Olympic image.

The 1993 master planning document for the Games, for example, refers to the Olympic Ring neighborhoods as low-income areas primarily made up of renters from single-family households that were "in substandard condition," with "streets, curbs and sidewalks" showing "widespread disrepair."[54] The report disparages the neighborhoods, suggesting, "Olympic Ring neighborhoods are trash-strewn, overgrown and an unsightly mess. No one has responsibility for them. Their appearance discourages residents and potential lenders and investors." This description suggests that residents were to blame for neighborhood conditions—as if it was dilapidated because of their failures to lift themselves out of poverty rather than a failure of government to provide basic services and resources. They imply what was needed was a different kind of resident along with "lenders and investors." In other words, Olympic organizers saw the neighborhood as a problem to be solved by the influx of outside residents, investors, and tourists who could help change the character of the neighborhood.

Rather than providing the kinds of infrastructure these neighborhoods actually needed to address long-standing underlying problems—such as sewage and wastewater runoff, vital needs of many of the Olympic Ring neighborhoods at the time—Games organizers proposed sporting infrastructure as the means to urban revitalization.[55] The "Facility Impact Report, Olympic Stadium" claimed the stadium was "designed to assist the neighborhood in revitalization efforts through the appearance of the Stadium and its relationship to the street," suggesting further, "The project will enhance the streetscape and add to the visual and aesthetic value of the neighborhood."[56] Like the sports that would be broadcast to viewers' TV screens, then, neighborhoods were themselves made subject to this mediatization. Space, spatial value, and the material transformation of space and citizens were hinged to its aesthetic and visual value as sites of sporting spectacle and performance.

While the stadium was tasked with transforming the visual and aesthetic value of the neighborhood, it also served as an infrastructural site for training and transforming citizens. Games organizers called for hiring neighborhood residents for stadium construction projects to provide job training and employment,[57] educational programming to youth,[58] and affirmative action policies that would provide job opportunities for racial and ethnic minorities and women.[59] The city's Black mayor, Maynard Jackson, pushed for the affirmative action plan after being pressured by neighborhood organizers who demanded government do more for the neighborhoods affected by Olympic infrastructure.[60]

Although these are perhaps laudable efforts to provide training and resources to neighborhood residents affected by the Games and stadium infrastructure, the proposal for revitalization largely fell on the uncompensated residents. Games organizers acknowledged there were limited resources allocated for revitalization, which was insufficient to address systemic issues in the Olympic Ring neighborhoods. Thus, organizers called for the use of volunteer labor by residents, encouraging an "adopt-a-block" program modeled on "adopt-a-highway" to provide regular maintenance.[61] The Corporation for Olympic Development in Atlanta (CODA) called for residents to take responsibility for their neighborhoods, suggesting that enlisting residents and neighborhood organizations in cleaning up their neighborhoods for the Olympics would help them become more self-responsible citizens in the long run. For example, CODA proposed that creating a "clean and green" program to pick up trash and a "paint-up/fix-up" program would "positively impact the appearance of neighborhoods and turn attitudes around in a positive way."[62] While they did call for human services, job training, and employment, much of the revitalization was about extracting volunteer labor of residents to transform them into self-responsible citizens, capable of creating neighborhood space that could be seen as a site of spectacle for Olympics viewers.

In contrast to the FCS's discourse of urban renewal and slum clearance, the Olympic stadiums hinged on a discourse of urban "revitalization" and "revival." Planners often acknowledged the harms of slum clearance and the detrimental effects they had on neighborhoods and displaced peoples. In a July 1993 CODA background memo on "Implementing Community Revival," for example, the organization notes:

The Olympic Ring Neighborhood revival plans will emphasize rehabilitation, not clearance, the preservation of neighborhood character and institutions, the creation of new ownership housing, and community improvements, such as streets, sidewalks, neighborhood parks and playgrounds.

RELOCATION: Unlike most redevelopment plans which required substantial relocation of families and businesses, it is anticipated that there will be little or no relocation in the Olympic neighborhoods.[63]

Yet, apparently unironically, right above this note the "redevelopment plan" requests reports on "property acquisition, including through eminent domain" and for the plans to "provide for rehabilitation or demolition." Thus, "revival" and "revitalization" still called for widespread displacement and relocation. Later reports on building Olympic Stadium parking demonstrate that despite claims that little or no relocation would be necessary, the city was indeed planning the contrary. In an October 1993 "Olympic Stadium Parking and Land Acquisition Update," Games organizers called for negotiating with landowners and homeowners for their properties, but should those negotiations fail within thirty days, they stated, "a condemnation petition will be filed" to enact eminent domain policies.[64] The report claimed the Metropolitan Atlanta Olympic Games Authority, the state authority tasked with overseeing the Games, would find replacement housing for those displaced within ninety days. However, Keating says little housing ever materialized; instead, as in earlier eras of stadium construction, funds were diverted to middle-class or mixed-income housing, leaving the poor with few options.[65]

The key difference between renewal and revitalization, then, was less about displacement and removal, since both strategies resulted in demolition and displacement. It was more about targeting some new populations as problems to be solved through rehabilitation rather than waste to be removed. Thus, Olympic revitalization and new urban sporting infrastructures became mechanisms for transforming citizens into empowered, responsible, healthy, and capable citizens, where displacement and relocation were characterized by elites as ways of "salvaging" the health of these populations and their neighborhood. Rather than problematizing the systems and structures that produce poverty and racism, Atlanta's Olympic-era urban revitalization programs problematized the city's people—namely, impoverished Black residents—and treated their displacement and the development that would replace their neighborhoods as a kind of gift of salvation. But those populations who would not, or could not, maximize themselves were further marginalized and displaced, exacerbating existing racial, class, and spatial inequities. Thus, Olympic revitalization of the downtown core was largely regarded as a failure as these neighborhoods continued to lose jobs and residents.[66]

These broader strategies of Olympic sportification of place are put into sharper focus when considering the Georgia Dome and Centennial Olympic Stadium (later, Turner Field). In both cases, the stadium served as a site for governing citizenship. Still, residents virulently resisted stadium-building efforts and, in so doing, drew on the cultural memory of resistance to FCS.

"You Can't Live in a Stadium": The Georgia Dome and Westside Atlanta

Building a new sports stadium for the football team, the Falcons, was part of the Olympic bid and revitalization strategy for the Olympic Ring. At the time of the bid, the Falcons were agitating for a new stadium and threatening to leave. Both the Falcons and the Braves, along with fans, complained that FCS's multipurpose design was conducive to neither baseball nor football, as it had poor sight lines and too much distance between fans and the action on the field. Moreover, since the city had built FCS primarily to attract an MLB team, the Braves had the better contract deal; as the primary tenant, they received all stadium revenue from parking and concessions, including from Falcons games. The Falcons wanted their own stadium, where they could access revenue streams beyond ticket sales. To prevent the team leaving for Jacksonville, Florida, the Georgia governor's office commissioned a study to determine a location for a new stadium. The study concluded that FCS was outdated and recommended building two new stadiums instead—one for the Braves and one for the Falcons. Soon, the city and the county government got involved in negotiations, with the county government ultimately approving and financing a new site for a Falcons stadium, what would become the Georgia Dome (the Dome), in Atlanta's downtown Westside, adjacent to the city's historically Black college and university campuses, in the Vine City, English Avenue, and Lightning neighborhoods.[67] The Georgia Dome, built and funded by a public-private partnership through the Georgia World Congress Authority, was a $214 million domed structure that could seat seventy-two thousand people.[68] It became a centerpiece of Atlanta's claim that it would have the infrastructure to host the Games.

The Dome sits at the cusp of the second- and third-generation stadium eras. The dome style, popular at the time, would soon go out of fashion as teams sought more iconic architectures that both stood out and helped define and signify the city in more place-specific ways. However, the Dome's translucent cable roof was innovative for the time. It consisted of fiberglass-reinforced, Teflon-coated material, "supported by the ring beam and a network of cables, hoop rings and steel posts."[69] The translucent material of the roof created, as one sportswriter remarked, "the closest thing to an outdoor atmosphere in an indoor stadium."[70]

The translucent roof and the seat-filled walls in the playing area therefore did not create a window effect to the downtown area, as do more contemporary stadiums, such as Mercedes-Benz Stadium (discussed in the next chapter), but instead reinforced more of a sense of being in a bubble—part of downtown Atlanta but not immersed within it. Fans were separate and protected. The divide between inside and outside reinforced a sense of spectacle—what happened in the stadium was constituted as private, special, and something distinct from the "real world."

Similarly, the Dome's integration of media technology also sat at the cusp between second- and third-generation stadiums, prioritizing the stadium's televisual capacities and connectivity to broadcasting, cable, and satellite technologies and integrating some elements of emerging digital technology. Teams and stadium executives were acutely aware the stadium still needed to compete with the televised experience, and the challenges of converting FCS to include new technologies other new stadiums were using helped the Falcons persuade legislators they needed a new stadium. The builders incorporated state-of-the-art technologies, including closed-circuit television, large screens (jumbotron), instant-replay-capable video systems, fiber-optic cabling, and teleconferencing.[71] However, digital and web technology developed rapidly in the 1990s, and those changes also greatly impacted televised sports entertainment. The technology used in the Dome was therefore quickly out of date. In 2003, analog systems built into the original stadium control suite and broadcast infrastructure were replaced with serial digital interface, a first step toward high-definition capability that enabled video and audio to be transmitted over coaxial and fiber-optic cable, to comply with new league standards.[72] The Dome underwent a more extensive $30 million renovation in 2006, including the integration of flat-screen plasma TVs and LED lighting along with additional luxury boxes and suites.[73]

The Dome aimed to make the stadium an entertainment destination to create experiences, where going to the stadium meant more than just going to watch a game. "Skybox" suites and club seats were especially crucial to the Dome experience, which provided more luxury experiences, with 203 suites and 5,800 club seats ranging from $20,000 to $120,000 annual lease rates.[74] The emphasis on suites enabled the team to generate more revenue. Luxury boxes were hence a major reason teams pushed for new stadiums at the time, arguing that renovating older structures to accommodate these luxury spaces would be more challenging and costly. The Dome's suites featured padded seats, catering, reserved parking, and private elevators to the suite level, where these special fans could enjoy private cocktails, fine dining, and restrooms while viewing the game on their own big-screen TVs.[75] Targeting businesses and executives, these luxury experiences both catered to and helped to produce precisely the kind of cosmopolitan, international citizen Atlanta boosters hoped to attract in their quest to become a global city.

Although it lacked architectural uniqueness and was similar to other domed stadiums at the time, stadium boosters argued that the Dome departed from the cookie-cutter designs of past stadium generations, such as FCS, because it was uniquely designed to fit into the downtown urban Atlanta landscape. However, what that meant at the time was that it fit in with other mega-event centers built in this period, such as the Georgia World Congress Center, World of Coca-Cola, CNN Center, and the newly renovated and reopened mall, Underground Atlanta. These structures were built to enable Atlanta to host and attract convention business and mega-events, such as the Super Bowl and the Olympics. Thus, the downtown architecture the Dome fit into wasn't attached to a sense of place for those who lived in the neighborhoods where these megastructures were built. Instead, they were attached to the image of Atlanta as an international city—a place created through its possibility of being a nonplace or anyplace. As will become clear in the discussion of Mercedes-Benz Stadium and Truist Park, this disregard for the culture and sense of place of the neighborhoods in which these structures were built distinguishes the Dome from more contemporary stadium-building rationales that mark the third generation.

As mentioned above, the Georgia Dome and its parking areas were built in an area that included the Vine City, English Avenue, and Lightning neighborhoods (see map 1.1). Like Summerhill, Mechanicsville, and Peoplestown—the neighborhoods razed to build FCS—the Dome-area neighborhoods consisted of predominantly Black, working-class residents. Likewise, these neighborhoods have a long history in Atlanta tied to civil rights and racial justice organizing, including several churches. While the Olympic bid instrumentalized this history to sell an image of Atlanta as an equitable space of Black success, building the Dome in the middle of these neighborhoods, like FCS in the previous decades, showed little regard for the actual people who lived there and the culture that contributed to that image. The city used the principle of eminent domain, the policy that enables government to seize private property for public use, to remove several churches and hundreds of residents from their homes. The Vine City and English Avenue neighborhoods had already been targets of urban renewal in the 1970s when several blocks were cleared and hundreds of residents displaced to build the Georgia World Congress Center. The Georgia

Dome thus continued patterns of privileging the interest of business elites over city residents, leading to further displacement and winnowing already scarce resources allocated to the neighborhood.[76]

The displacement caused by the construction of the Georgia Dome did not go uncontested. That resistance is palpable in a set of oral history interviews conducted by a humanities class at Booker T. Washington High School in 1987 and 1988 just as the planning for the Dome's construction was under way. In those interviews, Vine City residents, city council members, and clergy people voiced their concerns about the impending stadium. Overwhelmingly, those interviewed, whether they supported the stadium or not, conveyed concern about how it would contribute to further displacement of people in their neighborhood, especially the poor and elderly. Rebecca Jackson, an elementary school principal in Vine City, questioned whether the Dome truly brought in more opportunities, saying any opportunities it brought would "not overshadow the displacement of human beings in this area. Moving out from a neighborhood that they've been in for years."[77] As with so many urban renewal projects inflicted on the neighborhood previously, the planning for the Georgia Dome and the Olympic projects around the neighborhood excluded and disregarded their voices entirely. Reverend Howard Creecy Jr., the Fulton County assistant chaplain, supported building the Dome because he thought it could contribute to neighborhood revitalization, but he also voiced concerns that the project did not include the voices of the poor or the communities that lived there. Creecy claimed, "The project was conceived in the mind of some community, civic leaders who are neither indigent [sic] to their community or reflective of the color and kind of community. . . . From the very beginning, Vine City was not included in the planning and projection of this project."[78]

These oral histories convey a sense of deep mistrust of government and an agential voice of resistance to the ways the city, county, and state disregarded the value of their neighborhood. Residents contested how government and media portrayed the neighborhood, instead laying claim to the value of the neighborhood and the people living there. Mabel Austell, a Vine City resident, for example, said, "This has been a relatively nice neighborhood. We haven't had that much crime, even though they would like to label it that way . . . [with] students who go to college, teachers, postmen, small business owners. . . . These people are very dear to the community."[79] The sense of deep, affective connection to place is evident in many of the interviews and serves as a stark contrast to the disparaging ways governing and business elites portrayed the neighborhood and the blighted properties of the Olympic Ring. While many residents also described the neighborhood as troubled by blight and poverty, they attributed that blight to the fault of government, urban renewal, and disinvestment rather than residents.

Residents also drew on the cultural memory of how FCS affected the Summerhill neighborhood, using that history to demonstrate the hollow claims being promised by stadium boosters. Vine City commissioner Nancy Boxill, for example, conveyed her concerns that Vine City would end up looking like the FCS neighborhoods, "one huge parking lot on four sides of the stadium."[80] Rebecca Jackson forcefully argued, "I remember when they moved the people from Summerhill over there where the present stadium is located, they told the people that they were going to rebuild the area. They could then move back in. They never did that. It hasn't happened yet. If they did build the area up again, the former residents would not be able to afford the rent."[81]

While elites promised residents the stadium would be a boon to their neighborhoods, creating revitalization and opportunity, the residents laid bare how these stadium projects were, in actuality, revitalization and opportunity for *other* people and *other* parts of Atlanta. They promised opportunities by draining resources from the kinds of infrastructure and programs that would have created opportunities for the people who lived there. As Rebecca Jackson said, "The area has changed, but it cannot be improved by putting up a stadium. You can't live in a stadium. Kids can't go to school in a stadium."[82]

Despite widespread opposition, the Dome led to the demolition of virtually the entire neighborhood of Lightning and hundreds of homes and several churches in Vine City to clear the way for parking lots. Still, residents' resistance garnered some significant gains. Organizers in these neighborhoods teamed up with residents from Summerhill, Peoplestown, and Mechanicsville as well as other residents affected by Olympic infrastructure. Together, they formed an organization called Atlanta Neighborhoods United for Fairness (ANUFF). Along with several Black clergy members, ANUFF agitated for a greater say and participation in the decision-making process, an environmental impact study, and guarantees that residents would receive funding for relocation. Although there were initially no funds set aside for relocation, organizers eventually got the state to put aside $25 million.[83] They pushed for affirmative action programs in hiring contractors and stadium jobs. These gains laid the groundwork for the kinds of Community Benefits Agreements future organizers would demand.

Centennial Olympic Stadium/Turner Field

Like the Falcons, the Braves also threatened to leave Atlanta if they didn't get a new stadium. The city seized the Olympic opportunity to build a new stadium adjacent to FCS. After the Olympics, the city demolished FCS and replaced it with a parking lot while converting the newly built Centennial Olympic Stadium into a ballpark for the Braves.

The team named the new baseball stadium Turner Field after their owner, Ted Turner, and the stadium became affectionately known as "The Ted." Turner bought the Braves in 1976 and saw them through some of their most successful seasons.[84] When the stadium was built, the Braves were "practically synonymous with their owner."[85] Turner helped turn the Braves into a household name, christening them "America's Team" and broadcasting their games to a national audience through his Atlanta-based WTBS television station. Providing content for his TV stations was a primary reason Turner decided to purchase the Braves.[86] Turner would soon go on to found the twenty-four-hour news station CNN, the Cable News Network, in 1980, also located in Atlanta. Although CNN did not air Atlanta-based content as WTBS did—Charles Rutheiser proposes that CNN did not really represent Atlanta; it just happened to be where CNN was located—it did influence the city in significant ways, especially by transforming downtown Atlanta into the space that included CNN headquarters and attracting a whole new labor sector to the city.[87] CNN represented the kind of city Atlanta aspired to be: a global city and telecommunications hub through which capital and information flowed.

Turner Field is characteristic of the early stages of the third generation, as it is modeled on the retro ballpark design of Baltimore's Camden Yards. Architectural consultant Janet Marie Smith, who pioneered Camden's retro design, collaborated with Atlanta-based architectural firms Heery International, Rosser International, Williams-Russell and Johnson, and Kansas City–based Ellerbe Becket, to design Turner Field as a "classic-style" ballpark with modern amenities. As one designer noted, "The goal was to create a traditional urban ballpark, with a sense of intimacy and enclosure" but with a place for "modern entertainment aspects—food service, seating classifications, and interactive themed environments."[88]

Like Camden Yards, the stadium aimed to signify baseball's urbanism and tradition, modeled on first-generation ballparks like Fenway Park in Boston and Chicago's Wrigley Field. The stadium's red, white, blue, and dark green color scheme "was selected to evoke a traditional baseball ambience," thus emphasizing a sense of national and Atlantan identity and pride.[89] The nostalgic design further emphasized baseball's urbanism and a sense of being in Atlanta by creating views to downtown from most seats.[90] Though elements of Turner Field gestured toward placemaking and local Atlanta, it was also lacking in this area. Constructed on a tight timeline and to host the Olympics, the stadium so clearly took from the Camden Yards model that it was perhaps more of an iconographic representation of Baltimore than Atlanta. While Turner Field did to a degree become a topophilic place for some Atlantans, it "never quite captured the imagination of baseball fans comparing modern ballparks to one another. It was nice and pleasing, but much of its charm was manufactured and not truly original; there's no genuine signature asset to be found."[91]

Still, Turner Field aimed to create a sense of place by celebrating Atlanta as a sports town, theming areas of the park with design elements to represent the old stadium and featuring monuments to Braves history. The stadium featured a statue commemorating Hank Aaron's 715th career home run, preserved the fence from FCS over which he hit the run, and had an on-site Braves Museum and Hall of Fame. The ballpark design emphasized intimacy, bringing fans closer to the game, working to mirror the intimate and personalized view provided by television. Like Camden, Turner Field aimed to create a sense of connection between fans, team, and city by celebrating baseball and the team as a central part of Atlanta and national tradition.

The ballpark's nostalgic, classic design encouraged fans to view coming to the stadium as an essential part of baseball tradition itself, while modern amenities made attendance more on par with the television viewing experience. Integration of media technology to enhance game viewing and the stadium experience was a key component of this, including technologies to facilitate cable and broadcast production, video replay, and fifteen hundred feet of fiber-optic cabling for audio and video on the inside of the stadium and plaza. Additionally, the stadium contracted with Panasonic to integrate electronics, such as huge scoreboards, video screens, and matrix boards that were "twice the size of the main board used in the Fulton County Stadium," and custom speakers for a high-fidelity sound system.[92]

Like the Dome, and perhaps even more so, Turner Field was intended to be "a spectacular sports and entertainment destination."[93] Amenities focused especially on producing fans as consumers, encouraging them to come early, stay late, and spend more. This included luxury experiences through suite and club services. At the club level, fans enjoyed "an enclosed, air-conditioned/heated concourse" with "four food courts, upgraded interior finishes and furniture, a stadium club, and a restaurant/bar with waiter service."[94] For fans who could not afford the luxury experience, the stadium offered a range of lower-tier amenities, including various concessions, retail sites and an official Clubhouse Store, museum, and Scout's Alley. The latter space engaged fans in skill games involving Braves statistics, past and present, along with interactive educational stations complete with touch-screen kiosks. Together, the stadium included "eight electronic interactive games using Panasonic touch-screen monitors, plus six non-electronic games which use standard devices such as radar guns."[95]

Unlike the Dome, Turner Field did not have other structures in the neighborhood it was tied to. While the Dome was part of the downtown tourist bubble, Turner Field, like FCS before it, was its own bubble. It served as a stand-alone entertainment center, and that is how the Braves wanted it—they sought to ensure fans coming to the game spent their money at the stadium. This made Turner Field also distinct from the Camden Yards model, since although it was tied to discourses of neighborhood revitalization, it was also specifically detached from the neighborhood. Turner Field's neighborhood revitalization plan ultimately aimed to protect stadium-goers from the neighborhood. Constituting the stadium as a site for family-friendly fun, luxury experiences, and spectacular entertainment attracted upper- and middle-class Atlantans to a neighborhood they would otherwise avoid because of its reputed association with blight, crime, and impoverished Blackness. Simultaneously, promises of neighborhood revitalization assured those fans the stadium would be safer than FCS had been, while placating residents who were resistant to the disruption of a new stadium in their neighborhood with promises of resources.

Like the residents on Atlanta's west side who opposed the Dome, Summerhill, Peoplestown, and Mechanicsville residents virulently resisted the stadium plans, at least initially. Olympic organizers planning for the new stadium elicited support from the Summerhill Neighborhood Incorporated (SNI), a neighborhood organization formed as part of Atlanta's Neighborhood Planning Unit program, with promises to direct funding specifically to Summerhill. Keating argues that Olympic planners effectively co-opted the SNI "to provide themselves with political cover by appointing Doug Dean, head of SNI, along with a representative from a neighborhood not in the stadium area to the AOC [Atlanta Organizing Committee]."[96] Through Dean, the SNI agreed to support the stadium in exchange for moving the stadium site to the edge of Peoplestown but designating Summerhill as the primary stadium site. Keating says this put Summerhill in the position to gain resources while weakening the bargaining position of the other two neighborhoods, further isolating them and starving them of resources. This struggle over scarce resources between neighborhoods is a hallmark of the neoliberal city, where neighborhoods, like the residents who live there, must become entrepreneurs for themselves and compete to access funding and support.

Summerhill became a primary target for Olympic Ring revitalization. Despite striking a deal with the AOC, the Braves and the Atlanta Committee for the Olympic Games (ACOG) did not allow neighborhood representatives to participate in the planning process; thus the plans did little to address the real needs of the neighborhood.[97] Instead, like the broader neighborhood revitalization plan for the Olympic Ring, the revitalization plans for Summerhill called for further displacement of residents legitimated by the discourses of urban crisis that problematized the neighborhood as a deteriorating slum in need of sport-driven development. The 1993 "Summerhill Urban Redevelopment Plan," for example, describes the neighborhood as "appropriate for urban redevelopment because of blight, distress, and impaired development" and says, "The 'rehabilitation, conservation, or redevelopment, or a combination thereof, of such area or areas is necessary in the interest of the public health, safety, morals or welfare of the residents of the municipality or county.'"[98] The plan goes on to describe the neighborhood as an abject space through a discourse of disgust, problematizing the neighborhood as a space of blight, poverty, and social distress. These are coded references to the urban that construct it as a space of fear and Otherness. As Cortland Rankin writes, "The conflation of rundown urban environments with crime and social deviance both reflects and encourages the racist and classist criminalization of entire neighborhoods, particularly the low-income communities of color where abandoned buildings and empty lots tend to be located."[99] Thus, the discourses are not inconsequential; they had real, material impacts on the policies and practices of revitalization that affected the neighborhood and people who lived there.

Strikingly, the plan acknowledged that previous urban renewal efforts contributed to these conditions, noting the neighborhood did not recover from the "disruptions caused by the construction of Interstate Highways and the Fulton County Stadium."[100] The authors even went so far as to fault government for these infractions, arguing, "Many of the previous residents of Summerhill were displaced as a result of governmental actions." The authors boldly declared, "The time has come for public and private efforts to overcome the problems of the past and to create a new community in Summerhill."[101] Though these statements seem to place fault on government, the authors did not call for the government to repair those harms but, rather, for a public-private partnership to "create a new community." The existing community in Summerhill was therefore viewed as a problem to be overcome through the revitalizing transformation of the neighborhood. Existing conditions in the neighborhood were seen only through this lens of problematization—as threats to the life and health of the population, a disease that must be subjected to revitalization to be cured. What could not be cured would be removed, displaced. While the authors acknowledged that the new stadium could end up harming the neighborhood, they nonetheless forged forward in arguing for the same strategy for renewing the neighborhood as in the 1960s—a sports stadium—but with "proper planning."

But that planning replicated the earlier era by calling for the use of eminent domain to displace 26 homeowners, 307 renters, and 18 small businesses.[102] "Proper planning" also meant implementation of new technologies of governing. The "Summerhill Urban Redevelopment Plan" called for new programs to shape Summerhill's residents into ones more fit to participate in the neoliberal economy, including programs targeting homeownership, business entrepreneurship, the construction of shopping spaces, job training, public safety, health care, education, recreation, and social service programs.[103] Job training aimed to get residents "involved in the renovation and beautification of their own communities" through the revitalization efforts in the stadium neighborhoods.[104] The plan maintained that the goal of the broad set of programs they proposed was "to empower former and present residents of Summerhill by providing support and creating an environment in which the residents can rely on themselves and make their own decisions in building a stable, prosperous community."[105] In other words, it would produce self-reliant, neoliberal citizens who cared for themselves and did not drain public resources. These forms of citizenship, however, were distinct from those assumed of the stadium-going fans—neighborhood residents were thought of more as citizens who work for the stadium rather than the fans and citizen-consumers who take leisure in the stadium.

Parts of Summerhill gentrified as a result of the stadium's driving up rents and further displacing poor residents. According to Keating, the Summerhill revitalization project "reverses a long-standing policy of either tearing down such neighborhoods or simply neglecting them. And yet the Summerhill revitalization has not done a great deal for the neighborhood's original residents."[106] It created new racial, class, and spatial antagonisms that bear on the current era of stadium building in the neighborhood, as the Braves moved out to Cobb County and the city sold the Turner Field properties to Georgia State University, which I discuss in chapter 3.

As noted in the case of the Dome, residents of Summerhill, Peoplestown, and Mechanicsville resisted the stadium and agitated for a better deal. Though their initial efforts were geared toward preventing the stadium from being built altogether, after the SNI agreed to support the stadium a coalition of organizers, including ANUFF, the Olympic Conscience Coalition, the Task Force for the Homeless, and local unions, shifted to a strategy of garnering community benefits and trying to participate in the planning process.[107] The group won some concessions, including reducing the number of parking spaces allotted to the stadium, a portion of the parking revenue devoted to a community development fund, affirmative action hiring policies, the appointment of local Black administrators to top administrative positions in the ACOG, a minority contracting program, and job training for residents near the stadium. These were, perhaps, as Charles Rutheiser concludes, "more symbolic than substantive."[108] The stadium deal was ultimately a huge win for the Braves, who assumed no financial liability for the stadium and negotiated substantial revenue from parking and concessions. The Braves further inhibited development in the neighborhood, notoriously enacting their "no contest" clause in the contract to prevent businesses from opening, including grocery stores, in order to discourage spending outside the stadium so that the team could accrue all stadium-related revenue.[109]

Following the Olympics, antagonisms at the heart of the city's race, class, and spatial divides remained, and citizens would continue to articulate their own claims to place, neighborhood, and identity in efforts to construct an Other Atlanta, as they did in resisting FCS, the Georgia Dome, and Turner Field. The governing rationale and production of and resistance to sportified citizenship evident in these histories continues to influence Atlanta's contemporary practices of stadium construction in ways that both extend and depart from the strategies of these earlier stadiums. It is to those practices I therefore now turn.

CHAPTER 2

Governing the Fan-Advocate-Citizen in the Interactive Stadium

Despite the promises of revitalization made by stadium boosters, Turner Field and the Georgia Dome were largely considered failures in terms of urban economic development. Driven by discourses that demonized the Turner Field neighborhoods and imagined them as crime-ridden because of their association with Blackness and poverty, many white fans avoided all parts of the neighborhood except the stadium. Likewise, the downtown and Westside neighborhoods around the Dome did not become the vibrant, twenty-four-hour spaces developers claimed the stadium would create. Instead, the stadium and other tourist and convention-oriented structures remained sealed-off tourist bubbles.[1] Nevertheless, city elites once again turned to new stadium infrastructure in the 2010s under the same guise of revitalization, assuring residents that this time would be different. After a protracted debate, the Falcons brokered a deal with the city to fund a new stadium, Mercedes-Benz Stadium (MBS), adjacent to the Dome, in March 2013.[2] The Braves, on the other hand, made a stadium deal in August 2013 with suburban Cobb County, just outside Atlanta on its northern periphery.[3]

Notably, these stadium negotiations took place amid the controversy over Atlanta Hawks owner Bruce Levenson's leaked emails saying that his National Basketball Association (NBA) fans were "too Black," speculating to the franchise's other executives that "the black crowd scared away the whites and there are simply not enough affluent black fans to build a significant season ticket base."[4] Unsurprisingly, his comments spurred a major controversy and Levenson resigned from the team's ownership. Nevertheless, his comments laid bare the sharp racial and class divisions in Atlanta and the ways in which the city's sporting institutions and infrastructure have long valued white fans over Black ones, despite and alongside their investment in discourses of Atlanta as a Black Mecca.

As with Atlanta's efforts to become a national and international city in its previous eras of stadium construction, the new high-tech stadiums comprise a core strategy for bringing Atlanta, and its suburbs, into the future—one imagined to constitute the city as a global technology hub while also brandishing its image as a city of Black success and racial justice. While the Dome and Turner Field were on the cusp of second- and third-generation stadiums, incorporating aspects of both, these two new stadiums are more fully indicative of the third generation. Both are influenced by new urban regeneration schemes tied to placemaking, neighborhood, and locality along with digitization, interactivity, and media convergence. This emphasis on placemaking and positioning the stadium as a catalyst of urban (and suburban) regeneration turns the logic and culture of stadium space, and its mediatized, sportified technologies of citizenship and governing, outward to the neighborhood. On the one hand, this involves a "cleansing" of space, where the stadiums once again contribute to displacement by gentrifying neighborhoods, pushing out populations imagined to be drags on the neighborhood's economic potential, and continuing patterns of previous eras of stadium development. On the other hand, however, Atlanta's contemporary stadiums are also put to work to transform the populations in those neighborhoods in new ways. The governing logics of third-generation stadiums reconstitute neighborhood residents as subjects with capacity, fan-citizen-advocates who can produce new kinds of value for the city, the stadium, and, ostensibly, themselves.

This outward turn in citizenship and governing practices establishes a form of what Michel Foucault terms "biopower."[5] Whereas disciplinary power is targeted toward the production, monitoring, and regulation of the individual, biopower is directed at the production of population. Foucault suggests that biopower "designate[s] what brought life and its mechanisms into the realm of explicit calculations and made knowledge-power an agent of transformation of human life."[6] Thus, biopolitics acts as a technology of population in which the power to produce and maximize the conditions for life are tied to the production of knowledge about biological populations (e.g., demographics, health, behaviors, living arrangements, etc.) through which subjects are made into populations. Biopower constitutes life by determining that which should be made to live (according to dominant ideals of what comprises a good life) and that which will be abandoned and allowed to die because it is a threat to the health of the population and a good life. The marker between life and death, according to Foucault, is race—in other words, structures of racialization determine which populations will be invested in so as to produce the life and health of the population and which will be subject to more disciplinary forms of punishment, abandonment, or destruction.[7] Alexander G. Weheliye argues that racialization is fundamental to biopolitics. It is the central technology that constitutes "a set of sociopolitical processes that discipline humanity into full humans, not-quite-humans, and nonhumans."[8] Sport, sporting spaces, and sporting culture provide key vectors for the biopolitical production of the healthy city, as they are linked directly to the body and both ideals of and techniques for producing health and healthy bodies.

This chapter, along with the following, considers how Atlanta's third-generation stadiums produce city space in ways that invite a particular kind of body and discourage other kinds of embodiments to align with governing and citizenship ideals associated with the sportification of place. In both cases, the mediatized, mediatizing, and mediating elements of the stadium are put to work toward urban regeneration, citizenship, and governance, with sport and media culture core components of how those citizenship practices and technologies of governing are conceived and play out. In this chapter, I focus on the case of the Falcons Stadium (MBS, also home to the city's Major League Soccer team, Atlanta United FC [Football Club]). With the stadium built to produce a "frictionless fan experience," I propose that its design, architectural, and media logics are turned outward to the surrounding neighborhoods in order to produce citizens through the ideal of fandom—healthy citizens of capacity who, like fans for the home team, advocate for themselves and their neighbors. That transformation, in turn, works to brandish Atlanta's image as a Black Mecca and site of Black wealth generation and productivity, creating the neighborhood as both an urban entertainment destination and a space imagined to heal the city's racial-spatial divides. The enjoinment for residents to see themselves in terms of the idealized sportified citizen is mobilized by the circulation of topophilic affects of Black joy and pride produced by the stadium. In so doing, MBS throws a sharp focus on the complex and fraught cultural politics within Atlanta.

In contrast, as I argue in the following chapter, the Braves' move to suburban Cobb County, toward whiter fans and away from the historically Black neighborhoods of the Braves' former home at Turner Field, completes the other side of the coin of this biopolitical racial spatialization through segregation that cordons off what was imagined by city elites as a potentially threatening impoverished Black neighborhood. Together, these stadiums demonstrate the contradictory, but also complementary, strategies of sportification's urban, cultural governance and the significance of stadiums as urban media infrastructures in terms of how they participate in struggles over race, class, and place within Atlanta.

Brokering a Deal

Although the Falcons were just shy of fifteen years into their tenancy at the Dome, their owner, Arthur Blank, started hinting at a new stadium as early as 2006, predicting in an interview with the *Atlanta Journal-Constitution* that the team would be in a new home by 2015.[9] Reports suggest Blank wanted a greater share of revenue from the stadium, which was shared between the team and the Georgia World Congress Center Authority (GWCCA, the state-owned authority that operated the Dome). Blank sought to increase luxury suite revenues and to host the Super Bowl and other mega-sporting events, such as the FIFA (Federation International de Football Association) World Cup.[10] With the Falcons' lease set to expire in 2020, negotiations ramped up in the early 2010s. While the city debated renovations to the Dome, boosters argued that a new stadium was necessary to create a high-tech, state-of-the-art facility that could compete with a new generation of stadiums across the country, such as the retractable-roof stadium built for the Cowboys in Dallas, Texas, which opened in 2009 and cost over $1 billion.[11]

However, the tide for public funding was turning, with critics arguing that stadiums might produce new revenue streams for their owners, but they give little back to the city. Indeed, Atlanta was still paying down the bonds for the Dome. Criticizing the proposal for a new Falcons stadium in the city's newspaper, sports economist J. C. Bradbury said the plan was like "adding zero to zero," merely shifting the Falcons, who brought in little money to the city or state, from one venue to another.[12] What proceeded was a prolonged debate over the city's, county's, and state's contribution to the new stadium. Although the amount of contribution was called into question, there seemed little doubt that the legislature would support the stadium. The Falcons made it clear they preferred to stay downtown, but they also intimated they would look elsewhere if the city didn't deliver.[13] This put pressure on the legislature and the GWCCA to strike a deal.

Atlanta's then-mayor, Kasim Reed, was particularly keen to reach an agreement with the Falcons, a position that stood in contrast to his brokering with the Braves for their new home, as I detail in the following chapter. Reporters speculated this difference could be attributed to the fact that the Falcons had a strong Black urban and suburban fan base who regularly attended games. The fan base for the Braves, conversely, was (and remains) overwhelmingly white and suburban.[14] The Falcons boast one of the highest percentages of Black fans in the NFL, with about 25 percent of fans identifying as African American.[15] The team invests heavily in marketing to Black fans, inscribing the city's Black Mecca place-branding into the stadium and the franchise. In the 1990s and early 2000s, in particular, the Falcons played up the team's association with Atlanta's burgeoning Black cultural industries, including popular music and hip-hop, fashion, and film. This coincided with the reverse migration of middle- and upper-class Black residents from the Northeastern United States to Atlanta during this period.[16]

While Black Atlantans have long supported the Falcons, fandom had one of its greatest surges during Michael Vick's quarterback tenure between 2001 and 2006. Vick, one of the few Black quarterbacks in the NFL, represented an important symbol for Atlanta's Black community—the city's "huge black middle class, finally had a quarterback that looked like them."[17] Vick was released from the team and imprisoned after he was convicted for his involvement in a dog-fighting scheme in 2007. The Falcons replaced Vick with a white quarterback, Matt Ryan. While some Black fans rallied around Vick, wearing his jersey and speaking out on what they saw as an overly harsh penalty, the Falcons managed to gain back support when they brought home more winning seasons. In the words of one reporter, "Winning heals most wounds, however deep."[18]

Although the Falcons paid tribute to the idea of Atlanta as a Black Mecca and seemed to revere their Black fans, that representation remains bound up with the Atlanta Paradox and reveals the highly variegated complexity of Black identity, especially as it intersects with class and space, in the city. While some in the Black community, including fans, business elites, the legislature, and the GWCCA, seemed determined to keep the Falcons downtown, others, especially those from the impoverished neighborhoods around the Dome, pushed back against the proposals. Area residents complained that the neighborhoods had already been cut off from downtown from previous urban renewal projects and that a new stadium would only further isolate them. A particularly thorny issue for the Falcons was that their preferred site next to the Dome would require the purchase and demolition of two historically significant Black churches—Friendship Baptist and Mount Vernon Baptist.[19] After decades of mistrust and broken promises from previous development, including the Dome, the neighborhoods were skeptical of promises made by the Falcons and the city.[20]

The pushback from the neighborhoods forced the Falcons, GWCCA, and the city to negotiate, ultimately leading to some concessions. The financing package passed by the GWCCA and the city council included a provision for a community benefits plan where the Falcons agreed to commit up to $70 million for infrastructure costs, $20 million for property acquisition, and a pledge from the Arthur Blank Foundation for $15 million devoted to neighborhood projects, along with an additional $15 million from the Westside Tax Allocation District Community Improvement Fund. Though these were significant concessions, neighborhoods were skeptical from the get-go. For instance, the community benefits were passed as a "plan" rather than an "agreement" and therefore were not legally binding. While the Falcons and the city of Atlanta touted the community engagement measures, many community members were less enthusiastic. Deborah Scott, head of Georgia Stand-Up, a progressive nonprofit advocacy group, criticized the negotiations as "top heavy," claiming, "The way they're doing it in Atlanta is telling them what they're going to do and have two-hour sessions to talk about those issues without real authentic community buy-in."[21]

Despite pushback from the neighborhoods, the deal for a new Falcons and Atlanta United FC (Football Club) stadium went through. With the legislature balking at tax increases for the state's struggling public schools, they voted with little fanfare for a hotel/motel tax levied for the new stadium.[22] The city contracted the global architectural firm HOK and principal designer Bill Johnson to design a technology-centered stadium. Ground for the 1.9-million-square-foot, 80,000-capacity stadium broke in May 2014, with naming rights going to the luxury car company Mercedes-Benz. Construction was completed in 2017, and the Falcons played their first preseason game on August 26.

Designing the Frictionless Fan Experience

The design and architecture of the Atlanta Falcons/Atlanta United FC Stadium, MBS, is undergirded by a discourse of the "fan experience," a ubiquitous term in the stadium industry today. An MBS executive suggested the whole idea behind the stadium was to enhance the fan experience, noting that they employ a "vice president of fan experience" as evidence that fans are at the center of their thinking. The investment in fan experience is tied to lingering fears over competing with at-home sports viewing. Creating a multidimensional experience for the fan that can motivate them to come out to games, and pay a premium price for doing so, remains a major concern. The need to compete with the at-home experience accelerated with the expansion of satellite, digital, and streaming media into homes that enabled viewers to circumvent TV broadcasting blackouts of local games, a policy in place since the 1970s, as the league relied primarily on local ticket sales for revenue. The NFL maintained the blackout for local games if there were still tickets available at the stadium (encouraging fans to come to the stadium), but they suspended the policy in 2015.²³ An MBS executive cited the rollback of local blackouts along with the emergence of the "Red" channels (e.g., NFL RedZone, operated by the NFL Network, and the Red Zone Channel operated by Direct TV) as influential in the push to transform the Falcons Stadium into a more media saturated and digitally connected experience.²⁴ Under this logic, stadium executives imagine they need to provide more than just the game; they must provide a spectacular experience. Today this goes beyond the kinds of second-generation family-friendly entertainment provided at venues like the Dome; it encompasses thinking of each component of the stadium as a site of spectacular experience and interactive engagement. It also means creating tiered, and especially more premium and luxury, experiences that can generate more and differentiated revenue streams. But stadium executives are not merely responding to what fans want; they are producing it as well. The "fan experience" is both an impetus for and a product of the third-generation stadium. The stadium-produced fan experience is ultimately a model of governing and citizenship that responds to contemporary exigencies in sport, media, and city life.

The integration of a converged media experience is central to MBS. The stadium is designed to offer fans "an immersive, technology-driven game-day experience."²⁵ Whereas the second generation brought in TV and profit from broadcasting rights while also providing entertainment experiences at the stadium to enhance the live game (so that there could be crowds on TV), this third generation enfolds the televisual and digital media experience into the live experience itself, creating a converged multimedia experience that blurs the distinctions between the live and mediated stadium. The stadium is part of this immersive mediated experience, as it is built as an iconic piece of spectacular architecture designed to entice the senses of fans and citizens alike. The unique architectural design of the building, with its angular roof, intended to resemble falcon wings, stands out in the landscape (see fig. 2.1). Though the Dome stood out as well, MBS provides a unique and distinct shape intended to be an iconic skyline structure that signifies Atlanta and the team. That signification is further enhanced through the stadium's three key architectural features: the Oculus, the "Window to the City," and the Halo. Each of these features demonstrates the broader ways in which the stadium's architecture and its relationship to media culture and practices is involved in the production of citizen-subjects.

The Oculus is a retractable component of the stadium roof, built in eight sections designed as petals that seamlessly link to the angular roof (see fig. 2.2). The petals individually retract and open like a camera shutter aperture. HOK's lead designer on the project, Bill Johnson, "was inspired by the Pantheon and

Fig. 2.1: Mercedes-Benz Stadium's angular shape is meant to symbolize falcon wings. The Georgia Dome (prior to demolition) can be seen in the background. (Photo by Jonathan Brill, used with permission)

the way the circle of light hits the playing field."²⁶ But whereas the Pantheon is a piece of ancient architecture, this roof is made with futuristic technology and materials. The sixteen-hundred-ton panels are made of steel trusses covered in ethylene tetrafluoroethylene (ETFE, a transparent, fluorine-based plastic—a common material used for third-generation roofs). The panels operate at the push of a button. Johnson says, "The vision was that the opening would create a very tiny pinpoint of light on the Falcons' logo at the 50-yard line, and as the roof retracted, the spotlight would become bigger and bigger."²⁷ Whereas most stadium designs tend to start with seating or the field of play, it is the roof and ocular design from which the remainder of the building follows. Johnson notes, "The beam of light, cast by the roof on to the field of play, is the centrepoint and we have designed the building so that it feels like it's swirling and spinning around that centrepoint."²⁸ In specifically referencing the opening of the camera lens, the Oculus is thus designed as a theatrical device that self-consciously both creates and signifies a mediated sporting experience. It performatively demonstrates the blurred lines between the lived experience of the game and its mediated production along with the role of the stadium itself in that pro-

Fig. 2.2: Mercedes-Benz Stadium's retractable roof is an "Oculus," opening like the aperture of a camera. The Oculus is surrounded by a video board "Halo." (Photo by Jonathan Brill, used with permission)

duction. As the center point of the stadium, the Oculus structures the fan as a subject who watches and is watched, encouraging them to experience the live game as always-already mediated.

Surrounding the Oculus is a six-story, 63,000-square-foot, 360-degree screen video board called "the Halo" (see fig. 2.2). Because the Oculus prevented a center-hung scoreboard, the Halo was embedded in the building structure to encircle the Oculus. The religious signification here is not insignificant, as it speaks to how the stadium, and its embeddedness in media culture and practices, is a kind of religious experience. Christopher Thomas Gaffney claims, "Stadiums stand out in the collective imagination as sacred," as spaces of intensity and shared experience, as well as pilgrimage, rhythm, and ritual.[29] Just as institutions like religion and the church are waning in US American culture, stadiums provide collective spaces where individuals create affective connections to others by way of a kind of shared faith in team and city. The stadium also provides an institutional space where the values and behaviors of sport and fandom serve as a guide to societal morals. The Halo helps constitute the stadium spectacle and its sacred performances through excess—projecting images of the game as larger-than-life, sharp, intensified visuals to be consumed (worshipped) by the spectator.

The Halo aims to produce a particular kind of fan-subject—the digitally immersed and connected fan. According to Mike Gomes, senior vice president of fan experience for team owner Arthur Blank's company, AMB Sports & Entertainment Group:

> [The Halo] seems to be the thing people are mesmerized by. Wherever you are in those concourses you see that digital display. It's very anchoring. You're always connected to what's going on. There's [sic] very few places in the building where you don't have a view to the [H]alo. In the industry, one thing we're always confronted with is that connectivity. If you go to the concessions you don't want to miss something. There's a reluctance to leave your seats. I think this building will be transformational for the fans because of that connection. It's not about sitting in a row. It's wanting to move around and see the event from different perspectives.[30]

Unlike the devoted religious subject who passively consumes sacred spectacle, the Halo responds to the distracted, mobile, postmodern fan-subject—it ensures the fan is immersed in the spectacle regardless of where they are in the stadium, and it encourages them to move, congregate, and be active and engaged in the entirety of the stadium experience beyond the game. The Halo manages and channels distraction. That movement and immersion is further encouraged by twenty-five hundred large HD televisions interspersed throughout the stadium, as well as an additional one-hundred-foot-high column wrapped in a 3-D video board.[31] The third generation's idealized citizen-subject is an active and mobile subject whose potential distraction is funneled into a carefully choreographed digital immersion that connects them to the game, team, city, and other fans.

However, the mobility of fans can be a problem; it means that when viewed on TV the stadium sometimes appears empty on game days because fans congregate on concourses or in clubs watching the game on a screen rather than in their seats.[32] Coaches and team owners complained it made their teams appear less popular on screen than the actual attendance figures suggested. But MBS concourses are designed for congregating, not just facilitating the flow of people to and from their seats. There are multiple bars and restaurants, along with tables to stand at, socialize around, and watch the game. At the time of my interviews with them, stadium executives had not yet designed a solution to this problem. Instead, they indicated that broadcasts were showing fewer crowd shots, an aesthetic practice developed during the COVID-19 pandemic, when there were no crowds at all.

Fig. 2.3: The "Window to the City" provides sweeping views of the downtown Atlanta skyline, transected by a giant video screen board, with ample space for congregating in its open concourse. (Photo by the author)

A third key architectural feature of MBS is the Window to the City—a sixteen-story, 22,500-square-foot set of windows made of transparent ETFE panels that provide panoramic views of the city skyline from the stadium's west side (see fig. 2.3). This design feature opens to the city, creating a visual and physical connection between the stadium and downtown Atlanta. As Falcons team president, Rich McKay, explains, "We wanted transparency. We wanted it to be an invitation to come to this building, and a window to the city."[33] The panoramic view emphasizes that the stadium is not just anywhere—it is not just a site of contained sporting spectacle. Rather, it is *somewhere*; it is intentionally placed within Atlanta and a particular neighborhood. The window to the city is a hallmark of contemporary third-generation stadiums and, in McKay's words, is "the money shot on TV." Though it is perhaps part of a new cookie-cutter design for the contemporary stadium, it is also cookie-cutter via distinction—that is, it replicates by emphasizing what is unique to the stadium: the city itself and a visualization of a specific place, locale, and land.

The stadium's screens—whether the Halo, Window to the City, Oculus, column, TV screens dotted throughout the concourses, or the micro-personalized screen of the spectator's own phone—are all components of the stadium as spectacle, a space designed to stand out and attract the gaze as well as a space for producing and containing spectacle. These screens compose an "architecture of spectatorship" that organizes looking and predisposes the spectator to view the event as a site of spectacular consumption.[34] Writing about early cinema, Anne Friedberg theorizes the screen as constituting a virtually mobile gaze, or, in other words, a gaze predicated on the mobility of the screen and the immobility of the spectator. For Friedberg, the virtually mobile gaze of the cinema screen created new kinds of subjects related to shifts in urbanism, as it both produced and responded to anxieties over industrialization and the cultural changes it brought on. Similarly, the ubiquitous screens of the third-generation stadium are related to shifts in contemporary subjectivity and the urban. While the virtually mobile gaze might suggest that screens render spectators into passive viewers, screens in contemporary stadiums are instead figured as components of the stadium's digital infrastructure that seek to produce active and interactive spectators. The screens imagine a distracted viewer and aim to attract their attention while also directing that attention to engage in active productions of their own media (e.g., through social media posts) and data (where their movements, purchases, and activities can be mined for profit).

However, while today's stadium executives glorify the interactive spectator—enjoining them to post, repost, and participate—that participation is also structured by a desire to ensure that their interactivity unfolds in predictable (that is, profitable and brand-enhancing) ways and to ensure security of the stadium. I address how the direction of interactivity plays out in terms of branding in chapter 5 and in relation to surveillance and crowd control/security in chapter 8. What I want to emphasize here is how this interactivity is tied to governing and constituting citizenship practices, channeling the potentialities of collective fandom—which could be disruptive and resistant—into "appropriate" modes of individual fan experience.

MBS is architecturally designed to encourage "appropriate" behavior through design and architecture that integrates digital technology and facilitates a "seamless" experience for the fan to move among the live game, large video screens, individual screens, and to engage in the production of their own content. MBS designers and executives describe the stadium as "a fully integrated ecosystem,"[35] in which the integration of technology into the stadium is "as integral to the building as the concrete, steel and glass."[36] As one MBS stadium executive put it, "Where before static—your content was basically your big screen, your stadium board—[stadiums] now are living, breathing, digital content–producing entertainment" venues.[37] The stadium is powered

Fig. 2.4: Fiber-optic cabling runs throughout the stadium's subterranean infrastructure, with room to incorporate more and newer forms of technology as they are developed. (Photo by the author)

by a Gigabit Passive Optical Network that includes 4,800 miles of fiber-optic cabling connected to 15,600 Ethernet ports (see fig. 2.4), which powers more than 1,800 Wi-Fi access points, 700 registers, 590 security cameras, and 400 door security access points along with 4,200 speakers.[38] The network is capable of storing 4 petabytes worth of data along with 7 terabytes of random-access memory and is a gateway to IBM Cloud, which supports the stadium's mobile applications. Stadium executives claim this design enables the stadium to be "future flexible" in order "to support a future with increased data consumption needs whilst also being flexible enough to have locations to have cameras to be installed or the ability to take future technology even though we may not know exactly what that is."[39]

For MBS executives, the integration of this technology is key to enabling fan connectivity, which is their number one priority. They want fans to share their experiences with their social media networks. However, doing so creates a potential threat, since the executives are not able to control the messages that fans produce. In response, executives vigilantly watch social media on game day, collecting this data to respond to fan experiences in real time, as well as distributing postgame surveys that are analyzed to structure future responses.[40]

Along with data gathered throughout the stadium, this information is used to curate interactive participation that unfolds in more predictable ways. Thus, the digitization and datafication of the stadium enables stadium executives to carefully collect and preserve future experiences to minimize production of fan content that might threaten the brand.

The digitization of the stadium also turns it into a media production studio. MBS, as other stadiums, has a warehouse-like space where broadcasting trucks can pull up and plug directly into the stadium to access the network and to facilitate the production and broadcasting of content (see figs. 2.5 and 2.6). An MBS stadium executive suggests that the production of game day or another stadium event (e.g., the Super Bowl or a rock concert) is "not so different from a film production," noting, "You have the local location scouts" from the broadcast production companies to whom the stadium workers provide "the insider's view of how best to view the stadium and connect."[41]

But MBS is indicative of how teams and stadiums seek independence from legacy TV broadcasters as well. Stadium designs enable production of the team's own content and their own distribution channels.[42] While players from the teams are encouraged to produce their own content on their social media, each team—the Falcons and Atlanta United—also has their own content production arm. The Falcons built a studio (Ticketmaster Studios) in Flowery Branch, where

Figs. 2.5 and 2.6: Broadcasting trucks can pull right up to Mercedes-Benz Stadium and plug into the stadium's digital system.

the team practices, to facilitate additional content production that provides more intimate interactions with the players for fans. The studio is a "strategic investment the Falcons have made to deliver on growing demand for engaging content from fans, media, corporate and league partners across multiple fan touchpoints."[43] An MBS executive explained, "You're going to see more and more clubs producing more and more content themselves . . . to get their message out. You have your own . . . TV station that you produce content for. . . . It's all digital content. And . . . you see that as increasingly important for the team."[44] Production of their own content enables teams to control the message and reap additional revenue more carefully. It also influences the content that legacy media produces about the team. As the MBS executive noted, "How do we control that message . . . and make sure it's [what the team wants to say] versus what . . . ESPN wants to say or what Fox wants to produce? How do we really influence that?"[45] They see creating their own content that frames the broader message as a key strategy.

The team increasingly produces short- and long-form content and shares it on social media platforms like TikTok and Snapchat. Their content goes beyond sports. For example, one long-form piece of content—a two-part, twelve-minute video—created with one of the Falcons players, Hayden Hurst, focused on suicide prevention, a cause Hurst is actively involved in. "It was important for him to tell that story," the MBS executive noted, "and what better way than our own channels to do that? . . . It [had] over a million views, which is great for our brand. It's great for him . . . everybody wins in that situation, so it's becoming more and more . . . prominent."[46] This statement demonstrates how sport, sports content, and sporting celebrities are enmeshed in social and cultural life in ways that go well beyond the game. Hurst and the Falcons' suicide prevention video demonstrates how sporting institutions are technologies of governing, teaching citizens core values and behaviors in the wake of waning institutions that might otherwise provide this kind of pedagogical content. But the content is produced with an eye toward how it enhances the brand value of Hurst and his team by creating goodwill and generating sentimental affect among fans. Fans are then encouraged to share that content and to become marketers and distributors of this kind of affective value.

Along with screens, interactive technologies, datafication, and media production technologies, MBS also partnered with IBM to incorporate "smart" technologies into the stadium, including artificial intelligence.[47] Smart technologies create what is increasingly referred to as a "frictionless" experience, a complementary discourse to "fan experience" that is ubiquitous in the stadium industry, especially since COVID-19. "Frictionlessness" stems from the digital consumer technology industries, which put a premium on creating "seamless" experiences that enable more efficient processing and minimize both physical and digital "roadblocks." Frictionlessness encourages users to forget about the technologies, platforms, and systems that make their actions and interactions possible, as they fade into the background and enable the user to go about their everyday life. MBS executives try to create a frictionless experience through smart and automated technologies for things like concessions and security. Doing so, they reason, enhances the fan experience, as fans can grab a local beer from an automated marketplace without having to show an ID or pay directly. While frictionlessness could be considered part of the space-time compression associated with media communication technologies, imagined to detach people from the spaces and places of their everyday lives by minimizing interaction and increasing efficiency and mobility, frictionlessness in the stadium is actually meant to enhance people's connection to place. It encourages them to immerse themselves in the sociality of the game and the stadium experience while not getting caught up in the nitty-gritty of security checks or paying cashiers. But that mobility and efficiency, the lack of friction, is accorded to only the "right" bodies, and, as I detail in chapter 8, is predicated on the production of new hierarchies that create more friction for some while removing it for others.[48] Ultimately, though, the ideal of frictionlessness in MBS speaks to a kind of governing rationale—one whereby the work of governing is off-loaded onto invisible digital technologies.

IBM claims that MBS's "smart stadium is on a city-scale"; in other words, it is at a scale that enables it to be a testing ground for replication citywide.[49] Indeed, the Atlanta-hosted 2019 Super Bowl used the stadium to test the rollout of new smart city technology. This included large-scale surveillance technologies, called "Operation Shield," that enabled citizens and businesses to integrate their surveillance cameras into a city-run network to increase policing capacities during the game, as well as other forms of smart traffic control technologies.[50] Additionally, the weapons detection system Evolv, tested out in MBS, was later integrated into the city's public school system. The system "uses advanced sensor technology and artificial intelligence" to detect weapons in what is promised to be a more efficient and "dignified" screening process.[51] The stadium, along with its mega-events, is a core part of rolling out the city's smart city planning strategy, SmartATL, initiated in 2015. SmartATL frames Atlanta's problems as acute "yet solvable through the strategic implementation of smart technologies (e.g., sensors, data centers, and algorithms)—only if we act quickly and invest early." Its developers promise that the integration of smart technologies into the fabric of the city will improve mobility, public safety, and sustainability, and will grow the economy.[52]

Stadium design discourses encourage builders to think of the stadium in smart city terms, where its placemaking is interconnected with its "smart" capabilities. As one design guidebook suggests, "There is also demand to integrate the latest smart technologies and recognise the need to think bigger to activate sport's potential to become an integral part of urban regeneration, a catalyst to renewal. It is as much about place-making as it is about fan and athlete experiences."[53] Here, the connection between urban regeneration, placemaking, and stadium mediatization is made explicit. The integration of smart technologies into the stadium is rationalized as not only a means for enhancing the fan experience, making the stadium more efficient or safe, but, rather, for urban regeneration such that the experience, safety, and efficiency of all city residents and visitors is aligned with and replicating that of the stadium. Moreover, the stadium is imagined as more than just a component of regeneration; it is positioned as the catalyst. In this sense, the smart stadium helps to constitute the smart city, integrating the logics of the stadium into the wider city.

Black Joy and Dirty Birds: Mobilizing Affect

Taken together, the mediatization of the third-generation stadium constructs the sportified fan-citizen as an advocate—that is, not just a passive fan who likes a team but a passionate advocate who promotes the team and contributes to the production of its value.[54] This vision of the sportified fan as advocate models the kind of ideal citizen-subject of the neoliberal city—one who does not just passively live in and reside there (i.e., one who is entitled to rights and services because of their residence and citizenship) but rather an advocate for themselves and their city. Thus, Atlantans are encouraged to produce and maximize themselves as the kinds of engaged, active and interactive, entrepreneurial fan-advocate-citizen-subjects produced in the stadium. The ideal citizen becomes one modeled on the fan—stratified and tiered, frictionless and "smart," datafied and surveilled, and a passionate advocate for team and city, produced to maximize interactivity that is carefully curated to produce economic, cultural, and social value. Citizens are enjoined to internalize these ideals in a number of ways, from the design logic of the stadium and its surrounding infrastructure to specific programs generated by the stadium to train neighborhood residents to adopt idealized behaviors (discussed in more detail in the following section).

As a majority-Black city, the production of Atlanta's sportified fan-citizen-advocate is necessarily a part of the city's complicated racial politics, particularly as they intersect with class and spatial divides and the Atlanta Paradox. On one hand, these citizenship practices often play out in deeply unequal ways, continuing the kinds of displacement and impoverishment of Black neighborhoods produced by earlier generations through new logics and strategies. On the other hand, MBS's production of sportified citizenship is rooted in a meaningful and seemingly "authentic" mobilization of Atlanta as a Black Mecca, where the stadium is a space of emplacement and cultivating, circulating, and intensifying affects of Black joy and pride. Fans opt in to the interactive and surveillant demands of the stadium (and, by extension, the city), at least in part, because of its promises of joyousness.

Although there are numerous examples of how the Falcons cultivate Black fans and mobilize affects of Black joy and pride in MBS—including through music, fashion, design and architecture, and art—the politics at stake in its production are perhaps best exemplified by the "Dirty Bird," the Falcons' signature celebration dance and nickname for its fans. The name stems from Atlanta's burgeoning rap scene in the late 1990s. Darren E. Grem reports, "Throughout the 1990s, industry leaders and southern rappers promoted the Dirty South as a new type of rap music," blending Black, Southern cultural aesthetics with existing forms of East and West Coast rap. The Dirty South represented "rappers who felt estranged from Atlanta's economic and social progress and excluded by their southerness from competing in a rap-music market dominated by New York and Los Angeles. By the end of the 1990s, however, their unique coupling of regional and racial identity had earned them increased attention. . . . The next wave of southern rappers . . . preferred to promote the Dirty South as a loosely defined, inclusive concept and a lucrative set of attractive commodities."[55] The Dirty Bird signifies a particular identity embodied in and specific to Black, Southern identity, including its complicated and evolving cultural politics, especially among intersections of race, class, and upward mobility.

In addition to its relationship to Atlanta's rap roots, the Dirty Bird moniker emerged during the team's historic 1998 season, during which they bounced back from a losing record from the previous year to go 14–2 and ultimately clinch the NFC (National Football Conference) Championship, making it into the franchise's first ever Super Bowl. Though there is some debate about the dance's origination, running back Jamal Anderson is credited with its creation and popularizing it among fans. During a Week 8 game against the New Orleans Saints, after he made a particularly good play, Anderson started doing the dance—bouncing from one foot to the other and spreading out his arms and flapping them like wings. He called the dance the Dirty Bird. Anderson recalls, "It was so Atlanta. . . . What happened couldn't have happened anywhere else."[56] The dance became a sensation, taken up by fans who called for the players to do the Dirty Bird. Soon, fans earned the Dirty Bird nickname as they, too, performed the dance and costumed themselves like birds in the stands.[57]

Anderson's suggestion that the Dirty Bird is inherently Atlanta and couldn't have originated anywhere else demonstrates how the dance embodies topophilia, demonstrating a love of place by connecting the team and its fans to the city through stadium performance. What appears unsaid in his statement, though, is how this topophilia is tied to race and Atlanta's image as a Black Mecca. The celebratory dances of Black football players are part of a longer history of Black cultural performance, aesthetics, and dance traditions.[58] Furthermore, the 1998 season unfolded amid the city's flourishing Black cultural scene, especially in the hip-hop industry, with acts like OutKast cementing Atlanta as a hip-hop capital.[59] The Dirty Bird therefore represented not only the Falcons and their incredible season but also the rise of Atlanta's Black cultural class. In their research on African American expressive culture and basketball, Gena Dagel Caponi suggests, "The virtuosic individual performance is a social act, inspiring the team and the community."[60] As such, Joel Dinerstein argues that performances like the Dirty Bird are political, such that "individual achievement *reflects back on the community*; in other words, African American athletes often find ways to share the moment of scoring with a real or perceived audience."[61] The Dirty Bird thus celebrates not only the Falcons' and the athletes' performance but, rather, the Black community, and Black Atlantans in particular, by circulating topophilic affects of Black joy and pride.

Drawing from the writings of Zora Neale Hurston, Lindsey Stewart theorizes "the politics of joy as a response to [the] dialectic of Black enchantment and Black tragedy."[62] Stewart maintains that Black joy is evidence of a "lingering abolitionist discourse" that foregrounds a politics of refusal rather than of resistance. She notes, "While resistance foregrounds an oppositional relation between oppressed and oppressors, joy foregrounds a flourishing relation of the self to the self (or, in the case of Black joy, how Black folks relate to each other)."[63] In so doing, Black joy "cultivates a future apart and beyond white supremacy."[64]

Building on Stewart's theory of Black joy as refusal, the Dirty Bird can be read as an affective and embodied performance of Black joy shared between players and fans that is part of a tradition of cultivating Black liberation. When the NFL imposed a rule in 2006 penalizing players for "excessive celebrations," these rules could therefore be rightly criticized as linked to white supremacy and an effort to discipline and govern Black bodies, stemming the powerful affects and political potentiality of performance. Those rules, however, were rolled back in 2017. Players are now allowed to celebrate, including dancing, as long as their celebrations are neither considered offensive nor taunting the other team.[65]

This rule change coincided with the opening of MBS, and the Falcons have embraced the Dirty Bird in their new home, encouraging fans to identify themselves as Dirty Birds. In addition to building the "Dirty Bird Nest," "a general admission fan zone ... for enthusiastic Falcons fans," they've also turned the Dirty Bird into an official fan song and incorporated it into tailgating rituals.[66] It thus remains a central part of the mediatized stadium-going experience. Because it is connected to a seemingly organic tradition of Black cultural performance, the Dirty Bird creates a sense of authenticity and connection to the new stadium, constituting both the stadium and Atlanta more broadly as meaningful Black cultural spaces. Furthermore, the practice connects the Falcons and MBS to Atlanta's Westside neighborhoods, the site of histories of civil rights organizing and HBCUs (historically Black colleges and universities), to which the team also articulates to produce its image and sense of place.

Stewart warns, "Black joy in the South is still sometimes used against us. This can be seen in how a narrative of Black southern enchantment is frequently spun to evade the civil rights movement's demands for political inclusion and recognition in our institutions across the nation."[67] Arguably, MBS aims to mobilize affects of Black joy through the Dirty Bird to brandish its and Atlanta's image as a Black Mecca while, as I detail below, it contributes to displacement and gentrification. Still, I think it would be wrong to dismiss the Dirty Bird, as it manifests in the contemporary stadium as a mere commodification of authenticity, hegemonic capture, or subsumption of Black joy. According to Dinerstein, "The tradition of the black body on stage as exoticized or commodified Other is only one part of a complex story of framing African American athletic achievement."[68] Another part of that story is the political potentiality of Black joy, capable of exceeding or withdrawing from white supremacist efforts of capture. As Stewart writes, "The political devaluation of southern Black joy has its roots in an emancipatory Black political tradition that mandates an emphasis on our racial oppression in the public sphere."[69] That devaluation also intersects with gender, as affects of joy and love are culturally associated with the feminine and the personal, private sphere, seemingly devoid of political potentiality. Unsurprisingly, then, it has been Black feminists and feminists of color, such as Audre Lorde, bell hooks, Adrienne Maree Brown, Sara Ahmed, Stewart, and others, who have championed the politics of emotion and of joy, love, the erotic, and pleasure in particular.[70] While the Dirty Bird and football, more generally, might be read as displays of sporting masculinity, Black feminist readings instead encourage us to read the practice as a manifestation and cultivation of Black joy that politicizes the personal and embodied experiences of Black Atlanta and the stadium.

It is in this context, then, that I acknowledge the complex racial politics at play in the Dirty Bird and, by extension, the potential of joyous affects circulated in MBS and other third-generation stadiums. Following Stewart, those affects reside in the space in between "Black enchantment" and "Black tragedy." The Dirty Bird, and likewise the affects of Black joy cultivated by and circulating in the stadium, need not be disconnected from emancipatory and liberatory politics. Indeed, MBS's promise of "revitalization" and "community uplift" is so powerful precisely because it is carried out in the name of topophilia as joyous, thus further illustrating these fraught and complex cultural politics.

Transforming the Westside?

MBS is a core component of major new urban developments in Atlanta's downtown core. City elites backed Westside stadium district development to ensure Atlanta would be a 2026 FIFA World Cup site. In addition to MBS, there is a plan to revive Underground Atlanta into a mixed-use retail and residential space as well as the development of Microsoft's Westside campus, aimed "to build Atlanta into a U.S. hub of datacenters and tech jobs."[71] The city also backed a major Westside mixed-use office, residential, and shopping development called Centennial Yards, modeled on New York City's Hudson Yards. In Atlanta the eight-million-square-foot development will rise across the street from MBS, conceived as a "mini-city." The $5 billion project is backed by a $2 billion tax-incentive initiative from the city of Atlanta and will include residences, commercial space, retail and shopping, restaurants, and a hotel. The developers' aim is to "make the project 'the center of gravity for the ultimate fan experience,'" demonstrating how the logic of the fan is extended more widely.[72]

The Westside development will reshape downtown Atlanta, anchored by MBS, which is expressly put to work to "catalyze changes in neighborhoods surrounding the development."[73] An MBS executive explained that the stadium wants to be "a good steward of this community," attributing this sentiment to Falcons team and stadium owner Arthur Blank, pointing to the fact that Blank is invested in the stadium being a good neighbor and "part of something that is part of the community."[74] The MBS executives I spoke with indicated that the stadium worked toward those ends in multiple domains, including using the stadium as a vaccination and voting site, working with local food banks, bringing in local schools to use the stadium for hands-on lessons in STEAM (science, technology, engineering, art, and mathematics), and being an environmental steward through the building's LEED (Leadership in Energy and Environmental Design) certification and environmental sustainability projects.[75] But the most significant contribution the stadium makes in working with the community is in their Westside Development Initiative through the Arthur Blank Foundation.

MBS executives and Falcons team owners are very vocal about their desire to use the stadium as an urban development catalyst. But the executives I spoke with also characterized being a good neighbor in terms of trying not to bother the residents of the neighborhood either. They acknowledged that a lot of people who come to events at the stadium or at the neighboring GWCC are not from the neighborhood, and the traffic and infiltration into the neighborhood can be disruptive. Thus, "being a good steward to the community" was not so much about encouraging fans to filter out into the surrounding neighborhood restaurants and bars, as is often the justification for community impact in stadium development. Instead, the impact that MBS executives aimed to have on the community was through economic development, which would be orchestrated through a series of philanthropic initiatives.

Falcons team owner, Arthur Blank, said that if they managed to build the stadium but were "not successful in our community work on the Westside, then we would have failed. The stadium is one measure of success. The long-term measure of success will be transforming the communities around the stadium."[76] The stadium's website explains, "The Blank Family of Businesses is committed to leveraging Mercedes-Benz Stadium as a force for good and serving as a catalyst for positive, transformational change in Atlanta's Historic Westside Neighborhoods."[77] Undoubtedly, this rhetoric of investment in the surrounding community comes from decades of critique of stadium effects on surrounding neighborhoods, including those of activist groups who criticized the Dome, Turner Field, and FCS, as discussed in the previous chapter. Likewise, the Falcons' commitment to urban regeneration helped to create public buy-in for the $200 million in public subsidies contributed to building the $1.6 billion stadium. Although $200 million is relatively small in comparison to what some other cities pay to house their teams, there is a catch: The agreement came with a "waterfall fund" that enabled the team to continue to draw on collected hotel taxes in future years for "maintenance, operation, and improvement" expenses that could cost the city up to $700 million.[78] As George Lipsitz argues, those subsidies are a direct trade-off with other kinds of investment the city might make, such as in education, which might instead be invested in rectifying spatial injustice. The subsidies send a message that "the pursuit of unlimited profits for the wealthy counts for more than the basic needs of the poor."[79] The Falcons' investment in the Westside neighborhoods, coordinated largely through the Arthur Blank Foundation, serves to counter these critiques and to justify that public buy-in through programs intended to prevent gentrification and displacement. Table

Table 2.1. Arthur Blank Foundation's Westside "Community Impact" Programs in Atlanta

Westside Works[A]	Offers training and job placement in a variety of fields—education, construction, IT, culinary, CDA, CNA; assessment, training, and support to create and sustain job readiness; stadium jobs to Westside residents (through the "West Nest"—a stadium-based restaurant that provides on-the-job skills for individuals enrolled in the Westside Works culinary program and Westside Hiring Program)
Westside Ambassadors[B]	Provides internships for Westside youth; teaches "integrity, ownership, communication" and "employability skills"; partners with American Explorers, an outdoor leadership training program
The Home Depot Backyard[C]	A "shared public space" adjacent to the stadium with playground, pavilion, and tailgating space for game day; focused on providing event programming invested in "community uplift"
Westside Neighborhood Prosperity Fund[D]	A granting agency that provides funding for investment in the community

A. CareerRise, "When Workforce Works: Westside Works," n.d., https://careerriseatlanta.org/wp-content/uploads/Westside-Works.pdf; CareerRise, "Westside Works," https://careerriseatlanta.org/westside-works/, accessed January 13, 2025; Adina Solomon, "At Mercedes-Benz Stadium, West Nest Provides a Training Ground for Westside Works Students and Grads," *Atlanta Magazine*, January 31, 2019, https://www.atlantamagazine.com/dining-news/at-mercedes-benz-stadium-west-nest-provides-a-training-ground-for-westside-works-students-and-grads/.

B. Mercedes-Benz Stadium, "Westside Ambassadors," https://www.mercedesbenzstadium.com/community/westside-ambassadors/, accessed January 13, 2025.

C. Mercedes-Benz Stadium News, "The Home Depot and Mercedes-Benz Stadium Announce the Home Depot Backyard," April 21, 2017, https://www.mercedesbenzstadium.com/news/the-home-depot-and-mercedes-benz-stadium-announce-the-home-depot-backyard.

D. Arthur M. Blank Family Foundation, "The Arthur M. Blank Family Foundation Continues Investment in Atlanta's Historic Westside Neighborhoods," Arthur M. Blank Family Foundation, November 17, 2022, https://blankfoundation.org/the-arthur-m-blank-family-foundation-continues-investment-in-atlantas-historic-westside-neighborhoods/.

2.1 outlines the main components of the foundation's Westside community-building/transformation efforts initiated when the stadium was first built.

On the one hand, the Falcons' efforts to invest in the community are commendable. It's notable that they acknowledge that the predominantly impoverished Black Westside neighborhoods have a "rich history" of their own to be shared with Atlanta and already a "vibrant community."[80] The Westside is therefore not only figured as a problematized site in need of uplift from wealthier, white Atlantans; it is also valued for its community and culture in its own right. On the other hand, each of these programs is a form of biopolitical intervention into the neighborhood. They seek to transform the population into healthy, self-responsible neoliberal citizens in ways that draw on a cultural ontology of sport (active, healthy, theatrical, performative, creative, self-responsible, entrepreneurial) modeled on the ideal fan. These interventions are made possible through the production of space. City space is transformed into sportified space through stadium architectures designed to fold into neighborhood spaces and to encourage residents to engage in practices that might make them healthier and more productive, interactive, and entrepreneurial citizens who are prepared to be "advocates" for themselves and their communities. Like the tiered experiences provided by the stadium, the neighborhood constitutes another tier in which fan experience is extended outward to residents who enact their own tier-appropriate expression of sportified citizenship as fan-subjects. In the absence of the ability to perform those duties on their own, privately funded programs, like those offered by the Arthur Blank Foundation, provide expert training to help neighborhood residents help themselves through, for example, teaching "employability" skills.

"The Home Depot Backyard" is a notable component of these efforts. The foundation characterizes the project as a form of "Community Activation."[81] In a press release, executives emphasize that the Backyard makes the stadium available to those who might otherwise never go to a game, suggesting it gives back to the community by providing "year-round opportunities for the community to enjoy the space through arts, culture and entertainment events, military veteran appreciation activities and everyday access to a beautiful greenspace with play areas and fun activities."[82] The emphasis of giving back in terms of "community activation" (rather than "community activism") is significant. This discourse demonstrates how the site is bound up with neoliberal ideals of "empowerment" rather than histories of racial and class justice.

Further, this discourse of empowerment harnesses the neighborhood as a site of governing through community, displacing the role of government in caring for its citizens onto the community. Nikolas Rose refers to this practice as "ethopolitics," which "works through the values, beliefs, and sentiments thought to underpin the techniques of responsible self-government and the management of one's obligations to others."[83] The ethopolitical aims of Home Depot Backyard are evident in the kinds of programming promoted on the site's original website (now taken down): "arts and culture, health and wellness, communal education and service-oriented activations . . . daily fitness classes . . . events focused on uplifting the community."[84] While, arguably, "arts and culture" might be tipped toward activism and justice, the remainder of the programs are suggestive of how stadium space and its events are imagined to transform problematized bodies into sportified ones—in other words, those that are healthy, fit, creative, performative, and productive. In turn, it is expected that those bodies will then work to transform and contribute to the economic and cultural uplift of their neighborhood spaces through their labor and citizenship practices.

Frank Fernandez, vice president of community development at the Blank Foundation, further claimed that the Home Depot Backyard would rectify the divisions that had been created by the Dome, stating, "The physical and social barriers that once existed will be removed, unifying the people and places around Mercedes-Benz Stadium."[85] Fernandez's statement positions the stadium itself as a central, unifying force, supposedly rectifying the isolating and displacing harms of earlier forms of urban renewal by providing a new kind of connection. On the original website for the Backyard, the space was described as one that would provide "community uplift" and bridge the "physical and cultural divide" between the Westside and the rest of Atlanta. While the language of race and class is not used, both are implied (especially through the reference to a "cultural divide"), as well as a discourse of community that is indicative of Rose's ethopolitics; building community is imagined to rectify the systemic harms of racism and poverty (rather than structural or systemic change). It is worth emphasizing here that the Home Depot Backyard is not, in fact, a public space. It is a private space that is carefully controlled through heavy policing and surveillance. Undoubtedly, then, these practices ensure that "community activation" and "cultural uplift" play out in carefully monitored and controlled ways.

Similarly, the Blank Foundation's Westside Neighborhood Prosperity Fund, relaunched as the Westside Future Fund in 2022, is a laudable effort but whose embeddedness in neoliberal ideals of citizenship limit its potentials. In its original formulation as the Westside Neighborhood Prosperity Fund, the Blank Foundation partnered with the city of Atlanta to distribute funds ($15 million from the foundation in 2014 and another $15 million in 2017, along with $17 million from the city) to the neighborhoods "in areas focused on building human capital through workforce development, housing, education, health, entrepreneurship, and youth leadership. An additional $7 million has been invested in Westside initiatives through other foundation programming."[86] This description of the kinds of strategic investments the fund would make—in "human capital"—demonstrate their embeddedness in neoliberal logics of entrepreneurial subjectivity and self-responsibility.

While its efforts to invest in the Westside are laudable, the Blank Foundation's programs reflect how, under neoliberalism, neighborhood investment is predicated on the whims of wealthy philanthropists like Arthur Blank (and his foundation's public-private partnerships) rather than as a duty and responsibility of government to care for its citizens. This is emblematic of neoliberalism's affective economy produced by market-driven governance. Vincanne Adams argues that under these conditions, "The safety net becomes a kind of affective choice, rather than a civil right protected by regulations that are enforced by strong public sector policies and judicial protections. Helping others in need is seen as a moral virtue, while making profits on this work is seen as equally virtuous."[87] This form of market-driven governance demands precisely the kind of sportified citizen produced by the stadium, where residents are figured as "advocates," who, like fans of the home team and through the curation and tutelage of the Arthur Blank Foundation and the Westside resources, engage interactively as empowered users, entrepreneurializing themselves to provide for and govern themselves and their communities.

Notably, the $200–$700 million in public funds for the stadium far exceeds the Blank Foundation's financial commitment to the fund, estimated at approximately $57 million.[88] One wonders if the city would have been better off using the moneys to fund these projects themselves. Moreover, because of the deal the Falcons worked out with the county to vacate the Dome and build MBS, they do not pay any taxes, and the Falcons receive 100 percent of the revenue generated by the stadium (e.g., ticket sales, concessions, parking). All resource sharing is voluntary. But what happens when or if Blank decides he no longer wishes to "give back to" or share resources with the neighborhood? That question is especially pressing given that the stadium is part of an industry composed of disposable infrastructure that will inevitably become obsolete, no matter its "future flexibility."

Despite the efforts of the Blank Foundation and an explicit investment in countering displacement, MBS drove up rents and housing prices in the neighborhood. The population numbers overall continue to decline. Home prices reportedly increased astronomically, as houses that might have sold for twenty thousand dollars prior to the new stadium being built were going for eighty thousand dollars by 2019, and rent prices increased several hundred dollars monthly,[89] up by at least 20 percent since 2012 when the project was first announced.[90] While stadium executives and the city claim they are committed to community partnership and countering displacement, that is not how many residents feel, reporting they feel like gentrification is happening since the stadium was built. This sentiment speaks to how gentrification works not only as a material and economic process but also as a symbolic and affective one, where residents are made to feel like outsiders in their own neighborhood as it becomes populated with places designed to cater to wealthier, whiter populations. Further, the Blank Foundation's refusal to sign a binding community benefits agreement made housing activists feel like the community partnerships were a public relations stunt and that developers had ultimately concluded, "We're going to develop it the way we want to develop it and develop it for who we want to develop it for."[91]

It's important to emphasize that the stadium and its resulting development and displacement have not gone uncontested, as neighborhood residents, organizers, and activists still struggle to hold the Blank Foundation accountable to its promises to contribute funding and resources to the community and that the city and county provide for its residents. This politics of resistance complements the politics of refusal described above in relation to expressions of Black joy. Resistance draws on the longer histories of struggle outlined in the previous chapter as residents activate the cultural memories of the broken promises of the Dome, Turner Field, and FCS (Fulton County Stadium). Kate Diedrick and Christopher A. Le Dantec note that these cultural memories have helped organizers shift their tactics to "take steps to confront the stadium and subsequent development by learning from history, building shared identity and developing a right to occupy and contest space."[92] By sharing stories; organizing street events; and building shared identity, community, and capacity, residents have drawn on their history, cultural memories, and identities to contest their exclusion from decision-making about the stadium, resist displacement, and demand community benefits and resource sharing. Though residents were not able to stop the building of the stadium, they continue to organize and demand accountability and resources.

Likely in response to this pushback, the Blank Foundation's focus shifted more specifically toward a discourse of equity and addressing the effects of gentrification brought on by the stadium and its ancillary development. This shift was reflected in the relaunch of the Westside Neighborhood Prosperity Fund into the Westside Future Fund. The foundation's president, Fay Twersky, described the shift in priorities as a response to concerns raised by residents over gentrification, stating, "Many legacy residents . . . are vulnerable to displacement. . . . We want to support long-term residents to be more economically stable and benefit from the improvements in the community they've called home for years. As we spoke with residents and nonprofit leaders about how we could make the most difference, we heard that legacy residents do not want to be priced out of the neighborhoods. They want to have more economic opportunity and more affordable housing enabling them to have the genuine choice to stay."[93] Daniel Shoy Jr., the Blank Foundation's managing director of youth development and its Westside programs, describes the "refreshed strategy" as a refocusing of priorities, where "the goal is to increase the economic mobility of legacy residents living in the English Avenue and Vine City neighborhoods. . . . If we are not thoughtful about the equity piece, then not everyone will be able to benefit."[94] Toward these ends, the Westside Future Fund has since pledged $10 million toward affordable housing projects. This support complements a $753,000 grant given by the Blank Foundation to the Atlanta Housing Trust to build four affordable housing units, as well as $6.2 million to the Georgia Resilience and Opportunity Fund "In Her Hands" program (which provides a guaranteed income to women in the program) and $6.2 million to Westside Works.[95] Although these programs are still rooted in the affective economy and market-driven governance, they are notable for their shift from programs aimed to create citizens of capacity to more direct distributions of funds toward affordable housing and guaranteed income. Even more notable is that they reflect the strength of the neighborhood activists to effect change through their continued engagement in both a politics of refusal and Black joy, which lays claim to the value of the community, bodies, and histories of the neighborhood, and of resistance, which pushes back against the oppressive forces of gentrification and displacement.

CHAPTER 3

Entrepreneurialism through Abandonment

The Making of a Stadium District

In 2013 the Atlanta Braves announced they were leaving Turner Field in downtown Atlanta for a new facility in suburban Cobb County, thirteen miles north of downtown. The decision ignited a series of debates about the relationship between teams and their spaces. If sports stadiums are sites of topophilia and physical embodiments of the places they represent, then the decision by the Braves to move outside the city prompted the question: What and who, precisely, constitutes "Braves Country" and, by extension, Atlanta? The move thus laid bare long-standing antagonisms over race, class, and space and their inextricable ties to Atlanta's sporting culture.

Michael L. Butterworth argues that baseball's close association with white, middle-class masculinity was reinforced in the 1960s "when several new ballparks were built in and around 'suburban white refuges,'" thereby fueling "baseball's connection to the myth of American exceptionalism."[1] It is no coincidence that this period of stadium building coincided with a decline in Black interest and participation in baseball. Although there is a rich history of Black baseball culture (both playing and watching), including in Atlanta, the integration of Major League Baseball and the subsequent decline of the Negro Leagues initiated a period of declining Black participation in and fandom of baseball.[2] Thus, the Braves' claim that the move to Cobb County would bring them closer to their fans (read, white middle-class men) was not incorrect. But why, in a majority-Black city among a community with a strong historic connection to baseball, did the Braves fail to engage with the community that immediately surrounded them? Particularly in an era when teams were relocating closer to urban cores, celebrating the history of the sport as an urban phenomenon, what did it mean for a team to abandon a majority-Black city that was famously "too busy to hate"?

Truist Park, the name of the Braves stadium at the time of this writing, draws into sharp focus the continued racial, class, and cultural tensions that exist within Atlanta's urban/suburban landscape. In contrast to the case of the Falcons, discussed in the previous chapter, the Braves' departure to Cobb County demonstrates how efforts to entrepreneurialize metro Atlanta as a technology hub are also inextricably tied to what Henry Giroux calls the "biopolitics of disposability," a term that describes the abandonment and abdication of responsibility for people and neighborhoods deemed failures in the neoliberal city.[3] However, the pushback against the move and the call-out of its racialized impact by neighborhood organizers, like those surrounding Mercedes-Benz Stadium, also present a realm of possibility for critiquing this form of governing and citizenship through demands for binding community benefits programs.

Where Is Braves Country?

When the Braves announced they would be moving to Cobb County, it was no surprise that many residents and critics took the move as just one more slap in the face to the neighborhood that had given them a home and to the public that had funded the stadium only seventeen years earlier. The move continued the biracial coalition between elite white and Black policymakers and corporate executives at the expense of the city's working-class and poor Black constituents. Initially, city officials, fans, and residents in Atlanta were "shocked" by the decision, having been unaware the Braves were negotiating with Cobb County. The Braves made a deal with county officials instead of the city of Atlanta after a set of secret meetings and negotiations. When the team announced they were moving, Cobb County was 56 percent white, and the closest incorporated town near the new stadium site, Vinings, was 89 percent white. In contrast, 54 percent of Atlanta's population and 89 percent of Turner Field's Summerhill neighborhood identified as Black.[4]

Like the Falcons' justification for a new stadium, the Braves explained the move as an endeavor to enhance the "fan experience." In some ways, this mirrored how the team legitimated the necessity for the city to build Turner Field; for Turner Field, the Braves claimed the stadium needed to provide "fan comfort," which meant upgrading luxury and spectacular entertainment experiences. But what stood out in their move to Cobb County was their claim that the enhanced experience would be largely due to their moving closer to their fan base. This claim was supported with a widely publicized "heat map" showing that the largest share of the Braves fan base (based on ticket sales) was in Atlanta's northern suburbs. Andy Walter argues that the Braves' ticket holders map "drew lines that reflected enduring divisions (white/black, wealthy/poor) but imbued them with new meaning, distinguishing where the Braves seemed to belong and where they did not.... By strategically re-territorializing 'Braves Country,' the map effectively created new urban subjects (Braves fans 'here' and not 'there') and, thus, a new city."[5] The Braves' reliance on the "heat map" aimed to sidestep the issue of race by claiming powerlessness in the face of numbers, suggesting the team had an obligation to go where their fans were. S. Derek Schiller, executive vice president of sales and marketing for the Braves, espoused a color-blind discourse justifying the move, asserting, "We don't look at the exact makeup of the race, religion factor of that ticket buyer.... What we're concerned about as a business that sells tickets is where do our ticket buyers come from?"[6] Agnostic to race but concerned about geography, this statement belies the long-standing intersections of race, class, and space in Atlanta.

A central discourse running through the press following the announcement was the sentiment that the Braves were not leaving Atlanta, claiming that the less than thirteen-mile distance was a meaningless one (see map 3.1). In fact, through a quirk of planning, the new stadium retained an Atlanta zip code. In so doing, the team not only effectively relocated the center of Atlanta to its white, northern suburbs, but it also constructed a broader discourse of regionalism by suggesting that the distinction between Atlanta's suburbs and its downtown core was "obsolete." This was a key theme running through a *New York Times* article detailing the logic of the move, contending that Cobb County was in fact more urban than downtown Atlanta, or at least more urban in terms of contemporary New Urbanist logics of downtown revivals:

> "The Cobb County site is actually more in line with a new ethos of urbanism that rewards smaller, walkable communities," said Chris Leinberger, a professor at the George Washington University School of Business. This year, he released a study of new urban development patterns in the Atlanta metro area as part of his work for the Brookings Institution. In it, many parts of suburban Atlanta had a more urban feel than the city itself. "The whole concept of city versus suburb is a really obsolete concept, and moving the baseball stadium reflects that," he said.[7]

Notably, the Braves are not the only traditionally urban cultural institution that abandoned downtown Atlanta for Cobb County. The Atlanta Opera, Atlanta Lyric Theater, and the Atlanta Ballet each moved to the suburbs, all the while promising visitors an "authentic Atlanta" experience.

88 · ATLANTA

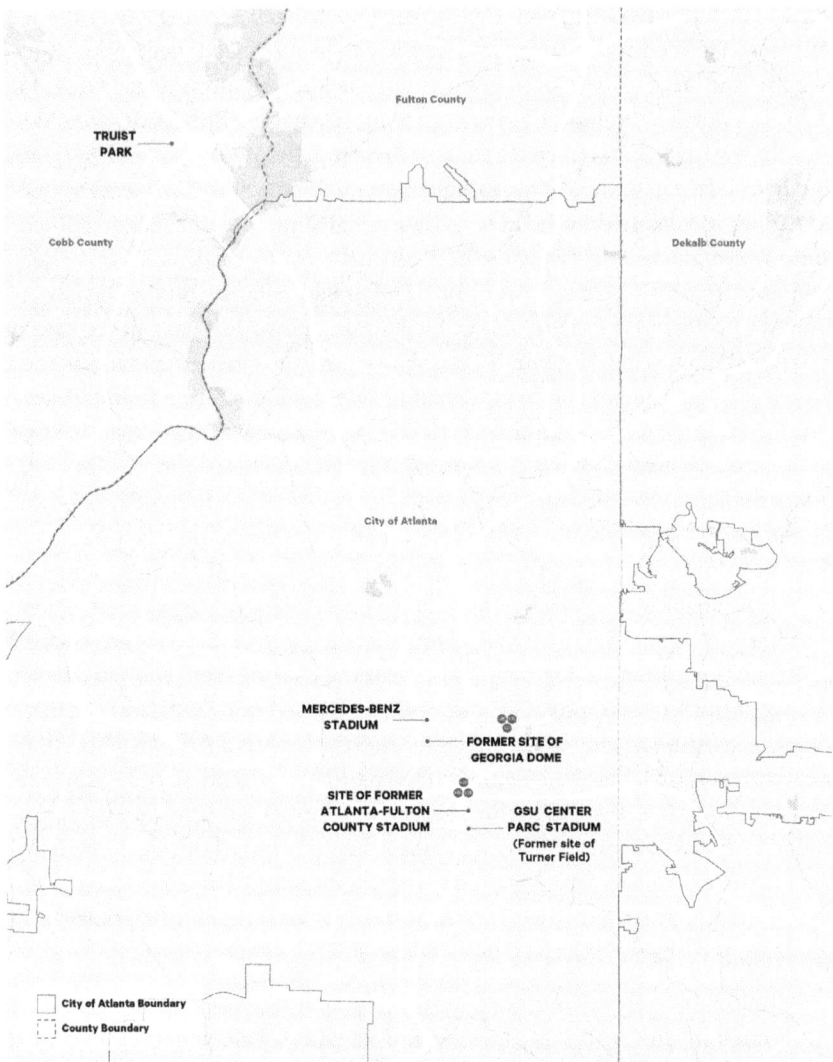

Map 3.1: Cobb County is a first ring suburb, 13 miles north of downtown Atlanta (Credit: Gillian Tiley)

The city of Atlanta refused to bargain with the Braves over public funding for a new stadium, since they had funded Turner Field twenty years earlier and had yet to see an economic return on their investment. But the Braves' move was nevertheless pitched by the team and Cobb County officials as not only good for Cobb County but good for Atlanta as well. They declared that the new stadium would still represent Atlanta and, in so doing, would help promote the city to fans at home and beyond. In fact, they claimed the move would help them to promote it even better because they could build a new development to incubate new media, digital, and technology industries to serve the city. The Braves seemed to want to both abandon downtown Atlanta but also to position themselves as "authentically" Atlantan, and, even *more* Atlanta than actual Atlanta. It thus drew upon and signified the kinds of aspirational images of Atlanta embodied in earlier stadium renewal and revitalization plans, but it projected those ideals onto a kind of blank canvas in the unincorporated town of Cumberland in Cobb County—a new place imagined to have no messy history or sense of place they would need to either clear or revitalize to conform to the aspired image. As one reviewer of the stadium noted in an Athens, Georgia–based news outlet, "There are no eyesores, no trash, no junk loitering anywhere. Just a comfortable environment with happy people all about—shopping, relaxing and emotionally stimulated by having the good fortune to work in such an uplifting environment."[8]

Unlike Turner Field, Truist Park is part of a mixed-use development with retail, dining, hotel, entertainment, and office space. It is a stadium district— that is, an urban space where the stadium serves as the center of broader neighborhood development. The creation of stadium districts is a hallmark of the sportification of place and third-generation stadiums. These districts respond to criticisms that stadiums alone do not economically benefit cities or result in significant forms of urban regeneration, especially given the enormous public expenditures they demand.[9] Mixed-use district developments, in theory, spread economic benefits to a wider sector of the city and economy. However, there is little evidence to suggest economic benefits exceed public expenditures; benefits remain unequally distributed, merely shifting consumption practices from one part of a city to another, thereby draining resources from other neighborhoods.[10]

Cobb County gave the Braves authority to approve what went into the stadium district, and the team generates revenue from the district rather than just the stadium. The stadium is therefore the center of a new urban space, The Battery Atlanta. Truist Park's stadium district offers a place-based "urban" experience in a carefully planned and controlled suburban environment. Although Truist Park is one of the only suburban stadiums built during this period, its design logic is still rooted in the Camden Yards–inspired nostalgia of the "retro" ballpark. It thus implicitly evokes signifiers of urbanism as a means of authenticating suburban space. As such, it emphasizes older ideals of suburban white flight but in an updated fashion by situating the suburban park as a site of urban development.

Urbanizing the Suburban

Truist Park's aim to make the neighborhood *feel* urban rather than suburban differentiates it from the earlier stadiums built in Atlanta. As discussed in chapter 1, earlier stadium iterations in Atlanta (and elsewhere during the second generation of development) mimicked suburban isolation but through contained spectacular entertainment in the urban core. In contrast, Truist Park turned the suburban into an urban space by producing an "authentic" experience of the local at the pedestrian and neighborhood level. This contrasts with the automobility and escape/division from the neighborhood prioritized in the second generation.

The area surrounding the park is a mixed-use development with an aim to create both an entertainment destination and a tech-hub incubator. Cobb County officials say they supported the development because of the Braves' promises to contribute to this development.[11] To an extent, the deal between the Braves and Cobb County demonstrated a shift in stadium funding in response to critiques of the tax incentive models of public funding. While the Braves still managed to garner public funding, they promised that in exchange they would contribute direct private investment in the surrounding area. The deal was heralded as a win-win, where Cobb County, the team, and its investors could profit from the development. Ultimately, Cobb County contributed approximately $400 million from bonds and transportation taxes for a $1.1 billion project, including the stadium itself and the adjacent urban development and entertainment destination site, The Battery Atlanta.[12]

The Battery is a "baseball-centric, live-work-play megaplex."[13] It is described as a "legacy destination" and a "lifestyle hub," anchored by the stadium and "designed for the community to live, work, play, stay, and cheer."[14] The Battery is indicative of New Urbanist design principles, as it is not merely an entertainment destination but is imagined as a place where people live, work, and play in walkable urban communities. Although New Urbanism espouses discourses of racial, ethnic, and class diversity, promising that designing mixed-use urban spaces to engender community will help break down segregation between suburban and urban spaces, in practice that has not been the case. Instead, research shows that New Urbanism increases displacement of racial and ethnic groups.[15]

The design of Truist Park and The Battery drew heavily on architectural and planning designs that evoked signifiers of the urban to create a look and feel that replicated "authentic" urban Atlanta (see figs. 3.1, 3.2). While there is on-street parking as well as a large garage, parking is largely out of sight and creates the sense of a walkable neighborhood. Three luxury apartment buildings provide

Figs. 3.1 and 3.2: The Truist Park Stadium District is designed to look and feel urban.

the feel of being in a dense area, interspersed with offices, shops, restaurants, and entertainment venues beyond the stadium, such as the Coca-Cola Roxy, which includes a movie theater, virtual reality experience (The Void), and an escape room. The development includes few major chains, instead featuring stores and dining establishments originating in Atlanta. These establishments construct the district as local, place-based, and, especially, tied to Atlanta. The Battery Atlanta website describes the area as a "carefully curated mix," providing both boutique and flagship offerings. These include the Terrapin taproom, a bar centered on the Atlanta craft brewery, and the Atlanta-based market Savi Provisions, which describes itself as "a neighborhood destination market."[16] The area also includes the Waterloo Sunset Vinyl Lounge, a store that buys and sells record albums, 45s, DVDs, blu-rays, and CDs, promising visitors, "We think like collectors because we are collectors. . . . We exhaustively winnow the chaff so only the finest material makes it to the sales floor, and what is there is mercurially identified and sorted so you can find what you're looking for."[17] Together, these destinations offer visitors something beyond the spectacular entertainment destination of the stadium as a suburbanized tourist bubble. Drawing instead on signifiers of "authenticity" and exclusivity, they promise a curated local experience tied to a unique sense of place and refined urbanity. In so doing, The Battery resignifies suburban Atlanta from a derided space of homogeneity, sprawl, and commodification to a hip, urbanized, and cool space. This is reflective of broader shifts in suburban development, especially influences of New Urbanist design and principles, which address the financial and demographic shifts in suburbia since the early 2000s, when population began shifting back into urban centers.[18]

The discourses constructing The Battery Atlanta as a lifestyle and entertainment destination connect the fan experiences in the stadium to those that they are encouraged to participate in outside of it. In this sense, Truist Park's stadium district, like that of MBS, cultivates fandom as a governing and citizenship practice through its connection to media culture, especially its "tech hub incubator." To build the park and stadium district, the Braves, owned by Liberty Media, partnered with media giant Comcast/NBC Universal. The district serves as a technology incubator site for Comcast, where its office building within the stadium campus aims to "help identify and nurture tech entrepreneurs who are creating the innovations of tomorrow" and to "get in on the action to find the next big thing in Atlanta tech."[19] The partnership also resulted in significant integration of media into the stadium itself, with an "all-fiber network and multi-terabit capabilities."[20] This integration promises to facilitate deeper fan and community engagement, as promoters argue the stadium's capabilities will help "meet our fans' high expectations for engagement, awareness and access. Shoppers, hotel guests and office tenants will also enjoy an experience unlike any other community."[21] The convergence of media and sport in and through the interactive stadium is thus imagined to both draw on and produce newly engaged and interactive fans *and* community members. The stadium itself serves as an incubator site, tasked with producing the kinds of creative and entrepreneurial citizens who will promote and bring Atlanta into the technological future.

The tech hub in the Truist Park/Battery Atlanta development is the primary site for producing these aims. Originally rolled out as The Farm, the space was described as providing:

> 12,000 sq. ft of work space for our co-workers and accelerator companies, a tricked out hardware lab for creative engineers, and various spaces for tech related events. We're ideally located in Battery Park across from the Atlanta Braves stadium, which give us one of the best views in Atlanta. Ping pong in the front, flying drones in the back, and a lot of brainpower solving problems in between. Come grab a bite to eat with a fellow innovator, watch the Braves' fans queuing up for the game as the marching band plays, and experience a day with founders who are changing the world through tech.[22]

It provided space, programming, accelerator programs designed for tech entrepreneurs and startups, coworking, mentorship, and a hardware lab.[23] The Farm (which now appears closed and relaunched as the Innovation Center at the Battery) was a component of Atlanta's broader efforts to transform the city into a technology hub, along with Atlanta Tech Village in Buckhead. One of the main draws of The Farm that still resides in The Battery Atlanta is SportsTech, a program aimed at supporting startups and entrepreneurs who are developing sports technologies to influence "the way sports are played, both on and off the field."[24] Through their twelve-week program, they promise to "bring your sports tech idea to life, get it to market, and provide players and teams with a competitive edge built on technology and innovation." They note that they are specifically looking for participants who are developing products with a technology focus, making an explicit call encouraging international applicants. The main investment areas they list include fan/player engagement, athlete/player performance, media and entertainment, venue and event innovation, coach success, business of sports, fantasy and sports betting, and e-sports.

SportsTech, and Comcast/Universal NBC's tech-hub incubator more generally, is perhaps the ultimate expression of the sportification of place. It is a quasi-urban space that is a product of the partnership between a major media conglomerate and a city's sports team. Through that partnership, the city extends the logic of sport and the stadium to entrepreneurialize and mediatize city space and residents. Notably, though, the program is aimed not so much at Atlantans as *any* potential entrepreneur, including "global" ones. Thus, while the incubator plays a role in entrepreneurializing Atlanta, using the stadium as a site for producing the city as a technology hub, it does so largely by working to attract labor and investment from outside Atlanta. Whereas Atlanta Tech Village makes an explicit call for Black entrepreneurs and efforts to highlight their Black founders, SportsTech makes no such effort.

The Truist Park Stadium District thus does not appear to invoke the discourse of Atlanta as a Black Mecca. The Braves were an early symbol of civil rights and baseball's integration, with celebrated Black players like Hank Aaron in the 1960s and 1970s and, in the 1990s, amid the rise of Atlanta's hip-hop scene, flush with rising Black stars. Yet, the twenty-first-century Braves franchise, in contrast to that of the Falcons, has shown little interest in connecting with Black fans. As one reporter quipped, "The crowds for Falcons and Hawks [Atlanta's professional National Basketball Association team] games, in the city's downtown, are filled with Black and brown faces. But the throngs of Braves fans who passed through on their way to Turner Field were noticeably whiter."[25] The reporter further suggested that the Braves' games can have a "Trump feel," a nod to how the campaign rally for former (and now current) president Donald Trump, which often take place in sports stadiums, "functions as a homosocial space and retreat for anxious whites."[26] Likewise, baseball, as in the case of the Braves stadium, works to produce and cultivate "fantasies of an unapologetic, omnipotent white masculinity" through the production of these kinds of affective spaces.[27]

The production of this kind of spatialized affect can be seen in the Braves fans' signature chant (beginning circa 1991), the "Tomahawk Chop," in which fans, often using foam instruments shaped as a tomahawk (a single-handled axe whose design is attributed to Indigenous peoples), move their arms up and down in a chopping motion to celebrate good plays and home runs. The chop is generally accompanied by a drumbeat and a repeated chant of "OHHHHH oh oh oh / Ohhh oh oh oh." Native American tribes have long criticized both the Braves name and the chant for how it "mocks the Native American cultural practices, trivializes their diversity and assaults their humanity";[28] they have also made clear that "Native people are not mascots, and degrading rituals like the 'tomahawk chop' that dehumanize and harm us have no place in American society."[29] Those criticisms have intensified in recent years as other teams changed their names and mascots in response to these protests, often dividing fans along political lines.

Nevertheless, the Braves franchise, Georgia's governing elites, and many of the team's fans have instead doubled down on the use of the Tomahawk Chop.

Shortly after the Braves moved to Truist Park and made it to the World Series during the 2021 season, Georgia governor Brian Kemp tweeted, "While Stacey Abrams and the MLB stole the All-Star Game from hardworking Georgians, the Braves earned their trip to the World Series this season and are bringing it home to Georgia. Chop On, and Go @Braves."[30] Kemp was referring to how the MLB moved the All-Star Game out of Atlanta in response to the state passing a law that made it more difficult for people to vote, criticized by many as disproportionately disenfranchising Black voters. His decision to use the Tomahawk Chop to make his political point, especially in contrast to the Falcons' Dirty Bird (discussed in the previous chapter), demonstrates how the Braves and their sporting home are bound up with performances of whiteness.

These cultural politics are made especially evident by the Braves' move to Cobb County. As opposed to slum clearance associated with urban renewal and Fulton County Stadium (FCS) and the neoliberal urban revitalization associated with the Dome and Turner Field, the Braves stadium in Cobb County is indicative of a distinct urban development logic that involves creating enclosure, containment, and "zones of human discard."[31] Truist Park is constitutive of a kind of biopolitics of disposability; Henry Giroux notes that the biopolitics of disposability is a hallmark of neoliberal racism. Describing how Hurricane Katrina made visible whole segments of the population—primarily impoverished Black people—that the government had abandoned, Giroux argues that the Katrina event revealed a new kind of politics, "one in which entire populations are now considered disposable, an unnecessary burden on state coffers, and consigned to fend for themselves."[32] Although the abandonment of New Orleans' impoverished, Black, and elderly citizens in the wake of Katrina is not necessarily comparable to the Braves' abandonment of Turner Field and its surrounding neighborhoods, it is nevertheless arguable that the move aligns with the same kind of logic the Bush administration operated with in the years leading up to Katrina. That is, the Braves treated these neighborhoods as irredeemable, sites to be enclosed and contained. Abandoning the neighborhoods altogether, the move revealed a shifting racial politics to a biopolitics of disposability that treats impoverished Black neighborhoods as waste to be disposed of rather than places to be revitalized and "redeemed," because they are imagined as threats to the health and vitality of the city. However, similar to how the "Katrina disaster... revealed a vulnerable and destitute segment of the nation's citizenry that conservatives not only refused to see but had spent the better part of two decades demonizing," the Braves' sudden departure from Atlanta revealed racial, class, and spatial injustices long denied and suppressed in the wake of decades of stadium development and Atlanta's urban growth machine.[33]

Contesting Sportified Citizenship

In the press coverage after the Braves announced the move, relatively more journalistic space was given to opposition to the move, especially from the perspective that it was driven by racist politics and assumptions, than to its benefits and justifications. This stands in contrast to the history of journalistic coverage of stadium projects, which tend to be overwhelmingly favorable and privilege perspectives of elites and stadium boosters.[34] First, critics pointed out that the city's public transportation system, MARTA, which is the primary means of transportation for much of the city's working-class urban population, does not run into Cobb County. The deal to build a stadium was made without any plan in place to improve either public transportation or the city's infamously congested highway system. The lack of public transport to the stadium was seen as particularly egregious as the Braves had made the issue of poor transportation links a key argument for why they needed a new stadium in the first place. Neither Cobb County nor Braves officials contacted planners about the transportation issues that the new site would present. That the Braves would choose to move to a site with even worse transportation links was seen by several journalists as a clear indication that the Braves' decision was about race and class. Critics pointed especially to the incendiary comments of Cobb County's Republican Party chair, Joe Dendy, who suggested, "It is absolutely necessary the solution is all about moving cars in and around Cobb and surrounding counties from our north and east where most Braves fans travel from, and not moving people into Cobb by rail from Atlanta."[35] As critics noted, this statement exposes the racist assumptions behind the move regarding who is considered and valued as part of the Braves fan community—whites from the northern suburbs—and that it would cater to this fan experience while isolating downtown and south Atlanta from this new form of urban revival. It "played into the notion that the neighborhood around Turner Field was somehow 'unsafe' for white suburban fans outside of their cars, despite the fact that the Summerhill neighborhood has a lower crime rate than most other urban Atlanta neighborhoods."[36]

Thus, many critics explicitly called out the Braves' move as a continuation of "white flight." As journalist Andrew Baggarly argued, "The Braves will make their white-flight move—and yes, that's precisely what it is—in 2017.... We're supposed to assume . . . that the 'heart of Braves country' must be a lot closer to the suburbs than the Old Fourth Ward or Sweet Auburn, where Dr. Martin Luther King Jr. was raised."[37] While some critics and commenters pushed back against critics who claimed the move had racist undertones by claiming that it was purely a business decision, the prevailing conclusion was that this business decision was steeped in racism.

While the Braves' departure treated the Turner Field neighborhoods as zones of discard, real estate speculators referred to the site as a potential "blank slate" from which to imagine a new mixed-use development. Mayor Kasim Reed speculated that "the site could become 'one of the largest developments for middle-class people that the city has ever had.'"[38] Despite the mayor's promise to include neighborhood stakeholders in a transparent conversation over the future of Turner Field, he was widely criticized for brokering a backroom deal with Georgia State University (GSU) to develop the area as a mixed-use campus with no community input. Imagining the site as a "blank space" absent of people, cultures, and histories ripe for the kind of backroom deals of the infamous Atlanta urban growth machine continues the historic injustices the neighborhood has faced for over six decades. GSU's deal with the city allowed for Turner Field's renovation to house the university's football team, the Panthers, and an $800 million development project designed to "revitalize the area, bringing a strip of new restaurants and shops and close to 1,000 new residences near the football stadium."[39]

The promises from this development are similar to those engendered by MBS, as discussed in the previous chapter. While a large portion of the housing built in this newly designed area is for GSU students, along with some luxury condominiums, developers promised a commitment to the neighborhood and working-class residents to mitigate displacement. On their website describing the development, GSU details the long history of the Summerhill neighborhood, citing the many instances of city elites failing the community and contributing to its destruction, including through various phases of stadium development. Despite noting that building FCS and its subsequent iterations in the neighborhood did little to address poverty, they herald GSU's takeover of the stadium as a "new era" in which Summerhill "saw the first signs of hope in more than a decade," promising GSU's presence in the neighborhood will help to "rekindle a community spirit" and connect old and new residents.[40] But GSU is hardly an unbiased entity. The university has long collaborated with city elites and business leaders by providing research and reports that support an urban growth and development model that benefits business at the expense of the poor.[41]

Unsurprisingly, then, many residents were skeptical of GSU's promises. They were particularly concerned about gentrification, which they began to see even before GSU completed its renovation. The shops and restaurants that popped up seemed to cater to a wealthier, and perhaps whiter, clientele.[42] Although some of these changes reflected the new GSU students moving into the area, others were more indicative of the kinds of residents expected to move into the $300,000–$700,000 condominiums under construction. Although they include a stipulation that 10 percent of residences must be made affordable to residents making 80 percent of the area's median income, these high prices mean that demographic changes in the neighborhood will be all but inevitable.

Before the GSU deal was finalized, these concerns were voiced largely through an organization called the Turner Field Community Benefits Coalition, which made efforts to ensure a voice for neighborhood residents and stakeholders in the future of the neighborhood. Comprised of a set of residents, neighborhood associations, and community-based organizations, the coalition waged a strategic media and political campaign on a three-point platform of inclusive planning, transparent development, and community benefits. Its website, which has since been taken down, included a cultural history of the area exposing the injustices imposed on community residents through racist urban renewal measures in the past along with goals and a platform for future development, which "values people first and foremost, both those who are here now and those yet to come. We honor diversity as a community imperative, honed by mutual respect, empathy, engagement [with] and service to neighbors, and tempered by shared bonds of culture, tradition and history."[43] The coalition focused especially on the necessity of including the voices of every resident in the planning process and, crucially, getting the city to sign a binding community benefits agreement that would guarantee neighborhood residents "jobs and job training, education initiatives, transportation, green spaces, sidewalk and lighting, and security issues" and that "would be signed by the purchasing entities and included in the planning of the new office, retail, housing, university and athletic buildings."[44] Privileging community benefits over corporate profit, the coalition argued, was a form of inclusive urban planning. The group used the fact that the city was awarded a Livable Cities Initiative grant to develop the area, which requires participatory planning, to hold the government accountable to neighborhood voices.

The possibility for the coalition to affect the outcome of the planning process, however, was relatively slim, particularly as the mayor maintained he was committed to an inclusive planning process only insofar as it did not impede development, telling the *Atlanta Journal-Constitution*, "I'm not going to have the process cost the community a quarter of a billion [to] a half of a billion dollars' worth of development."[45] He also refused to halt backroom talks with GSU and other developers who expressed no commitment in collaborating with the community.[46] Residents started receiving phone calls from real estate speculators wishing to purchase their homes; as one coalition member lamented, "They're treating us like a commodity, not a community."[47] The mayor, GSU officials, and developers continually refused to meet with organizers. The coalition ultimately staged a march and erected a tent city at Turner Field for sixty-three days (see fig. 3.3). Finally, GSU and the developer, Carter and Associates, agreed to meet with the group, promising to allow the tent city to remain but bulldozing it shortly thereafter. Ultimately, the Turner Field Community Benefits Coalition splintered into separate factions, some signing agreements with developers, with others still pressing for further commitments and transparence of who the investment would ultimately benefit.[48]

The coalition and affiliated organizations, although perhaps not entirely successful, nonetheless did alter the rhetoric and direction of the planning process to envision a new future for their neighborhood. While the GSU development affects the character of the neighborhood and remains a site of antagonism, the coalition used the rhetorical framing of the Braves' move as a racialized one as an opportunity to open up a wider discussion about histories and futures of urban planning and development in Atlanta. In so doing, they offered an important site of contestation to the sportification of place.

As the cases of Atlanta's stadiums show, sportified citizenship and governing is also tied to city image, symbolism, and branding. As in each case of the city's stadium history, the city's promotional image and, later, its brand have become part of what is being used to govern those citizenship practices and direct behavior while also serving as a site of contestation over who and what that brand represents. In the next section, I turn to the case study of Seattle, where I take up this role of image and branding more specifically.

Fig. 3.3: The Turner Field Community Benefits Coalition set up a tent city outside Turner Field after the Braves departed for Cobb County, contesting the displacement they feared would come from proposed new development. (Photo by author)

PART II

Seattle

Place-Identity and Branding

CHAPTER 4

Boosting the Northwest

With a population of just over 700,000 people and 3.5 million in the metro area, Seattle is generally viewed as a major cosmopolitan and high-tech city (though still not on the level of New York, Chicago, or Los Angeles). Seattle holds some of the country's most financially and globally significant technology industries, including Microsoft and Amazon, and is a global port connection to Asia and the Pacific Rim. Playing up its natural geographical location as a major urban center next to the Pacific Ocean, and tucked between the Olympic and Cascade mountains, Seattle markets itself as a "dynamic, urban city surrounded by unmatched natural beauty."[1] So too it often sells itself as a politically progressive city with a rich local, creative culture while also containing some of the world's wealthiest and biggest global industries.

But this conception of Seattle as a global cosmopolitan city was not always the case, and its history of provincialism is still evidenced in the seemingly contrasting images its current branding intimates. Up until the early 2000s, the city was considered an insular second- or even third-tier city, plagued with boom-and-bust periods, "always seemingly on the cusp of national and international prominence" but never quite reaching the aspirations of city boosters.[2] To counter its image as small-town and insignificant, boosters invested in trying to promote Seattle as "cosmopolitan, globally connected, economically robust, and eminently modern."[3] But this aspiration for national and international recognition was not desired by all. Seattle's early settlers also prided themselves on Seattle's "small town in a big city" feel, ruggedness, and geographical isolation, and that sensibility continued to influence the city's cultural identity as it developed. Shannon Mattern suggests that the city's "erratic economic growth" in its boom-and-bust periods manifested a city design characterized by these paradoxes—creating a landscape that both symbolized a desire to be a big city with "audacious and aggressive" design alongside more "timid and nondescript" architecture that manifests small-town parochialism.[4]

The constitution of Seattle materially and symbolically as a modern city depended, as Serin Houston contends, on destruction as much as development, whether through settler colonial efforts to clear the land and assert territorial control over Indigenous lands, the violent expulsion of the Asian population through forceful and legislative means, or the internment of the Japanese population in 1942 during World War II. These forces of violent oppression and expulsion enabled new kinds of development that produced modern Seattle.[5] City space in Seattle is thus contested, marked by complex and deeply uneven racial, ethnic, and class geographies, and, like Atlanta, historical anxieties and inequities that shaped the city are built into its architecture, design, and landscape.

Seattle's football and baseball stadiums are both emblematic of and have helped shape these inequities. It is a deeply segregated city. Mostly white and wealthy citizens reside north of downtown. South of downtown, where the city's stadiums are located, contains the highest concentrations of people of color and impoverished peoples. The stadiums are located in what is today called the SoDo neighborhood (so named for its location, south of the Kingdome), which buttresses Pioneer Square and the Chinatown-International District neighborhoods, which are some of the most socioeconomically as well as racially and ethnically diverse neighborhoods in the city.[6] The demographic trends in these neighborhoods are direct results of both history and policy, including redlining and slum clearance, that pushed impoverished peoples and people of color into these areas. Sports infrastructure plays a key role in producing and managing this uneven geography.

Marked by internal divisions that complicate any kind of universal place-identity, like many other cities, Seattle draws on sport and sporting infrastructure to promote a unifying sense of city identity across these fault lines. Historically, Seattle was not seen as a sports town, as the multiple contested fights over public funding for professional sports stadium infrastructure demonstrate. For many Seattleites and Washingtonians, rooting for the local university team—the University of Washington Huskies—was seen as sufficient to meet the needs of sports fans. However, since the 1960s, city boosters have turned to professional sports and sporting infrastructure to promote Seattle as a major city and to create a unifying identity tied to a sense of local authenticity *and* cosmopolitanism. As Terry Anne Scott claims, "Sports . . . just as much as any triumphant company or legendary musician, have rendered Seattle noteworthy, important, even exceptional. . . . Sports in Seattle promise to create and maintain global visibility. . . . Despite a constant struggle for credibility, Seattle exists as a preeminent sporting center."[7] Sports are used to create not only a unified city identity, which projects the Seattle image and brand, but a regional identity as well. Boosters use sports to unify the eastern and western parts of the state as well as crossing urban/rural divides.

There are two key periods when stadiums were used to catalyze Seattle's place-identity into the upper echelon of cities and to build a unifying sense of identity. First, in the 1960s and 1970s, as the city aimed to become "major league," Seattle renovated Sick's Stadium (home to Seattle's minor and Negro League baseball teams) and subsequently built the Kingdome as part of a broader urban renewal effort in which attracting an MLB and NFL team were key strategies. Second, in the 1990s and early 2000s, as part of Seattle's technology boom and renewed efforts to promote itself as a global, first-tier city, the Kingdome was imploded to make way for two new sports stadiums as part of a new round of urban revitalization. These two periods mark distinct moments in the relationship between stadiums and the construction of place-identity, in what Miriam Greenberg argues is a shift from urban boosterism to urban branding.[8] Greenberg notes that boosterism was an American phenomenon of the modern city that took hold in the late 1900s in which urban elites partnered with newly developing media and marketing companies to promote positive images of a city to attract workers, tourists, and investors. Whereas urban boosters were largely individual entrepreneurs, acting independently without formal institutional arrangements, urban branding emerged as part of the neoliberal city by formalizing public-private partnerships and linking them to broader economic development strategies and government restructuring. Seattle's two stadium-building periods had a major impact not only on Seattle more widely but on the neighborhoods surrounding the stadium in particular. The neighborhoods got caught up in the city's boosterism and branding efforts in ways that implicated how they were symbolized and how they were materially constituted and practiced in everyday life. In this chapter, I focus on the first period, historicizing Seattle's second-generation stadiums in the 1960s and 1970s, while the next chapter focuses on the 1990s–2000s and the city's third generation.

A Seattle-Style Quality of Life: Stadium Debates, the Forward Thrust, and Becoming Big League

Historicizing Seattle's stadiums begins on the heels of the 1962 World's Fair, the building of the Seattle Center, and the Forward Thrust urban renewal campaign, which the fair kicked off. In the 1940s, population in Seattle spiked. Whereas other parts of the US population decreased during wartime mobilization, the Pacific Northwest, as a staging center for waging war in the Pacific, saw a 45 percent population increase in workers, including Latinx and Black workers. This altered the racial makeup of a city that had been predominantly white after colonial settlement. The city also had a sizable Asian population, who settled in the late 1800s and early 1900s and worked mainly in canneries, lumber mills, hops farms, mining camps, and railroads.

After the war, the city aimed to capitalize on its importance to become a national and global city. Its major claim to this status was its relationship to the American empire and military. This was largely made possible by Boeing, a major US arms manufacturer, which was the city's largest employer, as well as nearby Bremerton's naval shipyard and Fort Lewis.[9] But soon after the war, suburbanization deeply affected Seattle. During the 1950s and 1960s, the metro area grew larger and more populous than the central city. In the late 1960s and early 1970s, Boeing also struggled financially, leading to major layoffs. This made the city's overreliance on Boeing as its primary employer glaringly apparent, and it spurred efforts to rethink and revitalize the city to diversify its industrial and economic base and bring people back downtown.[10] With major urban renewal campaigns, such as the sprawling Forward Thrust, which included a domed sports stadium, Seattle's identity was rethought and reshaped.

Major League Baseball was expanding in the postwar period to the south and west, and the American League was eager to get a franchise to Seattle, where they saw potential profits in the city's rising population. Boosters amped up major efforts to solicit city, county, and state support for professional sports and a new stadium in the mid-1950s, with newspapers and the general manager for the city's minor league team, the Rainiers, soliciting public and legislative support to publicly fund a new stadium. The world's fair supercharged these efforts, with stadium boosters pushing for a professional-grade stadium as part of the fair's infrastructure. However, there was little public support locally, especially since the city had yet to sign a team.[11]

Still, this did not subdue determined boosters. After the fair, boosters capitalized on rising discourses of the city as a cosmopolitan center to argue that it needed a professional team to be truly "big league." Seattle elites thought the city should be acknowledged as a rising city of the West, where a professional sports team and the infrastructure to support it would demonstrate that prowess and counter the image of Seattle as provincial. William Mullins notes, "Cities of middling size—growing urban centers a little unsure of themselves—are most anxious to be esteemed as big league. . . . In the 1960s, when Seattle first began to dream of a franchise, that meant a major league baseball or National Football League (NFL) club."[12]

Although boosters were eager to build a stadium to attract a professional team, it would take three rounds of voting to convince voters to put up the public financing. Political jockeying to garner legislative and public support for a stadium initiative continued throughout the 1960s. At this point, not only professional baseball was up for grabs but negotiations were under way for an NFL expansion team along with professional soccer and hockey teams. Stadium boosters mounted a full-force campaign to get voters to support the resolution; they brought in professional sports stars like Mickey Mantle to drum up support. Finally, on the third try, on February 13, 1968, the resolution passed with 62 percent of the vote, the majority of which came from the county's suburbs.[13] Therefore, there remained little support inside the city for the stadium. Seattle's local news outlets played an outsized promotional role, with nearly all coverage espousing the pro-stadium position.[14]

The stadium initiative couched the domed stadium as part of a broader urban renewal scheme, the Forward Thrust—a set of ballot initiatives proposing $815.2 million in improvements in transportation, parks, recreational facilities, and community centers.[15] The Forward Thrust Committee's founder, James Ellis, was a civic-minded Seattle-based municipal bond lawyer. Ellis pushed for adding the stadium to the program's bond initiatives because he believed it would drive people to the polls, given the controversy surrounding the stadium and the two prior failed votes.[16] The Forward Thrust planned not only to remake Seattle into the kind of national city of import that the city's new professional sports teams would symbolize but also to represent the city in response to the rapid changes taking place in Seattle at the time, including the postwar population boom as well as suburbanization and the beginnings of sprawl.

In addition, the Forward Thrust responded to broader discourses of urban crisis and decline taking shape in the United States at the time, exacerbated by national economic decline resulting from deindustrialization. Though Seattle was not affected to the extent of Rust Belt cities like Detroit, the rapid downturn of Boeing in 1970 as a result of airline cutbacks and Pentagon budget cuts left a marked impact on the city. The company removed sixty thousand Seattle-area jobs between 1969 and 1971.[17] While Seattle found itself on the precipice of emerging as a national urban leader after its successful hosting of the 1962 World's Fair—a boom time for the city—the Boeing layoffs once again left the city facing a bust period. The Forward Thrust and its stadium initiative thus sought to combat decline, diversify the city's economy, and create a modern city that would encourage investment and ease the mobile flow of both people and capital.[18]

The Forward Thrust was a neo-progressive, liberal reform aimed to improve Seattle's urban "quality of life" by building material infrastructure that planned for population growth. This quality-of-life discourse has since become central to Seattle's promotional identity. As described in one of the committee's promotional pamphlets, circulated to encourage residents to get out and vote for the bonds, the program was pitched as primarily responding to population growth and the consequent decline this would bring to the urban environment's quality of life. "When they're 21, it will be too late," reads the front of a pamphlet promoting the initiative, above an image of four frowning children, and continuing: "While they're growing up, Seattle and King County will be getting bigger, too. We'll add 750,000 people in the next 17 years. We can either get ready for this new growth or quietly sit by and watch this magnificent corner of America deteriorate under the pressure of jammed highways, blighted neighborhoods, over-crowded parks and beaches, and polluted air, water and land."[19] The Forward Thrust bonds, they promised, were the answer, providing "smart growth" to prevent this potential future. The pamphlet's discourse demonstrates the anxieties brought on by the city's postwar population boom and the tensions created between those who sought to preserve the city's past as a small regional city and those who wanted to thrust the city into the spotlight as a major city of import. The Forward Thrust worked to balance these competing visions by offering a set of measures they argued would enable Seattle to grow while preserving its character.

The program's quality-of-life rhetoric, however, was largely centered on ideals of white middle- and upper-middle-class consumer citizenship. The program offered few changes to address the quality of life of Seattle's impoverished.[20] Instead, they were treated as problems to be solved or barriers to quality of life. The architects of the Forward Thrust claimed the program was expressly "*not* urban renewal" but, rather, it was the "best alternative to urban renewal," stating in a document outlining the bond proposals that its neighborhood improvement bonds and low-income housing would "depend on individual neighborhood plans and wishes of residents."[21] This agenda aligned the Forward Thrust with President Lyndon B. Johnson's 1967–1974 Model Cities program, entitling Seattle to federal grants focused on neighborhood development and organization. Model Cities was part of Johnson's War on Poverty and effort to address race riots, failures of urban renewal, and the discourse of urban decline plaguing US cities.[22] However, even though Forward Thrust addressed poverty and other social issues, the program did not include any social or welfare programs. Instead, it focused on building material infrastructure capable of improving quality of life—and, by extension, poverty—with the ultimate goal of attracting business, investment, and financial growth.[23] The neighborhood improvement bonds, for example, called for "street, alley, sidewalk and street lighting improvements" to enable the city to qualify "for loans and grants to homeowners and businessmen to improve their property."[24] They were therefore focused on making material changes to neighborhoods that would enhance their appearance, making them more attractive sites for investment and encouraging residents to help themselves. Voters ultimately endorsed about half of the Forward Thrust bonds, including a new domed stadium.

Securing the stadium bond initiative convinced the American League to grant Seattle an expansion team, and thus they formed Seattle's first MLB team—the Seattle Pilots, who were to play their first season in 1969. However, since the stadium had yet to be built, the city worked out a deal with the league to renovate the existing minor league baseball stadium, Sick's Stadium, to get it up to league standards for the team to play until the new stadium was complete. Sick's was home to the Rainiers, who played as part of the Pacific Coast League, and to a Negro League team, the Seattle Steelheads of the West Coast Negro Baseball Association, who played when the Rainiers were on the road.[25] Built in 1938 on the site of Seattle's first baseball stadium, Dugsdale, which was built in 1913 and burned by an arsonist in 1932, the stadium was owned and named after Emil Sick. Sick owned the Rainier Beer Company and bought a minor league team to promote his business. Like most ballparks of this early generation, the stadium was privately financed. Dan Raley writes in his history of the Rainiers, "The team would become a needed part of the city's social fabric, a unifying force for an isolated baseball town in an unknown part of the country.... Practically overnight, Rainiers baseball had woken up a depressed, slumbering town."[26] Sick hired local talent for the team in order to create a bond between the citizens of Seattle and the Rainiers. The stadium became a key site of constituting this newly forming Seattle identity.

After Sick died, the city of Seattle bought the stadium and its surrounding property in 1965 as part of a land purchase for the interstate highway system that would become I-5.[27] When Sick's was first built, it was described as a "dream," with a field that put fans closer to the action than most ballparks.[28] By 1965, when the Pilots were set to move in, however, the stadium was in major disrepair. With public funds already committed to a new stadium, the refurbishment of Sick's and who should pay for it became the subject of much debate. Ultimately, the city promised $1.175 million for repairs, including increasing the eleven-thousand-seat stadium to twenty-eight thousand seats and creating ample parking. Renovations of the stadium, however, were rocky from the beginning, with bare bones and shoddy construction, the capacity was raised to only sixteen thousand and renovations were not complete by opening day.[29]

Part of the difficulty in completing the renovations, according to William Mullins, was due to contractors' perceptions of the neighborhood as a dangerous place.[30] Sick's was in southeast Seattle at the intersection of McClellan Street and Rainier Avenue (see map 4.1) in Rainier Valley. When the stadium was first built, it was a largely rural farming area nicknamed "Garlic Gulch," a low-income neighborhood composed of Italian and Japanese farmers.[31] By the time the Pilots came to play, Rainier Valley had a sizable Black population. Redlining made it one of the few neighborhoods they could inhabit, as they were pushed out of central Seattle into the south of the city. The neighborhood held two housing projects built during the postwar population boom. After the 1964 Civil Rights Act, there was a further wave of white flight from the neighborhood and southern Seattle. These forces influenced a discourse that constructed the neighborhood as unsafe, drawing on long-standing racist assumptions that equate Blackness with criminality, leading to the city's further disinvestment from the neighborhood and part of the reason why the stadium was in such disrepair. The association of the neighborhood with Blackness meant white Seattle residents also did not turn out for the Pilots, and the team made little effort to reach out to the neighborhood's Black population.[32] Poor attendance combined with the lack of a broadcast contract put the team in financial trouble from the start.[33] The team, with its lackluster fandom and subpar stadium, became a kind of laughingstock in the American League. Ultimately, the Pilots played just one season in Seattle. Leaving for Milwaukee in 1970, they became the Brewers after the Braves departed for Atlanta. Seattle thus found itself with a plan for a new stadium but again without a team.

Seattle ultimately brokered a deal for another team, the Seattle Mariners. The state and county filed a lawsuit against the American League for the Pilots' breach of contract.[34] Before the case went to trial, the state settled with the league, which granted Seattle an expansion team in 1976. In addition to professional baseball and football (the NFL's Seahawks), the city also attracted an NBA team, the Seattle Supersonics, who played at the Seattle Center starting in 1967, along with a North American Soccer League (NASL) team, the Sounders. The city was thus well on its way to showing itself as a major league city. However, baseball remained the prized sport. The Seattle Mariners, named in honor of the city's maritime history, eventually played their opening game in the new domed stadium—the Kingdome—in 1977. But getting there would not be easy.

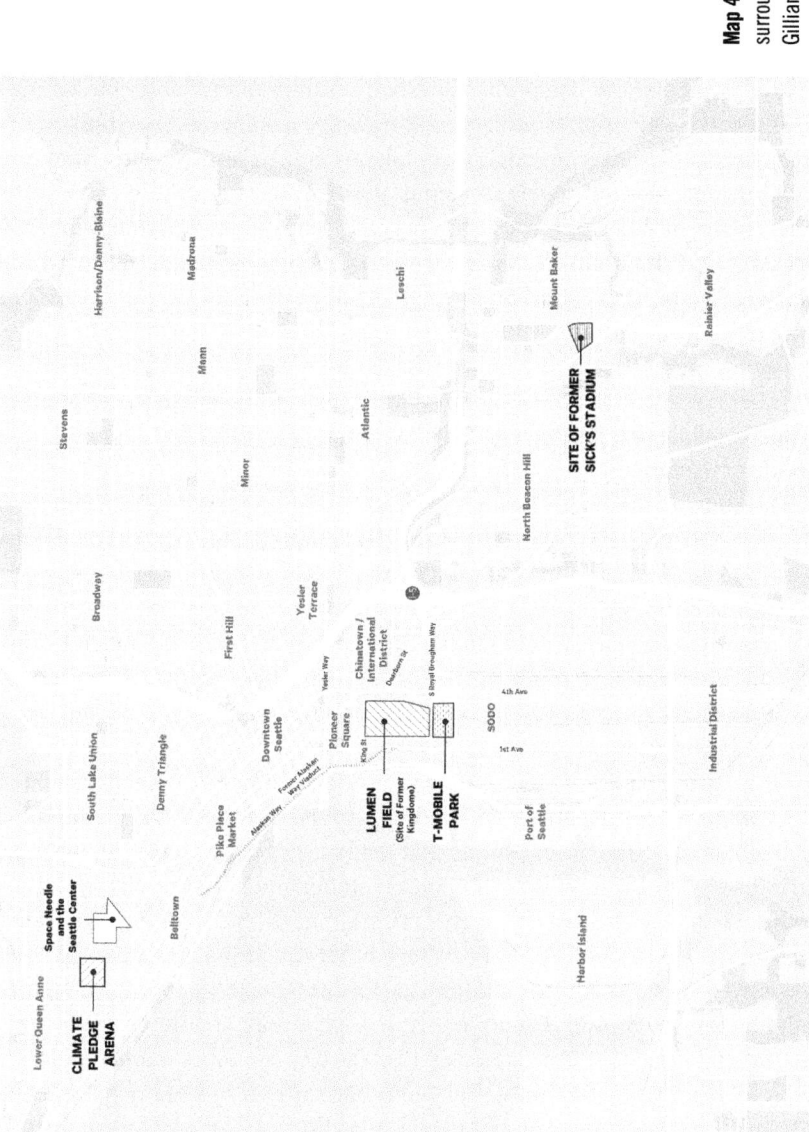

Map 4.1: Map of Seattle stadiums and surrounding neighborhoods. (Credit: Gillian Tiley)

The Where of the Dome: Competing Visions

The stadium bond vote did not end the difficulty in the march toward the Kingdome. Despite securing a positive vote for a stadium in King County, the battle over the stadium continued, especially over where the stadium would be located. The size and multipurpose function, which the voters approved as a contingency of public funding, limited potential sites. However, the location of the stadium also served as a site of struggle over the broader urban changes taking place in Seattle. Although the rise of the suburban stadium is a notable characteristic of second-generation stadium building, several stadiums were built in the urban core during this period as well. Like Atlanta's Fulton County Stadium, the Kingdome was ultimately located in the urban core as part of elites' aims to revitalize the city center, despite a heated debate about potential suburban locations. But suburban versus urban was not the only contested locale for the stadium. Even within the urban core, it seemed no one could agree on the right place to locate a stadium. Although there were broader social forces at play in this generation of stadium building that influenced these debates, the *where* was also a product of competing visions and historical circumstances specific to the parochial politics playing out at the time, especially elites' hopes for the Seattle of the future.

The state formed the Washington State Stadium Commission, which in March 1968 contracted Western Management Consultants, to work on selecting a site. The commission developed a list of selection criteria, including the environment, character, and "charisma" of the site, with a particular eye toward whether it would enable the stadium to promote the city's image and be a "visible landmark and focal point for the region."[35] The city of Seattle heavily campaigned for a central downtown location, as they were invested in bringing people back into the city and building up the downtown as a tourist and business hub.[36] However, the consultants first recommended a suburban location—South Park, which straddled King County's suburbs, Boeing, and Seattle. The consultants argued the downtown location that was being backed by the downtown business establishment risked displacing the poor and elderly and would create traffic congestion. Upon hearing South Park was a real possibility, Ed Carlson, a hotel and airline executive and city booster, formed the Ad Hoc Committee for the Seattle Center Stadium Site to lobby for downtown. The urban-versus-suburban location debate demonstrated the broader issue at stake: Was the city center an important space in an increasingly post-industrial, suburbanizing city? Although the commission ultimately selected a site at the Seattle Center, studies soon showed that costs would run upward of $80 million due to parking and traffic issues. The stadium bond vote, however, permitted spending up to only $40 million.[37] Resistance to the site thus began to brew almost immediately.

Spearheading this resistance was Frank Ruano, the bilingual son of Spanish immigrants, who was born in Miami and relocated to Seattle in 1950. A successful real estate agent specializing in commercial properties, Ruano was initially part of the stadium booster effort.[38] He developed a proposal to build the stadium at a King Street location, close to where the Kingdome eventually ended up. Ultimately, though, Ruano was sidelined by a downtown coalition of politicians and businesspeople who were pushing hard for the Seattle Center site. Ruano formed the group Committee to Save the Seattle Center to oppose the downtown stadium initiative and organized a petition to get a public vote. The group helped secure a "no" vote on the site on May 17, 1970.[39]

But Ruano was not alone in his resistance. Voters wrote in to then-mayor Wesley C. Uhlman between 1968 and 1970 on the stadium location. Many citizens contested the stadium and public funding altogether, especially the mayor's preferred Seattle Center site. Whereas some historians, such as Walter Mullins, represent those resisting the city's aims for a sports team and to become "major league" as standing in the way of progress, others, such as Jeffrey Sanders, suggest that resistance was part of a nascent urban environmental movement influenced by ideals of justice stemming from the civil rights movement, questioning who and what modernization and urban development was for.[40] It is this latter sentiment that is evident in many of the letters written to the mayor during this period. Writers were concerned about traffic and how the stadium would impact the environment of downtown, including contributing to air pollution and affecting the beauty of the city center. As one resident, Edna Hinkley of West Seattle, who thought the stadium should be built in the suburbs, argued, "We don't want air pollution and traffic added. The center is a beautiful place now. A stadium is no added beauty to crowded areas. It needs wide spaces. We have just about reached the point of not caring if we ever get a stadium."[41] While this sentiment aligned with the quality-of-life discourse espoused by the Forward Thrust, it also diverged from it, particularly as Hinkley also drew attention to the need for more social services and welfare programs in the letter. Numerous residents, including Hinkley, expressed concern about public expenditure on a stadium, suggesting the money could be better spent on other services. As one resident put it, the mayor should "expose the baseball stadium scheme for what it is—a plan for a few businessmen to make money at the expense of the city."[42] Similarly, Hinkley's letter continued, the stadium was "not a necessity for the welfare of our city," where the cost of living had "skyrocketed" over the previous twenty years, concluding that city money should be put toward things like raising unemployment amounts and social welfare programs.

Numerous residents also expressed that city elites' visions of making Seattle "big league" was out of step with their own sense of place. As one resident put it, "What will Seattle do with [a] stadium really[?] What good to us yokels who like to stroll around Seattle Center[?]"[43] Referring to themselves as "yokels" suggests a division between the more cosmopolitan elite, who favored a center stadium to symbolize Seattle's economic growth and prowess, and the local sensibilities of those perhaps blue-collar, provincial Seattleites more indicative of the city's working-class history. Similarly, another resident said, "One can enjoy 'sand-lot' baseball just as much as big league, and I feel that the money for big-league baseball and the stadium can much better be spent in a way that will better fulfill the needs of the entire population of the city."[44] Taped to their letter was a letter to the editor from one of the local papers espousing an anti-stadium view and writing:

> I, for one, would in no way be ashamed to have Seattle known as a city that got a major league baseball franchise and lost it. I care not for the opinions of those who judge a city by the presence or absence of a baseball team. I would like to see Seattle known as a beautiful city that takes advantage of its environment and has clean air, good schools, and prideful citizens living in harmony.[45]

This letter, like Hinkley's and others, exposes a tension between Seattle elites and the so-called yokels who contested their vision of Seattle as "big league." They show how that vision was tied to business and economic interests benefiting the few at the expense of most Seattleites. These sentiments demonstrate how some residents espoused other values and senses of place that did not align with the boosters' vision of Seattle.

Despite this resistance and the vote against the Seattle Center site, along with the loss of the Pilots, stadium boosters continued apace to find a location for the stadium, with promises from the American League of an expansion team. Again, the capability of the site to promote a particular image of the city that boosters were trying to sell was a key concern. The committee charged with choosing a site wanted a stadium "located so as to establish a regional focal point for the multipurpose stadium such that the community would identify with the facility in the same manner as it presently identifies with the Space Needle, Seattle Center, Mt. Rainier, Lake Washington, Puget Sound, etc."[46] These characteristics demonstrate how the stadium was imagined to be an iconographic symbol of Seattle, one that would communicate an image of Seattle not only to those who lived in the greater regional area but to those who lived in Seattle as well. Of note is how they positioned Seattle as a city of nature by drawing on a combination of built and natural environment. In so doing, the committee charged with site selection positioned the stadium to connect people to a seemingly authentic local identity that was deeply connected to its geographical location but also thoroughly modern and capable of capturing and subduing nature with its ability to build futuristic structures like the Space Needle and the stadium. The stadium was intended to balance this dualism of connection to Seattle's natural, "authentic" past while communicating its readiness to participate as a leading city of the future. This juxtaposition perhaps aimed to soothe anxieties expressed by those resistant to the stadium, such as those "yokel" residents, by stitching that history and sense of place-based identity and rural naturalism to a symbol of Seattle's future.

After considering three urban locations and two suburban ones, the King Street location was ultimately presented as the ideal site to the King County Council on January 22, 1971.[47] The council approved the site on May 17, 1971.[48] Ruano once again opposed this site and the public expenditure, forming the group Citizens Against the Stadium Hoax (CASH) in 1971, which tied up the stadium in litigation for years in protest against cost overruns. In addition to CASH, organizers and activists in the Chinatown-International District (CID) and Pioneer Square, the two neighborhoods adjacent to the proposed stadium site, were also staunch in their opposition to the stadium. Unlike Ruano, though, these neighborhoods had little political clout and access to the kinds of resources typically needed to influence the halls of government. Nevertheless, activists from these neighborhoods turned to both formal and creative means to have their voices heard and to lay claim to the value of their neighborhoods and their spatial practices. In so doing, they contested the image of both Seattle's history and its future promoted by stadium boosters and city elites.

Kingdome Protests

The King Street site was located in the industrial area of the city, adjacent to the city's port and to Pioneer Square and the CID. At the time it was chosen, the King Street area was referred to largely as the Industrial District. The location lent easy access to I-5 and State Route 99 (Alaskan Way Viaduct), both of which were components of earlier urban renewal programs that divided and cut off neighborhoods in South Seattle, including the CID, from the rest of the city.[49] The decision to locate such a large public infrastructure project in this area was thus part of a longer history of racial and class displacement justified by promises of urban renewal.

Residents and businesses in Pioneer Square and the CID, along with business owners in the port and industrial district, pushed back against the King Street choice, demanding an environmental impact study. The 1972 "Stadium Impact Study" noted that the site was not compatible with a massive sports stadium structure. "The incompatibilities of stadium scale with local district form," the report read, "would be staggering. . . . [The stadium] will not be located in a compatible environment; the scale and form of the surrounding area is distinctly different."[50] The study further showed that the area was already experiencing "upgraded commercial activities," thus risking further displacement and major changes to the character of these neighborhoods.[51] While the study suggested that Pioneer Square would be somewhat protected because it had recently received historic district status, the CID had no such protection. Residents in the CID argued that the stadium would increase housing prices due to business speculation, tourism, and hotel construction, risking pushing out the largely Asian population, especially the elderly, and thereby disrupting the neighborhood's culture. Residents further feared the stadium would negatively impact the district because it would "overwhelm the scale of their neighborhood, create noise and light pollution, clog the district with traffic, and escalate parking problems."[52]

Pioneer Square's historic district status meant there could only be minimal new building and development in the neighborhood. Nevertheless, residents and advocacy organizations were still concerned about the stadium's potential effects. Pioneer Square was the site of the city's original Skid Road, and it remained the home to much of the city's transient and unhoused population. It was where community and social welfare services that served these populations were located. Advocates for this population were especially concerned that the stadium and its influx of tourists would negatively impact a neighborhood already in transition due to historic preservation programs. The Skid Road Community Council, for example, pushed back on conclusions from the "Stadium Impact Study" that the impacts to the neighborhood would be "minimal," arguing that the study itself had acknowledged that the new stadium would "[create] substantial economic pressures, raise rents, produce an influx of new and sometimes incompatible commercial uses in the area, and lead to a population decline in the impacted areas."[53] Noting the populations the council represented "are least able to effectively influence public policy decisions," the council called into question the logic of the impact statement. In particular, they challenged the study's contention that Pioneer Square and the CID were well-established communities that catered to the needs of residents while also concluding that "both areas lack the amenities that constitute a desirable place to live." In pointing out this contradiction—how could they both provide for their communities and lack desirable amenities?—the council revealed how the most marginal residents and the cultures and sense of place embedded in these neighborhoods were deemed "undesirable," thus communicating that the populations themselves were undesirable in the vision of the neighborhood's post-stadium future. This point supported the council's and residents' concerns about displacement of a population that had already been severely displaced by freeway construction and urban renewal.

Bemoaning the city's late inclusion of voices from these neighborhoods for proposals on how to protect them, the organization made specific suggestions as to how the site could address the unique needs of Pioneer Square's population, including support for the Skid Road Shelter Project, allocation of tax funding for the social service needs of Pioneer Square residents, priority employment of neighborhood residents in construction and facility operations, and resident access to facility restrooms on a twenty-four-hour basis.[54] The proposal also included a recommendation to create a policy to address how the increased policing resulting from the stadium would impact Pioneer Square residents, who existed on the margins of society and were often subject to police bias and harassment. These expressions of concern for neighborhood residents demonstrate how the kind of neighborhood place being constituted by the stadium and its boosters risked further marginalizing the city's most marginal residents. Advocates contested that vision and made a claim to the value of those lives, the kinds of places they constitute, and, ultimately, their right to the city.

In response to concerns raised by Pioneer Square and the CID, the city's Department of Community Development agreed to prepare a "city strategy" to protect the neighborhoods from the stadium's potentially negative effects. The city formed the Citizen Action Force Group (CAF), composed of citizen and county representatives, in July 1972.[55] The CAF solicited and incorporated feedback and proposals from neighborhood residents, businesses, and organizations affected by the stadium. The CAF's final report considered several stadium impacts on the neighborhoods and made recommendations related to land use, social impacts, parking and transportation, and construction. The report also proposed a city council resolution of intent acknowledging the unique characteristics of Pioneer Square and the CID and a commitment to support them. In addition, they called for further historic district preservation measures, building and fire code amendments, and proposals to build an Asian cultural center, a bicentennial park with urban greenspace and cultural facilities, and a Skid Road Community Shelter facility in Pioneer Square.[56]

However, the group had little enforcement power and no real say on either the site or the building project. It was formed late in the process, with work on the site scheduled to begin just a few months from its formation. Critics such as Victor Steinbrueck, an architect and University of Washington professor who had been instrumental in historic preservation efforts around Pike Place and Pioneer Square and was a member of the CAF, argued that the group was a political ploy to lend credibility to the stadium project. In an August 1972 letter to the mayor and to county executive John Spellman, Steinbrueck claimed, "City and county politicians and officials are committed to proceeding with the project regardless of unacceptable adverse impacts" and the findings of the task force.[57]

Despite the minimal impact of the CAF, with the support of two city council members who had been vocal critics of the stadium deal—George Cooley and Jeannette Williams—the city council adopted a series of resolutions related to protecting Pioneer Square and the CID in 1972, including the one proposed by the CAF to acknowledge the unique characteristics of the neighborhoods. The resolution established a discourse envisioning a different kind of Seattle in contestation to the "big league city" discourse espoused by stadium boosters. The resolution stated that the city should give preference to "interests of historic preservation and cultural identity and well-being of existing residents" and conceded that development often benefits parts of the community while adversely affecting others. It thus called upon the city to "work to fulfill all the needs of the total community. This approach will encompass the life-sustaining social processes necessary to the existing residential communities." Notably, the resolution drew upon the same logic used by stadium boosters to argue that these neighborhoods were valuable not only to those who lived there but also to the broader identity and future of Seattle and the county as a whole: "They will be of incalculable value in preserving the heritage and identity of Seattle for our children and their children after them," where they will "stand as a symbol of and a key element in the larger commitment of the citizens and government to this city."[58] But it contested ideologies of urban development, renewal, and the quality-of-life discourse promoted in the Forward Thrust, which viewed this culture as a problem to overcome through projects instituting a "healthy" and "attractive" Seattle of the future. Instead, the series of resolutions expressed the value of the existing people and cultures within the neighborhood to Seattle's identity and image.

Neighborhood activists also used more direct measures to make their voices heard and defend their claim to city space. Opposition to the Kingdome in the CID was part of the nascent Asian American movement rising in Seattle at the time. During the official ground-breaking ceremonies for the Kingdome on November 2, 1972, approximately twenty-five Asian American youth protesters marched from the Asian drop-in center in the CID to the stadium site. There, they disrupted the ceremonies carrying signs reading "Hum Bows, not Hot Dogs" and threw mudballs at the stage and speakers.[59] The signs thus demonstrated the neighborhood activists' claims to place by showing how the stadium risked altering the culture and character of the neighborhood and making it inhospitable and alien to those who lived there. "Hum Bows, not Hot Dogs" revealed how displacement worked through forms of cultural and symbolic gentrification, not just materially. The protest led to more organized struggle as the group marched on the local Housing and Urban Development office a few weeks later to demand government funds to rehabilitate and preserve the neighborhood. While longtime neighborhood organizers worked with the city to mitigate the stadium's impact on the CID, young militant activists waged political demonstrations and marches, using the Kingdome to "expose society's neglect of Asian Americans" by demonstrating how the stadium would exacerbate the neighborhood's "lack of decent housing, inadequate social services and continuing discrimination."[60]

Although the protesters were too late to stop construction, neighborhood activists and organizers continued to pressure the city to follow through on its promises to support and protect the neighborhood. One of the main issues was parking, since the stadium parking plan ran south into the CID. Debates about regulating parking grew heated during stadium construction. While the city claimed that spectator parking in the neighborhoods would benefit businesses, many residents and business owners thought otherwise, pointing out how traffic, parking, and potential displacement would erode a sense of community.[61]

In September 1975, Mayor Uhlman established the Stadium Parking and Access Committee (SPARC) to oversee and implement the parking and access plan for the Kingdome. The city council held a series of public hearings on the plan, where CID and Pioneer Square neighborhood residents, organizers, and activists spoke out against not only the plan but also the broken promises from the city to the neighborhoods. One of the individuals to speak out was Bob Santos, a civil rights activist, longtime neighborhood organizer, and director of the International District Improvement Association (INTER*IM). Formed in 1968 by neighborhood activists and businesses, INTER*IM was part of the growing neighborhood organization movement in the city, informed by social justice movements, that advocated for the rights and needs of the CID. Neighborhood organizations in Seattle like INTER*IM built on preexisting local organizing structures and "complex and collective local neighborhood identity and history, ... [which] helped reinforce this sense of community and sense of place among people in an already diverse and active neighborhood."[62] Speaking at a public hearing, Santos and other neighborhood organizers articulated this sense of place to contest how the stadium would impact the neighborhood and residents' spatial practices. Santos argued that the stadium and parking plan "cut through the middle of this community, imposing difficultly for the residents. The community is composed of primarily low-income elderly, whose normal lives will be disrupted by additional traffic, resulting in the noise and air pollution and restriction of... activities."[63] Nemesio Domingo, representing the Alaska Cannery Workers Association and their members, many of whom lived in the CID, similarly argued that the stadium would impact the culture of the neighborhood, claiming, "If the International District cannot continue as a residential area of Third World people—and in many senses a regional shopping area for Third World people . . . the District will be lost and what we'll get, essentially, is a plastic commercial area that is pretty much signified by the Pioneer Square."[64]

Here, Domingo suggests that the historic preservation efforts in Pioneer Square had turned the neighborhood into a "plastic," or otherwise commercial and homogenized, site for tourists at the expense of the lived cultures of the everyday citizens of Seattle who populated the neighborhood. Fearing the same would happen to the CID, Domingo contested the dominant discourses surrounding historic preservation. Historic preservation, as it is often implemented by middle-class white gentrifiers, tends to value buildings rather than people.[65] Preservationists often legitimate increased surveillance, policing, and reformation of space to render it "safe" for white bodies and corporate capital.[66] Instead, Domingo laid claim to a different kind of preservation, emphasizing the preservation of culture and the ways of life of people rather than buildings.

At another hearing, Santos condemned the city for prioritizing other parts of Seattle over the CID, a relegation he claimed had happened for "far too long." Santos maintained that the CID was in "a position of a politically expedient football with a history of insincere commitments for its improvement and preservation," and he called on the city to "reprioritize" the CID so that it could put money toward building affordable housing and support the social welfare programs the city had promised them.[67] Santos connected the deprioritization of the CID to "racist economics," arguing, "The International District is a fragile, but important part of the City of Seattle. In a pluralistic society, steps must be taken to ensure the preservation of each culturally distinct... community. If we fall victim once again to the blind racist economics, the opportunity to preserve this unique part of the City will be lost to all of us forever."[68] Santos thus made it explicit that the economic promises of the city's investments into infrastructure like the stadium was not purely an economic decision; it was driven by racist assumptions with racial consequences. The stadium was just one of a long list of projects the city initiated that provided resources to other parts of Seattle at the expense of the CID, as it banked on the neighborhood's lack of political capital and the racist assumptions of legislators and residents alike to dismiss their concerns and claims to government resources. Moreover, it depended on racialized ways of framing the CID as a problem neighborhood, where crime and poverty were viewed as endemic of neighborhood culture rather than a result of the city's economic decisions on where to spend its resources. Instead, Santos and the other speakers at the hearings reversed this logic, laying claim to the value of neighborhood culture and residents' spatial practices and placing the blame of the neighborhood's problems on the city and its prioritizing of infrastructure projects like the stadium.

Organizing around the Kingdome galvanized the Asian American movement in the CID, which has remained a significant force in Seattle to the present day. As a result of their steadfast activism, the CID and Pioneer Square won some concessions, including an Asian cultural and community center, Skid Road shelter, and minority hiring for contracting jobs.[69] However, the city council's promises to protect the CID and Pioneer Square from the stadium was largely another broken promise to these neighborhoods. Although the city traced the progress on the resolution proposals over several years, it showed little political will to follow through on most promises. Still, the framework provided by these organizations and activists to lay claim to the city and their neighborhoods, to value its culture and the spatial practices, created a powerful alternative discourse of "Seattle" that the city, business, and stadium booster elites would have to contend with well beyond the Kingdome.

The Kingdome: Constructing a New Seattle

Stadium boosters heralded the opening of the Kingdome in 1976 as the start of a new era for Seattle. Hy Zimmerman, sportswriter for the *Seattle Times*, claimed in a commemorative magazine created for the Kingdome's opening that Seattle was "always a baseball town. . . . Seattle baseball, like water, ever has sought its level, which is top of the sports tank."[70] If major league baseball was perceived as the most important sport, as America's pastime, boosters maintained Seattle had always been a contender, even if it was only now entering the big leagues. Forming the "Big 3" of West Coast baseball with Los Angeles and San Francisco, Zimmerman said that Seattle's minor league team had already demonstrated its regional prowess. However, he claimed, "Seattle grew so rapidly it outgrew its minor league status. In its maturation, it demanded what was its sports due."[71] The Kingdome thus demonstrated that Seattle was ready to be acknowledged for the big-league city it was always meant to be.

Although the Kingdome was meant to project an image of "big league" Seattle, as with Atlanta's Fulton County Stadium, its design and architecture were driven largely by economics. Cost cutting produced an enclosed, five-inch-thick concrete shell; fewer restrooms than comparable facilities; mostly bench seats; and an industrial, almost brutalist, modern design aesthetic that appeared unfinished, with gray exterior walls and an unpainted concrete roof.[72] Modeled on the Houston Astrodome and the New Orleans Superdome, the county chose a dome design in large part for its multifunctionality: It enabled boosters to lay claim to the building's multipurpose function (thus legitimating public expenditures), as it could house multiple sports along with conventions, concerts, and mega-events.

An unintended consequence of the dome structure and its concrete roof, however, was its unique sound. The Kingdome's concrete roof reverberated the sound of the crowd to reach unprecedented levels. Describing the sound, one fan recalled, "It kind of rolled through almost like an earthquake."[73] Another fan wistfully recollected, "This dull roar becomes just an impressively loud thing. . . . It's the variation and the sudden swell of excitement that I miss the most."[74] The sound, especially during football games, became notorious for disrupting visiting teams. Adopting the "12th Man" moniker from Texas A&M University, the sound created by the Seahawks fans became synonymous with the Kingdome and its fans, and the team consequently retired the number 12 jersey in 1984 in honor of loud fans who were capable of influencing the game. In 1989 the NFL tried to regulate crowd noise after the Seattle crowd disrupted the visiting San Francisco 49ers quarterback three consecutive times, and the referee ruled a penalty against the Seahawks.[75] The sound of the so-called 12th Man became an unintended part of the Kingdome's boosterism of the city. As I discuss in the following chapter, this sound would be taken up in the next generation of stadium building more purposefully, put to the task of urban branding.

The Kingdome's stadium design team included a joint venture between three architectural and engineering firms, two from Seattle, Narramore, Bain, Brady, and Johanson along with Skilling, Helle, Christiansen, and Robertson, and one from New York, Praeger-Kavanaugh-Waterbury. The stadium could seat sixty-five thousand football fans, sixty thousand baseball fans through removable seating, and had fifteen thousand individually contoured chairs, while the rest were benches with backrests.[76] It included thirty-three concession stands, five cocktail lounges, a dining room, and a Hall of Fame Museum. To further the entertainment spectacle, the Kingdome boasted a jumbotron along with forty-five CCTV-connected screens throughout stadium concourses, thirteen high-output arena speakers, and dozens of low-output speakers. The Kingdome was also a video production studio, maximizing the building's televisual and video capabilities to produce the event as a multimedia, immersive, and spectacular experience. A promotional video for the stadium boasts that its telescreen room supported in-house CCTV that was "fully equipped with video electronics which are the equal of a small television station," with "four tape recorders, three color cameras, a $120,000 instant-replay, a Datavision message control... with an intricate computerized 'game in progress' scoreboard."[77] An Eidophor projector above the stadium floor screened giant images. The Kingdome also offered video production services through its Kingdome Video Productions arm, a "full service, broadcast quality, Video Production House" that provided live-action videos, including marketing tapes, permanent archival event records, broadcast-quality TV commercials, "behind the scenes" tape recordings, and live booth coverage for exhibitors at events.[78]

In addition to multimedia spectacles, the Kingdome also boasted other forms of entertainment. Its Hall of Fame Museum, for example, held sports memorabilia that featured the collection of local *Seattle Post-Intelligencer* sports reporter Royal Brougham, including Muhammad Ali's boxing shorts and baseballs autographed by Babe Ruth.[79] The museum, therefore, didn't focus just on Seattle sports but rather on a range of professional sports from all over the country. It placed Seattle into the national picture, demonstrating that the Kingdome and the museum were not aimed at constituting a specific and unique place-based Seattle identity rooted in its history but to homogenizing it as a sports city, linking it to a national network of sports, and constituting it as a major league/professional sports community. Similar to the architectural style of FCS and the Georgia Dome, the Kingdome was not meant to signify something particular about Seattle but to symbolize that it was on par with other national cities.

Toward these ends, the most distinguishing architectural feature of the Kingdome was its massiveness; it was a huge structure that made an arresting mark on the city's landscape. "It's impossible to ignore a building as big as this one had to be," Kingdome designer Bob Sowder remarked. "After all, it covers about nine acres . . . precisely one Roman stadia [sic], which was a unit of measurement in Caesar's time."[80] Promotional materials for the Kingdome's opening paid great attention to its massive size, as an "imposing landmark."[81] The bigness of the stadium undoubtedly aimed to symbolize Seattle as "big league," capable of great and pioneering engineering feats. Royal Brougham described the Kingdome as "a monument to man's daring imagination, ingenuity and intelligence."[82] Similarly, referencing Indigenous Americans, pioneer settlers, and gold rush prospectors, sports publicist Bill Sears claimed, "The imposing edifice has much in common with those hardy souls who inhabited this frontier a century ago. Its rugged exterior reflects the craggy countenances of Seattle's early citizens, and its hope for the future is no less ambitious than the dream of those who came here seeking passage to the Klondike gold fields."[83] This discourse demonstrates the balancing act of Kingdome designers, who were tasked with creating a symbol that connected the city's provincial history, drawing on the "hardy souls" of settler colonialists, while also reimagining that history for the present. Heralding the architectural feat of building such a massive structure, the Kingdome symbolized the rising prominence of business elites in the sports, entertainment, and experience economy as the new "pioneers" and "hardy souls" that would bring the city into that future through "daring imagination, ingenuity and intelligence."

As a massive structure, the Kingdome employed monumentality, with even its early plans on location siting titled "The Stadium: All-American Monument."[84] Monumental buildings "become synonymous with more than their function, perhaps with a city or a culture."[85] Massive, monumental architecture like stadiums are thus bound up with urban place-identity. Architect Rem Koolhaas theorizes that monumental "bigness" originated with the Manhattan skyscraper. Calling this practice "Manhattanism," Koolhaas contends that the skyscraper symbolized Manhattan's importance and significance, where demonstrating its capability to build these big structures was central to that claim.[86] Lorraine Farrelly suggests that massive urban monuments symbolize a city, but they also work to construct the very city they symbolize.[87] The Kingdome embodied the hopes, dreams, and imaginations of a particular aspiration for the city. It served as the physical manifestation of an imagined place-identity, which its materiality worked to manifest into real, lived experiences.

Though the Kingdome was monumental in its massiveness, it was also architecturally functional and homogeneous. "We've tried to express this stadium structure in its boldest form," designer Bob Sowder explained. "It's like a bridge where the function is dramatically apparent."[88] According to Benjamin Flowers, the massive bowl design, popular during this generation, promotes homogeneity, constituting a sense of unity among fans versus outsiders.[89] In the Kingdome that sense of unity was further communicated through bench-style seating. Though cost drove this architectural choice, it also played on working-class sensibilities and promoted feelings of togetherness (though there were some individual seats, which illustrated a desire to construct class-based hierarchies as well). The constitution of unity through architectural design helped to build rivalry between the home and away teams.

Whereas the ballparks of today hark back nostalgically to the origins of baseball, Kingdome boosters heralded the fact that these domed stadiums were distinct from baseball's past. Referencing historic baseball stadiums in Pittsburgh, Brooklyn, and, Seattle, for example, Seattle sportswriter John Owen reflected in the Kingdome commemorative magazine:

> Ebbets Field, we don't have. Our structure bears no resemblance to Forbes Field, the Polo Grounds, or, for that matter, to Sicks' [sic] Stadium, sports temples of another era. And that's just the point. That was another era, when spectators sat on a backless pine plank in the bleachers, and either baked or basked in the sun. Sports promoters determined some trends, not so many years ago. Customers began to complain about their comfort, the climate, and the pace of the game.[90]

The Kingdome's design thus purposefully broke from ballpark designs of the past, prioritizing middle-class comfort and spectator experience. Moreover, boosters argued that the Dome provided comfort by protecting spectators from the climate, providing air conditioning and dividing spectators from the cold, wet, and windy climate of the Pacific Northwest and thereby standardizing spectators' experiences in the Dome with other cities' stadiums. As will become clear in the discussion of Seattle's contemporary stadiums, the third generation reverses this desire to divide spectators from their surroundings, instead seeking to immerse them in the Pacific Northwest environment. But in the Kingdome era, promoting Seattle as "big league" and modern meant providing the same kind of place-based experience as other cities.

Nevertheless, promotional materials from the Kingdome opening demonstrate how urban boosters balanced the promotion of Seattle as a national, big league city but with a unique place-identity, drawing rhetorically on an invented history/tradition of what James Lyons calls the "natural Northwest"—an iconography that emphasizes Seattle's dualistic qualities of urbanism and nature, seemingly providing the best of both worlds while also demonstrating its capacity to capture and subdue nature for modern progress.[91] Seattle's promotional natural Northwest iconography has a long history bound up with settler colonialism. Marianna Christine Davison proposes that the city's symbolic and material use of nature in its early boosterism presented the city as modern but connected to an uninhabited wilderness that required the erasure of Indigenous place histories, ripe for colonial commodification and exploitation.[92]

Kingdome promotions produced Seattle and Western Washington as a commodified and commodifiable set of spectacles to be consumed—from nature to curio shops. In one promotional pamphlet, given out to event attendees and available in tourist and information shops, Washington's northwest corner is described as fresh and green, an "almost incredible display of rare scenic beauty," while also emphasizing its "lively cities with exciting entertainment, elegant shops, cultural attractions—concerts, opera and drama—superb restaurants, fine hotels, motels, and luxury resorts and friendly small towns exemplifying Americana at its best," ensuring visitors that most rain falls from November to March (outside baseball season).[93] The pamphlet's cover shows the Kingdome with the Seattle skyline peeking above the roof in the background, with the port and Puget Sound to the west, and parking lots dotted with cars in the stadium's foreground (see fig. 4.1). A dull gray marks the whole photograph, which lacks vibrancy—it looks drab and industrial. If the aim was to make Seattle and the Kingdome look exciting, shiny, and new, this image didn't really cut it. But the green border signifying nature and the pictures inside present a more vibrant vision of Seattle and the Northwest. Those pictures foreground people consuming and experiencing nature—someone waterskiing on Lake Washington framed by Mount Rainier in the background, people fishing, sailboats, a ferry making its way through the San Juan Islands, and people alpine skiing. These images promote the environmental and natural side of Seattle—its access to water and the mountains—as a site of recreation. The pamphlet is indicative of the city's and state's turn to tourism at this time as a key industry in its efforts

Fig. 4.1: Promotional materials for the Kingdome reveal the drab, brutalist architecture of the stadium in this circa 1976 brochure. (Stadium Administration Files, Series 473, Promotional Materials 1972–2000, box 1, folder 3. King County Archives, Seattle, Washington)

to diversify its economy. It constructs Seattle as a site of tourism where one can experience both nature and urban refinement.

In addition to featuring the natural part of Seattle's lifestyle, the pamphlet also featured its potential for cultivating urban refinement by featuring neighborhoods around the stadium, with a section titled "Historic Areas Near Dome," stating that the stadium was "expected to be an outstanding visitor attraction in itself" but that it was also on the "edge" of prime tourist areas in Seattle. Like the emphasis on nature, the discourse regarding urban neighborhoods surrounding the Kingdome was geared toward the consumer-tourist, driving people to revitalized areas of the city built to cater to the needs of the idealized postwar middle-class consumer and offering commodified and packaged bits of Seattle history and urban entertainment amusements. The pamphlet focused mainly on Pioneer Square, with a history of the area that brushed over its complexities, noting only briefly how this area of "Old Seattle," part of the city's original settlement, fell into disrepair and became the site of the original Skid Road when the center of downtown shifted northward. Noting the neighborhood was a "refuge for many of the less fortunate Seattle citizens who were 'down on their luck,'" visitors were assured how the neighborhood was "saved" by "an enterprising group of Seattle business persons" who made the neighborhood into a historic district.[94] The pamphlet highlights Pioneer Square's underground tour, restaurants, and shops along with the waterfront, and Pier 70's shops, stores, and restaurants, which served the interests and tastes of middle-class consumers.

The pamphlet describes the CID through an Orientalist discourse that is clearly not addressed to Asian residents or tourists but to white tourists who are invited to consume the Other.[95] Despite the Pacific Northwest being a site of a substantial Asian population and a gateway to the Pacific Rim, Asian culture is represented as an essentialized, commodified product for the white tourist to consume. For example, the pamphlet reads, "More than one visitor has been pleasantly surprised to see an elongated Chinese dragon slinking down streets fronted by Oriental [sic] bazaars and curio shops. Numerous festivals and celebrations occur in the international community, and many superb ethnic restaurants offer service in the early morning hours."[96] Although these neighborhoods were sold to stadium-goers as potential sites for tourism, boosters were also keenly aware that many white, middle-class residents imagined them as dangerous.

The Kingdome was therefore constructed with an eye toward security and surveillance, and boosters publicized these features to assure visitors they would be safe coming out to the Kingdome. In addition to architectural and landscaping design that communicated safety and protection, mediatization of the stadium communicated safety as well. While providing a spectacular experience, mediatization also enabled a sophisticated surveillance system. One article noted, "The Kingdome not only looks like a giant fortress, but hidden inside its foreboding concrete exterior is a highly effective security system that keeps the big domed stadium safe for spectator and participant."[97] The stadium employed a twenty-four-hour security force of off-duty police officers during events. Security, medical, operations, and maintenance staff used a portable two-way radio system to give "communications capability wherever they traveled in the big stadium complex," which was equipped with TACTEC two-way portables, an eighteen-ounce radio developed by RCA that operated on three UHF channels to "provide clear message traffic both inside and outside the structure."[98] While this enabled the Kingdome to employ fewer people through "efficient utilization of employees," this security apparatus enabled near-constant surveillance to provide "efficient crowd control."[99] The mediatization of the stadium thus also helped present an image of the Kingdome and downtown Seattle more broadly as safe and secure. But in so doing, this turned residents' fears about increased policing, voiced by activists in the run-up to stadium construction, into a reality.

The Kingdome thus had a major effect on these neighborhoods, as well as on the city more broadly. It was part of a much larger-scale development in the city, leaving an indelible material effect on Seattle well beyond the Kingdome. In 1979, for example, when the city lost a bid to host the Super Bowl because the league claimed there were not enough hotel rooms in the area, a frenzy of hotel building in the city began, with the planning commission fast-tracking development. In addition to hotel rooms, the 1980s also witnessed an unprecedented growth in downtown office development and retail construction, which Timothy Gibson contends was fueled by "a volatile combination of excess investment capital, an expanding demand for downtown office space, and a healthy dose of competitive ego" as Seattle "emerged as a node of international trade" with a number of Fortune 500 companies and white-collar jobs in informational and service sectors.[100] In addition to development, revitalizing the Seattle Center became a major focus in the mid-1980s.[101] Arguably, the Kingdome helped kick off this massive shift in Seattle's development. But the resistance to the homogenized, spectacular, consumer spaces it created, along with cultural, social, and economic shifts in Seattle and beyond, were signs that a new era was on the horizon.

The Fall of the Dome

Although much was made of the Kingdome upon its opening, the fanfare did not last long. It soon became an object of public scorn, both inside and outside

Seattle. Within twenty years of opening, plans for a new stadium were under way, despite the Kingdome being promoted as a "forever" stadium. As the dome style fell out of favor, and especially after Camden Yards was built, spectators determined that the Kingdome was an inferior place to see a game. With new ballparks arising in various cities, Seattle once again risked falling behind. The Mariners' owners were especially vocal, arguing they were not able to capture the revenues and profits necessary to operate the team.

Initially, the county kicked off a major renovation plan for the Kingdome in 1988.[102] However, on July 19, 1994, four 32" x 48" fiberglass tiles fell 180 feet from the Kingdome's ceiling three hours before a Mariners game. This would ultimately end the discussion of refurbishment, and a new round of stadium politics in Seattle would kick into high gear. This new round coincided with cultural, economic, and spatial shifts in the city in which new urban renewal schemes hinged on the logic of place and urban branding rather than boosterism and discourses of the homogenized "big league" city. Once again, sports stadiums would be a crucial component in the material transformation of the city into this new era, as I detail in the following chapter.

The Kingdome was ultimately imploded on March 26, 2000, to make way for Seattle's new stadiums. Yet, it continues to influence the city and its sense of place even though it is no longer a part of its material infrastructure. Although the Kingdome perhaps failed to live up to the lofty aims of its boosters, it remains a Seattle monument in many residents' cultural memories through the kinds of affective connections people made to it, perhaps precisely because it was not particularly beautiful. It embodied the aims of booster elites who wanted to symbolize Seattle's big-league status, but in its functionality and lack of artfulness it also provided a structure to which so-called yokel Seattleites could attach their own sense of place and spatial practices. Boosters encouraged this kind of affective connection, promoting the stadium as "the largest indoor peoples' place in the West, uniquely awesome in size and inspiring in its beauty ... owned by we, the people."[103] Referencing public funding, boosters legitimated the public outlay by promising affective value in exchange for the profits the stadium would produce for its owners. But that did not mean spectators would connect with the stadium in the way boosters intended. The Kingdome frequently generated widespread hate, with many decrying the fact that the stadium bond debt was not paid off until a decade after it was demolished. For many, the Kingdome is remembered as an inferior place to watch sports and an ugly structure, a place to which people are attached almost despite themselves. Still, perhaps even *because of* the Kingdome's failure and being an ugly object of scorn, many recall the Kingdome nostalgically, especially for how it represents a bygone era of Seattle and sporting culture.

These affects live on in how Kingdome stadium-goers commemorate its history on social media and fan websites. A surprising number of those nostalgic expressions reference the Kingdome's urinals, which, as one Reddit user described, were large troughs "with giant fake art deco midcentury style round urinals where you peed looking at other dudes."[104] Another shared a poem:

> Treading softly and with care
> Dodging puddles here and there
> Always careful not to splash
> Fearful I may get a rash[105]

This ode to the urinal is indicative of the irreverent affective tone in which people remember the Kingdome—a place they remember fondly, but that fondness is partly because of the stadium's lack of comfort, artfulness, and beauty. In other words, it is a love for the stadium's failure to live up to the ideals of its boosters (as well as, perhaps, a tribute to a nostalgic form of working-class masculinity). The one thing fans seem to universally agree on is that the Kingdome will be remembered for its unique sound, which, despite trying to replicate it in the new stadium, many argue remains inferior. While debates rage in the comments sections of Reddit and other web forums about whether the Kingdome is worthy of being missed and conjuring nostalgic sentiment or not, it's hard not to be struck by the sheer number of people seeking out these forums and sharing their memories and experiences of going to the stadium.

When the stadium was finally imploded, workers handed out chunks of the concrete and rebar, which people took home as memorabilia, with many fans boasting they still have a part of the Kingdome. These material artifacts, along with the cultural memories of the Kingdome's smell—a "mildewy mix of hot dogs, beer and piss," according to one fan—remain as powerful affects that continue to push up against and complicate the city's next generation of stadium building.[106]

CHAPTER 5

Place-Branding the Local

The idea for this book began when a colleague and I unintentionally booked a hotel in Pioneer Square next to the Seahawks stadium (then CenturyLink Field) for a conference in Seattle in the spring of 2014. At the time, I resided ninety miles north in Bellingham, Washington, and like many others in the northwest corner of Washington at the time, I was swept up in the excitement over the Seahawks' dominating Super Bowl victory over the Denver Broncos and the celebratory fandom of the team's so-called 12th Man. Wandering around the stadium and surrounding neighborhood, my fandom palpable, I was struck by the complex and multidimensional relationship between sports, place-identity, and the urban. The stadiums were a monumental and overwhelming presence in what was otherwise a neighborhood marked by both extreme poverty and homelessness and a touristified old town claiming to be the "original" center of Seattle. Yet, this spectacular touristification was also articulated to locality and discourses of authenticity. An area populated by eateries with regional cuisine, craft breweries, and distilleries alongside social service institutions and shelters, the spaces in and around the stadium were not merely impositions erasing a sensibility of the local, but, rather, they were constituting and celebrating it, all seemingly components of the broader culture of "the 12s."

My experience of the Seahawks stadium illustrates some of the core ways third-generation stadiums respond to broader cultural, economic, and political shifts since the second-generation era of the Kingdome. Just as the 1960s and

1970s presented a key turning point for Seattle, so too did the 1990s and 2000s, and again sports stadiums played a crucial role in bringing about changes to the city's infrastructure and culture. By the 1990s, Seattle was thriving economically. The city benefited from a "new economic wave" and became the site of emerging software, microelectronics, robotics, and biotech industries that positioned Seattle as a "global gateway" to the new economy.[1] A massive downtown office building spree, a growing population, and an expanding economy rapidly altered Seattle's spatiality. Seattle of the 1990s became a media and popular culture darling, making an appearance in a slew of magazine profiles and as the setting for popular films, such as *Sleepless in Seattle* (dir. Nora Ephron, 1993) and television series like *Frasier* (NBC, 1993–2004).[2] Part of Seattle's attraction during this time, according to James Lyons, was that it offered a representational alternative of a "livable" city that contrasted images of the post-industrial urban crisis that were plaguing media representations of other major US cities, including Los Angeles and New York, during this period.[3]

Whereas the Kingdome emerged when Seattle aimed to become a "major league city," the city's third generation took place as Seattle, like Atlanta, was poised to become a global city and center of transnational investment and capital distribution. It had a booming technology sector linked to Seattle-based companies like Microsoft, Amazon, Adobe, and Nintendo of America. It was a gateway to Asia, a major shipping container port, and the site of numerous industries with global reach. Sports also fostered worldwide connectivity, as sports industries were globalizing in the search for new markets. But Seattle's sports culture and sporting infrastructure, as elsewhere, also negotiated tensions between the global and local by promoting the city on a global scale while maintaining a sense of placefulness and connection to the local through a nostalgic urbanism rooted in rituals of fandom.

It was during this period that Seattle turned to strategies of branding, and the city's third-generation stadiums embody this shift. Seattle's city government, in conjunction with its convention and visitors bureau, was an early adopter of place-branding.[4] Urban branding took hold in the 1980s and 1990s in the wake of an increasingly competitive global economy, neoliberal models of municipal governance, and the growth of urban tourism industries. Branding became a popular economic development strategy to distinguish the unique characteristics of a city to attract tourists, investors, and residents. According to Miriam Greenberg, cities shifted from urban boosterism and *selling* cities to urban branding and the *marketing* of cities, "where local agencies and organizations try to reconstruct the city according to expectations of the types of consumers they want to attract."[5] Thus, urban branding also marked a change in approaches to urban revitalization with efforts to construct the built environment to attract the "right" people.

Central to the shift toward urban branding is a change in the role of media in the urban. While boosters used media to promote cities since at least the nineteenth century, in the postwar period cities came to recognize the significance of the symbolic and representational economy and started making more concerted efforts to use media to promote a cohesive urban image.[6] By the 1980s, officials partnered directly with media companies through, for example, the creation of state and municipal film commissions to attract film and TV production. Doing so, it was reasoned, would create intangible value through the affective intensities produced by the city's representations in media.

Although some cities have been more successful at attracting film and TV production than others, nearly every major city in the United States has been successful at attracting the production of sports media through professional sports. Through regular broadcasting of the city associated with a localized form of culture, cities capitalize on sports media and the affective connections it both draws on and works to reproduce as a form of civic identity. Likewise, media companies, especially those with heavy investments in television broadcasting and cable, depend on sports and are invested in partnering with teams, stadium owners, and municipal governments to maximize revenue streams and benefit from the affective values generated through place-based fandom. Stadiums play a crucial role in the generation of this value, as they provide the venues for sports to be broadcast. But they also work as powerful material entities that can curate, shape, and manage place meanings and spatial practices to ensure those meanings and practices produce brand value.

In this chapter, I focus on how stadium infrastructure constitutes place-brands in Seattle. Whereas much of the critical literature on place-branding emphasizes how urban branding commodifies culture, imposing a hegemonic ideology onto space, I instead focus on how third-generation stadiums' emphasis on placemaking and "authenticity" produces a more complicated, ambivalent, and contested practice of space. In so doing, I suggest that the place-branding practices embodied in the sportification of place are best understood as performative media infrastructures.

Place-Branding and Iconic Stadiums

Brands are arguably, as Adam Arvidsson suggests, a fundamental form of social organization of the twenty-first century.[7] Originating in corporate culture, brands pervade ever-widening systems of economic, cultural, political, and social life as more and more aspects of our lives are subjected to the logic of brands and branding. Brands are a ubiquitous part of the urban landscape. Indeed, branding the urban itself is a predominant practice across cities globally, where sports and stadium infrastructure (re)produce, materialize, and promote a city's brand. As a particular form of place-branding, urban branding involves an assemblage of cultural producers across public and private interests that work together to constitute a city's unique identity.[8]

More than merely promotional devices, brands are forms of informational capital that serve as "platforms for action" and interaction.[9] As technologies and interfaces of communication, Celia Lury writes, brands are indicative of the digital, new media era; the versatility and impact of the brand is parallel to and, indeed, relies on digital technology.[10] The value of a brand depends on its ability to communicate and circulate through interactive and participatory circuits of communication, create practical and material relationships, and thereby influence behaviors. Brands are hence a kind of new media object that function as "hardware, software, and protocol."[11] Just as brands and branding are interlinked with new media culture and technology, so too are they fundamentally spatial. Andy Pike explains how brands are tied to the spaces from which they originate as well as adapted to and by the spaces into which they enter and intervene.[12]

In an analysis of urban branding strategies in Washington, DC, Timothy Gibson contends that city leaders build stadiums to "broadcast spectacular urban images to global media audiences ... not so much for tangible economic reasons but rather for their more nebulous symbolic advantages."[13] Although stadiums are undoubtedly spectacular sites that can participate in the commodification of space through practices of signification, third-generation stadiums also present a more complex and nuanced practice of space. The turn toward place-based affects in stadium design and urban planning and subsequent shift from a theme park model to strategies of branding governed by logics of authenticity complicates the hegemonic and commodifying aspects of the stadium that are indicative of earlier generations. This is because, as Scott Lash and Celia Lury maintain, brands, as opposed to commodities, work via a logic of difference rather than of sameness/identity.[14] Whereas the commodity is produced, the brand is a source of production, tied to a range of products and through which they flow into and from. Brands are singularities whose value stems from their distinctiveness and relationality—that is, from the quality of the affective relationships they create rather than from the quality of the product. Branding is thus tied to cultural ideals of authenticity. As Sarah Banet-Weiser writes, branding "is about building an affective, authentic *relationship* with a consumer, one based ... on the accumulation of memories, emotions, personal narratives, and expectations."[15]

Stadiums and the brands they work to (re)produce manifest in the urban environment as material, relational, affective, and interactive.[16] The brand performs as infrastructure that connects and disconnects people and places, encourages and discourages certain kinds of movements and behaviors in and through the city, distributes and withholds resources and power, and elicits passionate affective allegiances (and enmities). Stadiums invite fans and residents not just to consume the place-brand but also to act as produsers (producer/consumer-users) who co-create the brand through practices of fandom and more quotidian practices of everyday life.[17] Extensive investment in brand management ensures that behaviors unfold in ways that enhance rather than detract from or threaten the brand and its potential values. Notably, though, not all people are invited to participate and co-create the brand; some subjects are deemed threatening to the brand and are actively discouraged and prevented from participating, subjected to more aggressive and disciplining techniques of management.

A core way in which stadiums participate in performative branding practices is through the construction of "iconic" stadium architecture. Leslie Sklair and Laura Gherardi define iconic architecture as "buildings and/or spaces that are famous, and that have distinctive symbolic and aesthetic significance."[18] The Guggenheim Museum in Bilbao, Spain, heavily influenced the use of iconic architecture as a technique of place-branding and revitalization. Frank Gehry, the museum's architect, intended the building to serve as an artistic, cultural, and creative hub to spur economic, social, and cultural development for a post-industrial, struggling city. It is part of the broader shift in urban development toward using culture as a revitalization strategy and of the "creative city" strategy, which involves building infrastructure to attract the so-called creative class. Popularized by urban planning scholars Charles Landry and Richard Florida, the creative class theory contends that post-industrial cities will be economically successful only if they are able to attract those working in knowledge-intensive and arts, design, engineering, and computing jobs. Florida reasons that the creative class wants to live in "hip," bohemian areas that are unique, artistic, multicultural, and tolerant, and if cities want to attract them, they need to build infrastructure that caters to them.[19]

In the 1990s, Seattle viewed "creatives" as key to building on the city's burgeoning technology boom and invested heavily in development aimed to attract this class, even partnering directly with Richard Florida.[20] The Kingdome, criticized as a homogeneous and placeless piece of architecture, was deemed insufficient. New stadiums, on the other hand, offered amenities and a unique experience thought capable of attracting "the right kind" of people to symbolize this new image of Seattle and to keep them there.[21]

Rather than the homogenized monumentality of the second generation's city boosterism, stadiums are now considered works of art in themselves, often products of "starchitects" (star celebrity architects, themselves brands), who draw on place- and site-specificity to create stand-out pieces of architecture on a city's skyline. Convergent media culture enhances the possibility of engineering iconicity; media serve as platforms for spreading images of the stadium, shrouding them in an aura of fame. Some architectural theorists claim the shift to iconicity is part of a postmodern loss of metanarrative, in which individual icons produce a fabricated meaning.[22] However, stadium iconicity is imbued with a placefulness that works to counter this feeling of detachment and being unmoored from metanarrative. Stadiums are endowed with deep place-narratives that aim to connect the subject to a history of team and place, as individual icons that express uniqueness and distinction, even though this strategy itself has become ubiquitous. However, the icon can also become detached from the local, and, indeed, that is part of its aim—to circulate globally via media distribution. The iconic third-generation stadium thus creates a tension between local and global, constantly negotiated via the brand and its connection to the circulation of media culture.

The production of authenticity, central to the iconic stadium, is a feature of neoliberal urbanism more generally. What makes the branding practices involved in the sportification of place unique in this capacity, though, is how they draw on nostalgic affects of team and place that make a stronger claim to city identity, history, and culture than other forms of neoliberal development that harness discourses of authenticity, such as efforts to link Amazon's (failed) proposed urban development to "authentic" Queens, New York, culture.[23] It is the stadium, rather than the city square, concert hall, or cathedral, where we find the largest urban congregations, at preordained times and at regular intervals, to witness sporting rituals and records, serving as sites of community/civic bonding. Urban branding converts these affective intensities into immaterial and economic value through the brand. Importantly, branding is never neutral and is always related to power. Urban branding in terms of the stadium benefits some areas of the city and some bodies more than others, often in ways that exacerbate racial, ethnic, and class differences in the name of a unified identity.

SoDo MoJo and That Hometown Feel: T-Mobile Park

Professional baseball was not the boon to the city's sports legacy that Kingdome boosters had imagined. Rather, for most of their time in the Kingdome, beginning in their first year the Mariners suffered major losses, with fourteen straight losing seasons. Game turnout was therefore unsurprisingly low; the Kingdome rarely filled to capacity during games.[24] Mariners owners, who complained of poor profits, intermittently threatened to relocate. Although a range of issues contributed to the Mariners' losing record in the 1980s, from poor management to financial negligence, owners blamed the Kingdome. Ennis Broadcasting owner, Jeff Smulyan, who had pioneered 24/7 sports radio, purchased the Mariners in 1989. He complained the Kingdome was substandard and could not financially support a baseball team, in part because it lacked the revenue-generating luxury amenities of newer stadiums, such as club suites, especially in the face of skyrocketing player salaries. However, given the Kingdome was by then less than twenty years old and the city had still not recouped its debt, there was little support for new public expenditures on a stadium. In 1991 Smulyan announced he was putting the team up for sale, with rumors circulating he intended to move the team to Tampa, Florida.[25]

The Mariners' lease required the team to be optioned to local buyers first, and a group of Seattle business elites formed the Baseball Club of Seattle (BCS) to find a buyer. After Boeing owners and Microsoft's founder, Bill Gates, declined to buy, the BCS learned Nintendo's owner, Japanese businessman Hiroshi Yamauchi (whose son-in-law, Minoru Arakawa, was head of Nintendo of America, located in Seattle), was interested in joining BCS and buying a majority stake. Arakawa suggested his father-in-law wanted to purchase the team as a thank-you to the state for their support of establishing Nintendo of America's US headquarters.[26] However, there was significant pushback against foreign ownership of a US sports team. As "America's pastime," foreign ownership threatened the image of baseball as inherently national. Anti-Asian sentiment and growing xenophobic fears that Japan was a threat to US economic dominance furthered resistance to the deal.[27] However, supporters of the venture argued that enabling foreign ownership would open up new markets and profitable TV and licensing deals.[28] Although the deal ultimately went through, Yamauchi was forced to reduce his voting ownership stake from 60 percent to 49 percent despite contributing the majority of financing.[29] Still, the Mariners' foreign ownership deal further positioned Seattle as an emblem of the new global economy. It also revealed the significant role sports would play in the city's transnational branding as Japanese ownership connected the team, and baseball more broadly, to a new network of capital and fandom.

After the tiles fell from the Kingdome ceiling in 1994, the new Mariners ownership took up the mantle of lobbying for a new stadium in earnest, using the ailing Kingdome as leverage to further their argument for a baseball-only structure. Neil deMause and Joanna Cagan show how sports reporting played a key role in lobbying the public for a new stadium in Seattle. By providing free advertising space for pro-stadium campaigns, funding pro-stadium lobbying efforts, and editorializing the stadium vote as if it was "a sporting event where the paper roots along with the home team," local newspapers like the *Seattle Times* acted as a public relations arm for the team to negotiate a deal.[30] In addition to favorable news coverage, the surprising success of the Mariners also played a role. In the run-up to the vote in 1995, the team had their most successful season to date—winning the American League Division Series against the New York Yankees before finally losing a close American League Championship game to Cleveland. After the loss, the team's manager wept, saying that people hadn't believed Seattle was a baseball town, but "we showed them otherwise."[31] Local papers picked up on this as well, branding Seattle a "baseball town" and enjoining residents to identify with the team as an emblem of the city's perseverance and newfound success.

Despite hope that the winning season might turn the tides, voters turned down the tax levy for a new stadium in September 1995 by a narrow margin.[32] Undeterred, Mariners owners took their case to the state's capitol in Olympia, lobbying Governor Mike Lowry, who called a special three-day legislative session, which met behind closed doors. During the session, legislators and Mariners owners hammered out a deal to finance the stadium with state funding and King County taxes.[33] Bypassing the public's no vote, the King County Council voted 10–3 to approve taxes to pay for a new ballpark.[34] In addition to the taxes, the council created the Washington State Major League Baseball Stadium Public Facilities District (PFD), a municipal corporation, to oversee the public's interest in the stadium.[35]

The PFD selected a location two blocks south of the Kingdome for the new stadium (see map 4.1.).[36] As the Seahawks negotiated a new stadium deal as well, officials decided to implode the Kingdome and build the new Seahawks stadium atop its former site, adjacent to the new Mariners ballpark. At the turn of the century, then, Seattle would have two brand-new side-by-side stadiums. Ground for the Mariners stadium broke in March 1997, with the first game played in the ballpark on July 15, 1999.[37] Naming rights for the stadium originally went to Safeco, a Seattle-based insurance agency. When the team renewed its lease in 2018, rights went to the telecommunication company T-Mobile, and the stadium was renamed from Safeco Field to T-Mobile Park, its current name at the time of this writing.

T-Mobile Park is a model of the third-generation era's "retro-modern" design and emphasis on placemaking. The Mariners' ballpark nostalgically harks back to design elements of the nation's early ballparks through its urban location,

Fig. 5.1: T-Mobile Park's "retro-modern" design aims to create an intimate feel and sense of place-specificity with sweeping views into downtown Seattle, Lumen Field, and the Space Needle. (Photo by author)

brick façades, asymmetrical field dimensions, natural grass fields, and clear sight lines. At the same time, it showcases modern engineering and technology, including the removal of structural columns supporting upper decks to improve sight lines and create greater seating capacity, along with amenities like club and luxury box seating, upscale concessions, and entertainment experiences. When it was built, the stadium was outfitted with sophisticated media technology, including advanced video and audio systems and fiber-optic cabling. Much was made especially of the ballpark's lighting system, featuring huge LED video screens and graphics and animation boards.[38] Over the years, the PFD upgraded the facility to integrate further advancements in media technology, including digitized ticketing and concessions like the Walk-Off Market—a partnership with Amazon that enables fans to preregister with Amazon One's technology to scan their palm, walk into the marketplace, and grab and go.[39]

Most significantly for my purposes, however, the Mariners' stadium draws on these amenities and design features to play up site- and place-specificity through place-branding. Whereas other sports have specific field dimensions, early baseball parks varied by site, with no two parks the same. This is because of how ballparks were built to fit within the dense, urban landscapes where they first emerged. As a result, a major part of spectatorship in baseball is centered on "the sights, smells, and sounds of the stadiums in which it is played."[40] The Mariners' stadium was designed with this place-specificity in mind, fitting it into the site rather than clearing the site to fit the ballpark, and aiming to make fans feel as if they were connected to and a part of a particular place. The ballpark is asymmetrically designed and fits within the existing street grid on three of the building's sides.[41] In their initial design proposal to the city, the leading architectural firm on the project, Naramore, Bain, Brady, and Johanson (NBBJ), said:

> The new Pacific NW Baseball Park will become a significant feature in the urban landscape of south downtown Seattle. It should not stand apart from, but should be integral with its surroundings, conditioned by the context in which it is built. The new stadium will create a unique place in the city, a place where the historical meets the industrial, where the daily life of work meets the leisure life of play—embodying the role baseball plays in our society. It can function as an asset to the community, enhancing the quality of the surrounding environments while acting as a catalyst to bring other desired development opportunities in the area.... The new ballpark can promote the creation of a "sense of place"—acting as a catalyst to enhance the economic viability of the surrounding areas while conserving the healthy elements already existing.[42]

NBBJ's statements show how they rationalized the ballpark in terms of a sense of place linked with Seattle and the surrounding neighborhoods through a logic of sport and urban branding, where place-based affects would create potential economic and social value.

Lead architect Dan Meis aimed to create a unique civic building for Seattle that had a "home town feel."[43] The Mariners' ballpark evokes this feeling through location and materials. The architects designed the structure to blend into and complement surrounding neighborhoods.[44] The brick façades on the west and north sides, for example, pay homage not only to the ballparks of yesteryear but also to the materials and architecture of neighboring Pioneer Square. Similarly, architects took inspiration from the port's shipping cranes, including four crisscrossed steel columns that rise above the field's name sign to support a set of LED lights as well as arched steel trusses that crisscross over the roof (see fig. 5.1). The ballpark connects Pioneer Square and SoDo, two seemingly distinct neighborhoods, forming a buffer between two versions of Seattle's history and charting a vision of its future in the sports and experience economy.

Mariners owners and the PFD believed a roof was necessary to court season ticket holders in a city famously known for rain.[45] However, they demanded

Figs. 5.2 and 5.3: View of open T-Mobile Park roof, from outside (5.2, left) and inside (5.3, right) the stadium, covering a portion of the BNSF Railroad. (Photos by author)

the roof be retractable to uphold an outdoor baseball aesthetic. Ultimately, architects created a 650-foot-span, umbrella-style retractable roof design that covers, but does not enclose, the ballpark. The "umbrella" accentuates the city's Pacific Northwest identity, signifying rain. The roof consists of three movable panels that slide on a set of steel wheels to tuck into each other over the BNSF Railway tracks that abut the stadium's eastern side (see figs. 5.2 and 5.3). This aesthetic situates the stadium within a particular place, highlighting its relationship to the industrial SoDo neighborhood and the railroad, where sounds of trains can be heard during games. Indeed, on the day I attended a Mariners game, the railroad engineer blew the train's whistle as it passed the ballpark, resulting in a wave of cheers from fans. These railroad sounds remind fans of where they are, connecting them to their surroundings.

While the umbrella roof signifies rainy Seattle, it also enables sight lines to the city's downtown skyline and the natural surroundings of Elliot Bay and the Olympic Mountains. When closed, the steel truss arches echo the rounded dome of Mount Rainier, views of which can be seen through the trusses when looking at the stadium from Elliot Bay. Like the railroad, the sight lines situate fans within a particular place and invite them to identify their affective experiences at the ballpark with Seattle and the surrounding Northwest environment, and vice versa. The views to the city and the mountains are purposeful; NBBJ refused to extend the brick façade to the north end of the ballpark behind the left field bleachers, even though it would have provided better support for the roof, in order to ensure fans could see the Seattle skyline whether the roof was open or closed.[46] The stadium's Rooftop Boardwalk provides an especially breathtaking view of the city, bay, and mountains, with the wooden walkway, brick encasings, and streetlamp-like lighting evoking Seattle's fishing village aesthetic and history. When proposed zoning changes to the Industrial District and Pioneer Square threatened these views by allowing building height increases, the Mariners' legal team protested, claiming, "The public views from the ballpark are an important City asset."[47] Moreover, they said these views were significant not only for those attending the game but for fans watching at home as well: "Each time a game is broadcast, the cameras are set up to show the view of the water, mountains, and skyline. This view is instantly recognizable as the essence of Seattle. This is the image of our city that is broadcast locally, across the country, and around the world." Thus, "the essence of Seattle" was tied to the stadium and its media promotion as the stadium's place-based construction blurred lines between mediated and lived experiences of Seattle as image. Other design features solidify the sense of place and the city's relationship to sports too, such as the image of Fred Hutchinson, a Seattle player for the Rainiers before going on to the majors, embossed in aisle-facing seats; a statue of Dave Niehaus, Seattle sportscaster and "Voice of the Mariners," sitting at his desk featuring his signature phrases; and artworks, many from Washington-based artists, throughout the stadium that pay homage to the city's baseball history.[48]

Like other ballparks of this generation, a major component is the inclusion of luxury amenities to extend and expand game day. But many of these, too, evoke a sense of emplacement. The seventy luxury suites, each named after Hall of Fame players, for example, are designed with Northwest décor, such as using local slate for countertops and local wood. Featuring interactive games and activities, the Bullpen Market includes local food vendors and a Fan Walk of personalized bricks, while Lookout Landing and the Outside Corner Picnic Patio provide views of the city and Puget Sound.[49] Distinctive concessions emphasize place. Although most of the concession businesses at T-Mobile Park offer typical ballpark fare, a few local highlights draw large crowds, including Marination, Ballard Pizza Co., Just Poké, Lil Woody's, Pure Acai, and Moto Pizza. The ballpark also features a plethora of craft beer, a signature Pacific Northwest commodity. The Craft Bar is dedicated to local craft brews, and an outlet features Chateau St. Michelle, Washington state's "founding winery." In addition, T-Mobile Park's museum highlights the Northwest region's sports history, including an exhibit on Sick's Stadium. This is distinct from the Kingdome's museum, which featured some Seattle sports memorabilia but was largely dedicated to sports in general. T-Mobile Park, in contrast, highlights the specificity of Seattle sports, making sports a key part of Seattle history and identity.

This sense of place is further reinforced through integration of media into the game-day experience, including through the ballpark's mobile app. Although the app is "bare bones" and does not invite much interactivity, it does help connect fans to place by inviting them to extend the game-day experience beyond the ballpark into the surrounding neighborhood. When I used the app's virtual assistant, an artificial intelligence (AI) backed "Ask a question" feature, to ask about game-day activities, it directed me to The Boxyard, suggesting I should "be sure to visit SODO's premiere pre- and postgame destination across the street from T-Mobile Park." An industrially designed space, The Boxyard is part of the Mariners' development expansion into the SoDo neighborhood and includes an event space, restaurants, a beer garden, microbrewery, and Seattle-themed sports bar and grill. In addition to food and beverage options, the sprawling facility also houses a baseball and softball training facility, opened in the summer of 2023. As the virtual assistant explains, "The Boxyard project is part of our larger plans to continue revitalizing the SoDo neighborhood and give our fans a great spot to hang out before and after Mariners games."

The Boxyard illustrates the Mariners' and the PFD's increasing focus on place and neighborhood, but this was not always the case. T-Mobile Park's design was carefully constructed to create a sense of regional rather than just city-based identity because more support for the stadium, and consequently for the Mariners, came from the county and broader region outside Seattle when the stadium was built. Joshua Curtis, executive director of the PFD, explains, "There's reluctance to focus too much on Seattle because so many of the fans come from outside of Seattle."[50] However, that logic has started to shift. Curtis suggests this was influenced by changing ideas about sports stadiums and their relationship to the city and place. He notes, "The former ownership group of the Mariners . . . didn't care as much about the neighborhood around them. They saw this purely as a business that they were running and that anything that was good for the Mariners was thus good for baseball and the region. . . . That is not the case anymore. . . . There really is a . . . new . . . way that we're starting to reorient ourselves."[51] The shift was also sparked by debates over Climate Pledge Arena, home of Seattle's hockey team, the Kraken. The arena reignited the conversation over sports stadiums and their obligation to the city, as well as over who was responsible for funding them (Climate Pledge was privately funded). In 2019 the PFD established a Neighborhood Improvement Fund as part of the Mariners' lease renewal. The fund supports projects that "enhance fan enjoyment and contribute to an economically successful, safe, desirable, innovative and walkable stadium neighborhood . . . through urban design, supporting neighborhood planning, and helping catalyze an improved mix of building types," increasing sustainability, fan experience, and supporting neighborhood groups through affirmative action programs for BIPOC (Black, Indigenous, and people of color) residents in stadium-related projects and public art.[52] These aims demonstrate how the ballpark is involved in productions of and struggles over neighborhood space.

Through its investments in the neighborhood, T-Mobile Park, along with Lumen Field (which I discuss below), provide contexts of consumption and interaction, effectively sportifying place. These environments turn the activities of those who go about the practice of everyday life, along with those who engage in spectacular game/event day experiences, into forms of affective labor that constitute the brand. Outside T-Mobile Park and Lumen Field, there are large congregating places that facilitate crowd movement while also creating public gathering space. Public artworks, murals, and other sporting ephemera invite identification with the teams and fandom while providing unique sites to visit and to consume culture. The area is well lit, with the stadiums themselves throwing off light, and ample street lighting in addition to decorative lights. Together, these elements constitute the area as active and fun—a place to be, perform, and play. They invite the visitor to engage in sportified activities like gathering and playing in public space.

The stadiums' location in SoDo make them particularly impactful on this neighborhood's sense and practice of place and its brand. SoDo is historically, and largely remains, an industrial neighborhood that services the port and manufacturing. Until the 1990s, SoDo was not an official neighborhood name; the area was, and sometimes still is, generally referred to as the Industrial District, the Duwamish Manufacturing and Industrial Center, or Greater Duwamish in colloquial discourse and official documents. Sports journalist Peter Miller coined the name SoDo in 1979. Taking inspiration from New York City's SoHo neighborhood (which stands for its geographical location south of Houston Street), SoDo was meant to describe the area "South of the Dome," referring to the Kingdome.[53] But it would not be until 2000, just after the opening of the Mariners ballpark, that the name SoDo would finally become meaningful and taken up by locals. This uptake was not necessarily organic either. Rather, it was part of a marketing campaign created by Mariners consultant Steve Cunetta. Tasked with coming up with a slogan for the team, Cunetta was inspired by the SoDo welcome signs he drove by on his way to work each day, put up by developers in the 1990s in another failed attempt to brand the neighborhood. He created the slogan "SoDo Mojo" for the Mariners, which was emblazoned around the stadium, on video screens, and around town. The slogan's introduction coincided with a ninety-one-game winning season and a spot in the playoffs for the Mariners, one of their most successful since coming to Seattle. Fans embraced the SoDo Mojo slogan, and the name started to stick. Soon, businesses moving into the neighborhood started using the neighborhood name in their own branding, from the SoDo Commerce Building to SoDo Pizza.[54] In 2013 the city established the SoDo Business Improvement Area (BIA) as part of its neighborhood development programs, making the branded name the official neighborhood name.

Suggesting, "There's magic where a team plays in town," Cunetta explains that SoDo Mojo is "a description of Mariners baseball, when magic and Mariners baseball happens in that part of town."[55] Cunetta's statement demonstrates how branding is parasitic on topophilic relationships between sport and place. Neighborhood branding transforms the "magic," or ethical surplus, of the affective intensities created by sporting places to create new forms of brand value. Those affective intensities do not only transform how a place is perceived, but they have real, material implications on how the space is developed and practiced as well. With the SoDo Mojo campaign, the neighborhood became visible in new ways and to new populations. People stopped calling the neighborhood the Industrial District, associating it instead with post-industrial economies of sports, entertainment, and leisure, which, in turn, made way for new kinds

Fig. 5.4: A graffiti mural reading "SoDo MoJo" in T-Mobile Park's lower level, The Pen, connects the team and ballpark to the neighborhood through an aesthetic of hip and cool urbanism. (Photo by author)

of (sportified) development in the area. These developments include large sports-themed bars and restaurants in the SoDo neighborhood surrounding the stadiums. Additionally, the neighborhood is a site of mediated theatricality and experience beyond sports as well, an entertainment playground of sorts, playing host to a rotating set of immersive experiences and entertainment venues.[56] Meanwhile, the Home Plate Center development, a 348,000-square-foot building that takes up a city block adjacent to T-Mobile Park, aims "to create a festive environment that will naturally be an extension of the stadium on event days," using "decorative paving, pathway and general illumination, glazed awnings, and café seating . . . adjacent to restaurant establishments, and decorative plants with seasonal color for informal separation of spaces" to create pedestrian interaction.[57]

The neighborhoods adjacent to SoDo are also subject to rebranding through sport and the stadium experience. The cultural histories and sense of place from these neighborhoods provide a richer meaning and a sense of authenticity to the stadium experience. Neighborhood brandscaping in the CID and Pioneer Square generally highlight their unique cultural elements and histories, which serve as another brand context through which the stadium is experienced. An example of this is a set of public works projects initiated by the Washington State Public Stadium Authority (PSA) that highlight neighborhood culture, including the construction of dragon sculptures in the CID, a dining and entertainment guide featuring neighborhood restaurants and entertainment establishments for stadium attendees, and interactive media terminals in high traffic areas around the stadium to promote neighborhood businesses to "fans, visitors and tourists."[58] Ultimately, these examples demonstrate how SoDo and adjacent neighborhoods draw on the stadium, and vice versa, to create a sense of local place and authenticity while infusing them with the meanings, affects, and practices associated with sports and stadiums. These practices are further evident in the case of Lumen Field, which draws heavily on the cultures of the surrounding neighborhoods to constitute the stadium's brand experience.

Lumen Field: Authentically Local?

Like T-Mobile Park and the Kingdome before it, the building of Seahawks, Sounders, and OL (Olympique Lyonnais) Reign Stadium—originally named Qwest Field, then later CenturyLink Field, and subsequently Lumen Field (in its iteration at the time of this writing) after CenturyLink's rebranding—was mired in a contested political battle.[59] Ultimately, Microsoft cofounder, billionaire, and Seattle resident Paul Allen stepped in and agreed to buy the Seahawks, as long as the state subsidized a new stadium, claiming a modern stadium where the team could reap more revenue was the only way the team could be profitable.[60]

The stadium deal included a public-private partnership between the state and the Seahawks by forming the Washington State Public Stadium Authority—a seven-member body representing the state's public interest—which partnered with First and Goal, Inc., the private, corporate group created by Allen to manage construction and operate the stadium.[61] Much of the Kingdome's rubble was recycled and used in construction of the new stadium, situating it within a discourse of environmental sustainability that marked the city's emerging brand.[62] The architectural firm Ellerbe Becket (now AECOM, one of the nation's leading sporting facilities architectural firms) designed the building and its grounds. It partnered with local Seattle firm Loschky, Marquardt, and Nesholm on the design. Paul Allen also purportedly had a major design influence.[63] He wanted the stadium to recreate the excitement and intimacy he felt going to see the University of Washington's Huskies games while growing up in Seattle. Further, Allen supposedly gave principal designer Jon Niemuth the directive to design an outdoor stadium that would be as loud as an indoor one.[64]

Lumen Field (see fig. 5.5) is first and foremost designed to provide a set of tiered luxury experiences. The shift toward greater luxury, VIP, and tiered

Fig. 5.5: Lumen Field and T-Mobile Park (in the background) are imposing marks on the city's landscape and adjacent neighborhoods. (Photo by author)

experiences in third-generation stadiums enables greater profitability, but it also constructs a branded experience that communicates Seattle's cosmopolitanism. Lumen Field features personalized viewing experiences, luxury boxes, private suites, and upscale restaurants and retail facilities. It contains seventy-seven hundred club seats (expandable to ten thousand) featuring twenty-four-inch padded high-back seats.[65] Patrons can also pay extra for a Red Zone suite, which, when the stadium was built, was the only field-level suite in pro sports. The increased luxury-level seating promotes more privatized and individualized stadium experiences, where fans need not integrate themselves among the masses. These changes transform sporting events and the stadium experience from a working- and middle-class family aesthetic to one that primarily caters to an upper-class business elite.[66] With $300 million in public financing, it is mostly public subsidies that enable this luxury experience—supported by a sports-related Washington State Lottery, King County sales tax, hotel/motel tax, deferred sales tax, and stadium and exhibition center parking and admissions taxes. The hardest hit by these kinds of taxes are generally the poor, who, in Washington and many other states, are disproportionately overburdened by local taxes, for which they contribute an outsized proportion of their finances.[67] This means those who are least likely to benefit from the stadium and its luxury experiences are the ones who arguably contribute the most in creating them.

While the luxury experiences provided by the stadium are standard for most contemporary football stadiums, what distinguishes the stadium is its emphasis on "Seattleness." Like the Mariners ballpark, Lumen Field promotes distinctive Seattle and regional characteristics. The architectural design reinforces connections to the cultural geography and landscape of Seattle and the Pacific Northwest. The stadium's U-shaped north-facing side provides views of the city's downtown and skyline, similar to Atlanta's Mercedes-Benz Stadium, which modeled its Window to the City on Lumen Field's.[68] This view creates the effect of being within the city, heightening the sense of connection between the stadium space and the city and visually and physically connecting the affective experience of sports fandom to the urban fabric. To the south and southeast, the design opens to a view of Mount Rainier, connecting the urban leisure experience of attending a stadium event to the recreational experiences offered in the Cascade Mountains, emphasizing Seattle's natural lifestyle.

Designs pay particular attention to how the stadium would stand out in the landscape as an iconic structure while also highlighting the built environment in ways that would help it fit into a sense of Seattle history and place. The stadium's principal architect, Ron Gans, explains, "Aesthetically, the new stadium must stand on its own merit by contributing to the exotic city landscape. Yet the building must also respect the existing context and urban fabric that blossoms around it. Design cues must creatively blend old and new while minimizing the impact this large structure will have on its neighbors."[69] The design aimed not only to reflect Seattle and its existing place-identity but also to contribute to its landscape, thus playing an active role in branding the city and contributing to its sense of place-identity by emphasizing *particular* aspects of place—notably, the surrounding neighborhoods. According to Gans, "The design of Seahawks Stadium draws its inspiration from historical precedent and the local context to create a contemporary facility grounded in historically significant districts." The stadium pays tribute to, and thereby promotes, distinctive characteristics of the neighborhoods adjacent to the stadium. For example, noting they had the "important goal . . . [to] draw upon the strong historical commercial and industrial context while enabling the stadium to create a place for itself within the urban context," Gans claims that the "site design creates connections both physical and visual to [its adjacent] neighborhoods and weaves the area together in a logical and coherent form."[70] He says it does this through design that enables views to neighborhoods, and through the masonry, such as the columns, beams, and punched openings, which mirror the architecture of Pioneer Square (see figs. 5.6 and 5.7).

Fig. 5.6: View from Lumen Field into neighboring Pioneer Square and downtown in background, with Hawks Nest seating in forefront. The stadium was constructed to make fans feel as though they are in the city. (Photo by author)

Fig. 5.7: View north from Lumen Field's western concourse into the port, Pioneer Square, downtown, and the Space Needle at the Seattle Center in the distance. (Photo by author)

Other cultural forms, including art and concessions, further accentuate connections to adjacent neighborhoods. Lumen Field incorporates local artists and food vendors to constitute a sense of uniqueness and emplacement in the city and community while also justifying public funding by claiming this inclusion of locals is a community benefit and public good. First and Goal Inc. contracted an art manager to lead a committee for the building's art acquisitions. Notably, artists were not encouraged to relate their work to sport, like most of the art in T-Mobile Park, but, rather, to the building and the community as site-specific art installations.[71] Many of those installations include art from Seattle and Pacific Northwest artists who specifically reference place and landscape in their subject matter, thus enhancing the stadium's sense of connection to a particular place. For example, Seattle-based artist Romson Egarde Bustillo's installation, *Barangay*, includes three large-scale paintings that explore Filipino culture in reference to the artist's heritage and upbringing in Seattle, where Filipinos make up a sizable population, particularly in the neighboring CID.[72] Several pieces can be viewed without having to buy a ticket to the stadium, thus constituting a form of public art and creative urban planning that demonstrates Seattle's and the neighborhoods' cultural and creative assets.

The most visible piece of artwork on the building, and the one most featured in images of the stadium circulated in media, is Bob Haozous's *Earth Dialogue*,

Fig. 5.8: Bob Haozous's Earth Dialogue stands on Lumen Field's north tower. (Photo by author)

an installation of four twenty-four-foot-diameter painted steel discs on the stadium's North Tower (see fig. 5.8). Haozous is a Native American artist based in Santa Fe, New Mexico, of Warm Springs/Chiricahua Apache heritage. Lumen Field's website describes the piece as speaking to Haozous's heritage while carrying forms and colors with universal meaning, "intended as a constant reminder of our deep connection to the earth."[73] Each disc represents a different component of Earth—cityscape, humanity, sun, and clouds—in dialogue. American Indian studies scholar Traci L. Morris-Carlsten describes Houzous's work in more political terms, maintaining that his work stimulates dialogue by questioning the status quo, often incorporating symbolism of the trickster as a sign of humor, irony, and inversion to expose dominant settler colonial culture and strategies of Native survival. Morris-Carlsten argues, "Haozous is not creating the dialogue; he is provoking it by his tricky actions. He is trying to get people to talk, and they in turn create the dialogue. He is trying to stimulate discussion only. An Indigenous Cultural Dialogue, or stimulating discussion about issues central to Native Americans, is the major focus of all of Haozous's work."[74] Seen in this context, *Earth Dialogue*, as a site-specific installation, stimulates dialogue around core questions of environment, climate change, and humans' relationship to nature, but it also begs the question of the stadium's relationship to those issues as well as its impact and dialogue with its neighbors and settler colonial histories. It is an agonistic piece, defying an easy resolution and instead calling the question. Incorporating this kind of piece into the stadium is thus a kind of risk, as it may stimulate criticism of the place-brand, the stadium, and its cultural value systems. However, part of brand culture is that stimulating dialogue itself helps to produce value, as the circulation of meaning and information constitutes the site as significant and iconic. It is thus perhaps worth the risk for stadium owners.

Furthermore, the stadium's description of Haozous's piece helps steer dialogue in less risky directions by emphasizing the artwork's environmental politics and directing visitors to consider the stadium's sustainability measures and community benefits programs with the neighborhoods. It thus encourages visitors to see the stadium and Seattle as environmentally friendly and in terms of the natural Northwest brand. This is a form of brand management, which, in Adam Arvidsson's view, tries to anticipate how consumers will use and relate to cultural goods and to direct those interactions in ways that contribute to brand value.[75] This practice works to capture an ethical surplus, or the excess of meaning, community, and value created through the consumer's affective relationship to and interaction with the brand. In the case of *Earth Dialogue*, the stadium's efforts to direct viewers to interact with the piece in particular ways aims to capture the affective intensities produced through the dialogue stimulated by the art to create value and meaning for the stadium, its sports teams, and for Seattle as an ethical and environmental brand, worthy of investing, visiting, and living in. But it is important to note that brand management is not always successful, and indeed part of the brilliance of *Earth Dialogue* and Haozous's work more generally is its subtle critique and subversion.

Haozous's *Earth Dialogue* is just one of many pieces of Native American/Indigenous artworks placed in and around Lumen Field. Like the Pacific Northwest and, indeed, the Americas more broadly, settler colonialism is a present-day force in Seattle, and the city's formal efforts to address this, particularly through the inclusion and incorporation of Indigenous peoples and Native practices into broader city events and into the built environment, are complex, often contradictory, and not easily parsed politically. Native American imagery and symbolism is ubiquitous in the region, in large part because there is a sizable and active Native American population throughout the Pacific Northwest. But Native American symbolism is also incorporated into many non-Native spaces and activities, where the unique imagery of the Coast Salish peoples, such as the wooden carvings on monumental totem poles and the distinctive use of form lines to depict natural forms and creatures indigenous to the region, is often used to sell non-indigenous products and events by giving them a touch of exotic indigeneity.

One of those products is the Seahawks team mascot and logo. The Seahawk is a symbol drawn from a Kwakwaka'wakw transformation mask from Vancouver Island.[76] Unlike other teams that have received significant pushback for their cultural appropriation of Native symbolism in their sporting mascots, the Seahawks, in contrast, have been generally left unscathed by those critiques. Micheal Rios, writing for the Northwest Indigenous news source *Tulalip News*, suggests, "Unlike those teams, whose logos are founded on stereotypes (as opposed to any specific aspect of one of Native America's 574 federally recognized tribes) the Seattle Seahawks' logo is that rarest of birds: a culturally accurate sports icon directly inspired from an Indigenous masterpiece—and embraced by the Indigenous People it is borrowed from."[77] The Seahawk is not considered a sacred creature, and thus its use is generally not seen as a sign of disrespect to Native culture. Rios contends a major reason for this acceptance is that the Seahawks contribute to the region's Native urban and reservation-based communities, particularly by engaging in youth-focused community projects. Further, Rios notes, several Native artists have reappropriated the Seahawks logo for their own artworks, reproducing the logo on a variety of cultural products from clothing to blankets and beaded jewelry to celebrate the team's links to Native culture. I do not want to suggest here that Rios speaks for all Native peoples in their feelings about the Seahawks or their use of Native American symbolism, and undoubtedly other Indigenous peoples likely have negative or complicated feelings about the team and their appropriation of these symbols. What I do want to point out here, though, is that the incorporation of Indigenous Coast Salish artworks into the stadium reveals the complex cultural politics of placemaking and brand culture within sporting spaces, as it both commodifies and appropriates local culture and Indigenous practices while also producing genuine affects and practices of community, connection, and dialogue.

That complexity is also reflected in the stadium's concessions program, which provides another example of its practices of branding the local and placemaking. Lumen Field's website describes their concession options as "inspired by Northwest flavors," promising fans they will "find local chefs and restaurants all throughout the stadium."[78] As part of the lease deal and public-private partnership with the PSA, First and Goal partnered with local food vendors to feature Seattle's unique food culture. The food vendor policy created a partnership between the stadium, teams, government, community organizations, and local businesses, promising to bring a sense of place driven by local creative culture to stadium attendees. The concessions reflect the wider Pacific Northwest region and the city's diverse neighborhoods, variably changing over the years in response to the shifting food cultures in the region and fan desires based on surveys and data collection. Many of the current concession options include local restaurant vendors in the CID, such as Mangosteen's chicken teriyaki and Din Tai Fung's Taiwanese soup dumplings. Kathleen Johnson, executive director of Historic South Downtown, an advocacy organization for the neighborhoods affected by the stadium, claims the inclusion of these vendors was part of a community benefits deal brokered by the PSA in partnership with advocacy organizations in the CID.[79]

Although local food concessions have always been part of the Seahawks' stadium offerings, the emphasis on localism, especially neighborhood-based locations, was supercharged in the mid-2010s and particularly as part of a 2017 concession project, promoted as a form of neighborly goodwill. The stadium's executive chef, Taylor Park, explains, "We're trying to help our local community, and in return they are helping us by serving great food."[80] In addition to more local food vendors, Lumen Field also features a Stadium Street Market with four local chefs for each game along with a Night Market, offering a "global twist," inspired by Chinese and Asian night market traditions. Night markets have a long history in many Asian cultures, providing inexpensive food and goods to largely working-class and often migrant populations, supporting small and informal businesses and creating temporary public spaces for marginalized peoples to make community.[81] Lumen Field's Night Market features restaurants from the CID, Pioneer Square, and SoDo. Although tourists often frequent night markets in cities around the world, they primarily cater to the ethnic communities they serve, making Lumen Field's Night Market, whose customers are primarily white, wealthy sports fans, a rather different experience. Still, the inclusion of this vernacular form of local culture enables the stadium to draw meaning from placemaking practices in order to authenticate its brand.

The Kingdome also promoted the adjacent neighborhoods, inviting visitors to sample the exotic "Oriental [sic] culture" of the CID. However, this homogenizing and pejorative rhetoric is distinct from how Lumen Field promises an "authentic" experience by including vendors in the building and the stadium and featuring food and cultural practices as part of a unique experience. This shift reflects the rise of the neoliberal city, where local cultures, particularly racial and ethnic ones, are viewed as valuable resources to distinguish a city as unique, hip, and diverse, and, thus, a globally competitive creative city. This practice constitutes what George Yúdice refers to as the "expediency of culture," where spaces and practices of racially and ethnically diverse cultures are characterized as marketable economic and social resources, valued in new ways in the global economy.[82] But that valuation often attaches to elements of culture that are depoliticized, forms of what Arlene Dávila calls "marketable ethnicity," or forms of culture that create returns on investment, evacuated of their relationship to histories of political struggle. Marketable ethnicity favors market-based solutions for what are really problems of inequity, as "neoliberal policies and developments draw on and capitalize pervasive discourses of race and ethnicity while ignoring them as bases for inequities."[83] Rather than attending to the very real problems of economic disenfranchisement and inequity in the CID through policies that address racism and discrimination, selling cultural goods in the marketplace is offered as the solution. Thus, forms of culture that might come into conflict with what might be marketable or palatable to stadium fans come under threat, risking erasure and displacement and altering the neighborhood and who it is for and how it is practiced.

Lumen Field's integration of local culture was achieved in coordination with neighborhood organizations and driven by discussions and input from neighborhood representatives.[84] This kind of collaboration reveals the complexity of marketable ethnicity, with communities having to take advantage of the resources they are offered. MaryKate Ryan, community preservation associate for Historic South Downtown, notes, "I don't want to sound crass, but I think there is a level of, if they just come [and] buy food here, and they don't really care about what the CID is, . . . they'll take the business. . . . They're small businesses. They survive on razor-thin profit margins."[85] The local food vendors from the CID might be concerned about commodification of their cultural resources, but they ultimately want and need the business. Yet, this too is complicated by the ways this collaboration can create competition for scarce resources, as well as infighting between and among groups over who gets to lay claim to representing the group or what forms of culture are considered authentic and deemed worthy of inclusion into the stadium-going experience. Moreover, though both Pioneer Square and the CID present value for tourism, the grittiness of the neighborhoods is often a barrier to investors who instead envision turning them into "new and shiny" spaces, prioritizing the experience of tourists over the people who live there. However, as Kathleen Johnson asserts, the neighborhood also has value for the people who do and will live there, and if that value is not nurtured, the tourist value will not manifest either. Johnson says, "This is an ongoing, vibrant, and living place. This isn't just a cultural hub. This is a place where people live and run their businesses, and they run those independent of the stadiums. We're not . . . just a tourist stop for people on their way to the stadiums."[86]

"We Are the 12th Man": Sonic Branding at Lumen Field

Although the stadium sells a notion of "Seattleness" through a number of strategies, including concessions, art, and architectural design, perhaps the most significant way its brand is constituted is through sound, especially the promotion of the passion, commitment, and volume of the Seahawks' "12th Man." Lumen Field's designers tried to replicate the unique sound of the Kingdome, which, as noted in the previous chapter, was known as loudest in the NFL and helped start Seattle's 12th Man phenomenon. Though fans suggest the sound in the new stadium doesn't match that of the Kingdome, Lumen Field's loud volume has nevertheless become an iconic symbol of Seattle. Perhaps most famously, the 2011 "Beast Quake," in which fans erupted so loudly in response to Marshawn Lynch's touchdown during an NFC Wild Card playoff game, registered earthquake-level seismic activity, cementing the stadium's sound and the 12th Man as core symbols of the Seahawks and Seattle.[87]

While the Kingdome's sound was incidental, the loud, reverberating sound of Lumen Field is part of its architectural design, particularly the roof and cantilevered seating. The stadium has one of the smallest footprints in the NFL, creating an intimate enclosed feeling by stacking the upper-level seating on top of the lower level to bring fans closer to the field. This feature reflects sound back onto the field off the bottom of the upper deck. The stacked seating, together with the roof canopy, covers more than 70 percent of the seats, which protects fans from Seattle's rain while keeping them outdoors and capturing the crowd's sound. The extension of the roof canopy over the seating bowl also allows optimal speaker placement, enhancing sound quality.[88] Further, the curvature and angles of the canopy divert the noise to the playing field, an effect lead architect Jon Niemuth claims was a "happy accident."[89] Adding to the sound, the Hawks Nest in the north end zone—a set of aluminum bleachers with the stadium's cheapest tickets—creates a particularly loud sound when fans stomp. Finally, there are the fans themselves. Stadium space, design, and sound influence fan behavior as fans experience the reverberation of the noise and scream louder, caught up in a shared affective experience.[90]

Thus, while architectural design and the speaker system might explain the loudness of the stadium, fans claim they are the ones who are truly responsible. One fan asserted, "The stadium designs serve to level out the playing field with other indoor/domed stadiums. What takes the volume at Seahawks home games to a whole other level has everything to do with the passion and commitment of the 12th Man."[91] While other teams have strong fan communities, only Seahawks fans believe they can affect the game.[92] During the Seattle Seahawks' successful 2014 Super Bowl campaign, much was made of the 12th Man effect and their formidable home record. Writing about the Seahawks in *Sports Illustrated*, Chris Ballard notes, "No other franchise spends as much time glorifying its supporters."[93] While the 12th Man might seem at times like an organic concept that sprang forth from fans, the team does not miss an opportunity to brand and market "the 12s." The 12th Man has its own section on the Seattle Seahawks website, which details the team's close relationship with its fans and touts their position as the loudest in the NFL.[94] Since 2003 the Seahawks have honored their fans by raising a 12th Man flag at every home game, including on the Space Needle during their 2014 Super Bowl run.

The house the 12th Man built in Seattle has created a seismic shift, made the *Guinness Book of World Records*, and induced the greatest number of false starts from opposing teams in the league.[95] Whereas the Kingdome's loudness led to efforts by the NFL to regulate crowd noise, the league now welcomes it. Loudness is a valuable affective resource that can be transformed into profits by increasing stadium attendance (one has to be there to feel it!) and remediating it to fans at home. Mack Hagood and Travis Vogan maintain that Lumen Field converts noise into affect in service of commercial goals, where that affect helps brand the team, stadium, and city as "more intimate, authentic, and egalitarian."[96] For the Seattle city brand, sonic affect constitutes Seahawks fandom as an identity, community, and sense of civic pride deeply connected to the team, city, and region/state, as home of the 12th Man—the loudest, most passionate, prideful fans in the NFL.

Sonic affect fosters placefulness, a kind of regional "everyman" and Northwest identity that elides the corporate elitism of the stadium. This sentiment is reflected in stadium designer Joe Niemuth's musings on the Hawks Nest and the effect of the aluminum bleachers: "Everything about that section was designed to be loud.... The sound is just down and dirty. Originally, it was intended to be no-frills pricing, but it got this great following. Joe Six-Pack loved it. It was this cult-of-personality section that took on a life of its own."[97] The characterization of the Hawks Nest and its fans as "down and dirty" and "Joe Six-Pack" marks a distinctly classed, gendered, and, arguably, raced discourse that speaks to the kinds of tiered experiences provided by the stadium, where the raucousness of fans enables the stadium to lay claim to the city's and sporting culture's masculinist working-class history and even to venerate it while simultaneously promoting a luxury stadium space designed with a very different type of classed subject in mind. But more so, this collective fandom produces an ethical surplus through sonic affect that is captured as brand value, creating revenue by encouraging fans to buy tickets to come to the stadium to experience the sound. So too this sonic affect attaches to the team and city to render it a vibrant place, connected to a particular history and activated community.[98]

Yet, crowd noise, sonic affect, and the classed and gendered embodiments it expresses are also part of the tension of the stadium's power dynamics. Crowd noise expresses the kind of emotional intensity released at sporting events that in most other spaces is disallowed. That intensity expresses a collective potentiality of fans/masses and threatens to disrupt elite systems of power on which the stadium is built; it demonstrates the power of the collective and their agential, political, and potentially violent capacities. That threat is subdued through brand management, which redirects that potentiality toward the brand via the 12th Man. The activated fandom of the 12th Man, emblematic of the city and region, constitutes Seattle and the Northwest as an active and participatory public whose citizenship is characterized by practices of fandom. This demonstrates how branding is related to governing, as the passionate fan dedicated to the brand, rather than protester or politicized agent, is the idealized version of active citizenship.

Although Lumen Field plays host to other events—music concerts, conventions, monster truck shows—the sonic affect they produce is distinct from sport. This is due to topophilia. Fans at the 2023 Taylor Swift concert also created loud enough sounds to shake the earth, but those intensities are not able to be converted to brand value for Seattle in the same way as Seahawks fans.[99] As an internationally renowned pop star, Swift is not identified with the city of Seattle, and thus the seismic shifts she creates generate her own brand value more so than the city's. However, when she plays in Nashville, where she (somewhat controversially) claims her hometown roots, those intensities arguably (re)produce Nashville's city brand as a music city. Still, the fact the earthquake-level seismic activity created during the Swift concert was in Seattle, rather than at another stadium, adds to the stadium's iconicity and, hence, its role in Seattle branding. Most of all, though, the Swifties demonstrate the core relationship between sporting infrastructure and the circulation of affect. The use of stadiums as sites for concerts and other forms of popular culture, as well as political culture—for example, Trump rallies—reveals how the sportification of place extends the affective intensities endemic to sport and sporting culture to other cultural and political realms.[100]

Branding Cascadia

I would be remiss not to mention the idea of how the fan as the 12th Man is in large part specific to US American football, but Lumen Field plays host to the city's professional soccer teams—the Sounders and OL Reign—as well.[101] The stadium serves to constitute urban branding via the city's soccer clubs in ways that are both similar to but also distinct from that of the Seahawks, reflecting the differing fan communities of the respective sports. Soccer is particularly popular in the Pacific Northwest and in Seattle, especially. Attendance at the

Seattle Sounders games, for example, far exceeds that for other Major League Soccer (MLS) teams.[102] While Seahawks fandom has a deep hold within the county suburbs and more rural parts of the region, soccer fandom is strongest within the region's urban centers.

Soccer thus constructs a different cultural geography within the Northwest—one best captured by the idea of "Cascadia," a regional identity, spatial construction, and cultural imaginary. Matthew Sparke suggests Cascadia is "not a state, but a state of mind."[103] Its boundaries are not easily mapped geographically, as conflicting interpretations of the concept include different parts of the region depending on the political aims for conjuring the idea of Cascadia. Most interpretations, though, include the Northwest region running along the forty-ninth parallel of British Columbia, Washington, and Oregon, with others also including parts of Northern California, Alaska, Alberta, Montana, and Idaho. Cascadia is a binational (US and Canada) movement supported by activists, nongovernmental organizations, and businesses to promote cross-cultural, environmental, and economic regional connections in the Pacific Northwest. It stems from a bioregional movement and includes a vibrant secessionist movement. The Cascadia Department of Bioregion, a nonprofit organization devoted to promoting bioregionalism and political advocacy around Cascadian secession, boasts, "Cascadia has been listed as #7 on *Time Magazine*'s top 10 most likely to succeed (at seceding) independence movements."[104] The movement can be traced to a longer history of political alienation and even rebellion in the Northwest, where residents perceive the federal government as indifferent to the unique conditions and needs of the region. During the Yreka Rebellion in 1941, for example, a group of miners, ranchers, and loggers at the California/Oregon border declared their independence.[105] Though the rebellion was short-lived, it spoke to disenfranchisement and a sense of identity tied to Northwest cultural geography that has persisted. That sensibility can also be gleaned from Ernest Callenbach's *Ecotopia*, a novel published in 1975 in which California, Oregon, and Washington secede from the United States to form "a progressive utopia built on thoughtful forestry, urban density, and a deep disdain of plastic."[106] The Cascadia movement really took hold after the first Cascadia Bioregional Congress, held in 1986, where "bioregional organizers, policy planners, feminists, anarchists and indigenous leaders" gathered to "address issues ranging from grassroots democracy, community building, forestry, recycling, nuclear concerns, to decentralized and local economics."[107] The movement continued to grow and has since become a core cross-border regional identity with which many Northwest residents identify, though not always in its secessionist forms. The advocacy group CascadiaNOW! a nonprofit devoted to "a resilient and inclusive Pacific

Northwest community," for example, advocates for cultural shifts rather than secession.[108]

Seattle's soccer clubs are strongly associated with and branded through symbols of Cascadia. Hunter Shobe and Geoff Gibson contend that Cascadian identity is constructed through ritualistic practices and rhythms of fandom in Seattle, Portland, and Vancouver, whose soccer cultures in turn constitute and promote the idea of Cascadia.[109] Much of this takes place within the stadium through, for example, the raising of the Cascadian flag—the "Doug flag," with a Douglas fir tree imprinted on blue, white, and green stripes—during games. The Seattle Sounders embrace the use of Cascadia as part of their team branding, marking the news section of their website "Cascadia News," suggesting the team itself is synonymous with Cascadia.[110]

The connections Cascadia creates between supporters and place also play a material role in the region's spatiality. Cascadia's branding of Seattle produces space differently from that of the 12th Man, as the brand emplaces fans within ideologies of the Cascadia movement and its ethics of bioregionalism. This plays out in the everyday spatial practices of supporters. In my interviews with local neighborhood organizations and stadium officials, each mentioned that soccer fans' movements through the city to the stadium and interactions within the stadium and its surrounding neighborhoods were distinct from those of football fans. Soccer fans are more likely to live in the urban core and to navigate to the stadium using bicycles or public transportation rather than automobiles. They do not break records for crowd noise at Lumen Field, nor do they generally participate in tailgating before and during game days. These factors, along with the lower number of attendees for games, make soccer perceived by area residents as generally less disruptive.

In these differences, one can discern conflicting brands in Seattle, which, in turn, translate to different kinds of claims on the city's broader sense of place and identity. These are variations on the Seattle brand, constructing Seattle not as a singular brand but as adapted and adaptable to different audiences and contexts.[111] That variability is built into the flexibility of the stadium space and its design, as it can be transformed from a space conducive to activating 12th Man fandom in one season and Cascadia in another. This flexibility is linked to post-industrial production practices that David Harvey terms "flexible accumulation." Responding to the rigidities of Fordist production and influenced by the growing role of media, communication, and information in economic production and value, which makes the production of image key to capital accumulation, Harvey theorizes the post-industrial economy is characterized by "flexible labour processes and markets, of geographical mobility and rapid shifts in consumption practices."[112] Under flexible accumulation, production is decentralized to facilitate mobility, change, and continued innovation, creating practices of adaptability and "just-in-time" delivery. As a form of flexible accumulation, the potentially conflicting soccer and football brands instead become an asset to marketability across different market segments. The rowdier 12th Man lays claim to the city's working-class history by grounding it in affects of nostalgia, including through evoking affects of Huskies games and the Kingdome through stadium design. These affects conjure a particular kind of US American cultural imaginary, drawing on football rituals and uses of city space as a distinctly US American game, and promote a cultural geography that bridges divisions between the urban/rural, eastern/western, city/county through this claim to Americanism. On the other hand, soccer, a global sport, challenges a US cultural imaginary by eroding nationalist distinctions through the promotion of Cascadia. It lays claim to a different history of Seattle, one associated with the Cascadia movement and its agitation against nationalist borders. It signifies and constitutes Seattle's brand as multicultural, global, cosmopolitan, and environmentally conscious.

Although more politicized bioregional ideals of Cascadia are at play in Seattle's soccer culture, that culture is also part of connecting Seattle to a global and transnational political economic system. Soccer itself contributes to these forces through, for example, the transnationalization of sporting and administrative labor, foreign ownership of teams, and global branding and merchandising. Soccer fandom contributes to transnational and global fandoms, which create new identities, hybridized local/global geographies, and global/diasporic fans who participate in global sporting rituals.[113] In this sense, soccer's branding of Cascadia also subsumes its bioregional constructions to support geoeconomic rather than geopolitical formations. Those formations, Sparke argues, produce "neoliberal, market-oriented, anti-state transmutation" to facilitate the transnational flow of capital and finance and to enable regional capitals like Vancouver, Seattle, and Portland, which perceive a "historical alienation from faraway federal capitals," to be globally competitive centers of finance and culture.[114] With the United States, Canada, and Mexico set to host the FIFA World Cup in 2026, the world's largest and most globally popular sporting event, and Seattle's Lumen Field chosen as one of the host sites, soccer's branding of Seattle demonstrates how sporting spaces are vehicles for constituting new global economic circulations and flows of capital, labor, and consumption.

PART III

Minneapolis
Stadiums as White Space

CHAPTER 6

White Flight

To the Suburbs and Downtown Again

As the preceding chapters have put forth, stadiums are contested sites; they are cherished, struggled over, and sometimes challenged and appropriated. Ultimately, though, I contend that stadiums are white spaces, animated by what George Lipsitz refers to as a "white spatial imaginary." Lipsitz suggests that the white spatial imaginary "structures feelings as well as social institutions. . . . [It] idealizes 'pure' and homogeneous spaces, controlled environments, and predictable patterns of design and behavior. It seeks to hide social problems rather than solve them . . . [and] promotes the quest for individual escape rather than encouraging democratic deliberations about the social problems and contradictory social relations that affect us all."[1] Modern stadiums embody and perform this structure of feeling "to a T." They are built around ideals of purity and homogeneity, represent some of the most controlled environments in the city, and are designed using data analytics that seek to both predict and shape the behaviors of those within and outside stadium space. Although stadiums provide public gathering spaces, they are designed to curate individualized experiences. Stadiums privilege individual consumption of spectacle while prohibiting democratic deliberation by concealing, displacing, or redirecting social problems that might disrupt spectacle.

Stadiums are thus, on the one hand, products of a white spatial imaginary. They are the products of tax incentives and zoning policies building on longer histories of housing discrimination and redlining that produced the modern segregated city, which concentrated public wealth in the hands of white elites. Stadiums contribute to those histories as structures of urban renewal, revitalization, and regeneration, facilitating displacement of BIPOC and working-class peoples. The white spatial imaginary thus influences the building, design, and use of the stadium and explains how urban media infrastructures like the stadium are the material things produced by white supremacy—they are the sociospatial material products of white dominance, where "whiteness is learned and legitimated, perceived as natural, necessary, and inevitable."[2]

On the other hand, stadiums are also productive of the white spatial imaginary, and, in turn, white supremacy.[3] Whiteness is productive; it does things, makes things, and intervenes into the material in ways that secure white racial dominance and produce white privilege and racism. It is this material intervention I am most interested in terms of how the stadium, as an urban media infrastructure, is involved in the "structural, material, and corporeal production of white racial hegemony."[4]

Arguably, each of the stadiums discussed in this book is a product of a white spatial imaginary. However, Minneapolis—as the site that sparked the nation's largest collective uprising against racial injustice since the civil rights movement after Minneapolis police murdered George Floyd in the summer of 2020—is a particularly revealing city through which to unravel the racialized dynamics of stadiums and their imbrication in the urban. Floyd was arrested by Minneapolis police officers on May 25, 2020, after a convenience store clerk reported he used a counterfeit twenty-dollar bill to purchase cigarettes. Officers pinned Floyd to the ground, where he repeatedly expressed that he could not breathe. Officer Derek Chauvin pinned him for approximately seventeen minutes under his knee until Floyd finally perished. A bystander filmed the event, and the video circulated on social and, later, legacy media, where it sparked widespread outrage and a resurgence of the Black Lives Matter (BLM) movement. In Minneapolis, people took to the streets, where a tense, multiday struggle played out as protesters called attention to the city's deep racial disparities.[5] As the protests around Floyd's murder revealed, Minneapolis and St. Paul, known as the Twin Cities metro area, are a deeply contradictory space—a city on the one hand lauded as "progressive" and invested in the politics of equity, while on the other hand being one of the most segregated and inequitable cities in the country. Referring to this contradiction as the "Minnesota paradox," Samuel L. Myers Jr. argues that Minnesota is "one of the best places to live in America" and, simultaneously, "one of the worst places for Blacks to live," particularly when it comes to wide disparities in education, health care, housing, and incarceration.[6] Although the state is often painted as cosmopolitan, welcoming to refugees and immigrants, and civic-minded, critics suggest this is a "progressive illusion."[7]

This progressive illusion is also connected to "Minnesota nice"—that affect of Midwestern polite friendliness tinged with passive-aggressive avoidance of conflict. Drawing on James Baldwin's idea of "nice white people," David Todd Lawrence suggests that Minnesota nice is a corruptive innocence, in which innocence "constitutes the crime." After living as a Black man in Minneapolis, who often experienced forms of Minnesota nice, Lawrence notes, "I came to understand that niceness was really a kind of imperceptible camouflage that allowed social violence against BIPOC folks to take place without anyone having to take responsibility for it."[8] Ultimately, Minnesota's whiteness and the racial gaps in its citizens' outcomes are not incidental—they are products of a long history of government policy, corporate collusion, and racist actions of prejudicial individuals. As Chad Montrie writes, "Racial exclusion of African Americans was and is foundational. . . . Minnesota Whites' largely successful efforts to exclude Blacks from their midst, or contain them in delimited areas, played the formative role in making the current racial order."[9]

Minneapolis's stadiums were and continue to be fundamental to this process as they participate in constituting the city's racialized geography. In this chapter, I historicize this process. I first analyze the city's original major league ballpark—Metropolitan Stadium, built in suburban Bloomington. I suggest that the location of Metropolitan Stadium in the suburbs illustrates a white spatial imaginary rooted in more overt forms of racism and white flight, while the Hubert H. Humphrey Metrodome (more commonly referred to as the Metrodome), built at the tail end of the second generation of stadiums to replace Metropolitan Stadium, shifted to a more inferential racial logic. Debates over the Metrodome deferred issues of race to coded signifiers rather than an overtly racist politics, aimed to attract the white suburban consumer back downtown. For a time, it seemed there would be no third generation and that the Twin Cities would have to live with the Metrodome as community activists drew on a discourse of values and social justice to resist new stadium construction in the 1990s and early 2000s. However, the stadium coalition also pivoted to values, turning to the place-based emphasis on neighborhoods indicative of the third generation, finally resulting in Target Field in 2010 and U.S. Bank Stadium (UBS) in 2016. This place-based neighborhood emphasis reflects a shifting racial logic as well, still rooted in a white spatial imaginary but one that is motivated by a color-blind and neoliberal racism tied to post-racial politics. I analyze that logic and how it plays out in the city's contemporary stadiums' design, architecture, and practice through surveillance and datafication in the following chapter.

Metropolitan Stadium

Minnesota's second-generation stadium, Metropolitan Stadium—known simply as "the Met"—opened in 1956. Prior to that, minor league Twin Cities teams—the American Association's St. Paul Saints and the Minneapolis Millers—played downtown in small ballparks (Lexington Park and Nicollet Park) in their respective city centers.[10] While the Met holds much in common with the other case studies discussed in this book so far, such as constituting Minneapolis as a "major league city" by building a stadium to attract a professional baseball team, it differs from Atlanta and Seattle in that it was built in suburban Bloomington. Atlanta and Seattle both invested in stadium infrastructure as the driver of urban renewal in the urban core to combat deindustrialization and white flight. The Met, conversely, is indicative of the second-generation move to the suburbs, joining the likes of Milwaukee, Houston, Kansas City, and several others.[11] The move toward suburban stadiums is inextricably tied to a white spatial imaginary, as the suburbs themselves were outposts for white flight. Driven by racially motivated fears of urban decay, sports teams and stadium owners contributed to that decay by divesting from the city and investing in white suburbia.

The white supremacist motivation of this suburban shift in second-generation stadiums is evident in the words of the original owner of the Minnesota Twins, Calvin Griffith. Speaking at a Lions Club meeting in 1978, Griffith explained openly that race was a driving factor for why he moved his Washington (DC) Senators team to Minnesota: "I'll tell you why we came to Minnesota, it was when I found out you only had 15,000 blacks here. Black people don't go to ball games, but they'll fill up a rassling [sic] ring and put up such a chant it'll scare you to death. It's unbelievable. We came here because you've got good, hard-working, white people here."[12] Griffith's comments, exposed again in the wake of the city's 2020 protests, prompted the Twins to take down his statue at Target Field. The team did not wish to be associated with its forebearer and his racist comments. However, his comments are not merely the result of individual prejudice and incidental to baseball's history. Rather, they are indicative of how baseball itself is constitutive of racial formation.

Striving to become a "high order urban center," elites believed a major league baseball team "would symbolize the Twin Cities' arrival on the national scene."[13] As major league baseball began expanding westward, Minnesota was eager to get a team. But like Atlanta and Seattle, it did not have a professional-caliber stadium. Minneapolis and St. Paul business elites set to work trying to hammer out a deal for where the stadium should be. But both cities were determined to house the stadium, fueling long-standing rivalries between them.

Unable to resolve the rivalry, the stadium search committee proposed suburban Bloomington as an alternative (see map 6.1). The site provided cheap land, was equidistant from the two cities, had ample room for parking, and was proximate to the interstate highway system in development.[14] While the move to the suburbs quelled the struggle between Minneapolis and St. Paul, it also fueled segregated geographies and policies of suburbanization. During the time the stadium was built, between 1950 and 1960, Bloomington's population grew five times. New cultural amenities, like the baseball stadium and a mall, helped drive population growth. Most Bloomington residents were white, with less than a dozen Black residents. According to Chad Montrie, "Developers, realtors, homeowners in Bloomington had colluded in all manner of overt and covert ways to prevent Blacks from disturbing the community's racial uniformity, and for a long stretch of years they were overwhelmingly successful."[15]

The Bloomington site was originally farmland. The Met became the only MLB ballpark where spectators could view a working farm. "The location and view," Kristin Anderson writes, "helped to reinforce the myth of baseball's pastoral and bucolic origins, increasingly difficult to achieve in the old urban parks."[16] The view, the design of the stadium as a striking, colorful structure, and its

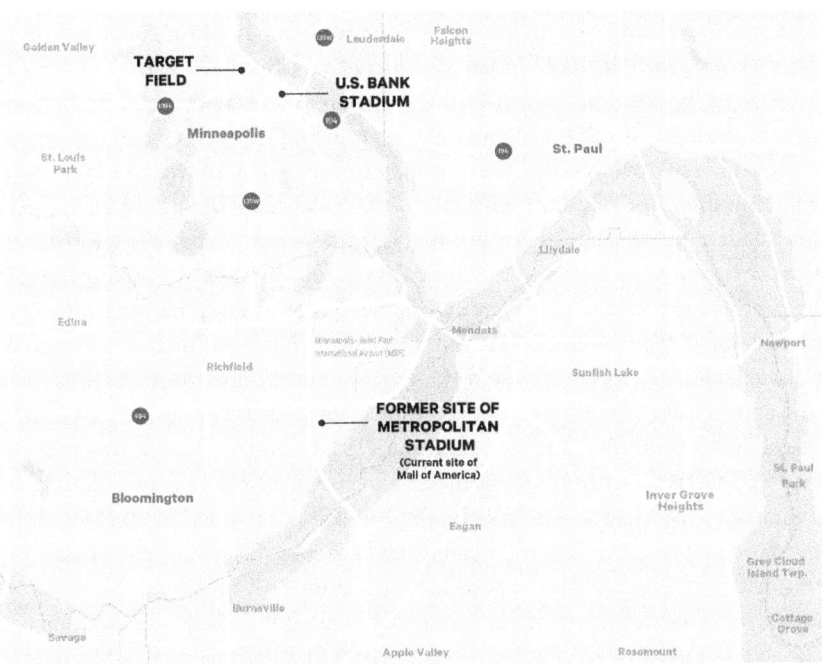

Map 6.1: Metropolitan Stadium was built in suburban Bloomington on the outskirts of Minneapolis. The site is now home to the Mall of America. (Credit: Gillian Tiley)

emphasis on enabling television production made the stadium constitutive of suburbanized entertainment and subjectivity rooted in an ideal of the white, middle-class family.

Although the suburban location resolved the St. Paul versus Minneapolis debate, it created a new rivalry between the downtown cores and the sprawling suburbs. The rivalry between the Twin Cities thus transformed into a trilateral one, which continued to play out in future debates over stadium locales. Moreover, even though the suburban location was meant to placate both Minneapolis and St. Paul, the latter ultimately refused to cooperate and opted to build a new minor league stadium in the city's Midway area. This left Minneapolis holding the bag, with its credit backing the general obligation bonds used to fund the stadium. The city of Minneapolis also paid for utilities and police services, and Bloomington requested a three percent admission tax diverted to the Bloomington general fund.[17] While Bloomington reaped financial benefits from the stadium location, it contributed nearly nothing to its costs. Instead, those costs fell on Minneapolis taxpayers. This inequitable distribution shows how the segregationist practices of Bloomington, and the consequent production of white space, depends on siphoning and depriving resources from other spaces.

Historians herald the Met's financing—via civic bonds—as a testament to Minnesota's strong civic pride. In their histories of stadium construction in Minnesota, journalist Jay Weiner and (eventual US senator) Amy Klobuchar believe the bonds demonstrate something unique about civic pride in Minnesota during this period. Weiner claims much of the money came from everyday citizens who pooled their money to buy five-hundred-dollar bonds, showing their pride and investment in a baseball team to put the Twin Cities on the map.[18] Klobuchar suggests this civic pride is part of the Minnesota tradition, wherein "the active role that the Minneapolis private sector has played in helping government to meet community needs has aroused national attention and esteem."[19] Klobuchar credits this successful collaboration to Minneapolis' smaller size, as a city where people know one another, creating a sense of pride and community. But most of all, she emphasizes this is made possible because the population is homogeneous, claiming, "In addition to being fairly small, the city's population is strikingly homogeneous. A 1980 census showed that the Twin Cities metropolitan area's population of about two million had less than five percent blacks, Indians, Chicanos, and southeast Asians. With such a low minority population, Minneapolis lacks the ethnic diversity which characterizes other American cities. People tend to come from similar backgrounds and they also share similar values, making it easier for business and government to pursue common objectives."[20] Homogeneity in this context means whiteness. What Weiner and Klobuchar are intimating here, but what is left unsaid, is that the civic pride constituted in and through the Met was one that was indicative of the shared backgrounds and values of *white* Minneapolis. These historians propagate a typical view of Minnesota—a space of progressive values and civic engagement—but this requires a kind of "willed amnesia" to the state's history of racial exclusion and containment. Performance of civic pride might therefore be read instead as a kind of white pride and the Met as a manifestation of the spaces produced by that collective investment in whiteness.[21]

When the Met opened in 1956, Minnesota didn't have a professional team. The Twin Cities initially backed the fledgling Continental League in a wager that it would convince the American League to grant them a team to stave off competition.[22] The gamble worked, and the league promised Minnesota a team if they built a professional-caliber stadium. They lured Calvin Griffith to move the Washington Senators to Minnesota in 1961, where they were renamed the Twins. That year, Minnesota also gained an NFL expansion team—the Minnesota Vikings—who also played in the Met. Quickly, however, the stadium was seen as out of date. Jay Weiner notes that critics started discussing plans for a new stadium as early as 1965. The Vikings were especially critical of the Met because the Twins had a more favorable lease agreement; the Twins received all revenue beyond ticket sales even during Vikings games. Those critics grew louder as a wave of domed multipurpose stadiums, which were easier to convert between the two sports, were increasingly returning to the downtown core as part of a renewed discourse of urban revitalization. That sentiment began to resonate more strongly in the Twin Cities as they began to see the suburbs as another rival.

The Metrodome

In contrast to some other deindustrializing cities, the Twin Cities were not subject to the urban decline discourse plaguing many cities in the postwar era. In part, this was because the Twin Cities were not dependent on one particular industry.[23] But it was also tied to Minneapolis' whiteness. The Twin Cities experienced the same kinds of urban unrest as other cities, as the civil rights and Black Power movements came to the fore, with protests emerging in 1966 around residential segregation in North Minneapolis and again in 1977 in St. Paul's Summit-University neighborhood.[24] Yet, the image of Minnesota as a space of whiteness, whether as Calvin Griffith's white utopia or Klobuchar's liberal, progressive, and civic-minded homogeneous community, along with the Cities' strikingly recalcitrant residential segregation, meant the urban core was not associated with the same kinds of socially constructed and imagined dangers of urban Blackness. Therefore, although civic elites feared the Twin

Cities could be at risk of the so-called urban decay taking shape in other cities, the area was largely viewed as thriving and a model for other cities.

Talk of a new stadium in the downtown core emerged at a time when the Twin Cities were investing in other kinds of urban infrastructure in the cultural realm, including the Guthrie Theater in 1963, Nicollet Mall in 1967, the Walker Art Center in 1971, and Orchestra Hall in 1974.[25] Stadium proponents saw a stadium as necessary to "gild that image" of Minneapolis as a thriving, sophisticated, and cosmopolitan city.[26] More important, they were fearful that not building a new, more modern stadium on par with other cities would risk Minneapolis' being demoted to a "minor league city." Stadium boosters evoked these fears to warn of potential financial and cultural consequences if that should happen. In his 1974 address to the annual meeting of the Minneapolis Chamber of Commerce, the chair of the Stadium Task Force, Harvey B. Mackay, warned if the Twin Cities did not build a new stadium, there was a real risk of losing their professional sports teams altogether. Mackay said such a loss would put the Cities "on our way to becoming a cold Omaha," thus stoking fears of the Twin Cities' demotion to a lower-tier city.[27]

By the late 1970s, there was a concerted effort by both the Twins and the Vikings, along with Twin Cities governing, business, and development elites, to build a new stadium downtown. However, stadium boosters found the public sentiment around stadium construction quite changed since the days of advocating for the Met. Rather than a wellspring of civic pride among "everyday citizens" to support a stadium that could gild the image of the Twin Cities as a cosmopolitan area, they instead ran into widespread opposition, especially to public funding. Further fueling the political struggle over the stadium was what Klobuchar describes as a strong council/weak mayor system in Minneapolis.[28] The city council had a much larger role to play in the stadium debate than in some other municipalities, and divisions within the council and between the council and the mayor's and governor's offices meant it was much more difficult to hammer out a deal.

Furthermore, most Minneapolis residents were against a new stadium. They expressed concerns over traffic, parking, pollution, and, especially, the taxpayer burden, calling into question the economic benefits that stadium proponents promised.[29] Opposition groups, such as Save the Met and Minnesotans Against a Downtown Dome (MADD), coalesced from a wide swath of the populace. They drew from fiscally conservative Republicans, socially progressive neighborhood groups, and fans opposed to indoor baseball and football or their commodification, forming a broad-based coalition to contest the stadium (see fig. 6.1).[30]

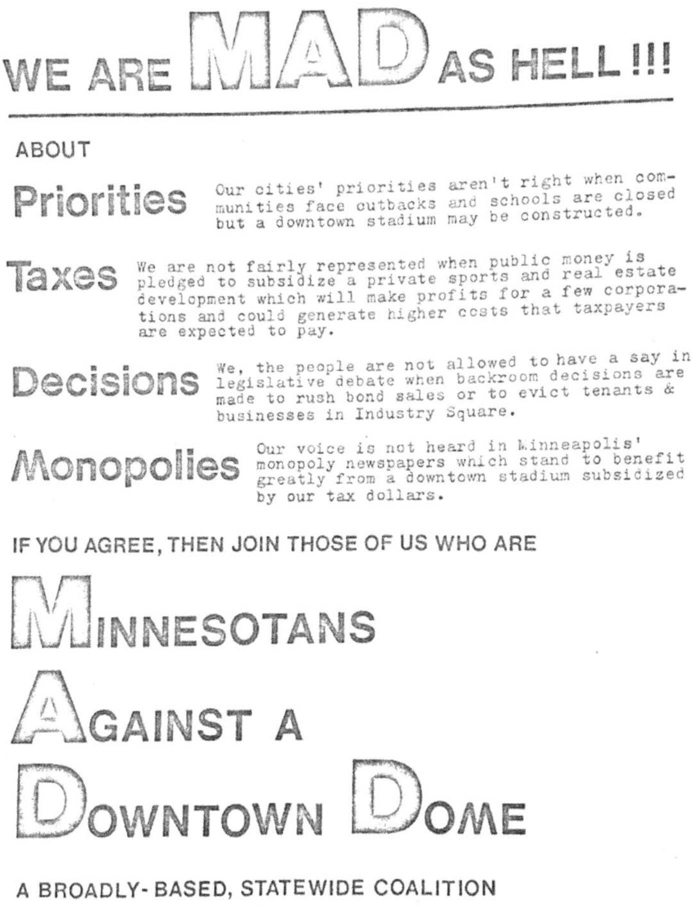

WE ARE MAD AS HELL!!!

ABOUT

Priorities — Our cities' priorities aren't right when communities face cutbacks and schools are closed but a downtown stadium may be constructed.

Taxes — We are not fairly represented when public money is pledged to subsidize a private sports and real estate development which will make profits for a few corporations and could generate higher costs that taxpayers are expected to pay.

Decisions — We, the people are not allowed to have a say in legislative debate when backroom decisions are made to rush bond sales or to evict tenants & businesses in Industry Square.

Monopolies — Our voice is not heard in Minneapolis' monopoly newspapers which stand to benefit greatly from a downtown stadium subsidized by our tax dollars.

IF YOU AGREE, THEN JOIN THOSE OF US WHO ARE

MINNESOTANS AGAINST A DOWNTOWN DOME

A BROADLY-BASED, STATEWIDE COALITION

Fig. 6.1: A flyer produced by Minnesotans Against the Downtown Dome (MADD), circa 1979. (Hennepin County Library, Minneapolis, MN)

Seeking to convince a disillusioned public to contribute to a publicly funded stadium, proponents, including the city, chamber of commerce, and downtown council, focused not only on economic benefits but also on social and "intangible" benefits. As with Seattle's stadium supporters, Twin Cities stadium proponents focused heavily on a quality-of-life discourse, suggesting that stadiums and professional sports were key to creating "social and economic health."[31] Boosters claimed the stadium would create entertainment and recreation activity that would be a "positive item in the comparative desirability of a community," which could in turn influence a company's decision to move or stay in the Twin Cities. Likewise, they said that the intangible benefits of a stadium downtown ensured "national publicity" through regular broadcasting on TV and radio. This would create "positive impact on regional prominence," leading proponents to conclude, "Socially and economically . . . we cannot afford to have the Vikings and Twins leave our state."[32]

Boosters wanted a downtown stadium to represent Minneapolis as a thriving cosmopolitan city, spark economic development, and revitalize the urban core.[33] They suggested that a downtown multipurpose stadium "would be a major economic stimulus to the city." Drawing on examples from Seattle, St. Louis, and New Orleans, they maintained that each city "encouraged new commercial buildings, hotels, restaurants, and retail stores in the area surrounding the stadium."[34] Further, the metropolitan council's 1977 recommendations on stadium locations argued that a downtown stadium would encourage more families to move downtown, expand downtown recreational activities, strengthen employment opportunities, and improve environmental quality through recreational development. Stating, "The Metro Centers are this Region's major source of identity," the council recommended that location and development priority should be given to projects, like a downtown stadium, that served to reinforce this status.[35]

This rationale represented Minneapolis as thriving and cosmopolitan while also responding to the rising competition from the suburbs and a belief that there needed to be the kinds of development that would attract middle-class families back to the city. It suggested the city's image needed to be constructed as safe for white, middle-class suburbanites. These discourses of a safe downtown full of recreation, entertainment, and culture are bound up with historically specific and racialized postwar fears of urban decline. Yet, they do not traffic in the overt racism at play in the Met.

Instead, the racial formation at work in the Metrodome's urban decline discourse draws on an inferentially racist logic. According to Stuart Hall, inferential racism refers to "naturalised representations of events and situations relating to race, whether 'factual' or 'fictional' which have racist premises and propositions inscribed in them as a set of *unquestioned assumptions*. These enable racist statements to be formulated without ever bringing into awareness the racist predicates on which the statements are grounded."[36] Inferential racism is a kind of "new racism," a term Eduardo Bonilla-Silva uses to describe the more subtle racism emerging in the 1970s after the implementation of civil rights legislation. The inferential nature of new racism defers race to coded signifiers in order to disavow accusations of bias.

This subtle coding can be gleaned in the idea of making downtown a safe and pleasant space, discourses ubiquitous across the archives on the Metrodome, including the promotional materials for the stadium once it was finally built. In the *Minneapolis Tribune*'s Metrodome Souvenir section, visitors are promised a "pleasant, safe, and enjoyable" visit, with "easy access, parking, entertainment, [and] shopping." The description of the Metrodome's downtown paints a bucolic view of Minneapolis, where visitors can "relax along the meandering tree lined Nicollet Mall or in one of over 16 atriums, plazas, or parks," promising them the best of both worlds: suburban agrarian life full of parks, beauty, and open spaces, with the shopping, culture, and entertainment of the urban. All the while, though, they are ensured safety through, for example, using the skyway system (started in the 1960s), ensuring they can "walk about downtown in comfort" without ever having to be a pedestrian, exposed on the street.[37]

These discourses drip of a white spatial imaginary, envisioning the stadium—and the urban it helps to produce more broadly—as a space secured for the enjoyment of the white, middle-class family. While whiteness and race are never explicitly mentioned, they reside in coded language that constructs the urban through appeals to a sensibility of white space as pleasant and safe. The kinds of subjects imagined to benefit from the stadium are likewise produced through seemingly innocent but racially loaded codes, as demonstrated in a 1977 document from the Sports Facilities Commission:

> The downtown business person can entertain his or her guest on a weekday or weekday evening by taking a cab or shuttle bus about eight blocks to the game. Because of the fast freeway system heading from all directions into Minneapolis, business people in other parts of the Metro area can drive downtown, catch a meal at the many fine restaurants, . . . and take in a game via shuttle bus or cab.
>
> People who like different kinds of entertainment will be pleased with planned multi-entertainment special events such as: Late afternoon games followed by a night at the Guthrie or Symphony Hall. All these facilities are already available in downtown.
>
> A lady who has a group of friends she wants to entertain by spending an afternoon at the Walker Art Center or Minneapolis Institute of Arts can have dinner at the Institute and then catch a cab to the stadium for a sports event that evening.
>
> Conventioneers will find it easy to walk or take a shuttle bus to the stadium. Senior citizens and young people from all over the Metro area can catch a regular route Metropolitan Transit Commission bus to the game. . . .
>
> On Saturdays and Sundays all persons attending the games will have an opportunity to enjoy the hiking trails and picnic facilities along the Mississippi river bank before and after the day game.
>
> People living downtown or in Loring Park or at the towers or in Cedar-Riverside will be able to walk or take a shuttle bus to the stadium.

>   For people who want employment, about 2,000 stadium jobs would be provided to people, many of whom would be inner-city youths. This is important to those families and youths.[38]

Notably, the racially coded language of "inner-city youths" seems to refer to Blackness and racial Otherness. Hence, the stadium was not envisioned through the same kind of white spatial imaginary as the first or second generation, which were more invested in segregation and explicit exclusion of Otherized bodies. Instead, Blackness and racial Otherness were included through a lens of racial uplift in the form of jobs. Black Minneapolis residents were not imagined to be the primary spectators who took their leisure time in and around the stadium—that was reserved for the businesspersons, ladies, and conventioneers—but, rather, as employees who served white fans.

While a downtown stadium was intended to participate in urban revitalization, the intent was never to engage in the kinds of placemaking practices we see in today's third-generation stadiums. Indeed, the Metrodome was never meant to respond to or benefit the neighborhoods around the ultimate site of the stadium, which were largely composed of working-class people and held a higher majority of people of color than other areas of the city. John Cowles, owner of the Minneapolis daily newspaper the *Minneapolis Star Tribune*, and a major stadium proponent, later reflected, "I don't connect the dots to the neighborhood around the stadium. I connect them to the central business district."[39]

Stakeholders tasked with selecting a location were largely driven by costs, seeking cheap downtown property (and where residents and businesses lacked political and economic capital to halt development). Still, while fighting with much of the public and within the legislature over public funding, stadium proponents argued vociferously over where the stadium should be located. Stadium legislation, agreeing to no more than $55 million in public financing, finally passed in 1977 only when the proposal included a "no site" proposal, where the Stadium Task Force insisted the location of the stadium was a "highly emotional" choice and therefore should not be decided by an unelected body.[40] That put the Metropolitan Sports Facilities Commission (MSFC), a new public entity created by the stadium legislation tasked with overseeing the public interest, in charge of choosing a site.

The MSFC struck a deal with business elites who agreed to set up a shell corporation—the Industry Square Development Company (ISDC)—to purchase land downtown adjacent to the Minneapolis Star and Tribune Company Building. John Cowles, president of the company and owner of both of the city's major daily papers, was a stadium proponent who headed the Stadium Site Task

Force. Cowles was already a controversial figure, as critics claimed he used his newspaper to persuade the public to support his own view on the stadium by publishing biased content and giving short shrift to stadium critics.[41] Cowles's ownership of the downtown property adjacent to the stadium meant he stood to benefit from the development more directly. Weiner notes that during the Metrodome debates, "Not only were cities in transition, but so were newspapers.... There was self-interest in maintaining population and strength in the urban core for Cowles."[42] According to Klobuchar, the ISDC was a unique public-private partnership that embodied the civic pride of Minneapolis' business elite, who were willing to take a loss (investors never expected to make a profit) in exchange for an investment in the public good.[43] In this sense, it bore the hallmark of early forms of neoliberal urbanism, ushering in an era of privatization of public space and inviting the question of whose interests were assumed by this ideal of "the public good."

Stadium opponents, especially those affiliated with neighborhoods being considered as potential stadium locations throughout the debates, raised this very question. The stadium opposition group MADD argued that the public's voice was excluded from the stadium debates. In one flyer, pictured in figure 6.1, emblazoned with the statement "We are MAD as Hell," MADD questioned stadium proponents' understanding of the public good, saying, "Our cities' priorities aren't right when communities face cutbacks and schools are closed but a downtown stadium may be constructed."[44] MADD organized public meetings and work committees, educational outreach and workshops, coalition meetings, lobbying at the capitol, and disrupted city meetings. Organized opposition influenced the legislature as well. The state senate staff published a critique of the Stadium Task Force in 1975, arguing that it wasn't representative of the public, since it included only business officials and labor leaders and had "no students, no jobless, no housewives, no teachers or medical professionals" representing the public's voice.[45]

Whereas Klobuchar claims there was nothing of significance in and around the stadium site—just "old warehouses, apartment buildings, and run down rooming houses"—and therefore the stadium "would not disrupt neighborhoods or business," neighborhood residents and activists suggested otherwise.[46] Residents in the areas of the proposed stadium sites rose up to contest the effects the stadium would have on their neighborhoods, declaring the stadium would neither revitalize nor improve quality of life but would instead harm their neighborhoods and siphon off already scant resources. The stadium, they said, was a "trade-off" with resources for other revitalization projects that had more direct benefits for the people who lived there. In contrast to the stadium proponents' white spatial imaginary, which viewed the city through a development lens, these groups offered an alternative imaginary rooted in neighborhood histories, a sense of place, and spatial justice.

These views are especially evident in a thirty-minute video program produced by Intermedia Arts Minnesota, a public access TV station located on the University of Minnesota's campus, titled *People and Causes: Citizen Participation and the Domed Stadium*. The host begins the program by explaining that *People and Causes* "is an open forum designed to let people be heard. It presents individual and citizen groups promoting, in their own way, the causes they feel are important."[47] This serves to undergird the main argument put forth by the activists opposing the stadium—namely, citizens had been left out of the debate. The program features a range of voices, from activists with the University District Improvement Association (UDIA), Leo Bernat (Housing and Redevelopment Authority commissioner for Minneapolis and former UDIA president), and state representative Phyllis Khan. All stress the significance of citizen participation in the stadium debate, pointing out that those from the neighborhoods who stood to be most impacted were never consulted.[48] The program also makes a strong case for the harm the stadium represents to what they suggest are already fragile neighborhoods. At the time of the video, one of the sites for the proposed stadium was in the Marcy Holmes neighborhood, located between downtown Minneapolis and the University of Minnesota's East Bank campus (see map 6.2). Rodney Loper, former president of the UDIA, asserted the stadium would be just one in a "long series of invasions of this community in terms of development." He said the stadium was "in the same class" as the Interstate 35-W freeway, which split the community in half and led to widespread dislocation and displacement in the heart of a residential community that continued to suffer.

Although the stadium was not ultimately located in Marcy Holmes, the neighborhoods abutting the Industry Square location were similarly fragile. Those neighborhoods—Elliot Park, Cedar-Riverside, and Phillips—coalesced to oppose the stadium, demanding an environmental impact study and decrying the stadium's potential harms. These neighborhoods have a long history as sites of the Dakota people, many of whom were displaced and forced westward when largely Scandinavian settlers first came to Elliot Park and Cedar-Riverside in the mid-1800s. However, the neighborhoods remain key to Indigenous life, providing spaces where numerous Native American peoples continue to reside and organize community life, politics, and culture.[49] The neighborhoods also include numerous working-class immigrant and Black peoples. That these neighborhoods were composed of higher numbers of poor people and people of color,

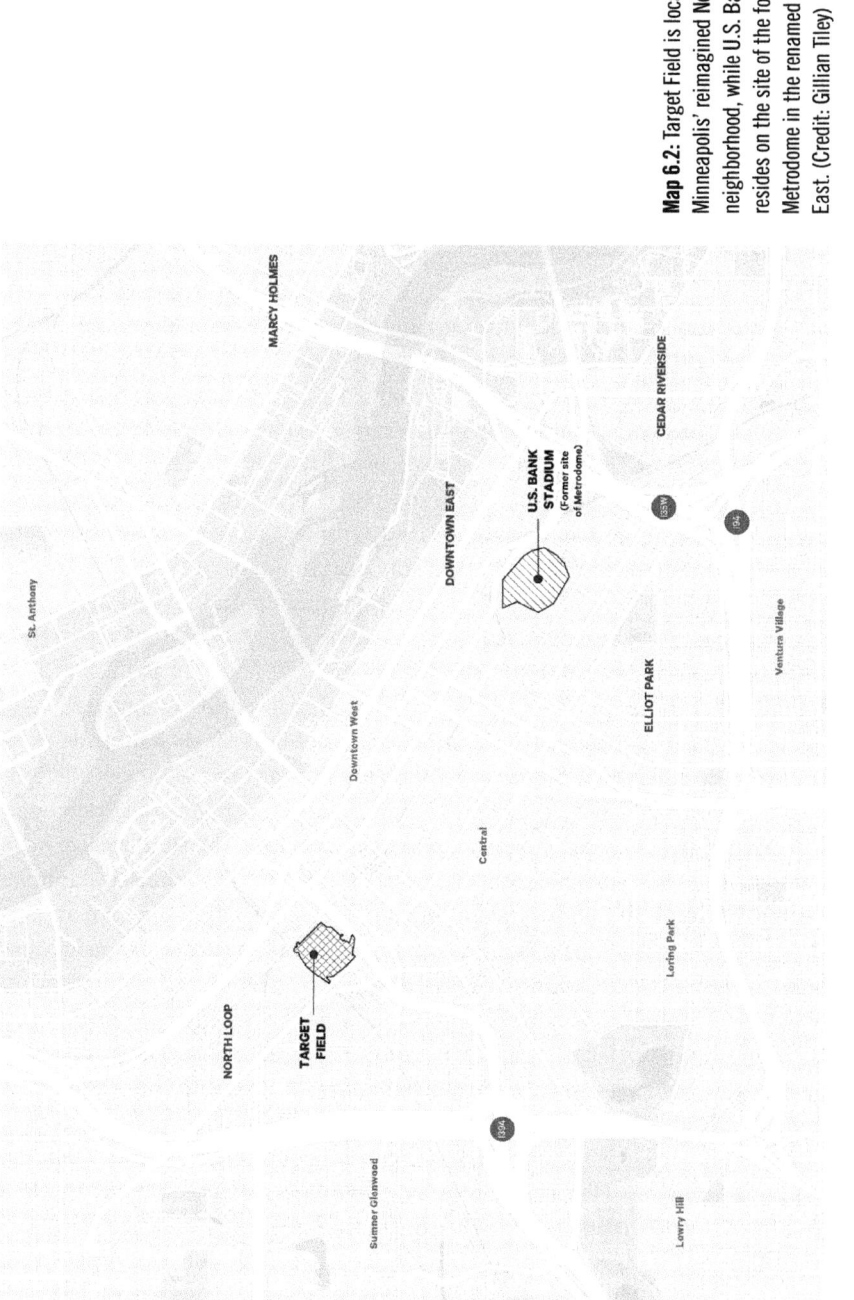

Map 6.2: Target Field is located in Minneapolis' reimagined North Loop neighborhood, while U.S. Bank Stadium resides on the site of the former Metrodome in the renamed Downtown East. (Credit: Gillian Tiley)

along with the systematic disinvestment in those neighborhoods, reflects the racialized geography of the Twin Cities more broadly. While for a time the area was home to wealthy elites during industrialization, the neighborhoods became largely working-class during the Depression and suffered further divestment as a result of postwar suburban white flight. The urban renewal programs of the 1950s and 1960s took a particularly hard hit on the area, creating displacement from the highway system. At the time of the stadium debates, the area, one of the more diverse in the Cities, was stabilizing, with sizable populations of newly arriving South Asian immigrants living alongside Indigenous peoples, refugees, and people of color in the city's more affordable housing stock.[50]

Opposition was especially strong in the Cedar-Riverside and the Elliot Park neighborhoods, closest to the Industry Square location. Cedar-Riverside residents had long been organizing around affordable housing. By the time the legislature decided on the stadium location and construction had started, neighborhood residents had waged a series of five rent strikes, some more effective than others, since 1974. The Cedar-Riverside Project Area Committee organized workshops to encourage citizen participation in the stadium debate where residents reflected on what the stadium would mean for them in terms of "cost, traffic, pollution," and "the social, environmental and economic impact of a stadium in Industry Square."[51]

Elliot Park raised similar concerns, largely organized by the Elliot Park Neighborhood Incorporated (EPNI), an organization of residents and businesses. In a series of letters to city officials in 1978, EPNI's then-president, K. B. Nowak, argued that officials were not taking the adverse effects of stadium construction seriously. Criticizing the draft Environmental Impact Statement, Nowak said the citizens who stood to benefit least from the stadium were going to be the ones most harmed, claiming, "In analysis of who uses stadiums compared to the city wide population you examine the disproportion of age, economic and educational factors without mentioning that in our neighborhood those disproportions are doubled. We have twice the city wide proportion of elderly, economically depressed and uneducated, and will thus benefit from stadium attendance less than anyone, even though we are closest in proximity."[52] Nowak also challenged the conclusion that the stadium would create economic opportunity and noted the potential for vandalism by rowdy fans after games. The Final Environmental Impact Statement conceded Nowak's claim that the stadium would have little benefit to the neighborhood. The statement noted that the city's predictions that there would be major development benefits and revitalization for the neighborhoods were overstated. The document drew from evidence from stadium construction in Pittsburgh and New Orleans to show that development in the adjacent area of Industry Square wouldn't necessarily be due to the stadium but to "continuing renewal efforts and other market considerations," concluding, "The stadium can serve as a major public use anchor in this otherwise marginal area and contribute to a changing image but it is not expected to directly induce adjacent development."[53]

Yet it was precisely this changing image that some organizers in these adjacent neighborhoods feared, as that image would mean the neighborhood would be gentrified and lack the affordable housing and service amenities that attracted the poor, working-class, transient, immigrant, refugee, elderly, and people of color who made up a disproportionate portion of the population. As noted above, stadium boosters did not consider neighborhood effects, as Nowak surmised, since they were invested instead in downtown development of the central business district. They saw the neighborhoods as problems to be overcome, seemingly seeing displacement as precisely what was needed. Nowak and Elliot Park's organizers contested this logic of space, staking a claim for rights of the people who lived there and their value to the city.

Once it was clear the stadium would be constructed in Industry Square with or without the neighborhood's acquiescence, organizers continued efforts to combat displacement and ensure the neighborhood would remain residential in character while also seeking other concessions from the city in the form of revitalization funds, prioritization of jobs for residents (especially residents of color), and mitigating traffic, parking, and air quality harms.[54] Even after the Metrodome finally opened in 1982, the neighborhood organization continued to try to mitigate its harms, advocating for and working to enforce critical parking zones and prevent displacement. In addition to using "direct action activities . . . to bring attention to the problems that will occur," the group used "press conferences, leafletting, picketing, etc." to make their voices heard, including putting out their own stadium guide to inform visitors about the neighborhood, their concerns, and how to respectfully engage with the space in ways that mitigated harm to residents and businesses.[55]

While stadium boosters made promises to the neighborhoods, most went unfulfilled. For example, they failed to follow through on hiring sizable numbers of people of color at the stadium, and they left it up to the neighborhoods themselves to enforce critical parking zones.[56] Moreover, the city failed to provide meaningful measures to prevent displacement. By December 1982, absentee landlords had already torn down three houses in Elliot Park to build parking lots.[57] While the *Minneapolis Tribune* covered the neighborhood's opposition and concerns about displacement in its special Souvenir section commemorating the Metrodome's opening, the paper described Elliot Park as an area consisting "mainly of older apartment buildings and houses that fill their lots, leaving little room for any lawns. Some blocks, with boarded up buildings, look similar to a ghetto. Other areas are undergoing renovation into attractive condominiums or small businesses."[58] The description of the neighborhood as a "ghetto" with a high transient population discouraged readers from identifying with the concerns of residents. Readers were instead encouraged to use a white spatial imaginary to associate Elliot Park with the urban Black underclass and to view displacement as a "benefit" that would turn it into a neighborhood full of attractive lawns and condos, signifiers of suburban, white, middle-class respectability.

This racial logic, and the production of space through a white spatial imaginary, is evident in the architecture and infrastructural design of the Metrodome. Critics noted from the beginning that the stadium was like a suburban outpost in downtown, failing to fit into the urban landscape at all. Like a mall, it was cut off from the surrounding neighborhoods, and it wasn't close enough to other downtown amenities to make it feel like it was a part of the larger urban fabric. The design prioritized access for the greatest number of spectators by connecting it to the highways, clearing surrounding land for large swaths of parking. Like Seattle's Kingdome, the widespread public opposition to public financing for the stadium meant cost-cutting heavily influenced architectural design. Architectural firm Skidmore, Owings, and Merrill (more recently known as SOM), which designed several other large buildings in the Twin Cities at the time, followed the cookie-cutter modernist style of other domes of the era.

While critics pointed to the design's lack of creativity, the integration of technology was heralded for its sophistication at the time. Noting its artificial turf and air-supported roof, Kristin Anderson writes, "The Metrodome represented a step forward into the modern technologies of local sports facilities, allowing Twin Cities fans to see in their own stadium some of the innovations already used earlier and elsewhere. When comparing the technologies of Metropolitan Stadium to those of the Metrodome, the leap seemed large and dramatic."[59] In contrast to the Met, the Metrodome placed a premium on comfort, including benches with contoured backs, some individual seats, and more bathrooms. However, as sports journalist R. T. Rybak noted in the *Tribune*'s Souvenir section, "Fans will find that it is not a luxurious building. That's the way the stadium commission wanted it."[60] Its bare-bones, modernist aesthetic and concrete catered to the middle-class fan and a Minnesotan sensibility of thrift and industriousness.

Whereas the destruction of Seattle's Kingdome sparked an outpouring of affection for the stadium, few fans lament and mourn the passing of the Metrodome with the same kind of sentimentality. Vitriol against the Metrodome as a space for watching and playing sports began even before it opened. However, the stadium was commended by some for its multipurpose uses. Governor Mark Dayton referred to the Metrodome as "Minnesota's Rec Room" and the nickname stuck, seeming to resonate with a sense that the building provided a place for the public to gather and recreate. When there were no games, the building hosted amateur sports, rollerblading and running, exhibitions and conventions, gatherings for Scandinavian and Hmong communities, monster truck shows, rock concerts, and religious events. Although the building was designed for and catered to sports fans, it was appropriated for other uses as well. However, some groups were able to access the space more than others. The Metrodome remained cut off, infrastructurally, architecturally, and symbolically, from the surrounding neighborhoods. What it meant for those neighborhoods was largely greater disinvestment, more nuisances in terms of parking and traffic, and increased policing.

Third Generation: Take 1

Although neighborhood activists did not prevent the Metrodome's construction, as with the activism opposing the other stadiums discussed throughout this book, opponents laid the groundwork and provided the cultural memory and discourses that informed the next generation of stadium opponents. And in this next round in Minneapolis, at least for a time, it seemed the opponents would clench a rare victory. The third-generation struggle over building a stadium positioned Minneapolis as a linchpin in the debate about stadiums and their role in the urban, not only around public funding and economic benefits but also with regard to cultural values.[61]

The Metrodome seemed doomed to fail almost from the beginning, and talk of a new stadium, particularly for the Twins, began almost as soon as the stadium opened in 1982. The Twins negotiated an "escape clause" in their thirty-year lease, which, they asserted, was necessary since stadium revenue deals favored the Vikings (whereas the Met gave the Twins a significant advantage). The escape clause enabled the Twins to break their lease if they failed to sell more than $1.4 million in tickets per year for three consecutive seasons, or if the team sustained an operating loss over three years.[62] To add insult to injury, the tide was turning on the multipurpose dome, and Minnesota found itself, like Atlanta, at the tail end of a movement. Once Camden Yards opened in 1992, the death knell rang—the Metrodome would not do. Thus, just ten years after the Metrodome opened, a new round of stadium building in Minneapolis seemed inevitable. By 1996, Carl Pohlad, the Minnesota Twins' owner since 1984, had gone public with a demand for a new ballpark, suggesting he would enact the escape clause if there weren't plans for a new stadium by 1998.[63]

But just as the tide had turned on multipurpose domes, so too had public funding for sports stadiums, especially in Minneapolis. Armed with research stemming from the stadium debates over the Metrodome, opponents in this next round also drew on an emerging academic consensus that stadiums were not good investments.[64] This research gave stadium opponents tools with which to counter proponents and demonstrate how stadiums benefit the few at the expense of many. In addition to academic research, the urban growth coalition in Minneapolis had also changed. While proponents for the Metrodome struggled to gather the same kind of civic leadership and investment they had been able to draw on to build the Met, when the time came to advocate for a third generation of stadium building in the Twin Cities, that coalition was even more fractured. Changes in both urbanism and economics intertwined to shift the Cities' civic leadership, particularly in the advent of globalization and financialization. The Twin Cities were not necessarily considered a global city, but they attracted businesses run by people and firms located elsewhere, making them less susceptible to affective arguments centered on civic pride. Together, these factors positioned Minneapolis as a litmus test and turning point for the next generation, at least for a time.[65]

While these conditions—the globalization of cities and new research showing stadiums' economic downfalls—were not unique to Minneapolis, other key site-specific historical contexts also shaped the nature of the third-generation stadium debate. Most notably, the Twin Cities' hockey team, the Minnesota North Stars, departed for Dallas in 1993, and St. Paul had already been lobbying for a new arena to bring hockey back. Meanwhile, Minneapolis built an arena at Target Center in 1990 for the city's new NBA team (the Timberwolves), but like the Stars, they too were threatening to leave for New Orleans.[66] Politicians and stadium proponents used a lot of their political capital lobbying for these infrastructures, and there was therefore little political will remaining to support yet another stadium, especially since the Metrodome was relatively new.

Stadium proponents initially relied on largely economic arguments for a new ballpark for the Twins, suggesting both the financing and style of ballparks had changed and put the Twins at a competitive disadvantage. Changes in mediasport—that is, the intertwined institutions and practices of media and sport—were also a factor. As Weiner argues, "Teams were owned by an increasing number of media companies.... If the economics of baseball were driven by ticket sales in the seventies and broadcast rights in the eighties, it was the stadium boom that fed the insatiable monster of the nineties."[67] In a 1997 document analyzing stadium options, the MSFC said that the Metrodome was "no longer a viable baseball stadium, especially compared to newer baseball stadiums such as Orioles Park at Camden Yards, Jacobs Field and Coors Field, all of which have far superior revenue-generating capacity," citing the Metrodome's poor sight lines along with lack of advertising and naming, suite, and parking revenue.[68] Proponents claimed there was a real threat of losing the Twins, once again invoking fears of Minneapolis becoming a minor league city, pointing to the departure of the Cities' professional hockey team, the North Stars, as evidence.

Initial designs released for the ballpark in January 1997 emphasized a baseball-only stadium replicating Camden Yards' retro-modern style. Although there was reportedly excitement over the initial plan, since it would bring outdoor baseball back to Minneapolis, news about the massive public funding required to build it quickly created controversy.[69] Proponents waged a major public relations campaign—called Minnesota Wins—to persuade the public to "Save the Twins." Critics, in contrast, questioned why the Twins owners, the billionaire Pohlad family, didn't save the Twins themselves. The stadium debate thus ignited class antagonisms in the Twin Cities, which had long been bubbling beneath the surface. The Minnesota Public Advocacy Research Team (MPART) noted, in their rhetorical analysis of the stadium debate of this era, that stadium proponents ultimately failed on several fronts: They had no clear leader or strategy, failed to identify who their audience was, and focused too much on sports economics.[70]

While stadium proponents waged a flawed campaign, credit is largely due to efforts of stadium opponents, who in this round of stadium debates organized a powerful opposition to public funding rooted in a question of values and identity. The group Fund Kids First, for example, was especially effective. The group drew on the ethos and moral authority of its founder, Reverend Ricky Rask, a fifty-two-year-old grandmother, to question why the public should fund a new stadium for a billionaire when the public schools were underfunded, kids were going hungry, and parents couldn't afford day care.[71] On getting involved in the stadium debate, Rask, who had fought for grandparents' rights to custody when children are taken into the care of the state, noted, "One morning I picked up the paper, and I saw they [the Twins] wanted $250 million. . . . I was just enraged. Something was clearly wrong with this picture in light of the fact I was living through meetings, and I was learning how little society regards children."[72] Rask framed the public funding as a matter of social justice, drawing attention to impoverished mothers and children, to show the stadium benefited a particular group of elite white men.

In MPART's view, the opposition effectively shifted the frame from corporate economics to values, labeling public funding of the stadium a matter of corporate welfare. Opponents pointed out how much of the stadium debate took place behind closed doors, without transparent or open discussion with the public. They reframed the debate from a perspective of grassroots economics and implored the public to question how public funds were used. Opposition groups, including Fund Kids First, Minnesota Alliance for Progressive Action, and Fans Advocating iNtelligent Spending (FANS), coalesced around equity and strategically engaged the local media to persuade the public.[73] By 1998, after multiple defeats in the legislature, it seemed any hope of a stadium deal was dead. Minneapolis became a primary example of a new era of political chaos that appeared to mark the third generation as well as the potential for opponents to organize and win.

Third Generation: Take 2

Although it looked like chances of a new stadium were defeated, proponents continued to strategize. In August 2000 the Minneapolis mayor, Sharon Sayles Belton, called for a new ballpark committee, the Committee of 17 (C-17), composed of seventeen residents and business representatives—four appointed by the mayor and the remaining members by the Minneapolis City Council. They were tasked with exploring "the possibility of designing and building an urban ballpark that would be privately financed, produce the revenues necessary for the baseball team and financiers, stimulate compatible urban development, and improve the urban fabric of Minneapolis."[74]

According to Nick Koch, C-17 was the turning point for the stadium debate. Koch was board chair of NuLoop Partners, a public-private organization born out of C-17 and committed to design and development in the North Loop neighborhood around Target Field. Koch claims C-17 created a new framework for the stadium focused on six key words: "transit oriented, compact ballpark, urban neighborhood."[75] Attentiveness to connectivity and the urban neighborhood represented a major shift. C-17 drew on discourses of placemaking and constructing a sense of urban neighborhood specificity. Even at this early date, the group was "thinking about urbanism, connection, fabric, . . . cities, housing, [and] living in an integrated urban neighborhood." For C-17 members, they saw what they were doing—planning for an "'urban neighborhood' scale ballpark that can be privately financed"—as "entirely new," a "departure from the way almost every other new major league ballpark has been conceived in the last decade."[76] Indeed, their emphasis on neighborhood placemaking as a key logic *was* a departure from earlier eras of stadium building, even if overstated, since ballparks like Seattle's T-Mobile Park, the Pittsburgh Pirates' PNC Park, and others drew on similar discourses.

Although not forgoing economic arguments altogether, like their opponents, stadium proponents shifted to the realm of values and affect, imagining the stadium as an urban infrastructure participating in city and neighborhood place-making. As C-17's report to the mayor and city council reads:

> Outside of any debate about the economics of baseball, the national pastime generates public goods. There are benefits that are hard to articulate, but easy to feel. This instinctive understanding of the benefits underlies the passion of ballpark proponents in arguments on the street, on the radio, and even in our committee meetings. The sense of something unique, something genuinely American, is fundamental to our experience of the game. To lose it would be sad.... We like having the Twins here—rooting for a team joins people together, gives people from all walks of life common ground.[77]

This refrain of the stadium bringing people together "from all walks of life," invoking nationalist ideals of a "genuinely American" pastime, constitutes an overarching logic in subsequent discourse on the stadium in Minneapolis. This discourse counters opponents' claims about the public good and where money should be spent, addressing specifically the kinds of claims made by Fund Kids First and others about inequity. This is because the C-17 discourse imagines the ballpark as a space for healing those inequities by bringing people together. But it rests on the contention that healing and connection is not accomplished merely by watching the game but through infrastructural changes and place-making practices enabled by the stadium.

The first rounds of the third-generation stadium debate were criticized as backroom deals made by elites, keeping the public out of the loop. C-17's meetings, in contrast, were open to the public, broadcast on public access television, and shared on the web. Tasked with setting the terms of engagement for the city, Koch says the group took its role seriously, including questioning the value of a stadium at all, and, if a stadium were going to be built, what kind of values would it embody? The group concluded a ballpark was worthwhile, but they called for it to be scaled down, provide public space, include community engagement, and be privately financed, including significant investment from the Twins. Their report acknowledged, "Ballparks are not good development generators" and, instead, recommended "the ballpark be used to enhance the development of existing entertainment venues in the city."[78]

Following C-17's report, in 2002 the MSFC published a *Stadium Issue Resource Guide* in another attempt to persuade the public they needed a new stadium. The report details the MSFC's "Town Hall listening tour," where they, along with Twins representatives (the Vikings opted not to participate), traveled around the state to seven communities in order to engage "the public in a statewide discussion on the future of professional sports in Minnesota and ultimately move toward the 'Minnesota solution.'"[79] They concluded that the public's tone was different from what it was in 1997, assuring readers the public did indeed want a stadium solution, but they wanted to shape it. While C-17 recommended private financing, the Twins and stadium proponents continued to seek other funding opportunities. With the Minneapolis City Council still refusing to participate in a funding package, proponents turned to Hennepin County. The county stepped in to offer a public-private partnership with the Twins organization and to levy county taxes to finance part of the stadium in January 2004.[80]

C-17's focus on how the ballpark could enhance neighborhoods and connectivity reflected the urban planning agenda in Minneapolis at the time. The 2003 "Downtown East/North Loop Master Plan," focused on the framework of "complete communities."[81] The plan reimagines downtown spatiality, creating a barbell-shaped area of focus for planning anchored by the two stadiums, noting that the two neighborhoods—Downtown East (site of the Metrodome and eventually UBS) and the North Loop (site of the future Target Field)—needed to be seen as "development pairs" to assess how the stadiums could reshape downtown as a whole but through a focus on neighborhood specificity. The plan defines complete communities as "neighborhoods or districts that are self-sufficient by virtue of interconnected transit and commercial environments that are, in turn, surrounded by a diversity of housing types, services, and amenities."[82] This discourse reveals an investment in neighborhood, a divergence from the rhetoric of the Metrodome, which focused on downtown. Instead, complete communities emphasize placemaking and neighborhood preservation, pointing to the need for affordable housing and diversity. However, the plan also warns of the dangers of "NIMBYism" (Not in my backyard) being enacted in the name of preservation, claiming, "Efforts must be taken to ensure that beneficial development is not stalled under the guise of 'neighborhood preservation.' . . . Neighborhoods are not static entities. . . . That sort of dynamism must be understood and embraced."

It is thus within this framework of connecting communities and the "six magic words"—transit oriented, compact ballpark, urban neighborhood—that Target Field took shape. The ballpark sits between the Warehouse District and the North Loop.[83] The dense urban location made construction technically challenging. This enhanced stadium boosters' claims that it represented a return to an "authentic" urban baseball experience. But for the Minneapolis City Planning Office, Transit Authority, and the Minnesota Ballpark Authority, that challenge also represented an opportunity, as the ballpark could be used to maximize transportation connectivity, connecting downtown to other parts of the city, and enhance public transportation and the pedestrian experience.[84]

After the Twins deal was finalized in 2005, the Vikings ramped up lobbying for a new stadium as well. When the Metrodome fabric roof collapsed in 2010 after a heavy snowfall, it seemed to be inevitable. Like the falling tiles in the Kingdome, this visual signifier of the Metrodome's failure—played repeatedly on TV and the internet—seemed to call out the stadium's death knell. The state's new governor, Mark Dayton, was also more favorable to another stadium. Eventually, the Vikings made a deal for $498 million in subsidies from both Minneapolis and the state.[85]

In his commemorative souvenir books for UBS and Target Field, Steve Berg, a Twin Cities journalist, says the arguments over this stadium-building generation in Minneapolis represented an identity struggle. Berg claims, "Minnesotans suffered through a kind of marathon therapy session in which they asked tough questions about themselves and their place in the world. . . . What kind of place should Minnesota be?"[86] On one side, Berg locates the "populists," referring to the provincial side of the Minnesotan identity with its "agrarian roots, our fierce populism, and piestic values," and on the other, the cosmopolitan, wanting to keep up with trends of other major cities. Berg suggests the "pragmatic" side won: Modern, forward-looking stadiums were built, enabling the city to keep up with its competitors, but with design elements and sensibilities that paid tribute to Minnesota as a unique place with its own history and identity.

Nevertheless, the stadiums represent more than a struggle over values and culture; they are also racial struggles, undergirded by a racial logic rarely acknowledged in Minnesota. The provincialism Berg refers to speaks to an underlying attachment to whiteness in Minnesota, while cosmopolitanism appears to open the city up to race and diversity. But the latter does so in a circumscribed way, rooted in diversity and a sense of place-specificity as market-based, erasing the kinds of diversity that already exist in the Twin Cities and in Minnesota more generally.

As Target Field and U.S. Bank Stadium mark a significant shift in the racial logic undergirding the stadium, the discourse animating these new stadiums recognizes the harms and faults of earlier generations, promising these stadiums will right those wrongs by connecting communities and healing cuts, especially in the case of Target Field. But recognition alone does not equal justice. As I describe in the next chapter, these stadiums enact new racial formations, logics, and practices of space, all of which remain rooted in a white spatial imaginary.

CHAPTER 7

Surveillance and the Datafied Stadium

Today's stadiums are some of the most secure buildings on the planet.[1] They are equipped with sophisticated technologies of surveillance, security guards, state and local police, stewards, ushers, and building materials and architectural designs that symbolically communicate and materially produce securitization. Spectators too are enjoined to play a role in securing the stadium, through self-regulation of their own and others' behaviors. Whether preventing and containing threats from outside or within the stadium, this securitization constructs the stadium as a space for "pure" sport through the identification and removal of threats. These practices, made possible through mediatization and datafication, produce the stadium as a white space; they mediate interactions between and among stadium bodies and orchestrate their behaviors to align with white, liberal citizenship ideals while subjecting those who threaten that ideal to more punitive forms of discipline and control. Consequently, fans are promised that technologies of surveillance, including harvesting their data, will create a more meaningful and fun fan experience.

In this chapter, I focus on how a white spatial imaginary structures Minneapolis' third-generation stadiums' design, architecture, and mediatization to organize bodies, structure practices of looking, and assign and constitute meaning. Specifically, I address how practices of surveillance and datafication constitute Target Field and U.S. Bank Stadium as sites that racialize, manage, and police bodies. The stadiums' surveillant and datafying capabilities work as forms of crowd control that "cleanse" and "civilize" stadium and urban space, producing both as white space.

Whereas earlier generations of stadiums (discussed in chapter 6) were rooted in historically specific racial logics—the more overt racialized spatialization of the Met and the inferential racism of the Metrodome—Minneapolis's third generation draws on logics of color-blind and neoliberal racism. Color-blind racism, defined by Eduardo Bonilla-Silva, is the enactment of racism through the repudiation of race and the denial that racial difference exists or matters.[2] It is tied to a politics of post-racialism: the rationale that racism ended with the enactment of civil rights legislation. Claims to a post-racial society are often legitimated by the apparent emergence of a Black middle class. While the inferential (or "new racism") of the second-generation era rearticulated overt racist impulses onto signifiers and codes of more subtle forms of racism, color-blind racism is "based on the superficial extension of the principles of liberalism to racial matters that results in 'raceless' explanations for all sort of race-related affairs."[3] Segregation, for example, is explained as a matter of choice and a desire to "self-segregate" rather than an effect of racist systems and structures.

This emphasis on choice and self-responsibility ties color-blind racism to neoliberalism, and its practice can also be described as a form of neoliberal racism. Henry Giroux writes:

> Neoliberal racism is about the privatization of racial discourse.... Neoliberal racism asserts the insignificance of race as a social force and aggressively roots out any vestige of race as a category at odds with an individualistic embrace of formal rights. Focusing on individuals rather than on groups, neoliberal racism either dismisses the concept of institutional racism or maintains that it has no merit. In this context, racism is primarily defined as a form of individual prejudice while appeals to equality are dismissed outright.[4]

Solutions to racial "problems" in neoliberalism therefore obfuscate state-based welfare solutions and instead promote individual entrepreneurial freedoms to redress economic and cultural exclusion. According to David Theo Goldberg, these shifts center on *race* rather than *racism*, eschewing broader structural critiques or antagonisms.[5] In mediasport, including the stadium, neoliberal racism manifests in discourses of the "post-racial," with celebrations of racial and ethnic difference as forms of consumable lifestyle while eliding histories of struggle and their politicization.[6]

As I detail in the remainder of this chapter, color-blind and neoliberal racism are what animate the third-generation stadium's white spatial imaginary through practices of surveillance and datafication. Specifically, I analyze three key practices: (1) crowd control measures produced by discourses of security and risk management, including the integration of surveillance technologies, boundary production, and zoning; (2) mediatized and datafied design and architectural practices that encourage identification with a white surveillant gaze; and (3) the integration of interactive technologies and practices framed through a discourse of the "fan experience" that enables data harvesting to manage and predict behavior. While celebrating diversity and ostensibly rectifying racial injustice, Minneapolis' third-generation stadiums hinge on practices of individualization and choice, deferring questions of structural racism to the seemingly objective reality of data. They are thus undergirded by a white spatial imaginary linked to color-blind and neoliberal racism. I conclude the chapter by reflecting on the possibilities and limitations of the teams' antiracism work.[7]

Race, Surveillance, and Datafication

Surveillance and the forms of power it institutes are inextricably tied to racial capitalism, settler colonialism, and anti-Blackness. Modern surveillance emerged out of colonization, the transatlantic slave trade, the plantation, and slave patrols that produced modern policing and prisons.[8] The racialized roots of surveillance subject BIPOC bodies to more punitive and carceral practices, as their bodies are always-already constructed as potential threats. It is the structural exclusion and denial of subjecthood to these bodies on which the "civilized" liberal subject is built. By its very nature, Catherine Zimmer argues, "surveillance is thus, at its origins, designed to produce identity along racial lines, while at the same time disavowing identity in order to maintain the racialized subject as object."[9] Surveillance thus participates in social ordering, upholding what Simone Browne suggests are "negating strategies that first accompanied European colonial expansion and transatlantic slavery that sought to structure social relations and institutions in ways that privilege whiteness."[10] Surveillance, backed up by the threat of policing, is central to white space and white supremacy.

While third-generation stadiums employ architectural and design measures to enhance surveillance capabilities, including boundary construction, lighting, and zoning, a major innovation for this generation of stadiums is its sophisticated integration of digital technology. This integration makes the stadium a site for the mass production of data and its harvesting. Innovations in big data and data analytics, "smart" technologies, and AI, now regular features of stadium construction and experience, make these practices possible. Stadium datafication is a component of datafying sport more broadly.

Big data, according to Mark Andrejevic, describes "the emergence of the prospect of making sense of an incomprehensibly large trove of recorded data—the promise of being able to put it to meaningful use even though no individual or group of individuals can comprehend it."[11] Data analytics—technologies that enable data to be sorted to find patterns—makes this possible; big data is used in conjunction with smart technologies to put data analytics into use. Smart technologies are "equipped with sensors, actuators and pre-programmed controllers" and rely on communication networks that enable "a structure to adapt to unpredictable external loading conditions."[12] The integration of smart technologies into the stadium produces a "smart stadium," where, according to Chamee Yang and C. L. Cole, "games are no longer just an object of commodified spectacles but an ongoing site of data exploitation and experimentation that involves athletes, stadium managers, fans, and researchers who either voluntarily or unknowingly contribute to the overarching regime of innovation."[13] The integration of digital media technology, including fiber optics, computer and networking systems, high-speed Wi-Fi, high-definition video, and GPS into the fabric of stadium infrastructure makes the smart stadium possible. Smart technologies are integrated into ticketing, parking, restrooms, concessions, surveillance, and more. They enable an instantaneous response to immediate needs and guide the design and implementation of practices to respond to future needs. This response requires the ubiquity of digital "touchpoints" to enable the constant collection, monitoring, and sorting of data.

Increasingly, stadiums are equipped with AI, which has rapidly expanded and developed in sophistication and use. AI refers to machine learning, where machines can make changes and decisions on their own, without human input, based on what they learn. Increasingly, stadiums integrate AI not only in their more conventional use—e.g., for data analytics—but also in more novel forms of generative AI. These technologies allow real-time responses and recommendations for fans and teams alike, turning the constant monitoring and collection of data into generative responses.[14] Such forms of AI are used in stadiums in a multitude of ways, from immersive virtual reality experiences, stadium navigation, personalized content, biometric heart monitoring (to determine when fans are most excited), ticketing, and parking assistance.[15]

Access to data analytics, smart technology, and AI, however, is not available to all, creating what Andrejevic refers to as the "data rich" and the "data poor." He maintains, "Putting the data to use requires access to and control over costly technological infrastructures, expensive data sets, and the software, processing power, and expertise for analyzing them. . . . The era of big data . . . ushers in powerful new capabilities for decision making and prediction unavailable to those without access to the databases, storage, and processing power."[16] Big data's power dynamics are therefore asymmetrical, creating a division between those who do the sorting and those who are sorted, the latter often without knowledge or consent. Moreover, because big data analytics is thought to be devoid of human subjectivity and error, it is viewed as more objective. Yet, as research shows, data analytics relies on algorithms produced by humans, thereby often importing existing bias.[17] This is true for smart technologies and emerging forms of AI as well, which rely on data and informational sets that can include preexisting biases.[18] In response to these criticisms, within the policing and sports worlds especially, those who use data analytics focus on its use in crowd surveillance. This makes it appear as though it is drawing on aggregate data rather than targeting individuals or social groups. However, as Hidefumi Nishiyama argues in his study of crowd surveillance practices in Japan, this claim is misleading, since it "does not capture the subtler relations between urban surveillance and forms of racism."[19] Specifically, Nishiyama points to how "racial coding operates in the classification of a particular crowd abnormality," such as racializing public loitering or coding BIPOC neighborhoods as security threats.[20] Encoded biases, and the obfuscation of that bias through appeals to discourses of objectivity and aggregation, are evident in Minneapolis' stadiums.

Crowd Control and Risk Management

A central feature of third-generation stadiums is securitization and risk management strategies that perform crowd control. The stadium design firm Populous, which designed Minneapolis' Target Field, notes that the "destructive impulse which may arise in crowds of otherwise civilised sporting fans is ... nothing new." But, they assure readers, "nowadays we have a more systematic understanding which can be applied to both the design of stadiums and their management."[21] The designs instill specific rules and orchestrate emotions to unfold in predictable ways. Thus, stadiums ensure "they only enable a collective 'release of emotion' within certain boundaries of intensity."[22] Those boundaries reinforce norms of "civility" through their juxtaposition to constructs of "destructive" behavior. It is these rules—some spoken, some unspoken—and the orchestration of them through a stadium's design, mediatization, and datafication that produces the stadium through a white spatial imaginary.

Although safety has always been a component of modern stadium discourse, since the COVID-19 pandemic and the protests surrounding George Floyd's murder, stadium officials in Minneapolis have doubled down on discourses of security. These include calls for police to crack down on crime around the stadiums, despite the protests aimed to demonstrate racial bias in Minneapolis' policing.[23] Thus, while Floyd's murder and the protests it ignited made racism and racial justice a central talking point among Minneapolis' stadium executives, neither team disengaged their policing contracts. Indeed, David St. Peter, Twins president, noted in our interview, "We work very closely with the Minneapolis Police Department, . . . the Met Transit Police Department, as well as the Downtown Improvement District . . . to coordinate and collaborate" around safety concerns.[24]

In addition to partnering closely with police, St. Peter suggests they have invested heavily in their own security apparatus, insisting the Twins were "ensuring that we're doing our part to provide a level of security and ultimately safety for our fans and employees at our ballpark. . . . It's not the type of thing we think of [as] exclusively being outsourced. It's something we're taking our own responsibility for. . . . I think of it more as a network of community, of security and public safety and we're playing our part as part of that network."[25] This statement shows how the kind of affective community the ballpark aims to produce is predicated on its networking to this security apparatus. When asked to provide more specific details on that apparatus—what companies, technologies, techniques, or practices were used—St. Peter claimed it was "proprietary" information. His response demonstrates the stadium's asymmetrical power relations, with stadium owners and executives requiring fans, workers, players, and attendees to submit to monitoring while shielding themselves from being monitored. It also demonstrates the increasing privatization of security in policing in the neoliberal city as unelected, profit-driven corporate entities take on the duties of managing public security.

The emphasis on securing third-generation stadiums and conducting crowd control is linked to discourses of risk management, which attends to threats both within and outside the stadium. Risk management strategies govern how stadiums are designed to contain threats to ensure both safety (*for* those within the stadium) and security (*from* those positioned as "outside," where outside can also be indicative of the outside within).

In the Institution of Civil Engineers' stadium guidebook, stadiums are discursively constructed as spaces at risk from "multiple threats" inside and outside the stadium, naming "direct action protest" in the same vein as biological terrorism.[26] Populous uses the discourse of "riot," a classed and racially coded term, to warn designers of the potential for the "crowd to become a mob, and that mob to become a riot."[27] Consequently, Populous encourages designers to build facilities for "mass arrest." When BLM protests erupted in Los Angeles in the summer of 2020, police used the mass arrest facilities at UCLA's Jackie

Robinson Stadium to detain protesters.[28] The irony of using that particular stadium, named after the first Black baseball player to break the color line in the MLB, for the mass arrest of people protesting anti-Black police brutality, was not lost on protesters. But the materiality of the stadium, built with the express purpose of enabling this kind of suppression of mass resistance, reveals how the stadium's symbolic naming works to incorporate a sense of racial diversity and inclusion while policing real political struggle.

Three key techniques of crowd control and risk management that produce a white spatial imaginary are worthy of noting here: surveillance technologies, boundary management, and zoning.

SURVEILLANCE TECHNOLOGIES

The most significant technique of risk management to conduct crowd control is surveillance, enhanced through the integration of digital technology and datafication. Integrating media technology through broadcast television and the institution of CCTV revolutionized the stadium as an efficient space for surveillance, where, as John Bale notes, "surveillance provide[s] knowledge while knowledge provide[s] power and control."[29] CCTV connects surveillance cameras in Target Field and UBS to the surrounding area, making the stadiums and their neighborhoods some of the most heavily surveilled areas in the state. At its opening, UBS boasted sixty-five 16-megapixel cameras able to zoom in and create high enough definition to read text on a fan's T-shirt. This is in addition to the more than three hundred surveillance cameras placed throughout the venue.[30] The ubiquity of cameras in contemporary sporting and urban contexts ensures that each spectator (and worker and player) knows they are always potentially being watched. They are encouraged to internalize the surveillant gaze of the camera in order to self-regulate their behavior and emotions.

The surveillant capabilities of CCTV in today's stadiums are augmented with sophisticated technology to enable efficient and individualized modes of surveillance. To determine camera placement and usage, security managers for UBS "took a deep dive into our video analytics" to create "situational awareness"—that is, security "can investigate incidents by analyzing motions that set off an alarm that is then investigated."[31] Equipped with smart technology, the cameras enable more efficient use of CCTV than in past generations; they do not depend on an individual observer to watch endless hours of footage. Rather, personnel are automatically alerted through smart systems to conduct crowd control and identify suspicious activity.

The Vikings also use operations management provided by 24/7 Software, a global operations and safety management company catering to large venues.

The software provides a "centralized repository, live mapping, and real time communication and reporting" to venue operators, also networking to third-party software.[32] The platform includes, among other means of tracking, incident management and reporting, live mapping, real-time communication, and activity tracking, promising clients that the platform enables "proactivity" rather than "reactivity." Billy Langenstein, director of event services for UBS, reports that the software alerts them to an average of 750 incidents per game, noting that the software "syncs directly into the IMS [Information Management System], along with our facial recognition, 3D visualization, elevator and escalator alarms system, and our panic buttons around the property. If a drone or a fight is spotted via our camera system, it's entered into the IMS in real time, which instantly enhances our communication because a notification is sent to need-to-know personnel for faster response."[33] In addition to enhancing stadium security, risk mitigation, and response, 24/7 Software enables surveillance of workers and vendors, maximizing the venue's profitability to ensure return on investment (ROI). As the company described in one of their webinars, venues can use the platform's data analytics "to prove performance and ROI to stakeholders by showing labor hours or how much a product is being used."[34] Referred to as "chargeback"—because the metrics can be used to charge companies back if the work is not equivalent to what they were initially charged—the dashboard "can clearly illustrate work orders to show exactly how much work is being done."[35]

BOUNDARY MANAGEMENT

By creating fortress-like structures that clearly demarcate between inside and outside, stadium architecture creates an enclosure that enables risk management via enhancing surveillance capacities. Boundaries communicate that what happens inside the stadium is something special, disconnected from the "real" world. Populous notes, "Stadium performances . . . are essentially escapist. Their enjoyment can be heightened by visually disconnecting the audience from the outside world."[36] Stadium boundary construction between inside and outside is intended to create a sense of "other-worldliness" that produces strong emotional responses and a sense of belonging.[37] Those boundaries, today largely managed through media technologies, also turn the stadium into a site of spectacular escape through securitization and ensuring anyone/anything that doesn't belong can be identified and removed.

UBS's boundary is secured and demarcated by a fence and road closures that create a one-hundred-foot perimeter around the stadium during events. When I visited UBS, in June 2018, I thought the fence was for the X Games, a sporting event scheduled to take place shortly after my visit, which included some outdoor events in the perimeter. However, the fence was still there during a fall 2022 visit. Fans and residents complain the fence detracts from the visual iconicity of the stadium and sends a message of exclusion to neighborhood residents. Langenstein explains, "We're space constrained. . . . We don't have huge parking lots where we can put up fences. Instead, we have to do temporary road closures to secure our perimeter. Yet, we are fortunate that we get to work with new security equipment to help us do our jobs."[38] Thus, boundary creation works in conjunction with more sophisticated forms of security techniques.

Stadium boundaries work as enclosures that make policing possible by compartmentalizing space "into socially homogeneous areas" that structure the stadium into a panoptic form that produces docile bodies.[39] As described by Michel Foucault, the panopticon is a spatial form of power derived from Jeremy Bentham's rendering of the ideal prison.[40] Prison guards are located in a central tower surrounded by prison cells in which prisoners can be subject to constant surveillance. As the window shades or two-way mirror in the tower prevent prisoners from knowing if the guard is there or not, the panoptic form institutes self-monitoring and disciplining from the prisoners themselves, who internalize the gaze of the guard and take on that gaze as their own, producing the individual as a docile body. Foucault claimed this form of disciplinary power was not unique to the prison; it was indicative of the whole social form of modern society and its liberal institutions. The discourse of safety structured the modern stadium as panoptic through enclosure and individualization (e.g., fencing around the stadium site, separating the field from stands, individual seating), which rendered the stadium as capable of instituting practices of surveillance that could be distributed at both a mass and an individualized scale. John Bale suggests, "The compartmentalization of space into socially homogeneous areas serves to reinforce boundaries between such groups and people come to literally know their place, . . . encouraging docility and a status quo view of the world."[41]

Although third-generation stadiums, like their predecessors, have clearly demarcated boundaries, they are also increasingly marked by a discourse of blurred boundaries between inside and outside the stadium. On the one hand, these blurred boundaries are imagined to create a sense of place. *Stadium Buildings* from DOM's Construction and Design Manual series encourages designers to consider that "although previously stadiums were always in self-contained buildings, today there are frequent moves to open stadiums up to the surrounding scenery, integrating them harmoniously into their surroundings and achieving a fantastic view for spectators."[42] Likewise, designers are encouraged to emphasize place-specific design elements in the stadium itself, such as in the use of Minnesota limestone in Minneapolis' Target Field, and to create more fluid buffers between the stadium and its surroundings.

Like the other case studies discussed in this book, Minneapolis' stadiums' dramatic views of the city skyline—principally, iconic ones that create a sense of site-specificity—produce this blurred boundary. This boundary blurring is visible in Target Field (see fig. 7.1), designed intentionally to connect spectators to their surroundings. Iconic city buildings, including the IDS (Investors Diversified Services) Tower, are visible from the ballpark. The ballpark's dense urban location—with the smallest footprint in the MLB—enjoins spectators to "absorb and savor their surroundings" through what is, "in effect, a big 'picture window.'"[43]

Target Field's blurred boundary aims to make the stadium feel like it is a part of a vital urban neighborhood rather than cut off from or displacing that neighborhood. Steven Berg, in the ballpark's commemorative souvenir book, says the ballpark "reaches out to grab the space of the city, but the neighborhood is also invited back in," enjoining spectators "to relearn the joys of city life that decades of suburban life have conditioned man to forget. For urban life—and urban baseball—it's not just about the destination; the journey is part of the

Fig. 7.1: Target Field's small footprint creates a blurred boundary between inside and outside, immersing the spectator in the city. (Photo by author)

experience."[44] Berg and stadium officials note that people are more likely to walk to the stadium, seeming to reimagine the fan along the lines of Walter Benjamin's urban flâneur or engaged in the spatial practices of Michel de Certeau's pedestrian.[45] The baseball spectator, the fan, is imagined as the new ideal urban citizen, a flâneur of sorts who takes their time, enjoying the journey, produced by and producing the urban as a space of wonderment and vitality.

Yet, as Henri Lefebvre reminds us, lived space remains dominated space, and though the everyday practices of pedestrians might seek to write their own text onto the city, urban planning in and around the stadium aims to harness those potentialities and to orchestrate their movement. As I've argued elsewhere, whereas de Certeau theorized the spatial practices of the pedestrian as a tactical form of resistance to challenge oppressive productions of dominant space, urban planning and regeneration has shifted to the tactical realm as well, aiming to capitalize on "the tactical encounters of the quotidian in order to transform city space and culture."[46] This move to the tactical has refocused contemporary urbanism and stadium construction away from the strategic plans of "fantasy cities" and "mallparks" to the more quotidian "creative placemaking" and "authentic" culture.[47] While this is part of how the sportification of place produces new forms of sportified citizenship and governance as well as city and neighborhood branding, it is also constitutive of making the urban feel safe and secure for white suburban spectators. As Berg's commemoration of Target Field's reinvention of the urban continues, "Baseball gives us a chance to reintroduce ourselves. We need to let people from greater Minnesota know that they can be comfortable here in the city."[48]

While the blurred boundary aims to bring suburban outsiders into the city, it also responds to contemporary anxieties over divisions within the urban. Each of the stadium stakeholders I spoke with in Minneapolis emphasized the importance of connecting the ballpark to the surrounding neighborhoods. A large public plaza, what Berg describes as the ballpark's "front porch," provides connectivity between the stadium and city over the I-394 highway, reversing the trend of second-generation stadiums, where the highway acted as a hard boundary between stadium and city. Thus, despite there still being a hard boundary to make the stadium more secure, there is an overarching effort to "right the wrongs" of earlier stadiums by connecting the ballpark to its surroundings. Dan Kenney, executive director of the Minnesota Ballpark Authority, which manages the public interest in Target Field, claims that city planning around Target Field intended to "heal that cut" from the I-394 highway, which "cut downtown off from what was going to become the North Loop and the existing Warehouse District."[49]

Much of the discourse around this connection is framed as a means of "community cohesion," where the material connectivity the stadium creates to the surrounding city is imagined to produce a more connected and cohesive community. This is linked to the belief that baseball itself is a means to cohesion. Describing sports as "magnets for communities," Twins president, David St. Peter, says, "Twins baseball brings community together. The world is a very divisive place, and baseball . . . helps mitigate that divisiveness and brings people together from all walks of life, different political persuasions, etc. [to] cheer on the hometown team."[50] As discussed in the previous chapter, though, there is also a material dimension to how the ballpark is imagined to create connectivity, as it was designed as a transit-oriented, compact ballpark in an urban neighborhood. Thus, the ballpark was from the start created as an infrastructure of connectivity, reterritorializing the city in a logic that circulated in and around the ballpark. Community cohesion is further constructed through other material means as well, such as using local materials in construction, contracting local labor with an emphasis on hiring women and people of color (especially in construction through the local construction company Mortenson), nostalgic tributes to local "legends" and a Twins Hall of Fame, and featuring local concessions, such as Kramarzuk sausages and Minnesota State Fair favorites (e.g., fried cheese curds) in the stadium.[51] As discussed in previous chapters, this emphasis on hyperlocalism is a component of sportified branding, citizenship, and governance, but here it is worth noting that the focus on place and localism as a form of community cohesion is also tied to racial and class politics. The community cohesion created by the stadium is imagined to bridge cultural, racial, and class divides via sport and sporting spaces. But the bridging of those divides is animated by a white spatial imaginary, as the permeable boundary and openness is marked by other forms of enclosure, surveillance, and exclusion that work to reinforce rather than ameliorate divides.

Whereas Target Field uses a blurred boundary, UBS takes that blurring to the next level (see figs. 7.2 and 7.3). The design creates a spectacular illusion of being both inside and outside through its translucent ETFE roof, glass façade, and ninety-five-foot pivoting doors. In the stadium's commemorative souvenir book, Steven Berg describes the experience: "Your senses lead you to expect contrast when passing through a major doorway. . . . But here, it's the absence of contrast that boggles the mind. 'Am I indoors or outdoors?' you may ask yourself. You are in a truly indoor-outdoor zone of sensual confusion."[52] The stadium's pivoting glass doors on the southwest can open on nice days, which further enables a sense of "seamless transition" between indoors and outdoors. The intended effect is to create an illusion of an absence of a boundary—a space

Figs. 7.2 and 7.3: U.S. Bank Stadium's translucent exterior and roof creates dramatic views into the city and aims to create a feeling of being outside while inside. From the club level (7.3, right), fans can experience the outside directly on the open-air terrace. (Photos by author)

for free movement and connectivity between sport, stadium, and the urban, and a sense of freedom intimately connected to imagined ideals of Minnesota's rugged, cold, outdoor lifestyle and the freedom one feels when engaged in vigorous sporting activity—thus, an illusion of the absence of control. However, that control is displaced onto a digital exterior and datafied logic, rendering its surveillant and controlling features largely invisible through affects of permeability and connectivity.

Like Target Field, UBS's blurred indoor/outdoor boundary provides dramatic views from the stadium into the city. Wealthier spectators who can afford club seats can access barrier-free views from a terrace outside. The blurred boundary creates a kind of "virtual window." Anne Friedberg explains that the virtual window "is reliant not on its transparency but on its opacity; its highly mediated modulation of light provides an aperture: not to a reality, but to a delimited virtuality."[53] Friedberg theorizes the screen as architecture, "as an expansion of material built space through the 'virtual window' of the film, television, or computer screen."[54] She contends that computer and digital technology shifted to the post-perspectival, which suggests a radical shift in how we perceive and interact with space and time, as these technologies produce images that are received in "spatially and temporally fractured frames."[55] Thus, the virtual window produces new kinds of subjects—users rather than viewers. For these users, distraction is the norm in a world where multitasking becomes possible through the shifting possibilities of the multiple windows. It is precisely this kind of post-perspectival experience that UBS's translucent architecture seeks to create, positioning the spectator as an active user rather than a passive viewer, while enabling the near-complete digitization and datafication of the stadium.

As Friedberg suggests, the virtual window is opaque rather than transparent, and UBS is similarly opaque, with its glass exteriors creating a mirroring effect so that those inside can see out but those outside cannot see in. Spectators consume city sites through their objectifying vision while remaining invisible to those outside, enhancing a sense of power and hierarchical superiority to those who cannot afford to attend the event. The mirroring effect of the glass also serves as a mirroring of the city (see fig. 7.4). Standing in front of the building, one sees oneself amid the city, producing a sense of urban flânerie and a "selfie-like" image. It is a kind of participatory architecture, inviting the spectator to interact with it. Like Friedberg's virtual window, then, the stadium

Fig. 7.4: The exterior of U.S. Bank Stadium creates a mirroring effect. (Photo by the author)

produces multiple windows, all performing at once to engage all the senses of the distracted, yet participatory, user.

The mirroring effect of the stadium enables anyone—the resident, tourists, passersby—to experience and interact with the stadium spectacle. This demonstrates how the stadium, like Target Field, is envisioned as a vehicle of community cohesion, particularly as it serves to unite disparate geographies. Berg notes in the souvenir book that he hopes the stadium will be "a unifier and an attractor. Maybe it can be for Minnesota a common 'living room' that unifies city, suburb, and countryside."[56] Despite gesturing to connectivity, however, those connections are animated by a color-blind and neoliberal racism such that the city's inequities and divisions are framed as matters of choice—tiered experiences, as I describe below—rather than products of social and political inequality. Blurred boundaries conceal the asymmetrical power dynamics of the stadium, eliding how sophisticated forms of security apparatus actually create a firmer boundary between the stadium and its surroundings, making it more and more difficult for those without the "right" kinds of access to enter into the stadium space.

ZONING

Increasingly, the production of boundaries, between inside/outside and within the stadium itself, are thought of in terms of zones. Stadium designers' emphasis on zoning and demarcation between zones (and the intensive policing of zones) demonstrates how the seeming openness communicated by a blurred boundary is subject to, and indeed predicated on, structured exclusions and, ultimately, a white spatial imaginary. Populous, for example, advises stadium designers to construct at least five zones—the playing field, spectator seating/standing areas, concourses (restaurants, bars, social areas), circulation areas between structure and perimeter, and the open space outside the perimeter. Within each zone, further zonation is also encouraged, such as VIP access areas for luxury guests within the spectator area.[57] Zoning within and outside the stadium governs the movement of bodies, and architecture and surveillance technologies symbolically communicate and materially influence those movements. Digitization further enables "collections of analytically arranged and segmented territories that distribute, locate, and separate bodies in a system wherein every individual is observable in their ascribed, purchased, or allotted place."[58]

Although one can get a ticket for the cheap seats at Target Field (high in the vertigo-inducing stands in front of the scoreboard) for as low as $20, for a premium price, fans can access a variety of suite and club levels that will grant them entry to exclusive stadium zones. These zones range from approximately $3,000 to $30,000 annually, enabling the fan to "choose" their level of elite access. The ballpark's Annual Suites—each named after a Minnesota lake and a number of a Twin and designed by a local artist—are pitched as "great" places to do business, with "partnerships being formed, deals being made, and relationships getting stronger."[59] Most are owned by corporations, although individuals can also purchase suites. The 120-person capacity Delta SKY360 Suite, on the other hand, is advertised more to the individual, described as "a highly exclusive area," promising ticket holders access to a "stylish" cabana, in-seat technology, and all-inclusive food and beverage from a chef-inspired menu.[60] For approximately $5,000, fans can also purchase an annual membership to the Delta SKY360 Club, where they are ensured "an elite experience."[61] The most exclusive zone, "for those who expect only the best," is the Thomas Reuters Champions Club, directly behind home plate, with individual seats priced between $19,035 and $27,945 annually.[62] The Champions Club boasts a private entrance, the best seats closest to the action, and access to an "elegant" private club with fine dining. Club and suite-level seating is available only through digital tickets, ensuring data harvesting of these valuable VIP members. Regular fans with no suite or club-level access are barred from entering these areas, which are secured through digital ticketing checkpoints, ushers, signage, and architectural design (e.g., one has to navigate to a different floor to access the suites).

While Target Field nods toward baseball egalitarianism with its $20 seats, football has become ever more out of reach for the everyday fan, as the zoned, tiered luxury experiences provided in UBS demonstrate. The stadium boasts 29 seating options, with individual per-game seat prices ranging from $50 to $9,500. The stadium has 131 private suites, with six levels of suite access, including 31 suites on the turf level whose per-season prices are between approximately $250,000 and $500,000. The 9,300 club seats are designed to communicate both their corporate and Minnesota-themed brands. Themes especially emphasize the juxtaposition of Minnesota's rugged outdoor lifestyle and its technological, cosmopolitan identity. For example, the Sukup Club emphasizes state-of-the-art video; the Buffalo Wild Wings Club has a "cooler, icy vibe"; while the Mystic Lake Club Purple "buzzes with technology, emphasizing real-time fantasy league information."[63] Like Target Field, access to these suites is strictly monitored and digitized. Even on the tour, we were able to enter only the Vikings' owner suite, since it was owned by the stadium.

Both Target Field and UBS therefore rely on an architectural design of zones to create tiered experiences of luxury, rationalizing those divisions through a discourse of choice. Dividing the stadium into zones produces a fragmentation of access, as one guidebook suggests, to create a "smooth and safe functioning of events" where "different categories of people require different structural conditions."⁶⁴ Thus, zoning ensures the security (and different categories of people and spaces) through surveillance and datafication, while also reinforcing a stratifying logic of fans—an ironic turn in the professed "community cohesion" constituted by stadium space. Strikingly, David St. Peter describes these zones in terms of neighborhoods:

> The ballpark is a melting pot of different people. And, ultimately, we knit together. What I have, we like to think of it as different neighborhoods. Which ... are just seating sections or experiences that are all kind of part of the overall Target Field experience.... I'm thinking about spaces within a ballpark.... Different seating sections, different hospitality spaces, different entitlement zones. They're all part of a ballpark experience.... People choose places to live because they like the environment, they like the views, they like the people around them. I think the same can be said for fans that come to ballgames.⁶⁵

Although he suggests the stadium is a "melting pot," the remainder of the statement belies this characterization, showing that stratified divisions remain while justified by a logic of individual choice. The analogy to neighborhoods is telling, as it turns on a post-racial and color-blind logic that erases the political struggle over neighborhood segregation and the inequitable resources distributed across urban neighborhoods, figuring them instead as a matter of choice. Likewise, it elides the lack of choice that many, especially poor people and people of color, have in making choices about the neighborhoods in which to live due to affordability and practices of discrimination in lending, leasing, and property value assessment.

Thus, although the class dimensions of zoning and its production of tiered luxury are perhaps obvious, there are intersecting racial dimensions as well. Classed spaces are, arguably, always raced spaces in the white spatial imaginary. Black and brown bodies are routinely policed within spaces deemed to be reserved for the upper class as they are assumed to not belong there and therefore pose a threat. The modern conception that Black bodies do not belong in wealthy spaces has a material dimension as the production of postwar wealth in the United States was built on a racial divide that facilitated capital investment into spaces designed for white bodies while systematically disinvesting from Black spaces.⁶⁶ Further, zones work to divide the bodies of the largely working-class people of color who make up the stadium's service workers from largely white spectators. So too both groups are further divided from the athletes and from each other. Social status therefore governs one's place in the stadium. In so doing, the stadium "of today mirrors the social order of society as a whole, right up to its mechanisms of exclusion."[67] Yet, stadium design rationales circumvent this critique through seemingly objective divisions of space and bodies by zoning practices that make them appear apolitical and free from racial or class distinction.

Surveillant enclosures, boundaries, and zoning are more than mirrors of societal exclusion—they produce those social relations. Exclusions transform the stadium into a "pure and homogeneous space"—a core logic, Lipsitz argues, of the white spatial imaginary—by removing, marginalizing, and managing populations that threaten its purity. Stadium design, architecture, and mediatization further encourage spectator identification with the white surveillant gaze.

Visual Regimes of Whiteness: Identifying with the Surveillant Gaze

While ubiquitous CCTV cameras encourage spectators to self-regulate through their internalization of the surveillant gaze, they are also invited to identify with that gaze and become surveillants themselves. The physical separation of the field from the spectators elevates the spectator in a position of power, as the bearer of the gaze. The double move of encouraging both distance and identification through managing the spectator's view aims to arouse the excitement of the viewer, creating sport as spectacle while situating spectators within a position of power in their ability to see and consume the play and individual players on the field. It enables them to be surveilled and to surveil. Spectators are encouraged to accept the former for the privilege of the latter, normalizing surveillance and enjoining them to identify with the surveillant gaze. Monitoring, surveillance, and datafication are presented not only as an assurance of safety but also as objects of identification and desire.

Omnipresent screens direct and orchestrate the gaze of the spectator. Giant screens invite spectators to see themselves as they are watched and take pleasure in watching others through close-ups of spectating fans or the "kiss cam," which produce surveillance as "fun." More recently, though, this practice is done through digital and mobile media, such as the digital platform Fancam, which both the Vikings and Twins use. As the company's website explains, Fancam "combines high resolution, 360° gigapixel imagery with custom branding and engagement features to become the ultimate crowd selfie. Fans are able to zoom in, find themselves in the Fancam, and then share with the world. With high viral potency, Fancam gives teams and brands the opportunity to reach a targeted audience and be part of the game-day experience. High levels of exposure on social media facilitates peer-to-peer sharing and amplifies the viral nature of

Fancam."⁶⁸ Fancam seamlessly connects the stadium's CCTV networks and surveillance apparatus to social media, encouraging the fan to view surveillance as part of creating a meaningful and memorable experience. Fancam explains that brands love their platform because of how it creates viral potency, targeted digital content, and data capture, while fans love it because it feels "authentic and personal" and creates a "sense of belonging."⁶⁹ These affective expressions demonstrate how the stadium helps spectators to identify with, and indeed feel like their lives and identities are made more meaningful through, technologies of surveillance. To access the team's Fancam, though, users must log in, thereby giving over their data for these "meaningful" experiences.

Notably, it is not only spectators who are subject to these surveillance practices; they are also designed to facilitate the spectators' (both in the stadium and at home) and management's surveillance of athletes. Indeed, professional athletes constitute some of society's most carefully monitored and tracked bodies.⁷⁰ UBS, for example, fully digitized its locker room, which includes an x-ray room that instantaneously transmits digital images directly to Vikings coaches.⁷¹ Spectators are situated as surveillants of players on the field, whose bodily displays are figured for the voyeuristic pleasure and consumption of fans. VIP spectators are promised even more intimate access to surveil players. For example, the Target Field Champions Club "features exclusive views into the Twins private indoor batting cages and the Twins' Treasure Island Radio Network studios where the radio pre- and post-game shows originate."⁷² Players in UBS must pass through the Delta SKY360 Club to reach the field, submitting themselves to the more intimate surveillant gaze of VIPs.

Stadium screens further orient the spectator's view of players, often by providing close-ups of individual players and plays, encouraging the spectator to view and surveil them through the lens and perspective of the TV camera. Simultaneously, teams' mobile apps provide even more refined data points on the player, urging the fan to sign up for the app (and hand over their data) with the promise of more detailed and real-time player stats and exclusive team content. On the Minnesota Vikings' mobile app, for example, users can access injury reports, a depth chart, game notes, and individual player stats, enabling the passionate fan or fantasy football player to gain access to timely and fine-grained data points on players. Players are also expected to provide more than game content for the consumption and analysis of fans well beyond the pre- or postgame interview or press conference. On their social media, along with the team's own media platforms, such as the Vikings Entertainment Network (a television, radio, online, and in-stadium platform that can also be streamed through the Vikings Now app), players are expected to exploit their living labor as content for fans' viewing pleasure.⁷³

Encouraging Good Behavior

While stadium surveillance and crowd control techniques work as forms of disciplinary power to regulate unruly behavior and encourage the internalization of and identification with a white surveillant gaze, stadium surveillance and datafication practices are also used to encourage good behavior. As Populous suggests, "It helps if the building itself does not provide opportunities for misbehavior, and perhaps even encourages people to behave well."[74] Fans are encouraged to freely give over their data not through a disciplinary command that they "must" (although they are required to provide some data if they want to enter the stadium), but, rather, through a discourse of fan experience, spectators are encouraged to view this data sharing as a vehicle to enjoyment ("you may").[75] Providing your personal information and locational data to the Vikings or Twins on their mobile apps, for example, is not framed as a requirement. Instead, doing so promises the spectator a more engaged and interactive experience. The MLB Ballpark app prompts users to share their location so that they can "stay informed and connected" with their favorite team, directing them toward what team owners and stadium executives perceive as "good behavior."

Although stadiums' more disciplinary measures are orchestrated through a discourse of risk management and crowd control, this biopolitical production of "good behavior" uses datafication in the name of fan experience. That is, datafication treats spectators and crowds not as a threat to be regulated but as collectives who, through data analytics, can be segmented into ever-refined data points so that the stadium can better cater to their desired experience. In discussing how technology can revolutionize the stadium experience, Populous suggests, "The stadium's computer would also store key information on the spectators attending, including age, sex, address, and event preferences. From this database of information, the stadium management could then form a precise profile of who attends which events, allowing them to target exact socio-economic groups for future events."[76] Stadium designers are encouraged to use this data not only to cater to the desire of existing fans but also to predict that desire. Moreover, as the data influences who the stadium imagines it caters to, and therefore its design, it also produces this ideal spectator.

"Fan experience" discourse is central to this kind of technology being integrated into the stadium. This discourse rationalizes digitization and datafication as a means to create a more personalized, seamless, and connected fan experience that enhances the game and fans' desire to come to the stadium. The frictionless fan experience, as described in chapter 2, makes the infrastructure facilitating fan movements and choices appear invisible. In so doing, it discourages fans from thinking critically about how the stadium is mining and using their data. Instead, the spectators are encouraged to view datafication as apolitical, merely invested in maximizing their experience.

Both Target Field and UBS officials use discourses of the frictionless stadium through employing "invisible" technologies. The Vikings, for example, started using the Crowd IQ platform in UBS through a rationale of improving the frictionless fan experience. An outgrowth of the popular Fancam platform, Crowd IQ uses Fancam's 360-degree gigapixel photography to track and analyze fan attention. The company's CEO claims that the technology enables "per-second analysis of where everyone is looking."[77] According to the company's website, teams use the data to "improve ticket sales, optimize the game day experience, articulate value to sponsors, and future-proof organizations."[78] For example, teams can use the data to create dynamic pricing for advertising on the jumbotron at times when they know people are more likely to have their attention on the screen. The Vikings' director of business analytics says the team uses Crowd IQ to "fill in the gaps" in the team's data, stating, "For some of those unidentified people sitting in the seats, at an aggregated level, it's really good for us to also know the age, the demographics, where they're sitting, where they're looking and all that."[79] The Vikings' director of business strategy, Genette Sekse Amar, used gender as an example of how the technology fills in gaps, noting, "In some of those night time games, we saw a gender shift" in Crowd IQ's analysis of looking.[80] This data, suggesting women fans were staying later than men ticket holders, wasn't showing up on ticketing data. The Vikings therefore planned to orient their late-night advertising and screened engagements to appeal to women. While my response to this granular data of where my eyeballs are focused during a game incites a degree of panic, the Vikings and other teams who use Crowd IQ believe fans will not resist its use because it will enable the stadium to provide them with more customized experiences. This demonstrates how what might otherwise be seen as Orwellian forms of surveillance are normalized by the highly charged affective environment of the stadium.

Crowd IQ's emphasis on gender, as well as age, at the seat level is also notable. It shows the increasing emphasis sports teams place on cultivating women and younger fans. But it is also interesting that Crowd IQ does not purport to, at least publicly, collect racial or ethnic demographic data. Assumedly, especially in baseball where game attendance among people of color is generally low, teams would be interested in expanding into this market. While I am not suggesting the company should collect racial data—I would prefer it did not collect data on gender or age either—what I want to point out is how the reticence to use racial demographic data seems undergirded by a logic of color-blind racism. It invites the conclusion that sports are post-racial, as if all races equally watch the game, which we know is not true, thereby reproducing, and leaving unchallenged, the idea of the stadium as white space.

In addition to more obviously surveillant technologies like Crowd IQ and Evolv (the AI-powered detection system discussed in chapter 2), stadiums' increasingly individualized and "narrowcasted" appeal to fans through interactive technologies, mobile apps, social media, and virtual reality in the name of creating a "customized fan experience" further enables data harvesting. Teams are encouraged to send "text, imagery, commentary to mobile phones and devices live during matches as well as afterwards."[81] At UBS, interactive media includes network-supported mobile apps and artificial intelligence. The Vikings app engages fans before, during, and after the game. Before the game, fans can purchase tickets, plan their stadium trip, and find and pay for parking. During the game, the app provides ticketless entry and directs fans to restrooms; food and shopping venues; how to navigate the stadium (i.e., where they do and don't belong); and provides notifications encouraging them to engage with team content, including ways to merge that content with their own and to share it on social media pages while tagging the stadium and team (thus encouraging further engagement with their own content). After the game, fans can use the apps to book transportation through a ride-share service, buy merchandise, and engage with game highlights and new content. Each of these actions creates a digital touchpoint, ripe for data mining.

Along with the app, UBS integrates AI. For example, fans can chat with "Vik," the team's AI chatbot, which will answer questions or direct you to a "live team member" to ensure your positive fan experience. Team mobile apps and their AI chatbots reinforce a micropersonalized experience for the spectator, and they invite them to see themselves as a partner in producing spectacle through their interactive participation in fandom. This is especially supercharged in the case of fans who are involved with fantasy football, and the stadium appeals to these hyper-engaged fans. In UBS, for example, Club Purple was originally marketed as a fantasy football lounge, complete with "TVs and a ticker where you'll be able to follow your fantasy football team . . . [and] fantasy football experts to give fans lineup advice on which players to start and which ones to sit."[82] Persuading fans to provide their personal data with the promise of a better fan experience provides data that helps them produce more hyper-engaged forms of fandom. This marks the other side of crowd control and risk mitigation in stadiums' surveillance and datafication; it reveals how the production of "fan experience" orchestrates "good behavior" by producing ideal fan-subjects.

Target Field uses augmented reality (AR) and interactive forms of gamification to enhance the fan experience. Using the AR app ARound, another digital touchpoint for data mining, fans in the stadium participate in interactive, immersive, and shared stadium experiences, such as through competitive games throwing virtual hot dogs and interactive content that appears during major points in the games.[83] ARound simulates the experiences of fans being together, using their individual mobile devices to participate in a "shared" virtual experience. But it also aims to connect fans to the stadium as a material place.

Stadium owners and teams use the data harvested by technologies like ARound, Crowd IQ, mobile apps, and other touchpoints to understand what spectators have done at the stadium and use that information to predict what they will do in the future. This is part of big data's capability to produce predictive analytics or predictions of behavior rather than just analyses of behavior that has happened in the past. In the stadium, predictive analytics is used to both anticipate potential risks as well as to produce the good behavior of the ideal fan. Predictive analytics in the stadium is still emerging. The Vikings, for example, partnered with the Denver-based data management firm SSB Consulting and their Central Intelligence platform, which caters to the data management needs of the sports, performing arts, and gaming industries. Together, the Vikings and SSB aim to use predictive analytics "to build solid forecasts of where fans go once they enter the stadium, to promote sales more effectively ... to adapt with fan feedback."[84] Andrejevic suggests that the goal of predictive analytics is "to extract non-predictable patterns that emerge only via automated processing of data sets that are too large to make sense of otherwise."[85] He says this is leading to new forms of power relations tied up with what he calls "emergent social sorting," or "the ability to discern un-anticipatable but persistent patterns that can be used to make decisions that influence the life chances of individuals and groups."[86] Predictive analytics is controversially used in policing, where it has been shown to reify existing racial biases.[87]

In the case of its use in stadiums, predictive analytics could exacerbate existing social hierarchies as well, building spaces that encourage certain types of fans to see themselves in some places while policing and keeping out other types of fans. What is most dangerous is that predictive analytics and emergent social sorting eschews criticism through their apparently neutral claim to technological objectivity—that is, they are believed to be more accurate because they are free from human error and bias. This claim to objectivity is ubiquitous in the data industry, including from those who work with data in the Twins and Vikings. In describing their "chargeback" metrics created by their worker surveillance capabilities, the 24/7 Software company, used by UBS, said, "It's tough to argue with hard metrics."[88] The stadium's director of event services further noted that the team owners were just "letting the technology do its job."[89] These statements inhibit critical thinking, shielding them from critiques of bias by an appeal to data objectivity. However, as research shows, this claim to objectivity is patently untrue—data and predictive analytics reproduce the biases of their algorithmic programmers as well as the data sets used to make predictions.[90]

A particularly controversial feature is the use of facial recognition. Despite this controversy, Brett Hutchins and Mark Andrejevic contend the stadium has served as a key space for testing facial recognition and biometric technologies.[91] Pitched as both a tool for risk and threat management as well as for creating and maximizing sales and profit, Hutchins and Andrejevic suggest that the affective connections people have to sport and the space of the stadium make them ideal spaces for testing out these technologies that might otherwise be considered threatening for future dispersion in broader societal uses because of the affective connection of fans to sports. The stadium serves as a site of "least resistance," normalizing these technologies to pave the way for their integration into everyday life. Sporting venues and events therefore often serve as testing grounds for the integration of surveillance technology into the city more generally.[92] Reports from Minneapolis confirm this conclusion. According to Minnesota journalist Tony Webster, emails from the Hennepin County Sheriff's Office "discussing surveillance technology repeatedly reference the 2018 Super Bowl at the new U.S. Bank Stadium in Downtown Minneapolis, which could be classified by the U.S. Department of Homeland Security as a National Special Security Event. As locals know from St. Paul's hosting of the 2008 Republican National Convention, guests may go home, but an influx of federal funding for new law enforcement equipment does not, changing policing for years to come."[93] The construction of UBS and the city's hosting of the 2018 Super Bowl were thus used as opportunities to integrate more controversial forms of security technology, including facial recognition and biometric scanning.

Still, teams are wary about integrating facial recognition due to privacy concerns. As a result, the stadium executives I spoke with largely framed facial recognition and biometrics as a choice, where fans could "opt in" to its use in order to "enhance their fan experience." At the time of this writing, reports suggest nine stadiums were actively using facial recognition technology for ticketing and in-stadium payments.[94] Those reports do not show Target Field or UBS using facial recognition, but my research suggests otherwise. The Fancam, used by both the Twins and the Vikings (and most sports venues in the United States today), makes use of biometric technology, though the teams using it are quick to note they do not collect identifying data from its facial recognition capabilities—yet—but, rather, aggregate data. On a stadium tour of UBS, my tour guide said facial recognition is used in the stadium, and published statements by the stadium's director of event services, Billy Langenstein, also made note of the facility's facial recognition capabilities and use.[95]

When I interviewed Mercedes-Benz Stadium (MBS) executives in Atlanta, they had yet to implement facial recognition, though they were hoping to do so in the future. Their hesitation largely involved the problems of facial recognition in recognizing the faces of people of color, especially Black faces. In a majority-Black city fraught with racial tensions, they noted, the stadium would not implement facial recognition until this aspect of the technology improved, suggesting, "The last thing that we want is that we would do anything that people would feel is discriminatory."[96] Since that interview, the stadium shifted gears and is now using facial recognition and other forms of biometrics. Apparently, they have been assured of its now more sophisticated abilities to differentiate Black faces. Their roll-out of facial recognition reinforces the effect of surveillance as fun as they have integrated the technology into a security robot built to look like a dog, which they've affectionately named Benzie the DroneDog. Softening the fear over facial recognition monitoring and sorting with affection and cuteness, Benzie is programmed to "autonomously patrol 11 acres and send back real-time video during 30-minute shifts. The video feed has 1080p color and night vision capabilities," and it can recognize license plates as well as "sniff" out bombs and narcotics.[97]

While MBS executives were initially concerned about facial recognition not being able to recognize Black faces, they made no note then, nor have they since, of the concerns over how facial recognition is implicated in racialized surveillance and policing, which have been at the center of the Black Lives Matter movement and calls for racial justice. Indeed, none of the executives I spoke with seemed worried about these issues. Instead, they rationalized concerns over biometrics, facial recognition, and data analytics through the color-blind discourse of the fan experience—risks were outweighed by benefits of personalized and frictionless experiences. As the MBS executive suggests, these technologies make the fan "feel special . . . valued . . . like, wow, this place really cares about me."[98] This production of affect is significant—the datafication of the stadium produces and extracts affective value from the fan who feels cared for and, in turn, then produces their own kinds of affective value in their care for the team, stadium, and the city. It is that capability of maximizing affective connections that makes the stadium such an ideal site for testing and normalizing the use of these kinds of technologies.

Drawing on Gilles Deleuze, Sybille Frank and Silke Steets say the stadium's datafication indicates a shift of the stadium from one of panopticon and disciplinary society to a control society, where "the forms of exercising power have become more flexible, while remaining continuous and limitless, and the structures of power have receded from view, while remaining omnipresent."[99] In the control society, individuals become "dividuals"—increasingly atomized data points rather than individual bodies—who "not only *control* themselves, but also *optimize* themselves as commodities for the market."[100] But dividuation is predicated on a biopolitical division between citizen-fans who are "empowered" and "optimized" through this kind of activity and those Others who are deemed threats to be excised. That is, fan empowerment is predicated on the ever more sophisticated security apparatus that seeks to predict threats before they occur and to punish those that do.

So too a rhetoric of maximizing choice and freedom of movement in and around the stadium sits alongside increasingly secured entry points that determine which bodies can and cannot gain access to that freedom. Populous, for example, points out, "The trend in stadium design is away from fixed relationships between customer class and service type, towards freedom of choice between a wide range of services."[101] But only the luxury-tiered fans are given that freedom of choice, and everyone else will consistently run into barriers and be corralled back into their appropriate zones, lest they become identified as potential threats. Dividuated access in the stadium, itself produced through data analytics that drive design, thus (re)produces social hierarchies.

Policing remains a key means to assert control. Most stadium stakeholders I spoke with commented on the importance of police networks—and not only on game day, since the goal is to create a vibrant, 24/7 stadium-based neighborhood. Often, they seemed to see increased policing as a gift to the neighborhood—part of their effort to be a "good neighbor" by ensuring resident safety. But in a city where the racial bias and police brutality sparked worldwide protests, it is difficult to understand this logic, especially when research shows that police stops and arrests are disproportionately higher in the areas around Minneapolis' stadiums.[102] While the researchers conducting this study on stadium and police stops concluded that this means sports increases criminal activity, it might be better interpreted to show that stadiums increase policing. Crime does not necessarily happen more in one geographic area than in others; rather, increasing policing in an area, and priming police to be on the lookout for crime, will lead to increased arrests, leaving criminal activity in other areas (especially white-collar crime) unpoliced.

Yet, the shift of surveillance to a medial space marked by data analytics, coded entry, and access points enables surveillance and policing to appear deracialized and objective, as it replaces the racist Jim Crow laws that structured stadium access overtly by race to a seemingly post-racial one. Following Natalie

Byfield, these surveillance technologies and their predictive analytics might be considered constitutive of a new form of scientific racism.[103] Within the realm of sport, already a space in which scientific racism lingers through biological theories of race, data increasingly serves as a vector for new forms of scientific racism, with data analytics seemingly "proving" the truth of racial identity and difference.

Community Engagement and Philanthropy

In response to the widespread protests in the summer of 2020 in Minneapolis after the police killing of George Floyd, the city's sports teams took a more vocal stance on racial justice. Although neither the Twins nor the Vikings acknowledged the role of the stadium in perpetuating injustice directly, both set out major initiatives in community engagement and philanthropy explicitly tied to antiracism. The Vikings proclaimed their commitment to racial justice by announcing a series of social justice initiatives in 2020 in support of voter registration, education, and criminal justice and police reforms, but the Twins took a more specific stance. Although Twins president David St. Peter suggested a desire to maintain the ballpark as an apolitical space, stating, "People coming into a sporting event are not necessarily coming here for politics," he nevertheless said the organization felt "it's important at times to . . . take action, to take stands, to demonstrate values that we think are important," for both their fans and their employees. Acknowledging the Twins had a big platform, he said it was important to stand up for "social equity and racial justice." The Twins posted a sign in the ballpark that reads "End Racism."[104] The 2020 opening day also included signs on the right field fence reading "Black Lives Matter: United for Change" and "Justice for George Floyd" and sold T-shirts with the Twins logo that read "Epicenter for Change." The team stayed in the foul lines rather than on the field during the national anthem, and some players and a manager took a knee.[105] Just a month before, the Twins also removed the statue of Calvin Griffith from Target Field over his resurfaced racist remarks from 1978 (discussed in chapter 6) in the wake of the Floyd protests. On the decision to remove the statue, a Twins representative remarked, "Our decision to memorialize Calvin Griffith with a statue reflects an ignorance on our part of systemic racism present in 1978, 2010 and today," and apologized, claiming, "His disparaging words displayed a blatant intolerance and disregard for the Black community that are the antithesis of what the Minnesota Twins stand for and value."[106]

These are noteworthy and not insignificant actions from the Twins acknowledging racial injustice, their responsibility to address it, and even their complicity in it. Still, it is not altogether clear what they mean by gestures such as the stadium sign that encourages spectators to "end racism." St. Peter says the team is "pretty vocal around the efforts to obviously ensure that this is a ballpark for everyone," suggesting that ending racism is less about ending systemic and institutional racism and violence like police brutality—the aims of movements like BLM—and more about liberal forms of inclusion and equal representation. While it is important for the ballpark to be open to everyone, doing so will make little headway in the matter of "ending racism," as the team claims to be doing, and in fact it is unlikely the stadium would be open to everyone without *first* ending racism. Rather than trafficking in practices of antiracism, the Twins espouse a discourse of neoliberal multiculturalism, a hollowed-out equality that emphasizes market-based measures of equality while effacing the structural, political, and material forces that produce inequity.[107]

It's tempting to read teams' and leagues' responses to protests against racism as efforts at brand management—in other words, as efforts to save face from criticism, wherein those in power proclaim their allegiance to racial justice to manage risk. Rather than instituting systemic policy change, these efforts ensure their brands remain profitable, and ultimately unthreatened, by protest. Notably, since the uptake of these discourses by sporting elites, protests by players in the stadium have waned.[108]

Still, I would be remiss to set aside their actions as merely shallow efforts at brand management. While the Twins' rhetoric on racial equity is vague, the philanthropic work of the Pohlad Foundation, run by the Pohlad family, who owns the Twins, and the Twins Community Fund, the team's philanthropic organization, take a more explicit antiracist stance on actions to rectify injustice. Bill Pohlad, the foundation's president, says, "Black people have experienced oppression and racism for far too long in this country"; he argues that there needs to be "structural change" and promises that the foundation will work with organizations to "change the systems that create racial inequities and marginalize people of color."[109] Reportedly moved by protests in the wake of Floyd's murder, the Pohlad family reorganized their foundation to include a major focus on racial justice. A representative from the Pohlad Foundation explained that because the Pohlads are from the Twin Cities (the Vikings owners are from New Jersey), they felt a special obligation to respond to what was happening in Minneapolis. A foundation representative noted that the unrest around Floyd's murder "was very eye-opening for them," and the Pohlads felt the need to "do something."[110] While the foundation had been focused on housing since 2017, after Floyd's murder in 2020 they pledged $25 million to racial justice efforts in the Twin Cities.

The foundation's reorganization included both a shift in the makeup of the Pohlad Foundation, by hiring a more diverse staff and advisory board members, with Bill Pohlad acknowledging that "real change must start within," as well as a change in how the foundation chose its funding focuses and the distribution of its funds.[111] Previously, the Pohlad family made those decisions. After the reorganization, the foundation turned to the expertise of advisory board members.[112] The foundation emphasizes that their racial justice work is community-led, drawing on an advisory council led by Dr. Brittany Lewis, a senior associate at the University of Minnesota's Center for Urban and Regional Affairs, to work with communities on what kinds of funding and projects they most need. Their emphasis is on ensuring that their funding is helping BIPOC organizations, people, and businesses. Foundation representatives acknowledge they are not in the best position to know where the money should go, instead believing BIPOC organizations already doing the work are "closest to the issues [and] need to really have input on the solutions."[113] So far that has translated into grants in the areas of rebuilding and recovery to BIPOC-led organizations and businesses affected by the 2020 protests, public safety "to transform policing through the Collaborative Solutions Initiative," and support to individuals and organizations doing racial justice work.[114] The foundation further notes their investment in Black home ownership, racial justice fellowship, and Black mental health.

The Pohlad Foundation does not have a place-centered strategy, instead focusing on home ownership and racial justice in terms of the Twin Cities more broadly. In contrast, the Twins Community Fund (TCF), with the help of the Pohlad Foundation, revamped its strategy in 2020 in response to the protests to be specifically place-focused on BIPOC neighborhoods around the stadium, especially the predominantly Black neighborhood of North Minneapolis, which TCF's executive director, Kristin Rortvedt, described as the ballpark's "backyard."[115] The demographic makeup of North Minneapolis is not incidental; it is a product of racist segregationist policies and redlining as well as strategic disinvestment.[116] Prompted by the 2020 protests in Minneapolis, Rortvedt suggests, the organization began to recognize "there's a whole lot of work that we need to do in our own hometown."[117]

TCF therefore shifted to "commit more hyperlocally," a radical change from how they had been thinking about community engagement previously, with a focus on large quantities of events and connections. Instead, they turned to more micro-level engagement at the hyperlocal level, focusing on local youth in softball and baseball clinics and mentoring in North Minneapolis. They also partner with other nonprofit organizations, such as Pillsbury United Communities and the Northside Achievement Zone, to fund scholarships and youth-oriented programs, including for older kids, often neglected in outreach efforts. They also shifted their focus in terms of partnerships, working to be more proactive about the organizations they partner with to align with their focus on hyperlocal impact. In Rortvedt's view, this focus on youth engagement is part of an effort to diversify the Twins organization, TCF, and baseball more generally: "I think there's a recognition that right now there's not a great pipeline for young people who want to work in this industry.... We want to make sure that we're helping create a pipeline to the workforce for them."[118]

Like the Twins' "End Racism" sign, I am not entirely sure what to make of the work of the TCF and the Pohlad Foundation. It is undeniable that both were deeply affected by the racial protests following Floyd's murder in 2020. It's admirable they've responded to the racism that event exposed through commitments—both financial and material—to racial justice. The Pohlad Foundation's investment in housing equity, especially, and their commitment to community-led decision-making and solutions seems promising. However, the extent of their impact is still too early to tell. Hopefully, they will also acknowledge the stadium's harms to these neighborhoods and work toward mitigating and rectifying those harms. Unsurprisingly, given their positions, those I spoke with were reticent to acknowledge that the stadium itself might play a role in racial injustice.

As activists and community organizers engage with the stadium, its officials, and philanthropic entities, it's worth remembering that their rights to the city and their neighborhood should not be preconditioned on their entrepreneurial fitness nor the philanthropic whims of charitable organizations. As with the case of the Arthur Blank Foundation and Atlanta's Westside neighborhoods (discussed in chapter 2), the turn to philanthropy, nonprofit organizations, and charity for social welfare turns rights of citizenship into acts of moral choice.[119] This absolves government of responsibility and far too often exacerbates social inequities. Although I am hopeful about the Pohlad Foundation's efforts to work with BIPOC grassroots organizations to meet the housing needs of BIPOC Minneapolis residents, I also see this as a grossly inadequate abnegation of governmental responsibility, making housing a matter of moral choice rather than a right (not to mention that organizations like the Pohlad Foundation and TCF are not accountable to the public or voters). This cannot be a long-term solution for racial justice in Minneapolis nor elsewhere.

Conclusion

In the spring and summer of 2020, sports and stadiums shut down in the wake of the global COVID-19 pandemic and then again in response to protests led by Black players supporting Black Lives Matter after the police killings of George Floyd, Breonna Taylor, and many others. In the wake of these intertwining events, it was difficult not to interpret the use of stadiums as temporary hospitals to contain the overflow of affected COVID patients—of which Black, Indigenous, and people of color made up a disproportionate margin—as containers of disposability. Stadium-hospitals laid bare societal inequities, where public expenditures on those very stadiums undoubtedly led to trade-offs in investments in public health.[1] Instead, we were encouraged to be thankful for the goodwill of private stadium owners who opened their spaces for the public good.

At the same time, however, protesters, especially those affiliated with BLM, made stadiums sites of resistance in ways that palpably revealed these broader inequities. These protests no doubt took inspiration from the Take a Knee movement, where players, influenced by San Francisco 49ers quarterback Colin Kaepernick's 2016 on-field protest, kneel during the national anthem to protest police brutality against Black communities.[2] Protests outside U.S. Bank Stadium in Minneapolis just before kickoff for the 2018 Super Bowl LII, for example, highlighted the stadium's role in the city's racial disparities. Protesters blockaded the light rail station near the stadium, demanding divestment from police. Organized by the Black Visions Collective, the protesters took a knee and chanted, "We stand with Black athletes that kneel for Black Lives."[3] The protesters explicitly linked the stadium to urban disparities, "protesting how the city has diverted public resources into a private, corporate event and demanding allocation of resources to the 'people that live here, the homeless people, the people of color, the trans folks, the queer folks, and everybody who is vastly more deserving than anybody who is in that stadium right now of the resources and the amount of money contributed.'"[4]

This was not the first time in the BLM movement when stadiums served as sites of protest; in 2016, for example, after police shot and killed eighteen-year-old Michael Brown in Ferguson, Missouri, stadiums were sites of clashes between BLM protesters and white nationalists.[5] The resurgence of BLM also influenced a rise of antiracist activism by athletes inside the stadium, including Take a Knee. In August 2020, professional basketball players went on strike, refusing to play their opening games, after police shot Jacob Blake, a twenty-nine-year-old Black man, in Kenosha, Wisconsin. Baseball, hockey, tennis, and soccer players stood in solidarity with the protests and deferred game play to highlight racial injustice.

These protests demonstrate how the stadium can be a site of contesting US racial logics and ideologies. As I have argued throughout this book, the sportification of place limits this political potentiality through architecture, design, and logics that serve as urban media infrastructures to govern and contain citizens, direct their behaviors through the brand, and encourage identification with a white spatial imaginary. Those within the stadium are invited to embody performances of white, masculine, middle-class citizenship and disidentify with protesters.

Even though third-generation stadiums are fully securitized, they are not, in fact, safe spaces. Although a *Washington Post* study showed that fan violence is a major issue in stadiums, with an average of six arrests per game, media rarely cover this violence.[6] When they do, they treat it as acts of a few bad apples or overconsumption of alcohol. They do not cover this violence as indicative of white masculinity and the affective intensities the stadium encourages. While surveillance, fan codes of conduct, policing, and crowd control can identify and punish violent (white) fans, it is as if these kinds of behavior are expected—anticipated as the inevitable outcomes of sporting rivalries.

Given the production of the stadium as a white space through practices of surveillance that encourage fans to identify with the racialized security apparatus, it is perhaps unsurprising the instances in which collective expressions and uprisings occur within the stadium tend toward the reproduction of white supremacy rather than racial justice. For example, in response to Take a Knee, we have yet to witness widespread collective kneeling on the part of spectators in football and baseball stands, nor a collective of fans chanting "Black Lives Matter" (although the latter has happened at WNBA [Women's National Basketball Association] games). While we see much collective resistance outside the stadium and on social media, fans inside the stadium are more likely to chant "USA," collectively boo, or engage in overtly racist acts such as using racial slurs or symbols of lynching in response to antiracist protests from players or other fans.[7] Even as the tide shifted in terms of the NFL's stance on Take a Knee after the 2020 protests, many fans collectively booed during a moment of silence held for racial justice at a Kansas City Chiefs game.[8]

Although these collective responses are perhaps indicative of the largely white fan base for both football and baseball, they also point to how stadiums have always been tied to the containment of collective potentiality that threatens the dominant social order by constituting practices of ideal white liberal citizenship. When spectators, as well as athletes, step outside of the boundaries of those ideals, such as when activists unfurled a banner at Fenway Park in Boston declaring that "Racism is as American as Baseball," they are treated as threats to be disciplined, contained, and removed.[9] Similarly, when protesters in Minneapolis unfurled a banner protesting the Dakota Access Pipeline, standing in solidarity with Native American protesters, they were quickly arrested.[10] Although one of the protesters noted they were met with some support—thumbs up and fists in the air—they were also met with boos and arrest.

Even when protests take place outside the stadium, they are deemed a potential threat to fan enjoyment and the "purity" of the game. During the protests organized by the Black Visions Collective in Minneapolis before the 2018 Super Bowl, police broke up the protests and arrested seventeen people.[11] When a group of people staged a mock funeral to protest police brutality outside the Cowboys stadium in Dallas, nine people, almost all BIPOC, were arrested, even though they were reportedly following police orders to disperse.[12] In St. Louis, after Michael Brown was killed and protests erupted in Ferguson, protesters outside the Rams stadium were confronted by fans and a clash ensued, but it was two Black protesters who were arrested for inciting violence, even though observers claimed that it was white fans coming out of the stadium who started the conflict.[13]

In these examples, protests are constructed as dangerous; protecting the "purity" of the game is secured through maintaining the stadium's "purity." However, in 2020, if you googled "NFL fan protest," you would have been inundated with thousands of images of white fans holding up signs protesting *against* protests in the stadium, reading, for example, "Proud American, I stand";

"Play football, not politics"; "Protest on your own dime, not my time"; and "The Silent Majority *Stands* with Trump." The unstated presumption that the stadium is a white space allows *these* protests to be read as apolitical (and therefore nonthreatening). This is a white supremacist logic; it figures the stadium as a space where whites are entitled to enjoyment, escape, and the "purity" of the game without having to be bothered by racial strife or antagonism.

Stadiums are ultimately imbued with an implicit anti-Blackness that becomes visible only when BIPOC bodies are in those spaces in ways that do not conform to their norms of whiteness. Protests against racial injustice in the stadium renders its whiteness visible. The backlash from white fans, team owners, sponsors, and journalists to these protests, which chastises players for not keeping their protests off the field, thus works as gatekeeping that maintains the stadium as white space by demanding Black players adhere to white norms and values of behavior, including the norm that they do not speak out against white supremacy. This is why those protests represent such a threat: They risk revealing how sports, the stadium, and the sportification of place more broadly are involved in upholding white supremacy.

In this context, players taking part in Take a Knee could arguably be read as practicing a kind of "sousveillance," or surveillance from below, by shifting the power relations of looking. Steve Mann, Jason Nolan, and Barry Wellman describe sousveillance as an "inverse panopticon" and "reflectionism," effectively holding up a mirror to the panopticon to uncover and undercut "its primacy and privilege" and to relocate "the relationship of the surveillance society within a more traditional commons notion of observability."[14] Mann, Nolan, and Wellman suggest sousveillance emerges when the surveilled use the tools of those surveilling them to surveil the surveillants. Although they largely focus on surveillance and data-gathering technologies, such as wearable devices or mobile cameras, the practice of sousveillance can be considered in more analog terms as well; it ultimately speaks to the unequal power relations of surveillance and the techniques those with less power use to respond to, make visible, and undercut the power of the gaze.

In taking a knee, players perform a looking back at the spectators, cameras, and officials, marking them, and the stadium itself, as complicit with the police violence their performative activism seeks to critique. Mann explains sousveillance is a "looking from below"—in other words, those with less power are looking "uphill" at those who possess the power of the gaze. In taking a knee, the players quite literally perform this looking from below, demonstrating in visual and embodied form a subjugated position of power. But in defying the expectations of the surveillants, triggering—both literally and affectively—the systems of risk management and security, they refuse their subjectification by and to that gaze. Instead, they turn their own gaze back onto their surveillors. The ubiquity of mobile devices and the stadium's enjoinment for spectators to share content further enables the sousveillant properties of Take a Knee, as their actions are captured on camera and virally shared online. It demonstrates that these players have power—not only in their voice and message but in their bodies and access to space. It shows they can transgress the boundaries of the zoned expectations of their performance.

These sousveillant performances express what Samantha Sheppard refers to as "critical muscle memory," both an analytical tool and a descriptor to understand Black representation and performance in sport. "Black memory," she argues, "becomes a muscle trained, flexed, and disciplined by colonialism, enslavement, and racial terror, as well as collective Black struggle, achievement, and cultural engagement."[15] Players taking a knee seem to understand, as if from muscle memory, the weight of the burden of representation they bear—the longer history of Black representation in mediasport—while also aiming to exceed that burden and its histories through their performance. It is a citational practice, citing these generic and narrative expectations of their bodies, drawing from histories of refusal in those expectations (such as the 1968 Olympic performance of Tommie Smith and John Carlos, who held Black Power salutes during the national anthem ceremony), and their own and collective, embodied performances of a vision of Black futurity and potentiality. In that sense, there is a degree to which taking a knee constitutes what Simone Browne calls "dark sousveillance," or "the tactics employed to render one's self out of sight, and strategies used in the flight to freedom from slavery as necessarily ones of undersight."[16] Like the forms of dark sousveillance Browne analyzes, such as Negro spirituals and abolitionist handbills, taking a knee is "a site of critique" that draws on "black epistemologies of contending with antiblack surveillance" so that they can be "appropriated, co-opted, repurposed, and challenged in order to facilitate survival and escape."[17] Taking a knee takes advantage of the surveillant gaze produced by the stadium to turn that gaze back, to render it visible, and to wage a wider critique of systemic and institutionalized anti-Black violence in order to imagine Other futures and spatialities.

Inspiring Change and Ending Racism?

Although there continued to be resistance to players taking a knee, during the COVID-19 pandemic, popular discourse shifted. The WNBA and NBA led the way in these shifts when they went on strike in support of BLM. While Take a Knee had not yet pervaded the more predominantly white sport of baseball, BLM reportedly took "center stage" on the MLB's 2020 season opening day as coaches and players collectively took a knee to demonstrate their resistance to police brutality. Athletes also became more vocal about the racism they experienced in the stadium, demanding teams do more. In a somewhat unprecedented move, the Boston Red Sox acknowledged that racism at their stadium was "a real problem," and they painted a 254-foot "Black Lives Matter" billboard on the highway-facing side of Fenway.[18] This is especially notable because MLB players have singled out Fenway as a site in which the team's primarily white fans engage in overtly racist behavior toward Black players, to the extent that many Black players in the league had a clause preventing their being traded to Boston.[19] Even NFL commissioner Roger Goodell reversed course on Take a Knee, acknowledging he was wrong to ban kneeling and should have listened to Kaepernick.[20] In some ways, then, the brief shutdown of sports in the wake of the pandemic and the subsequent closure of sports stadiums to fans seemed to open up sports to a more honest conversation about racism.

For now, the NFL and MLB are adopting messages of racial justice and bringing them into the stadium themselves. During the 2021 Super Bowl, for example, the NFL posted a sign reading "End Racism" and "It Takes All of Us" in the end zone and premiered a racial justice–themed commercial, titled "Inspire Change." The commercial features a voice-over from Ladanian Tomlinson's NFL Hall of Fame Induction speech, stating, "Football is a microcosm of America. All races, religions—living, playing, competing, side by side. I pray we dedicate ourselves to be the best team we can be. Let's choose to be for one another. To fulfill the promise of one nation. To be part of the solution. Be part of the change. To try harder, show up, dive in and stay in it."[21] The speech is accompanied by close-ups of Black and brown football players and ordinary people, then shifts to scenes from football games with Black and white players working side by side, followed by racial justice activists protesting police brutality on the streets. The music comes to a climax as scenes shift to the stadium, with those protests brought onto the field (notably, though, Colin Kaepernick is nowhere to be seen). Referees are wearing hats emblazoned with "End Racism" and football players don helmets with the names of Breonna Taylor, Elijah McCain, and Eric Garner, Black citizens killed by police. The commercial ends with what are seemingly efforts of the league to engage in racial justice–oriented community outreach, such as voter drives, and a statement of its commitment to social justice. Ultimately, the signs and the commercial acknowledge, in general terms, racial injustice with a similarly vague commitment to give $250 million to "end systemic racism." However, "Inspire Change" promotes football, and sport more generally, as a meritocratic space in which anyone, regardless of race, religion, and so forth, can compete "side by side," thus fulfilling the promise of "one nation." Importantly, it does so through sportification, suggesting viewers see themselves in sportified terms—as part of a "team"—enfolding citizenship into the subjectivity of the sporting fan. As in how neoliberalism shifts justice work to the market—imagining the market as the space in which racial justice is best achieved—this sportified logic imagines sport as the space in which social problems are best taken up and resolved, not through political struggle but through depoliticizing them by turning them into sporting rivalries. While the signage and commercial brought racial justice discourses into the stadium space, they did so by disavowing sport's involvement in that injustice and reifying the mythos of sport's apolitical ability to bring us together beyond politics.

In 2022 the Super Bowl once again put race front and center when, in partnership with hip-hop mogul Jay Z's Roc Nation entertainment company, the event featured hip-hop as the main halftime event for the first time in Los Angeles's SoFi Stadium, home of the Rams and the Chargers, which opened in 2020. In a nostalgic throwback to the history of West Coast rap, the show featured Dr. Dre, Snoop Dogg, Mary J. Blige, and Kendrick Lamar, with East Coast rapper 50 Cent and Detroit's Eminem also making an appearance. Roc Nation's control over the performance was the result of an agreement between Roger Goodell and Jay Z, with the former looking to improve the league's image on race after many high-profile acts (e.g., Rihanna, Cardi B.) refused to play the 2017 show in protest of how Kaepernick was treated by the league.[22] Since Roc Nation's takeover of the show, performers have brought racial politics directly into the stadium. The 2022 hip-hop performance made political overtures, including Eminem taking a knee and Kendrick Lamar's performance of "Alright," which critiques police brutality and served as a "cry of unity at Black Lives Matter protests."[23] But critics also questioned these gestures, contending they were effectively brand management while racism, rampant in the league's structures, remained in place and unquestioned. The show came on the heels of Brian Flores, then–head coach of the Miami Dolphins, calling the NFL a "plantation system" for its discriminatory hiring practices that kept Black players and coaches out of positions of power. Cornel West claimed that the performance, though a welcome celebration of Black experience and musical talent, was "also a missed opportunity for truth-telling about Brian Flores' challenge to the NFL's plantation system. . . . The political silence of our artists was sad!"[24]

Significantly, the show was not only a tribute to hip-hop but to Compton, a historically Black neighborhood in Los Angeles just ten miles west of SoFi Stadium, where many of the artists performing that day claim their roots. The set design featured classic bungalow-style homes that dot the landscape in Compton, a replica of the neighborhood's Martin Luther King Jr. memorial and

Tam's Burgers (a neighborhood restaurant) signage. A map of the neighborhood covered the stage floor. The performance demonstrated aurally and visually the significance of neighborhood space to hip-hop and Black experiences.[25]

In some ways, though, the performance was an ironic tribute. SoFi Stadium is part of a new stadium district development adjacent to the iconic Kia Forum, replacing the Hollywood Race Track. In addition to the football stadium, the Clippers, LA's NBA team, built a new arena there, the Intuit Dome. The district is in Inglewood, one of the few historically and majority-Black and Hispanic neighborhoods remaining in Los Angeles. Now the neighborhood is a site of real estate speculation and gentrification. For the Super Bowl, police cleared encampments set up by people experiencing homelessness in the neighborhood, many of them Black and Hispanic. In an ironic twist, then, the Super Bowl halftime show, with its tribute to Black and brown Los Angeles and courting fans of color, was predicated on the forced removal of some of those same communities.[26] Still, the performance could arguably be read as commenting on this practice, demonstrating a tactical sousveillance, critiquing the district.

While the meanings of the halftime show and the MLB's and NFL's incorporation of racial justice into the stadium are debatable, these practices demonstrate the complex intertwining of media, place, and identity as they are imbricated in sports and stadium space. The meanings of the performance cannot really be understood outside the broader material, urban media infrastructures in which they are implicated. As the epicenter of film and TV production, home to numerous iconic sports franchises, and an urban landscape marked by significant racial and class divides, Los Angeles is in many ways the ultimate example of the sportification of place. From the building of Dodger Stadium (opened in 1962) and the resulting so-called Battle of Chavez Ravine—which ensued in response to government efforts to use eminent domain to displace a Mexican American community to build the stadium—to the contemporary debates over SoFi Stadium and the gentrification of Inglewood, the city has a long history in which its mediatized, mediating, and mediated sporting spaces produce and govern citizenship as well as brand and racialize urban space. My hope is that theorizing these imbrications as the sportification of place can throw focus onto these dynamic and complicated systems of power as they play out in struggles over identity and place.

Globalizing the Sportification of Place

As this example of Los Angeles illustrates, the sportification of place is not limited to the case studies discussed in this book. Rather, it is a framework that can be used to think through the site-specific implications of stadiums across the

United States, and perhaps globally. As noted in the introduction, the industrial, economic, and infrastructural histories and contexts of US sport stadiums distinguish the particular ways the sportification of place plays out nationally. However, just as those contexts require further contextualization in the site-specificity of individual cities, and even neighborhoods, where stadiums are built, so too it could be argued that the insights from this book could be applied in site-specific ways to global sporting cultures and their stadiums. Especially as sporting venues globally integrate sophisticated media technologies, practices, and experiences while emphasizing place-based affects and practices, the sportification of place is perhaps evident in stadium infrastructure more generally.

The renovation of Barcelona's football (soccer) stadium—Spotify Camp Nou—is arguably a shift toward a sportification of place, though, again, in site-specific terms. The stadium opened in 1954, and it and the football club have served as sites of Catalan nationalism, a place-based identity and secessionist movement. According to Hunter Shobe, Camp Nou demonstrates the complex interweaving of the global and local as it plays out around Catalan nationalism.[27] On the one hand, the stadium serves as global branding, promoting the team to global fans and drawing on transnational corporate brands in service of those aims. Likewise, though, the stadium creates a local, place-based identity. Yet, these are not separate; place-based localism tied to Catalan-specific identity is a key component of the team's global branding and vice versa. These complex negotiations among global/local, nation/city, and city/neighborhood are further reinforced in the stadium's renovation. The renovation was rationalized as necessary for Barcelona to compete with Europe's other premiere clubs, including Madrid, which were integrating more sophisticated technology and revenue-generating features. The €1.5 billion renovation will increase capacity and VIP seating, generate revenue 365 days of the year, and put it "at the avant garde of technology."[28] The renovation also aims to integrate the stadium more deeply into the neighborhood, Les Corts, "with no barriers between the two thus allowing fans to move freely through the whole area."[29] A major component of the renovation is the Barca Innovation Hub, a technology incubator hub akin to Atlanta's Truist Park Battery development.

The renovations of Camp Nou thus seem to embody a sportification of place. They position the stadium to constitute and govern citizenship, city and neighborhood branding, and mediatization that enables more sophisticated forms of datafication and surveillance in ways that are increasingly global *because of* their embedded ties to place-based locality and placemaking. The sportification of place might thus be considered a component of broader shifts related to how contemporary media participates in both emplacement and displacement, constituting new ways for us to practice and engage our place-based localities in and through how it connects us to other places. And it is perhaps this capacity of sport—as simultaneously global and local—that makes it serve as such a powerful vector for enacting these forces in our contemporary moment.

Thus, if the sportification of place does indeed play out globally, it does so in site-specific ways that are not entirely comparable to the case studies discussed here. For Camp Nou, those specificities pertain to the history of football culture and spaces in Europe more generally and in Spain and Barcelona specifically. The distinct industrial context of football culture and its regulatory bodies present different demands and conditions, such as, for example, in soliciting support for renovating the stadium, which largely does not rely on public tax dollars but rather club support, bank loans, and investors.[30] Likewise, the club's context and its particular history matter for the kinds of place-based identity and affect that are both drawn upon and produced in the sportification of place, just as they mattered distinctly for Atlanta, Seattle, and Minneapolis.

Camp Nou, a football/soccer stadium, is also distinct from the case studies here, which focused on US football and baseball. These sports are tied to US cultural identity, and their sports spaces are key components of that identity. However, sports are changing in the United States, with European football becoming more popular, in part because of its promise to connect to a global media audience. Basketball is also increasing in fandom and viewership, and it has long been the most popular sport among Black sports fans. Notably, the NBA is also the most watched US sports league globally, outpacing the NFL and MLB by significant margins. That global reach is due in large part to the league's efforts to connect with global audiences, which Steven Secular says includes an emphasis on mediatization and digital platforming to intertwine local and global branding.[31] Like the site-specificity required to understand the potential global implications for the sportification of place, however, the basketball or hockey arena, tennis stadium, or football (soccer) pitch require a site-specific analysis as well. Their imbrication in unique sporting cultures and the development of these sports and their venues are unique and deserving of their own careful analysis. Yet, their increasing roles as part of a mediated, mediating, and mediatizing infrastructure also suggests that theorizing them as a sportification of place can be a starting point for that analysis.

A Fourth Generation?

The role of other venues both in the United States and globally to sportify place also raises another question: Are we at the beginning of a fourth generation? Just as some of the stadiums here stood at the cusp of the second and third generations, such as Turner Field, some of the more recent stadiums discussed in this book might be on the cusp between a third and fourth generation. Certainly, there is a difference between a stadium like Lumen Field, which opened in 2002, and Mercedes-Benz Stadium, opened in 2017. While Lumen Field has undergone numerous renovations to integrate technologies like those built into Mercedes-Benz Stadium, the latter's original integration of fiber-optic capacity, artificial intelligence, Halo board, and other mediatization that emphasize datafication and interactivity perhaps make it more of a Web 2.0 (emphasizing user generation and interactivity) stadium, whereas Lumen Field was Web 1.0 (emphasizing content consumption). Still, interactivity and datafication is just one element of the stadium, and the other elements that focus on governing citizenship and branding in place-based terms remain. We thus may be on the cusp of a new generation, but the stadiums considered here continue to exhibit core elements of the third generation.

So what might a fourth generation of sports stadiums look like or include? The influence of the COVID-19 pandemic on sports, which meant stadiums with no crowds and efforts to use stadiums for other capacities (e.g., vaccination sites or makeshift hospitals) will undoubtedly influence a new wave of thinking about how stadiums should be designed and used. We are already seeing how stadium designers and owners have fully embraced the idea of a "frictionless" and "touchless" experience in stadiums, largely due to the desire to make fans feel safe returning to crowded stadiums. As Steven Secular notes, the "bubble" the NBA created during the pandemic—moving teams to Disney property to produce a confined, COVID-safe space—demonstrated how the NBA endeavored to bring all elements of the sport's production under its purview.[32] The pandemic thus created the conditions of possibility for the further conglomeration and convergence of media and sport industries and their ancillary infrastructures. So too the doubling down on interactivity and fantasy leagues is in part drawn from efforts to get fans back into stadiums. Likewise, teams are augmenting stadiums with virtual reality to simulate fans and crowd noise, techniques developed during the pandemic. Not only do these efforts entice fans back to the stadium, but they are also pitched as enticements to return to normal.[33] In this way, the return to the stadium is about much more than a return to sports; it signals the ways sports have pervaded our very sense of being, as the return of sports as normalcy demonstrates the sportification of life more generally.

Of note as well is an increasing emphasis on green technology and mitigating climate change. Many of the stadiums considered in this book, especially those built after 2010, stress environmental sustainability. That discourse is central to these stadiums' branding as well as mediatization, where the latter speaks to the technological solutions deployed in the quest for sustainability. The sustainable stadium, then, might be the major impetus toward new kinds of stadium architecture, design, and mediatization, just as news and radio, television, the internet, and interactive media have been to previous generations. Sport's relationship to health and the body makes it an ideal vector for environmental governance. However, like the shift to private philanthropy as solutions to racial inequity, the emphasis on green stadiums reifies logics that make climate mitigation a matter of private choices on the part of billionaires, who, at the same time, are able to justify construction of multibillion-dollar sporting facilities whose very construction contributes to environmental degradation. This is a form of greenwashing, as Toby Miller suggests; sporting institutions and elites "endeavor to legitimize the harm they cause by promoting themselves as good environmental citizens."[34]

Although it is perhaps too early to tell what the next generation of sporting stadiums will bring, it is no doubt coming. With Oriole Park at Camden Yards—the stadium that kicked off the third generation—having celebrated its thirtieth anniversary in 2022, many of the facilities at the early end of the third generation are nearing the point of age in which discourses of obsolescence are no doubt on the horizon. Indeed, the Orioles released a "wish list" of renovations, such as a field-level suite and restaurant, as part of their 2023 lease negotiation, leaving some critics to think "How much of that can be done and still preserve that classic feeling?"[35] One wonders if what it will really mean is a new stadium altogether. Perhaps, as in the case of Camp Nou, the fourth generation will shift to more large-scale renovations rather than demolition and new construction. Demolishing and building new stadiums complicates the affective connections people build to stadiums and the role they can play in fostering a sense of urban and place-based identity. That identity becomes subject to fluctuation and fluidity, destruction and recreation, rather than permanence and history. Stadium designers, owners, and city officials invested in stadium monumentality must therefore think carefully about how to balance these aims—rendering stadiums sites for constituting a sense of place and city pride connected to history but with an eye toward some future aspirational identity. Perhaps this challenge explains why the third generation shifted toward architectures of placefulness rather than homogeneity, as there is a recognition that their ephemerality requires extra efforts to connect to place in order to use stadiums to constitute identity. The fourth generation might aim to capitalize on these affective sensibilities, as well as on discourses of environmental sustainability, through major renovation rather than demolition.

While a fourth generation of stadium building is still a question mark, the sports stadium will no doubt continue to play a meaningful role in our cities and neighborhoods. Critics questioned if sports would rebound after COVID-19, and the answer seems to be in: They did. Sport remains a vital part of our lives and our culture, and the spaces that sport produces are central manifestations of both that vitality and sporting elites' efforts to capitalize on it. I hope the framework of the sportification of place provides some insights for thinking about this agonistic tension and some tools for parsing out its stakes in struggles over racialized forms of governance and citizenship, branding, and datafication and surveillance and efforts to negotiate, refuse, subvert, and transgress sportifying practices.

The sportification of place demonstrates not only the significance of sporting spaces but of space and place more generally in media and communication studies. Thinking of sports stadiums as urban media infrastructures speaks to how other kinds of media work infrastructurally and, vice versa, how infrastructure constitutes mediating, mediatizing, and mediated practices. A robust literature on media infrastructure, from undersea cables to prisons, is already burgeoning.[36] Theorizing the stadium as an urban media infrastructure is a move toward looking at other kinds of major urban infrastructure—public libraries, universities, museums, hospitals—in new ways, as each are bound up with media culture and the urban with distinct and site-specific histories and contemporary practices and stakes. Hopefully, this book thus provides media scholars an impetus to take up these spaces, along with some tools for thinking about their cultural and political stakes.

Notes

Introduction

1. Jani Vuolteenaho, K.H.A. Leurs, and Johanna Sumiala, "Digital Urbanisms: Exploring the Spectacular, Ordinary and Contested Facets of the Media City," *Observatorio (OBS*) Journal* 9 (2015): 1–21.

2. There is a long history of partnership and ownership stakes among newspaper, radio, and television companies and sports teams, which can be traced to the advent of modern sports. There are numerous examples of media companies owning stakes in sports teams: The *Minnesota Star Tribune* (owned by parent company, Gannett, and formerly the *Minneapolis Star Tribune*) had a stake in the Minnesota Twins; CBS owned a majority stake in the Yankees in the 1960s and 1970s; Fox (under Rupert Murdoch's News Corporation) owned the Dodgers in the late 1990s and early 2000s; Walt Disney Company owned the Ducks until 2005 and the Angels until 2003; Comcast still owns the Philadelphia Flyers; Ted Turner, WTBS station owner, also owned the Braves, which I discuss in chapter 1. Regional sports networks like the New England Sports Network (owned by the company that owns the Boston Red Sox and its primary broadcaster) also exemplify long-standing connections between media and sports team partnerships. The more recent turn to sports teams starting their own media companies and becoming media ecosystems in and of themselves therefore has a longer history of this close relationship between media and sports.

3. David Rowe and Brett Hutchins, "The Mediat(izat)ion of Urban Leisure: Screening the Event," in *The Routledge Companion to Urban Media and Communication*, ed. Zlatan Krajina and Deborah Stevenson, 283–91 (New York: Routledge, 2020).

4. B. Joseph Pine and James H. Gilmore, *The Experience Economy: Competing for Customer Time, Attention, and Money* (Boston: Harvard Business Review Press, 2020).

5. David Rowe, "New Screen Action and Its Memories: The 'Live' Performance of Mediated Sport Fandom," *Television & New Media* 15, no. 8 (2014): 752–59, https://doi.org/10.1177/1527476414527835. A counterexample to how contemporary stadiums invite interactive media use in the stadium is Intuit Dome, home of the LA Clippers and owned by Microsoft CEO, Steve Ballmer. The design of Intuit Dome discourages second screen use, as Ballmer suggests he wants the stadium to be for "hard core" basketball fans who are in their seats with their "heads up." Bret McCormick, "Ballmer's in the Details," Sports Business Journal, February 19, 2024, https://www.sportsbusinessjournal.com/Articles/2024/02/19/facilities.

6. Pine and Gilmore, *Experience Economy*.

7. Daniel Taylor, "Selhurst Park at 100: Why One of England's Least Loved Grounds Really Matters," *New York Times*, https://www.nytimes.com/athletic/5724054/2024/08/29/selhurst-park-crystal-palace-100-years/.

8. Ivo Jirásek and Geoffery Zain Kohe, "Readjusting Our Sporting Sites/Sight: Sportification and the Theatricality of Social Life," *Sport, Ethics and Philosophy* 9, no. 3 (2015): 257–70, https://doi.org/10.1080/17511321.2015.1065433.

9. Jirásek and Kohe, "Readjusting Our Sporting Sites/Sight," 257.

10. Norbert Elias and Eric Dunning, *Quest for Excitement: Sport and Leisure in the Civilizing Process* (Oxford: B. Blackwell, 1986); Norbert Elias, *The Civilizing Process* (Oxford: B. Blackwell, 1982).

11. Joseph Maguire, "Sportization Processes: Emergence, Diffusion and Globalization," *Schweizerische Zeitschrift Für Soziologie* 21, no. 3 (1995): 577–95.

12. Jirásek and Kohe, "Readjusting Our Sporting Sites/Sight," 258.

13. On theories of mediatization and its conceptualization in communication and media studies, see Nick Couldry and Andreas Hepp, "Conceptualizing Mediatization: Contexts, Traditions, Arguments: Editorial," *Communication Theory* 23, no. 3 (2013): 191–202, https://doi.org/10.1111/comt.12019.

14. Couldry and Hepp, "Conceptualizing Mediatization," 258.

15. Henry Jenkins, *Convergence Culture: Where Old and New Media Collide* (New York: New York University Press, 2006), 2.

16. David L. Andrews, Ronald L. Mower, and Michael L. Silk, "Ghettocentrism and the Essentialized Black Male Athlete," in *Commodified and Criminalized: New Racism and African Americans in Contemporary Sports*, ed. David J. Leonard and C. Richard King, 69–94 (Lanham, MD: Rowman & Littlefield, 2012).

17. Michael L. Butterworth, "Public Memorializing in the Stadium: Mediated Sport, the 10th Anniversary of 9/11, and the Illusion of Democracy," *Communication & Sport* 2, no. 3 (2014): 203–224, https://doi.org/10.1177/2167479513485735.

18. My selections were also partly based on my own relationship to the cities, as they are either cities I've lived in (Twin Cities), near (Seattle), or have connections that made it possible for me to access primary resources (Atlanta). I acknowledge

my subjective positionality in relation to the research, sometimes drawing on my personal and affective connections to these spaces for critical reflection. I hope readers will see this as a benefit, as sports themselves are deeply affective. I acknowledge my experiences might at times influence and limit the conclusions that can be drawn from these insights, as well as from the lack of knowledge and experience I might have with regard to particular cities and teams. In those instances, I hope the book's larger grounding in archival research, interviews, and documentation will compensate for these limitations.

19. Lawrence A. Wenner, *MediaSport* (London: Routledge, 2010).

20. Sut Jhally, "The Spectacle of Accumulation: Material and Cultural Factors in the Evolution of the Sports/Media Complex," *Insurgent Sociologist* 12, no. 3 (1984): 41–57, https://doi.org/10.1177/089692058401200304.

21. David Rowe, *Sport, Culture and the Media*, 2nd ed., repr. (Maidenhead: Open University Press, 2004), 4.

22. Victoria E. Johnson, *Sports TV*, Routledge Television Guidebooks (New York: Routledge, 2021).

23. Brett Hutchins and David Rowe, eds., *Digital Media Sport: Technology, Power and Culture in the Network Society*, Routledge Research in Cultural and Media Studies 51 (New York: Routledge, 2013); Brett Hutchins and David Rowe, *Sport beyond Television: The Internet, Digital Media and the Rise of Networked Media Sport*, Routledge Research in Cultural and Media Studies 40 (New York: Routledge, 2012).

24. Johnson, *Sports TV*, 3.

25. Nick Couldry and Anna McCarthy, *MediaSpace: Place, Scale, and Culture in a Media Age* (London: Routledge, 2004).

26. Michael Serazio, *The Power of Sports: Media and Spectacle in American Culture* (New York: New York University Press, 2019); Dave Zirin, *A People's History of Sports in the United States: 250 Years of Politics, Protest, People, and Play* (New York: New Press, 2009).

27. Butterworth, "Public Memorializing in the Stadium."

28. Harry Edwards, *The Revolt of the Black Athlete*, 50th anniversary ed. (Urbana: University of Illinois Press, 2017; Serazio, *Power of Sports*; Zirin, *People's History of Sports*. The controversy over players' Take a Knee movement (where players, inspired by San Francisco 49ers quarterback Colin Kaepernick in 2016, kneel during the national anthem) demonstrates this antagonism.

29. Kevin Hylton, *"Race" and Sport: Critical Race Theory* (London: Routledge, 2009); David J. Leonard, *Playing While White: Privilege and Power On and Off the Field* (Seattle: University of Washington Press, 2017); David J. Leonard and C. Richard King, *Commodified and Criminalized: New Racism and African Americans in Contemporary Sports* (Lanham, MD: Rowman & Littlefield, 2012); Edwards, *Revolt of the Black Athlete*.

30. Ben Carrington, "'What I Said Was Racist—But I'm Not a Racist': Anti-Racism and the White Sports/Media Complex," in *Sport and Challenges to Racism*, ed. Jonathan Long and Karl Spracklen (Basingstoke: Palgrave Macmillan, 2011), 90.

31. Steve Macek, *Urban Nightmares: The Media, the Right, and the Moral Panic over the City* (Minneapolis: University of Minnesota Press, 2006).

32. Macek, *Urban Nightmares*, xv–xvi.

33. David L. Andrews, Ronald L. Mower, and Michael L. Silk, "Ghettocentrism and the Essentialized Black Male Athlete," in Leonard and King, *Commodified and Criminalized*, 70.

34. Andrews, Mower, and Silk, "Ghettocentrism," 76.

35. Michael Omi and Howard Winant, *Racial Formation in the United States: From the 1960s to the 1980s*, Critical Social Thought (New York: Routledge & Kegan Paul, 1986), 61.

36. David Morley, "For a Materialist, Non-Media-Centric Media Studies," *Television & New Media* 10, no. 1 (2009): 114–16, https://doi.org/10.1177/1527476408327173.

37. Lisa Parks, "'Stuff You Can Kick': Toward a Theory of Media Infrastructures," in *Between Humanities and the Digital*, ed. Patrik Svensson and David Theo Goldberg, 355–74 (Cambridge, MA: MIT Press, 2015).

38. See, for example, Lisa Parks, *Cultures in Orbit: Satellites and the Televisual* (Durham, NC: Duke University Press, 2005); Naomi Schiller, "Urban Media as Infrastructure for Social Change," in Krajina and Stevenson, *Routledge Companion to Urban Media and Communication*, 204–214; Nicole Starosielski, *The Undersea Network*, Sign, Storage, Transmission (Durham, NC: Duke University Press, 2015).

39. Steven Secular, *The Digital NBA: How the World's Savviest League Brings the Court to Our Couch*, Studies in Sports Media (Urbana: University of Illinois Press, 2023), 7.

40. Secular, *Digital NBA*, 55, 56.

41. Dave Colangelo, *The Building as Screen: A History, Theory, and Practice of Massive Media*, MediaMatters (Amsterdam: Amsterdam University Press, 2020).

42. Shannon Mattern, "Scaffolding, Hard and Soft—Infrastructures as Critical and Generative Structures," *Spheres* 3 (2016), https://spheres-journal.org/contribution/scaffolding-hard-and-soft-infrastructures-as-critical-and-generative-structures/.

43. Schiller, "Urban Media as Infrastructure for Social Change," 207.

44. Schiller, "Urban Media as Infrastructure for Social Change," 207.

45. Scott McQuire, "The Politics of Public Space in the Media City," *First Monday*, 2006, https://journals.uic.edu/ojs/index.php/fm/article/download/1544/1459#p3; emphasis in original.

46. Scott McQuire, *The Media City: Media, Architecture and Urban Space* (Los Angeles: Sage, 2008).

47. Myria Georgiou and Jun Yu, "Subjectivity in the Media City: The Media Life and Representation of the Cosmopolitan Stranger," in Krajina and Stevenson, *Routledge Companion to Urban Media and Communication*, 117.

48. Erica Stein and Germaine R. Halegoua, "Introduction: How to Do Things with Media and the City," in *The Routledge Companion to Media and the City*, ed. Erica Stein, Germaine R. Halegoua, and Brendan Kredell (London: Routledge, 2023), 1.

49. Much early media cities scholarship focused on representation. See, for example, David B. Clarke, *The Cinematic City* (London: Routledge, 1997); Tony Fitzmaurice

and Mark Sheil, *Cinema and the City: Film and Urban Societies in a Global Context* (Oxford: Blackwell Publishers, 2001). More recent work considers how other forms of media, e.g., television and digital media, constitute the urban. See, for example, Charlotte Brunsdon, *Television Cities: Paris, London, Baltimore* (Durham, NC: Duke University Press, 2018); Germaine R. Halegoua, *The Digital City: Media and the Social Production of Place* (New York: New York University Press, 2018).

50. See Nanna Verhoeff, "Screens in the City," in *Screens: From Materiality to Spectatorship: A Historical and Theoretical Reassessment*, ed. Dominique Chateau and Jose Moure, 125–39 (Amsterdam: Amsterdam University Press, 2016); Halegoua, *Digital City*; Germaine R. Halegoua, *Smart Cities*, MIT Press Essential Knowledge Series (Cambridge, MA: MIT Press, 2020).

51. See, for example, Helen Morgan Parmett, *Down in Treme: Race, Place, and New Orleans on Television* (Stuttgart: Franz Steiner Verlag, 2019), https://elibrary.steiner-verlag.de/book/99.105010/9783515121828; Helen Morgan Parmett, "Site-Specific Television as Urban Renewal: or, How Portland Became *Portlandia*," *International Journal of Cultural Studies* 21, no. 1 (2018): 42–56, https://doi.org/10.1177/1367877917704493; Ipek A. Celik Rappas, "From *Titanic* to *Game of Thrones*: Promoting Belfast as a Global Media Capital," *Media, Culture & Society* 41, no. 4 (2019): 539–56, https://doi.org/10.1177/0163443718823148; Ipek A. Celik Rappas and Sezen Kayhan, "TV Series Production and the Urban Restructuring of Istanbul," *Television & New Media* 19, no. 1 (2018): 3–23, https://doi.org/10.1177/1527476416681500; Noelle Griffis, "Music City Makeover: The Televisual Tourism of Nashville," in *Media Crossroads: Intersections of Space and Identity in Screen Cultures*, ed. Paula J. Massood, Angel Daniel Matos, and Pamela Robertson Wojcik (Durham, NC: Duke University Press, 2021); Elizabeth A. Patton, "Portland at the Intersection: Gentrification and the Whitening of the City in *Portlandia*'s Hipster Wonderland," in *Media Crossroads: Intersections of Space and Identity in Screen Cultures*, ed. Paula J. Massood, Angel Daniel Matos, and Pamela Robertson Wojcik (Durham, NC: Duke University Press, 2021).

52. Brian Larkin, "The Politics and Poetics of Infrastructure," *Annual Review of Anthropology* 42, no. 1 (2013): 327–43, https://doi.org/10.1146/annurev-anthro-092412-155522.

53. Michel Foucault, "Governmentality," ed. Paul Rabinow and Nikolas Rose, *The Essential Foucault* 229–45 (New York: New Press, 2003).

54. Foucault, "Governmentality," 328.

55. Foucault, "Governmentality," 333.

56. Nigel J. Thrift, *Non-Representational Theory: Space, Politics, Affect* (London: Routledge, 2008), 13.

57. Gilles Deleuze and Félix Guattari, *A Thousand Plateaus: Capitalism and Schizophrenia* (Minneapolis: University of Minnesota Press, 1987), xviii.

58. Brian Massumi, *Parables for the Virtual: Movement, Affect, Sensation*, Post-Contemporary Interventions (Durham, NC: Duke University Press, 2002), 72.

59. Carrie Rentschler, "Affect," in *Keywords for Media Studies*, ed. Laurie Ouellette and Jonathan Gray (New York: New York University Press, 2017), 12.

60. Melissa Gregg and Gregory J. Seigworth, eds., *The Affect Theory Reader* (Durham, NC: Duke University Press, 2010), 1.

61. Rentschler, "Affect," 12.

62. See, for example, Gregg and Seigworth, *Affect Theory Reader*; Massumi, *Parables for the Virtual*.

63. Sara Ahmed, *The Cultural Politics of Emotion* (New York: Routledge, 2004).

64. Mike S. Schafer and Jochen Roose, "Emotions in Sports Stadia," in *Stadium Worlds: Football, Space and the Built Environment*, ed. Sybille Frank and Silke Steets, 229–44 (Milton Park, Abingdon, Oxon: Routledge, 2010).

65. Massumi, *Parables for the Virtual*, 71.

66. John Bale, *Landscapes of Modern Sport* (Leicester: Leicester University Press, 1994); John Bale, "Space, Place and Body Culture: Yi-Fu Tuan and a Geography of Sport," *Geografiska Annaler: Series B, Human Geography* 78, no. 3 (1996): 163–71, https://doi.org/10.1080/04353684.1996.11879706.

67. John Bale, "The Spatial Development of the Modern Stadium," *International Review for the Sociology of Sport* 28, no. 2–3 (1993): 121–33, https://doi.org/10.1177/101269029302800204.

68. Yu-Fi Tuan, "Space and Place: Humanistic Perspective," in *Philosophy in Geography*, ed. Stephen Gale and Gunnar Olsson (Dordrecht: Springer Netherlands, 1979), 387.

69. Tuan, "Space and Place," 415.

70. Doreen B. Massey, *Space, Place, and Gender* (Minneapolis: University of Minnesota Press, 1994).

71. Anita Berrizbeitia, "Re-Placing Process," in *Large Parks*, ed. Julia Czerniak, George Hargreaves, and Harvard University (New York: Princeton Architectural Press; in association with the Harvard University Graduate School of Design, 2007), 378.

72. Berrizbeitia, "Re-Placing Process," 379.

73. Anna McCarthy, *Ambient Television: Visual Culture and Public Space* (Durham, NC: Duke University Press, 2001), 2.

74. See, for example, Thomas F. Carter, "Interrogating Athletic Urbanism: On Examining the Politics of the City Underpinning the Production of the Spectacle," *International Review for the Sociology of Sport* 46, no. 2 (2011): 131–39, https://doi.org/10.1177/1012690211398167; Michael T. Friedman, *Mallparks: Baseball Stadiums and the Culture of Consumption* (Ithaca, NY: Cornell University Press, 2023); Timothy A. Gibson, *Securing the Spectacular City: The Politics of Revitalization and Homelessness in Downtown Seattle* (Lanham, MD: Lexington Books, 2004); Harvey K. Newman, "Race and the Tourist Bubble in Downtown Atlanta," *Urban Affairs Review* 37, no. 3 (2002): 301–321, https://doi.org/10.1177/10780870222185351; Daniel Rosensweig, *Retro Ball Parks: Instant History, Baseball and the New American City* (Knoxville: University of Tennessee Press, 2005).

75. Undoubtedly, the accounts given in some interviews are likely to be a more official discourse. However, this is consistent with the broader aim of this research, which is to track the official discourse from the stakeholders involved in stadium construction who have some degree of power in shaping the discourse and in impli-

cating the production of space in the city. Yet, I've also tried to include where possible representatives or documentation from organizations who advocate for those who are usually shut out of these conversations as well. I acknowledge that the perspectives presented here are not wholly constitutive of the diverse views of stakeholders.

76. Michel Foucault, *The Archaeology of Knowledge* (New York: Pantheon Books, 1972), 28.

77. Henri Lefebvre, *The Production of Space* (Oxford: Blackwell, 1991), 26.

78. Lefebvre, *Production of Space*, 39.

79. Bale, *Landscapes of Modern Sport*.

80. Mark Dyreson and Robert C. Trumpbour, *The Rise of Stadiums in the Modern United States: Cathedrals of Sport* (London: Routledge, 2013).

81. Benjamin Sitton Flowers, *Sport and Architecture* (London: Routledge, 2018), 17.

82. Bettina Kratzmuller, "'Show Yourself to the People!': Ancient Stadiums, Politics and Society," in Frank and Steets, *Stadium Worlds*, 37.

83. Geraint John, Rod Sheard, and Ben Vickery, *Stadia: The Populous Design and Development Guide* (Abingdon, UK: 2013), 6.

84. John Bale, *Sports Geography* (London: Routledge, 2006), 133.

85. See Rod Sheard, Robert Powell, and Patrick Bingham-Hall, *The Stadium: Architecture for the New Global Culture* (Singapore: Periplus, 2005).

86. See, for example, Michel Desbordes, "The Establishment and Management of Sports Arenas: A Neo-Marketing Approach," in *Global Sport Marketing: Contemporary Issues and Practice*, ed. Michel Desbordes and André Richelieu, 156–86 (Abingdon, Oxon, UK: Routledge, 2014); John, Sheard, and Vickery, *Stadia*; Robert C. Trumpbour, *The New Cathedrals: Politics and Media in the History of Stadium Construction* (Syracuse, NY: Syracuse University Press, 2007); and Tim Chapin, "The Political Economy of Sports Facility Location: An End-of-the-Century Review and Assessment," *Marquette Sports Law Review* 10, no. 2 (2020): 361–82.

87. The relationship among sport, stadiums, and media has long been co-constitutive. On cinema and sport, see Dan Streible, *Fight Pictures: A History of Boxing and Early Cinema* (Berkeley: University of California Press, 2008). On stadiums, news, and radio, see Trumpbour, *New Cathedrals*. See also Michelle Hilmes and Lauren Rabinovitz on how radio and cinema spaces served as key sites of citizenship training, similar to stadiums. See Michele Hilmes, *Radio Voices: American Broadcasting, 1922–1952* (Minneapolis: University of Minnesota Press, 1997); Lauren Rabinovitz, *For the Love of Pleasure: Women, Movies, and Culture in Turn-of-the-Century Chicago* (New Brunswick, NJ: Rutgers University Press, 1998).

88. Serazio, *Power of Sports*, 252.

89. Benjamin D. Lisle, *Modern Coliseum: Stadiums and American Culture* (Philadelphia: University of Pennsylvania Press, 2017).

90. Cory Hillman, *American Sports in an Age of Consumption: How Commercialization Is Changing the Game* (Jefferson, NC: McFarland, 2016).

91. Sheard, Powell, and Bingham-Hall, *The Stadium*, 107.

92. Interstate highways were themselves frequently built by bulldozing Black and poor neighborhoods in the city in the name of "slum clearance," disposing of economically struggling neighborhoods that could then be seized by private capital and investment for profit.

93. George Lipsitz, *How Racism Takes Place* (Philadelphia: Temple University Press, 2011).

94. Chapin, "Political Economy of Sports Facility Location."

95. On post-racialism and neoliberalism, see Sarah Banet-Weiser, "What's Your Flava? Race and Postfeminism in Media Culture," in *Interrogating Postfeminism Gender and the Politics of Popular Culture*, ed. Yvonne Tasker and Diane Negra (Durham, NC: Duke University Press, 2007); Eduardo Bonilla-Silva, *White Supremacy and Racism in the Post–Civil Rights Era* (Boulder, CO: L. Rienner, 2001); Henry A. Giroux, *The Terror of Neoliberalism* (Boulder, CO: Paradigm, 2004); David Theo Goldberg, *The Threat of Race: Reflections on Racial Neoliberalism* (Malden, MA: Wiley-Blackwell, 2009); and Herman Gray, *Cultural Moves: African Americans and the Politics of Representation* (Berkeley: University of California Press, 2005).

96. John, Sheard, and Vickery, *Stadia*, 21.

97. Martin Wimmer, Inka Humann, and Anna Martovitskaya, *Stadium Buildings Construction and Design Manual* (Berlin: DOM Publishers, 2016), 14.

Chapter 1. Going Major League, Going Global

1. Michael Dobbins, "Race and Class in Atlanta-Style Development: Promoting Inclusion and Justice," in *Planning Atlanta*, ed. Harley F. Etienne and Barbara Faga (Chicago: American Planning Assoc., Planners Press, 2014), 113.

2. Maurice J. Hobson, *The Legend of the Black Mecca: Politics and Class in the Making of Modern Atlanta* (Chapel Hill: University of North Carolina Press, 2017).

3. Dylan Jackson, "Atlanta Has the Highest Income Inequality in the Nation, Census Data Shows," *Atlanta Journal-Constitution*, November 28, 2022, https://www.ajc.com/news/investigations/atlanta-has-the-highest-income-inequality-in-the-nation-census-data-shows/YJRZ6A4UGBFWTMYICTG2BCOUPU/.

4. David L. Sjoquist, *The Atlanta Paradox* (New York: Russell Sage Foundation, 2000), 2.

5. Dobbins, "Race and Class in Atlanta-Style Development," 113.

6. Larry Keating, *Atlanta: Race, Class, and Urban Expansion* (Philadelphia: Temple University Press, 2001).

7. The Creative Media Industries Institute, "Building Georgia's Digital Entertainment Future" (Georgia State University, 2023), https://issuu.com/gsumag/docs/cmii_digital_georgia_report_06-05c-23.

8. Nicquel Terry Ellis, "'Hollywood of the South': After a Decade, Industry Leaders Succeed in Making Atlanta a Hub for Filmmakers of Color," *USA Today*, March 1, 2020, https://www.usatoday.com/story/news/2020/03/01/industry-leaders-say

-tyler-perry-has-paved-the-way-for-filmmakers-of-color-to-succeed-in-georgia/4747702002/.

9. Ryan Zickgraf, "Tyler Perry's Wealth Is Not Trickling Down to Black Residents of Atlanta," *Jacobin*, December 4, 2023, https://jacobin.com/2023/12/tyler-perry-atlanta-tax-breaks-trickle-down-race-income-inequality.

10. Tyler Perry, "BET Ultimate Icon Award Acceptance Speech," "Nettye Johnson: Help Somebody Cross," June 23, 2019, https://nettyejohnson.com/2019/06/help-somebody-cross.html.

11. Zickgraf, "Tyler Perry's Wealth Is Not Trickling Down."

12. Keating, *Atlanta: Race, Class, and Urban Expansion*, 2.

13. Charles Rutheiser, *Imagineering Atlanta: The Politics of Place in the City of Dreams*, Haymarket Series (London: Verso, 1996), 4.

14. Rutheiser, *Imagineering Atlanta*, 52; Harvey K. Newman, "Race and the Tourist Bubble in Downtown Atlanta," *Urban Affairs Review* 37, no. 3 (2002): 301–321, https://doi.org/10.1177/10780870222185351.

15. Michael Lomax, "Stadiums, Boosters, Politicians and Major League Baseball's Reluctance to Expand: An Exploration of Post–Second World War US Trends," *International Journal of the History of Sport* 25, no. 11 (2008): 95, https://doi.org/10.1080/09523360802299260.

16. Keating, *Atlanta: Race, Class, and Urban Expansion*, 99.

17. Vartin G. Vartanig, "Atlanta Rushes to National Role," *New York Times*, November 16, 1964, City of Atlanta, Program and Policy Records (hereafter, CAPPR), series 15, box 14, folder 3, James G. Kenan Research Center at the Atlanta History Center, Atlanta, Georgia.

18. "Atlanta: Major League All the Way . . . Including Newspapers," *New York Times*, November 17, 1964, CAPPR.

19. Rutheiser, *Imagineering Atlanta*, 49.

20. Bell & Stanton Inc., "Atlanta Braves Opening Atlanta Stadium: An Operations Manual on the Job to Be Done, Prepared for the Atlanta Chamber of Commerce," February 20, 1966, CAPPR.

21. Bell & Stanton Inc., "Atlanta Braves Opening Atlanta Stadium."

22. Atlanta–Fulton County Recreation Authority (hereafter, AFCRA), "Atlanta Stadium: Special Dedication Edition," circa 1967, Atlanta–Fulton County Stadium Collection, 1966–1996, MSS854f, folder 1, James G. Kenan Research Center at the Atlanta History Center, Atlanta, Georgia.

23. AFCRA, "Atlanta Stadium," 50.

24. AFCRA, "Atlanta Stadium," 22. It's worth noting how underdeveloped computer technology was at the time, making its use in stadium construction an innovative use of computing. This demonstrates how stadium construction has long been a testing ground for rolling out new technologies.

25. AFCRA, "Atlanta Stadium," 22.

26. AFCRA, "Atlanta Stadium," 22, 23.

27. AFCRA, "Atlanta Stadium," 24.

28. AFCRA, "Atlanta Stadium."

29. Will Butler, "The Black Crackers: Atlanta's Negro League Baseball Legacy," Atlanta History Center, June 30, 2021, https://www.atlantahistorycenter.com/blog/the-black-crackers-atlantas-negro-league-baseball-legacy/.

30. AFCRA, "Atlanta Stadium," 24.

31. Ronald H. Bayor, *Race and the Shaping of Twentieth-Century Atlanta* (Chapel Hill: University of North Carolina Press, 1996), 74.

32. Newman, "Race and the Tourist Bubble."

33. Dobbins, "Race and Class in Atlanta-Style Development"; Keating, *Atlanta: Race, Class, and Urban Expansion*.

34. AFCRA, "Atlanta Stadium," 24.

35. Bayor, *Race and the Shaping of Twentieth-Century Atlanta*, 74–75.

36. William G. Holt, "Planned to Fail: Creating the Global South in American South Communities," in *Handbook of Emerging 21st-Century Cities*, ed. Kris Bezdecny and Kevin Archer (Cheltenham, UK: Edward Elgar Publishing, 2018), 205–221. Estimates suggest approximately 68,000 people were displaced; see Keating, *Atlanta: Race, Class, and Urban Expansion*, 93. On Summerhill's history, see Marni Davis's multimedia project, "Streetscape Palimpsest: A History of Georgia Avenue," https://www.arcgis.com/apps/MapJournal/index.html?appid=b907a20ea0564aaa921ecd208ec746bf.

37. Keating, *Atlanta: Race, Class, and Urban Expansion*, 92.

38. Keating, *Atlanta: Race, Class, and Urban Expansion*, 101.

39. Rutheiser, *Imagineering Atlanta*, 61.

40. Irene V. Holliman, "From Crackertown to Model City? Urban Renewal and Community Building in Atlanta, 1963–1966," *Journal of Urban History* 35, no. 3 (2009): 370, https://doi.org/10.1177/0096144208330402.

41. City of Atlanta Department of Planning and Development and Corporation for Olympic Development in Atlanta (hereafter, ADPD/CODA), "Master Olympic Development Program for City of Atlanta" (Atlanta, Georgia, October 19, 1993), 2, Maynard Jackson Papers (hereafter, MJP), box 108, folder 13, Atlanta University Center Robert W. Woodruff Library, Atlanta, Georgia.

42. Rutheiser, *Imagineering Atlanta*, 180.

43. Saskia Sassen, "The Global City: Strategic Site/New Frontier," in *Democracy, Citizenship, and the Global City*, ed. Engin F. Isin, 48–61 (London: Routledge, 2000).

44. Neil Brenner and Nikolas Theodore, *Spaces of Neoliberalism: Urban Restructuring in North America and Western Europe* (Malden, MA: Blackwell, 2002).

45. Kevin F. Gotham and Jeannie Haubert, "Neoliberal Revitalization: Prison Building, Casinos, and Tourism in Louisiana," in *Urban Communication: Production, Text, Context*, ed. Timothy A. Gibson and Mark Douglas Lowes, 27–28 (Lanham, MD: Rowman and Littlefield, 2007).

46. Nikolas Rose, "The Death of the Social? Re-Figuring the Territory of Government," *Economy and Society* 25, no. 3 (1996): 330–31, https://doi.org/10.1080/03085149600000018.

47. Regional/Urban Design Assistance Team, "Atlanta R/UDAT" (Atlanta, Georgia, September 14, 1992), MJP, box 114, folder 1.

48. Sarah Dylla, "Venues and Impact: Planning the Sites of '96," Atlanta History Center, August 24, 2020, https://www.atlantahistorycenter.com/venues-and-impact-planning-the-sites-of-96/.

49. Keating, *Atlanta: Race, Class, and Urban Expansion*, 150.

50. Diversity and multiculturalism were key criteria used by the IOC during this era. See Dobbins, "Race and Class in Atlanta-Style Development," 113.

51. Dylla, "Venues and Impact."

52. International Telecommunications Union, "Atlanta 1996," https://www.itu.int/newsarchive/wtd/1996/atlanta.html.

53. Rutheiser, *Imagineering Atlanta*; Keating, *Atlanta: Race, Class, and Urban Expansion*.

54. ADPD/CODA, "Master Olympic Development Program for City of Atlanta."

55. Rutheiser, *Imagineering Atlanta*; Keating, *Atlanta: Race, Class, and Urban Expansion*.

56. Atlanta Stadium Design Team, "Facility Impact Report, Olympic Stadium" (Atlanta, Georgia, January 8, 1993), MJP, box 111, folder 20.

57. Atlanta Stadium Design Team, "Facility Impact Report, Olympic Stadium."

58. Atlanta Committee for the Olympic Games, "Getting Schools Involved in the Olympics," *ACOG Torch*, January 28, 1993, MJP, box 106, folder 17.

59. Atlanta Committee for the Olympic Games, "Equal Economic Opportunity Plan (EEOP): Year End 1992 Executive Summary" (Atlanta, Georgia, March 12, 1993), MJP, box 106, folder 9.

60. Michan Andrew Connor, "Metropolitan Secession and the Space of Color-Blind Racism in Atlanta," *Journal of Urban Affairs* 37, no. 4 (2015): 436–61, https://doi.org/10.1111/juaf.12101; Keating, *Atlanta: Race, Class, and Urban Expansion*.

61. ADPD/CODA, "Master Olympic Development Program for City of Atlanta."

62. ADPD/CODA, "Master Olympic Development Program for City of Atlanta."

63. Corporation for Olympic Development in Atlanta, "Implementing Community Revival, Background Memo" (Atlanta, Georgia, July 13, 1993), MJP, box 106, folder 21.

64. Corporation for Olympic Development in Atlanta, "Olympic Stadium Parking and Land Acquisition Update," October 6, 1993, MJP, box 112, folder 1.

65. Keating, *Atlanta: Race, Class, and Urban Expansion*.

66. Rutheiser, *Imagineering Atlanta*, 5.

67. Keating, *Atlanta: Race, Class, and Urban Expansion*, 166.

68. Georgia World Congress Center Authority, "Georgia Dome Facts, Figures, and Records," https://www.gwcca.org/wp-content/uploads/2017/10/Georgia-Dome-General-Fact-Sheet.pdf/, accessed January 13, 2024.

69. Elyse Umlauf, "Georgia Dome Team Scores a Success," *Building Design and Construction*, 1993, http://bi.gale.com.ezproxy.uvm.edu/essentials/article/GALE%7CA13369270?u=vol_b92b.

70. Len Pasquarelli, "INSIDE: New Stadium Impresses Falcons with Spacious, Fan-Friendly Design," *Atlanta Journal and Constitution*, March 18, 1992, sec. Sports.

71. "Atlanta Set to Open the New Georgia Dome," *PR Newswire*, July 31, 1992, sec. State and Regional News.

72. Beverly Wilson, "The Georgia Dome," TVTechnology, January 1, 2004, https://www.tvtechnology.com/miscellaneous/the-georgia-dome.

73. "Falcons to Pay for Georgia Dome Facelift," *Atlanta Business Chronicle*, September 14, 2006, https://www.bizjournals.com/atlanta/stories/2006/09/11/daily32.html.

74. Umlauf, "Georgia Dome Team Scores a Success."

75. "Georgia Stadium Corp. Releases," *PR Newswire*, December 2, 1987.

76. Kate Diedrick and Christopher A. Le Dantec, "Atlanta's Westside Residents Challenge the Rules of Sport Mega-Development," *Third World Thematics: A TWQ Journal* 2, no. 1 (2017): 57, https://doi.org/10.1080/23802014.2017.1367261.

77. Booker T. Washington High School, Center for the Humanities (hereafter, BTWHS), "Oral History Collection" (Atlanta, Georgia, 1989 1988), Oral History Collections on the Construction of the Georgia Dome in Vine City, MSS611, box 1, James G. Kenan Research Center at the Atlanta History Center, Atlanta, Georgia.

78. BTWHS, "Oral History Collection."

79. BTWHS, "Oral History Collection."

80. BTWHS. "Oral History Collection."

81. BTWHS, "Oral History Collection."

82. BTWHS, "Oral History Collection."

83. Newman, "Race and the Tourist Bubble," 317.

84. Turner owned the team until 2003 when he sold it along with Turner Broadcasting to AOL/Time Warner, who in turn sold the team to Liberty Media in 2007.

85. "Who Is the Owner of the Atlanta Braves?" 11Alive.com, October 9, 2021, https://www.11alive.com/article/sports/atlanta-braves-owner-world-series/85-3c5c8ba8-dcc8-4b13-914d-a72707b975df.

86. "Yachtsman Turner Purchases Braves," *New York Times*, January 7, 1976, sec. Archives, https://www.nytimes.com/1976/01/07/archives/yachtsman-turner-purchases-braves-yachtsman-buys-braves-for-at.html.

87. Rutheiser, *Imagineering Atlanta*, 69.

88. William Weathersby Jr., "Turner Field," *TCI*, May 1997.

89. Weathersby Jr., "Turner Field."

90. "The New Stadium: Stadium Q and A," *Atlanta Journal Constitution*, October 27, 1992, sec. Sports.

91. "The Ballparks: Turner Field," *This Great Game* (blog), https://thisgreatgame.com/ballparks-turner-field/, accessed October 25, 2022.

92. Weathersby Jr., "Turner Field."

93. "It's Official . . . New Home of the Atlanta Braves to Be Named Turner Field," *PR Newswire*, December 13, 1996, sec. Financial News.

94. Weathersby Jr., "Turner Field."

95. Weathersby Jr., "Turner Field."
96. Keating, *Atlanta: Race, Class, and Urban Expansion*, 173.
97. Keating, *Atlanta: Race, Class, and Urban Expansion*, 144.
98. Joseph G. Martin, Altamira Design and Common Sense, and Linda D. DuBose, "Summerhill Urban Redevelopment Plan" (Atlanta, Georgia, October 1993), 1, MJP, box 114, folder 14.
99. Cortland Rankin, *Decline and Reimagination in Cinematic New York* (New York: Routledge, 2023), 25.
100. Martin, Altamira Design and Common Sense, and DuBose (herafter, MADCSD), "Summerhill Urban Redevelopment Plan," 3.
101. MADCSD, "Summerhill Urban Redevelopment Plan," 5.
102. MADCSD, "Summerhill Urban Redevelopment Plan," 21.
103. MADCSD, "Summerhill Urban Redevelopment Plan," 4–6.
104. Summerhill Neighborhood, "Job Training and Community Enhancement Program" (Atlanta, Georgia, January 7, 1993), 3, MJP, box 107, folder 1.
105. MADCSD, "Summerhill Urban Redevelopment Plan," 5.
106. Keating, *Atlanta: Race, Class, and Urban Expansion*, 159.
107. Rutheiser, *Imagineering Atlanta*, 328.
108. Rutheiser, *Imagineering Atlanta*, 253.
109. Holt, "Planned to Fail."

Chapter 2. Governing the Fan-Advocate-Citizen in the Interactive Stadium

1. Harvey K. Newman, "Race and the Tourist Bubble in Downtown Atlanta," *Urban Affairs Review* 37, no. 3 (2002): 301–21, https://doi.org/10.1177/10780870222185351.
2. Tim Tucker and Ernie Suggs, "New Developments Falcons Stadium; City OKs Stadium Deal," *Atlanta Journal-Constitution*, March 19, 2013, sec. News.
3. Tim Tucker, "Braves Move to Cobb County: Stealth, Speed Sealed Deal," *Atlanta Journal-Constitution*, November 18, 2023, sec. News.
4. Robert Weintraub, "We Love Our (White) Fans," *Slate*, September 10, 2014, https://slate.com/culture/2014/09/hawks-owner-bruce-levensons-email-reveals-how-atlantas-sports-franchises-think-about-race.html.
5. Michel Foucault, *The History of Sexuality: An Introduction*, vol. 1 (New York: Vintage Books, 1990).
6. Foucault, *History of Sexuality*, 143.
7. Michel Foucault, *Society Must Be Defended: Lectures at the Collège de France, 1975–76* (New York: Picador, 2003).
8. Alexander G. Weheliye, *Habeas Viscus: Racializing Assemblages, Biopolitics, and Black Feminist Theories of the Human* (Durham, NC: Duke University Press, 2014), 4, https://doi.org/10.1515/9780822376491. Weheliye, rightly, criticizes how Foucault's theorization of biopolitics is rooted in Eurocentrism and fails to address its imbrication in coloniality. See also Ann Laura Stoler, *Carnal Knowledge and Imperial Power: Race and the Intimate in*

Colonial Rule (Berkeley: University of California Press, 2002); Peter Redfield, "Foucault in the Tropics: Displacing the Panopticon," in *Anthropologies of Modernity: Foucault, Governmentality, and Life Politics*, ed. Jonathan Xavier Inda, 1st ed. (Hoboken: Wiley, 2008), 50–78.

9. Tim Tucker and Maria Saporta, "Owner of Falcons Thinks Out of the Dome; Blank Says New Stadium Necessary by 2015–16," *Atlanta Journal-Constitution*, September 7, 2006, sec. News.

10. Leon Stafford and Jeremiah McWilliams, "Prospects Rise for New Falcons Stadium," *Atlanta Journal-Constitution*, February 23, 2011, sec. News.

11. Leon Stafford, "NFL Boost Just a Part of Equation; Critics Question Need for New Football Venue," *Atlanta Journal-Constitution*, November 13, 2010, sec. News.

12. Michael E. Kanell and Leon Stafford, "'Just Adding Zero to Zero'; They Predict Taxpayers and Region's Economy Would Score Little," *Atlanta Journal-Constitution*, February 27, 2011, sec. Metro News.

13. D. Orlando Ledbetter and Leon Stafford, "Falcons Like Open-Air Stadium Idea; Official Tells AJC That Team Prefers to Stay Downtown," *Atlanta Journal-Constitution*, May 20, 2010, sec. News.

14. Richard Fausset, "In Atlanta, Debating Race and Sports," *New York Times*, September 10, 2014, sec. U.S., https://www.nytimes.com/2014/09/10/us/in-atlanta-debating-race-and-sports.html.

15. "Ethnicity of NFL Fans U.S. 2020," Statista, https://www.statista.com/statistics/1174759/ethnicity-nfl-fans-team/.

16. Since then, the Falcons continue to promote their association to Black culture through, for example, partnering with Samuel L. Jackson to lead a gospel choir singing the team's theme song, "Rise Up," and rolling out a new black uniform in 2020 in a nod to Black players and fans. See Errin Whack, "The Atlanta Hawks' Audience Problem Is That It Isn't Black Enough," BuzzFeed, September 9, 2014, https://www.buzzfeed.com/errinwhack/atlanta-hawks-audience-problem; Myrydd Wells, "Back in Black: A Brief Look at Atlanta Falcons Uniforms throughout the Decades," *Atlanta Magazine* (blog), April 14, 2020, https://www.atlantamagazine.com/news-culture-articles/back-in-black-a-brief-look-at-atlanta-falcons-uniforms-throughout-the-decades/.

17. Julian Harden, "Is It Time for the Atlanta Falcons to Retire Number 7?" *The Signal* (blog), February 18, 2020, https://georgiastatesignal.com/is-it-time-for-the-atlanta-falcons-to-retire-number-7/.

18. Fausset, "In Atlanta, Debating Race and Sports."

19. Tim Tucker and Katie Leslie, "Falcons Stadium; Church OKs Stadium Deal," *Atlanta Journal-Constitution*, September 20, 2013, sec. News.

20. Leon Stafford, "Study Targets New Stadium Impact," *Atlanta Journal-Constitution*, April 8, 2011, sec. Metro News.

21. Katie Leslie, "Tensions High over $30M for Stadium Neighbors," *Atlanta Journal-Constitution*, August 3, 2013, sec. News.

22. Jay Bookman, "State Picks Stadiums over Schools," *Atlanta Journal-Constitution*, March 16, 2010.

23. Kevin Patra, "NFL Suspends Local Blackout Policy for 2015," NFL.com, March 23, 2015, https://www.nfl.com/news/nfl-suspends-local-blackout-policy-for-2015-0ap3000000480822.
24. Author interview with Mercedes-Benz Stadium executive, March 28, 2022.
25. "Mercedes-Benz Stadium," *Architect*, August 25, 2015, https://www.architectmagazine.com/project-gallery/mercedes-benz-stadium-6468.
26. James Billington, "Super Bowl LIII: The Story behind How Mercedes-Benz Stadium Was Built," *Stadia Magazine* (blog), January 30, 2019, https://www.stadia-magazine.com/features/super-bowl-mercedes-benz-stadium.html.
27. Nina Tory-Henderson, "Mercedes Benz Stadium," *Danish Architecture Center—DAC* (blog), n.d., https://dac.dk/en/knowledgebase/architecture/mercedes-benz-stadium/, accessed November 30, 2022.
28. Tom Walker, "Stadia Design: Meet the People behind the Mercedes Benz Stadium," *CLADMAG*, 2017, issue 4, http://www.cladglobal.com/features?codeid=32299.
29. Christopher Thomas Gaffney, *Temples of the Earthbound Gods: Stadiums in the Cultural Landscapes of Rio de Janeiro and Buenos Aires* (Austin: University of Texas Press, 2010), 26.
30. Billington, "Super Bowl LIII."
31. Walker, "Stadia Design."
32. Author interview with Mercedes-Benz Stadium executive.
33. Billington, "Super Bowl LIII."
34. Nanna Verhoeff, "Screens in the City," *Urban Screens: Situations, Practices, Concepts* (Amsterdam: Amsterdam University Press, n.d.), 126, https://uplopen.com/reader/books/pdf/10.1515/9789048563630; Anne Friedberg, *The Virtual Window: From Alberti to Microsoft* (MIT University Press, 2006), 50.
35. Phil Guido, "The Ultimate Fan Experience: Turning Fans into Advocates," IBM THINK Blog, August 15, 2017, https://admin02.prod.blogs.cis.ibm.net/blogs/think/2017/08/42501/.
36. "Atlanta Stadium," Atlanta Stadium, October 22, 2018, https://www.ibm.com/sports/atlanta-stadium/.
37. Author interview with Mercedes-Benz Stadium executive.
38. "Security and Storage Take Center Stage at Atlanta's Premier Sports and Entertainment Venue," IBM Global Technology Services, April 25, 2019, https://www.ibm.com/case-studies/mercedes-benz-stadium; Shaun Behrens, "Connecting Sports Fans: The Infrastructure Inside the Stadium of Super Bowl LIII," https://blog.paessler.com/infrastructure-inside-the-stadium-of-super-bowl-liii/, accessed January 12, 2025.
39. Tom Bassam, "How IBM Created the Optimal Fan Experience at Mercedes-Benz Stadium," *SportsPro* (blog), July 12, 2018, https://www.sportspro.com/insights/features/from-the-magazine/mercedes-benz-stadium-fan-experience-ibm/.
40. Author interview with Mercedes-Benz Stadium executive.
41. Author interview with Mercedes-Benz Stadium executive.

42. In many cases, teams partner with legacy providers, such as Truist Park and the Atlanta Braves partnering with Comcast, to maximize their content production capabilities.

43. "Atlanta Falcons Open Ticketmaster Studios," https://www.atlantafalcons.com/news/atlanta-falcons-open-ticketmaster-studios/, accessed January 12, 2025.

44. Author interview with Mercedes-Benz Stadium executive.

45. Author interview with Mercedes-Benz Stadium executive.

46. Author interview with Mercedes-Benz Stadium executive.

47. Bassam, "How IBM Created the Optimal Fan Experience."

48. Frictionlessness also distracts users from awareness of the ecological and labor exploitation at work in the production and distribution of digital technology, an exploitation often borne out by the Global South. See Jakko Kemper, *Frictionlessness: The Silicon Valley Philosophy of Seamless Technology and the Aesthetic Value of Imperfection*, Thinking/Media (New York: Bloomsbury Academic, 2024).

49. Chamee Yang and C. L. Cole, "Smart Stadium as a Laboratory of Innovation: Technology, Sport, and Datafied Normalization of the Fans," *Communication and Sport*, August 4, 2020, 8, https://doi.org/10.1177/2167479520943579.

50. Sarah Wray, "Atlanta Puts Smart City Tech to the Test for Super Bowl," Smart Cities World, February 3, 2019, https://www.smartcitiesworld.net/special-reports/special-reports/atlanta-puts-smart-city-tech-to-the-test-for-super-bowl-.

51. Dalia Perez, "A Look at How Metro Atlanta School Districts Are Working to Keep Students Safe," 11Alive.com, January 10, 2023, https://www.11alive.com/article/news/local/atlanta-public-schools-weapons-detection-system/85-751a358d-bf6e-487a-93a1-06e2baac41d4.

52. Renee Shelby et al., "The Conjoined Spectacles of the 'Smart Super Bowl,'" *Engaging Science, Technology, and Society* 6 (2020): 312–19, https://doi.org/10.17351/ests2020.295; "SmartATL: A Smart City Overview and Roadmap," https://www.tmforum.org/wp-content/uploads/2016/09/11.30-Torri-Martin-Smart-City-Strategy.pdf.

53. Alf Oschatz, "Introduction," in *Stadium and Arena Design*, ed. Peter Culley and John Pascoe, Second (London: Institution of Civil Engineers Publishing, 2015), xiii.

54. Guido, "Ultimate Fan Experience."

55. Darren E. Grem, "'The South Got Something to Say': Atlanta's Dirty South and the Southernization of Hip-Hop America," *Southern Cultures* 12, no. 4 (2006): 16.

56. Gavin Godfrey, "Super Bowl 51: How 'Dirty Bird' Dance Became an Atlanta Falcons Legend," *Rolling Stone* (blog), February 3, 2017, https://www.rollingstone.com/culture/culture-sports/super-bowl-51-how-dirty-bird-dance-became-an-atlanta-falcons-legend-108084/.

57. There is some debate about the origination of the Dirty Bird. The Falcons claim O. J. Santiago started it during a Week 10 game in the 1998 season. See Amna Subhan, "25th Anniversary of the 1998 Falcons: How the Dirty Bird Celebration Dance Got Its Name," Atlanta Falcons, November 29, 2023, https://www.atlantafalcons.com/

news/25th-anniversary-1998-falcons-how-the-dirty-bird-celebration-dance-got-it. In Anderson's retelling of its history, though, Santiago's performance was just the one that took off and went viral among a wider fan base. Most agree Anderson popularized the performance and is the figure most associated with the Dirty Bird.

58. Joel Dinerstein, "Backfield in Motion: The Transformation of the NFL by Black Culture," in *In the Game: Race, Identity, and Sports in the Twentieth Century*, ed. Amy Bass (New York: Palgrave Macmillan, 2005), 169–89.

59. Godfrey, "Super Bowl 51."

60. Gena Caponi-Tabery, ed., *Signifyin(g), Sanctifyin' and Slam Dunking: A Reader in African American Expressive Culture* (Amherst: University of Massachusetts Press, 1999), 5.

61. Dinerstein, "Backfield in Motion," 182; italics in original.

62. Lindsey Stewart, *The Politics of Black Joy: Zora Neale Hurston and Neo-Abolitionism* (Evanston, IL: Northwestern University Press, 2021), 7.

63. Stewart, *Politics of Black Joy*, 8.

64. Betty Jean Young, "Black Performance as Creative Place-Keeping: A Case Study of Three Atlanta Gentrifying Neighborhoods" (PhD diss., University of Georgia, Athens, Georgia, 2023), 80, https://www.proquest.com/docview/2861144594?%20Theses&fromopenview=true&pq-origsite=gscholar&sourcetype=Dissertations%20.

65. Scooby Axson, "New NFL Celebration Rules Explained," *Sports Illustrated*, September 7, 2017, https://www.si.com/nfl/2017/09/07/new-nfl-celebration-rules.

66. "Dirty Birds Nest," https://www.atlantafalcons.com/tickets/dirtybirdsnest; Derek Helling, "Falcons: History of 'The Dirty Bird,'" Heavy.com, January 22, 2017, https://heavy.com/sports/2017/01/atlanta-falcons-dirty-bird-jamal-anderson/.

67. Stewart, *Politics of Black Joy*, 3.

68. Dinerstein, "Backfield in Motion," 187.

69. Stewart, *Politics of Black Joy*, 6.

70. Sara Ahmed, *The Cultural Politics of Emotion* (New York: Routledge, 2004); Adrienne Maree Brown, *Pleasure Activism: The Politics of Feeling Good* (Chico, Edinburgh: AK Press, 2019); bell hooks, *All about Love: New Visions*, 1st William Morrow paperback ed. (New York: William Morrow, 2018); Audre Lorde, "Uses of the Erotic: The Erotic as Power," in *Sister Outsider: Essays and Speeches*, Crossing Press Feminist Series (Trumansburg, NY: Crossing Press, 1984); Stewart, *Politics of Black Joy*.

71. Andy Peters, "Some Developers Bet Downtown Atlanta Is Finally Ready for Long-Awaited Comeback," CoStar, September 6, 2022, https://www.costar.com/article/744891873/some-developers-bet-downtown-atlanta-is-finally-ready-for-long-awaited-comeback.

72. Josh Green, "Centennial Yards Megaproject Vows to Be Mostly Complete for World Cup," Urbanize Atlanta, July 7, 2022, https://atlanta.urbanize.city/post/centennial-yards-development-mostly-complete-world-cup.

73. Tory-Henderson, "Mercedes Benz Stadium."

74. Author interview with Mercedes-Benz Stadium executive.

75. Author interview with Mercedes-Benz Stadium executive.

76. Maria Saporta, "Frank Fernandez to Lead Westside's Rebirth for Arthur Blank's Foundation," SaportaReport, January 20, 2014, http://saportareport.com/frank-fernandez-to-lead-westsides-rebirth-for-blank-foundation/columnists/marias metro/maria_saporta/.

77. "Community," Media Hub, Mercedes-Benz Stadium, https://www.mercedesbenzstadium.com/media-hub.

78. Neil deMause, "Why Are Georgia Taxpayers Paying $700m for a New NFL Stadium?" *The Guardian*, September 29, 2017, https://www.theguardian.com/sport/2017/sep/29/why-are-georgia-taxpayers-paying-700m-for-a-new-nfl-stadium.

79. George Lipsitz, *How Racism Takes Place* (Philadelphia: Temple University Press, 2011), 94.

80. Arthur M. Blank Family Foundation, "Giving Area: Atlanta's Westside," https://blankfoundation.org/wp-content/uploads/2024/09/Westside-AMBFF-FINAL.pdf, accessed January 13, 2025; Arthur M. Blank Family Foundation, "Atlanta Grants: Atlanta's Westside," https://blankfoundation.org/area-of-giving/atlantas-westside/, accessed January 13, 2025.

81. Mercedes-Benz Stadium News, "The Home Depot and Mercedes-Benz Stadium Announce The Home Depot Backyard," April 21, 2017, https://www.mercedesbenzstadium.com/news/the-home-depot-and-mercedes-benz-stadium-announce-the-home-depot-backyard.

82. Mercedes-Benz Stadium News, "Home Depot and Mercedes-Benz Stadium Announce."

83. Nikolas Rose, "Community, Citizenship, and the Third Way," *American Behavioral Scientist* 43, no. 9 (2000): 1399.

84. Mercedes Benz Stadium, "The Home Depot Backyard," https://mercedesbenzstadium.com/the-home-depot-backyard/, accessed August 8, 2020. Note: This website has since been changed, and the list of programming is no longer available on the site.

85. Kofi Stiles, "New Park Will Connect Westside Atlanta to the Downtown Area," *The Signal* (blog), May 9, 2017, https://georgiastatesignal.com/new-park-will-connect-westside-atlanta-downtown-area/.

86. "Mayor Reed and Arthur M. Blank Announce Additional $32m Worth of Investments in Atlanta's Historic Westside Neighborhoods," September 14, 2017.

87. Vincanne Adams, *Markets of Sorrow, Labors of Faith: New Orleans in the Wake of Katrina* (Durham, NC: Duke University Press, 2013), 11.

88. By 2017 the Blank Foundation had committed $37 million to broader Westside renewal efforts. Ken Belson, "Building a Stadium, Rebuilding a Neighborhood," *New York Times*, January 12, 2017, https://www.nytimes.com/2017/01/12/sports/football/atlanta-falcons-stadium-arthur-blank-neighborhood.html. Since 2017, the foundation claimed to commit an additional $27 million and subsequently $5 million per year for the next ten years. See Maria Saporta, "Blank Foundation Doubles Down on

Efforts to Improve the Westside," November 17, 2022, https://saportareport.com/blank-foundation-doubles-down-on-efforts-to-improve-the-westside/sections/reports/maria_saporta/.

89. Josh Green, "Five Years after Mercedes-Benz Stadium Broke Ground, Is Atlanta's Westside Revival Working?" Curbed Atlanta, January 31, 2019, https://atlanta.curbed.com/atlanta-photo-essays/2019/1/31/18201601/super-bowl-liii-atlanta-gentrification-poverty-blank.

90. Belson, "Building a Stadium."

91. Belson, "Building a Stadium."

92. Kate Diedrick and Christopher A. Le Dantec, "Atlanta's Westside Residents Challenge the Rules of Sport Mega-Development," *Third World Thematics: A TWQ Journal* 2, issue 1 (2017): 55.

93. Saporta, "Blank Foundation Doubles Down."

94. Saporta, "Blank Foundation Doubles Down."

95. Arthur M. Blank Family Foundation, "Giving Area: Atlanta's Westside."

Chapter 3. Entrepreneurialism through Abandonment

1. Michael L. Butterworth, "Race in 'The Race': Mark McGwire, Sammy Sosa, and Heroic Constructions of Whiteness," *Critical Studies in Media Communication* 24, no. 3 (2007): 232, https://doi.org/10.1080/07393180701520926.

2. David C. Ogden and Michael L. Hilt, "Collective Identity and Basketball: An Explanation for the Decreasing Number of African-Americans on America's Baseball Diamonds," *Journal of Leisure Research* 35, no. 2 (2003): 216, https://doi.org/10.1080/00222216.2003.11949991.

3. Henry A. Giroux, *Stormy Weather: Katrina and the Politics of Disposability* (Boulder, CO: Paradigm, 2006).

4. Eric Brown, "The Atlanta Braves' Move to Cobb County Is about Race, Not Transportation," *International Business Times*, November 14, 2013, https://www.ibtimes.com/atlanta-braves-move-cobb-county-about-race-not-transportation-1470814.

5. Andy Walter, "Mapping Braves Country," *Atlanta Studies*, November 2, 2015, https://www.atlantastudies.org/2015/11/02/mapping-braves-country/.

6. Ray Henry, "Atlanta Braves' Move Caters to Their Fans," *Berkshire Eagle*, December 14, 2013, https://www.berkshireeagle.com/sports/local_sports/atlanta-braves-move-caters-to-their-fans/article_dac820cc-afe7-565b-b83a-a9328dc31bf4.html.

7. Kim Severson, "With Braves Set to Move, a Broader Look at Atlanta," *New York Times*, November 16, 2013, sec. U.S., https://www.nytimes.com/2013/11/17/us/with-braves-set-to-move-a-broader-look-at-atlanta.html.

8. Loran Smith, "Truist Park and the Battery Are Impeccable Venues for N.L. East Winning Atlanta Braves," *Online Athens*, October 7, 2022, https://www.onlineathens.com/story/sports/mlb/2022/10/07/atlanta-braves-truist-park-and-battery-perfect-matches/8198040001/.

9. Timothy Kellison, "Enduring and Emergent Public Opinion in Relation to a Suburban Stadium District: The Case of Truist Park–Battery Atlanta," *Journal of Global Sport Management*, March 4, 2021, 3, https://doi.org/10.1080/24704067.2021.1886685.

10. Timothy S. Chapin, "Sports Facilities as Urban Redevelopment Catalysts: Baltimore's Camden Yards and Cleveland's Gateway," *Journal of the American Planning Association* 70, no. 2 (2004): 193–209, https://doi.org/10.1080/01944360408976370.

11. "Fiscal Impact of SunTrust Park and The Battery Atlanta on Cobb County" (Cobb County Chamber of Commerce, September 2018), Georgia Tech, Center for Economic Development Research, https://cdn.newswire.com/files/x/21/1e/f9ed7f4ffb021c87e ae14db828e6.pdf.

12. Gabe Lacques, "As Braves Open SunTrust Park, Here Are Seven Numbers to Know," *USA Today*, April 14, 2017, https://www.usatoday.com/story/sports/mlb/2017/04/14/braves-new-stadium-suntrust-park/100442650/.

13. Sean Richard Keenan, "Georgia Tech Study: SunTrust Park, Battery Rake in $19M Annually for Cobb County," Curbed Atlanta, September 19, 2018, https://atlanta.curbed.com/2018/9/19/17878808/georgia-tech-suntrust-park-battery-19m-annually-cobb-county.

14. Kate Weimer, "Entertainment Is in Season Year-Round at The Battery Atlanta," *Atlanta Magazine* (blog), November 11, 2019, https://www.atlantamagazine.com/news-culture-articles/entertainment-is-in-season-year-round-at-the-battery-atlanta/.

15. Scott N. Markley, "New Urbanism and Race: An Analysis of Neighborhood Racial Change in Suburban Atlanta," *Journal of Urban Affairs* 40, no. 8 (2018): 1115–31, https://doi.org/10.1080/07352166.2018.1454818.

16. "Company: Savi Provisions in the USA," Savi Provisions, accessed October 26, 2022, https://www.saviprovisions.com/company/.

17. "Atlanta, GA: Food, Drinks, Shops + More: Waterloo Sunset Vinyl Lounge," November 4, 2020, https://vinings.thebattery.sandysprings.atlfeed.com/waterloo-sunset-vinyl-lounge/. As of this writing, however, this store is now listed as "temporarily closed."

18. Jon C. Teaford, *The American Suburb: The Basics* (New York: Routledge, 2008).

19. Leon Stafford, "Comcast to Open Tech Incubator at SunTrust Park," *Atlanta Journal-Constitution*, March 23, 2017, http://www.ajc.com/news/local-govt-politics/comcast-open-tech-incubator-suntrust-park/PAO38JNW319YenaItP5sVN/.

20. Comcast Corporation, "Atlanta Braves and Comcast Team Up to Power Nation's Most Technologically Advanced Ballpark and Mixed Use Community," March 17, 2015, https://corporate.comcast.com/news-information/news-feed/comcast-braves-partnership.

21. Comcast Corporation, "Atlanta Braves and Comcast Team Up."

22. Comcast/NBC Universal: The Farm, "The Space: The Farm (A Culture of Innovation)," https://thefarmatl.com/about/program/, accessed January 13, 2025.

23. Comcast/NBC Universal: The Farm. "The Space: The Farm."

24. "Comcast SportsTech, The Premier Sports Accelerator Backed by Comcast," https://www.comcastsportstech.com/, accessed August 7, 2021.

25. John Blake, "The Atlanta Braves Won the World Series. But They Face a Tougher Opponent off the Field," CNN, October 31, 2021, https://www.cnn.com/2021/10/31/us/atlanta-braves-history-racism-blake/index.html.

26. Kyle W. Kusz, "'Winning Bigly': Sporting Fantasies of White Male Omnipotence in the Rise of Trump and Alt Right White Supremacy," *Journal of Hate Studies* 14, no. 1 (2019): 120, https://doi.org/10.33972/jhs.127.

27. Kusz, "'Winning Bigly,'" 115.

28. Cornel D. Pewewardy, "The 'Tomahawk Chop': The Continuous Struggle of Unlearning 'Indian' Stereotypes," presented at the 24th Annual Conference of the National Indian Education Association, Albuquerque, New Mexico, November 15–19, 1992.

29. Fawn Sharp, quoted in Nicquel Terry Ellis, "'Dehumanizing and Racist' Native Leaders Decry Braves' 'Tomahawk Chop' ahead of World Series Game in Atlanta," CNN, October 28, 2021, https://www.cnn.com/2021/10/28/us/atlanta-braves-tomahawk-chop/index.html.

30. Blake, "Atlanta Braves Won the World Series."

31. David Wilson, *Cities and Race: America's New Black Ghetto* (London: Routledge, 2007), 3.

32. H. A. Giroux, "Violence, Katrina, and the Biopolitics of Disposability," *Theory, Culture and Society* 24, nos. 7–8 (2007): 309, https://doi.org/10.1177/02632764070240072510.

33. Giroux, "Violence, Katrina, and the Biopolitics of Disposability," 306.

34. Robert C. Trumpbour, *The New Cathedrals: Politics and Media in the History of Stadium Construction* (Syracuse, NY: Syracuse University Press, 2007).

35. Brown, "Atlanta Braves' Move to Cobb County."

36. Brown, "Atlanta Braves' Move to Cobb County."

37. Andrew Baggarly, "Shame on the Braves for Using Turner Field Like a Disposable Diaper," *Comcast Sportsnet*, May 5, 2014, http://www.csnbayarea.com/giants/shame-braves-using-turner-field-disposable-diaper.

38. Stephanie Garlock, "In Atlanta, Two Stadiums Collide with Dreams of a New Downtown," Bloomberg, February 19, 2014, https://www.bloomberg.com/news/articles/2014-02-19/in-atlanta-two-stadiums-collide-with-dreams-of-a-new-downtown.

39. Espen Indrisano and Nate Harris, "Summerhill: Georgia State's Downtown Expansion," *The Signal* (blog), November 12, 2019, https://georgiastatesignal.com/summerhill-georgia-states-downtown-expansion/.

40. Torie Robinette, "Summerhill's Next Act," *Georgia State University Magazine*, August 27, 2019, https://news.gsu.edu/magazine/fall2019/summerhills-next-act.

41. Charles Rutheiser, *Imagineering Atlanta: The Politics of Place in the City of Dreams*, Haymarket Series (London: Verso, 1996), 57.

42. Matt Kempner, "Atlanta Neighborhoods around Old Turner Field Face Big Changes," *Atlanta Journal Constitution*, March 31, 2019, https://www.ajc.com/news/local/turner-field-neighbors-hopeful-skeptical-about-area-transformation/mFAftTrtN8J3dQ63wVWqsJ/.

43. "Community Benefits," *Turner Field Community Benefits Coalition* (blog), accessed March 22, 2016, original link: http://www.turnerfieldcoalition.org/?page_id=270. This site has since been taken down and, perhaps in an ironic twist, the link has been changed to direct the user to a salon website whose home page features women who appear largely white and European.

44. Dianne Mathiowetz, "Fight for Affordable Housing Not Over," *Workers World* (blog), June 5, 2017, https://www.workers.org/2017/06/31590/.

45. Katie Leslie, "Turner Field; Neighbors Seeking Stadium Sale Delay," *Atlanta Journal-Constitution*, July 8, 2015, sec. News.

46. Bill Torpy, "GSU's Plan for Turner Field Always Had the Inside Track," *Atlanta Journal-Constitution*, December 31, 2015, sec. Metro News.

47. Anna Simonton, "New Coalition Challenges GSU's Turner Field Development Plan," *Atlanta Progressive News* (blog), June 5, 2015, https://atlantaprogressivenews.com/2015/06/05/new-coalition-challenges-gsus-turner-field-development-plan/.

48. Becca J. G. Godwin, "Neighbors at Odds over GSU–Turner Field Agreement," *Atlanta Journal-Constitution*, April 27, 2017, sec. Metro.

Chapter 4. Boosting the Northwest

1. "Visit Seattle Washington," Visit Seattle, https://visitseattle.org/, accessed February 16, 2023.

2. James Lyons, *Selling Seattle: Representing Contemporary Urban America* (London: Wallflower, 2004), 3.

3. Serin D. Houston, *Imagining Seattle: Social Values in Urban Governance* (Lincoln: University of Nebraska Press, 2019), 36.

4. Shannon Mattern, "Plurality in Place: Activating Public Spheres and Public Spaces in Seattle," *InVisible Culture*, no. 6 (2003), https://www.rochester.edu/in_visible_culture/Issue_6/mattern/mattern.html.

5. Houston, *Imagining Seattle*.

6. SoDo includes 40 percent nonwhite residents compared to 30 percent overall in Seattle, 57 percent are renters in comparison to 53 percent citywide, and the neighborhood has a lower overall median income. See Janelle Ligrani, "SODO Census Data 2020," *SODO* (blog), November 9, 2021, https://sodoseattle.org/sodo-census-data-2020/. Pioneer Square is approximately 50 percent nonwhite, over 95 percent renter households, and 44 percent of the neighborhood's population lives below the poverty level compared to 14 percent citywide. See "Pioneer Square: Neighborhood Snapshot" (City of Seattle: Department of Neighborhoods, May 2018), https://www.seattle.gov/documents/Departments/Neighborhoods/Districts/Neighborhood%20Snapshots/Pioneer-Square-Snapshot.pdf. The Chinatown-International District is close to 75 percent nonwhite, 81 percent renter households, and close to 30 percent live below the poverty line. See "Chinatown International District: Neighborhood Snapshot" (City of Seattle: Department of Neighborhoods, July 2018), https://www

.seattle.gov/documents/Departments/Neighborhoods/Districts/Neighborhood%20 Snapshots/Chinatown-ID-Little-Saigon-Snapshot.pdf.

7. Terry Anne Scott, *Seattle Sports: Play, Identity, and Pursuit in the Emerald City* (Fayetteville: University of Arkansas Press, 2020), 4.

8. Miriam Greenberg, *Branding New York: How a City in Crisis Was Sold to the World* (New York: Routledge, 2008), 21, 35.

9. John M. Findlay, "Pioneers and Pandemonium: Stability and Change in Seattle History," *Pacific Northwest Quarterly* 107, no. 1 (2015): 4–23.

10. Mattern, "Plurality in Place."

11. William H. Mullins, *Becoming Big League: Seattle, the Pilots, and Stadium Politics* (Seattle: University of Washington Press, 2013), 34.

12. Mullins, *Becoming Big League*, 7.

13. Documentary West Productions, "King County Multipurpose Dome Stadium: Capsulized Version from 1957 through November 1973," April 14, 1974, Stadium Administration, Series 473 Promotional Materials, box 2, folder 3, King County Archives (hereafter, KCA).

14. Documentary West Productions, "King County Multipurpose Dome Stadium"; Timothy A. Gibson, *Securing the Spectacular City: The Politics of Revitalization and Homelessness in Downtown Seattle* (Lanham, MD: Lexington Books, 2004).

15. Shaun Scott, "Forward Thrust Part 3: Big League City," The Urbanist, May 18, 2018, https://www.theurbanist.org/2018/05/18/forward-thrust-part-3-big-league-city/.

16. William H. Mullins, "The Persistence of Progressivism: James Ellis and the Forward Thrust Campaign," Center for the Study of the Pacific Northwest, 2014, https://www.washington.edu/uwired/outreach/cspn/Website/Articles/Mullins/Forward Thrust.html.

17. Gibson, *Securing the Spectacular City*, 37.

18. The revitalization of Pike Place Market and the transformation of Pioneer Square into a historic district were two other major initiatives concurrently under way that, like the Forward Thrust, responded to discourses of postwar urban decline. See Jeffrey C. Sanders, *Seattle and the Roots of Urban Sustainability: Inventing Ecotopia* (Pittsburgh: University of Pittsburgh Press, 2010), 37–38.

19. Decision Committee for Forward Thrust, "Forward Thrust, Voter Information Supplement," circa 1968, Baseball Litigation Records: New Multi-Purpose Stadium, box 3, folder 21, Seattle Municipal Archives, Seattle, Washington (hereafter, SMA).

20. Mullins, "Persistence of Progressivism."

21. Forward Thrust Staff, "Estimated Bond Issue Projects," circa 1968, Baseball Litigation Records: New Multi-Purpose Stadium, box 3, folder 21, SMA; underlining in original.

22. Sanders, *Seattle and the Roots of Urban Sustainability*, 66.

23. Mullins, "Persistence of Progressivism."

24. Forward Thrust Staff, "Estimated Bond Issue Projects."

25. David Eskenazi and Steve Rudman, "Wayback Machine: Seattle Steelheads' Short Life," Sportspress Northwest, February 5, 2013, https://www.sportspressnw.com/2145947/2013/wayback-machine-seattle-steelheads-short-life.

26. Dan Raley, *Pitchers of Beer: The Story of the Seattle Rainiers* (Lincoln: University of Nebraska Press, 2011), 29.

27. Hanna Brooks Olsen, "Sicks' [sic] Stadium: How Did 40 Years of Baseball History Become a Hardware Store?" Crosscut, September 25, 2018, https://crosscut.com/2018/09/sicks-stadium-how-did-40-years-baseball-history-become-hardware-store.

28. Raley, *Pitchers of Beer*.

29. Raley, *Pitchers of Beer*.

30. Mullins, *Becoming Big League*, 134–35.

31. Raley, *Pitchers of Beer*, 20.

32. Mullins, *Becoming Big League*, 134–35.

33. Chris Donnelly, "Winless in Seattle A History of the Seattle Mariners, 1977–1994," in *Seattle Sports: Play, Identity, and Pursuit in the Emerald City*, ed. Terry Anne Scott (Fayetteville: University of Arkansas Press, 2020), 13–38.

34. Mullins, *Becoming Big League*.

35. "Criteria for Stadium Site," August 14, 1970, Traffic and Engineering Subject Files, Stadium Preliminary Site Selection, box 11, folder 4, SMA; see also "The Kingdome, Commemorative Magazine," March 1976, Stadium Administration, Series 473 Promotional Materials, box 1, folder 34, KCA, Seattle, Washington.

36. Mullins, *Becoming Big League*, 167.

37. "The Kingdome, Commemorative Magazine."

38. Athima Chansanchai, "Frank Ruano, 1920–2005: Stadium Opponent Was 'First Suburban Rebel,'" *Seattle Post-Intelligencer*, April 25, 2005, https://www.seattlepi.com/sports/baseball/article/Frank-Ruano-1920-2005-Stadium-opponent-was-1171677.php.

39. Ruano later admitted that his exclusion from this group precipitated his hard feelings and fueled his decades-long opposition. See Mullins, *Becoming Big League*, 180.

40. Mullins, "Persistence of Progressivism"; Sanders, *Seattle and the Roots of Urban Sustainability*.

41. Edna C. Hinkley, "Letter to Mayor Uhlman," January 8, 1970, Records of the Office of the Mayor, Subject Files: Baseball Stadium, 1970, box 161, folder 9, SMA.

42. D. Eugene Hokanson, "Letter to Mayor Uhlman," January 26, 1970, Records of the Office of the Mayor, Subject Files: Baseball Stadium, 1970, box 161, folder 9, SMA.

43. K. McDowell, "Letter to Mayor Uhlman," 1970, Records of the Office of the Mayor, Subject Files: Baseball Stadium, 1970, box 161, folder 9, SMA; underlining in original.

44. Helen Baker St. John, "Letter to Mayor Uhlman," January 22, 1970, Records of the Office of the Mayor, Subject Files: Baseball Stadium, 1970, box 161, folder 9, SMA.

45. Mrs. Frederick Cheney, "Letter to the Editor: Costly 'Shot in the Arm,'" *Seattle Times*, circa 1970, Records of the Office of the Mayor, Subject Files: Baseball Stadium, 1970, box 161, folder 9, SMA.

46. "Kingdome Project Pamphlet, 1972–1972," August 1972, Seattle (Wash.), City Clerk, box 3, folder 1025, SMA.

47. The urban sites were Dearborn Street, King Street Station, and, once again, the Seattle Center. The two suburban locations were Longacres East and Riverton.

48. See Documentary West Productions, "King County Multipurpose Dome Stadium: Capsulized Version from 1957 through November 1973"; State Stadium Commission Technical Committee, "Criteria for Stadium Site," August 14, 1970, Traffic Engineering Subject Files, box 11, folder 4, SMA.

49. Monica Guzman, "What Was Seattle's Most Disruptive Construction Project?" *Seattle Post-Intelligencer*, January 4, 2010, https://blog.seattlepi.com/thebigblog/2010/01/04/what-was-seattles-most-disruptive-construction-project/. Note: This article is no longer on the website.

50. "The Stadium: All-American Monument, Stadium Impact Study," 1972, 34, Land Use Director's Records, Model City Land Use Project: Stadium, 1971–1972, box 1, folder 9, SMA.

51. "Kingdome Project Pamphlet, 1972–1972."

52. Heather Macintosh, "Kingdome: The Controversial Birth of a Seattle Icon (1959–1976)," HistoryLink.org, March 1, 2000, http://www.historylink.org/index.cfm?DisplayPage=output.cfm&file_id=2164.

53. Bruce Zielsdorf, "Initial Review and Comment of Stadium and Convention Center Impact Study," June 30, 1972, Jeanette Williams Subject Files, Land Use and Urban Development, Sports Arenas-Stadium-Cooley/Williams Statements, 1972, box 18, folder 3, SMA.

54. Richard C. Locke, "Letter to Jerry Hillis, Chairman of Citizen Action Force," September 5, 1972, New Multi-Purpose Stadium, Baseball Litigation Records, box 4, folder 5, SMA.

55. Mullins, *Becoming Big League*, 254.

56. Citizens Action Force, "Citizens Action Force Recommendations on Alternative Solutions to Stadium Impact Problems," 1972, Baseball Litigation Records, box 4, folder 5, SMA.

57. Victor Steinbrueck, "Letter to Mayor Uhlman and John Spellman," August 29, 1972, New Multi-Purpose Stadium, Baseball Litigation Records, box 4, folder 4, SMA.

58. Bruce K. Chapman, "A Resolution Recognizing the Unique Nature of the International District and the Pioneer Square Historic District," Pub. L. No. 23782 (1972), http://clerk.seattle.gov/~archives/Resolutions/Resn_23782.pdf.

59. "Hum Bows" refers to a type of steamed bun, a Chinese pastry. The phrase "Hum Bows, not Hot Dogs" therefore lays claim to the cultural character of the neighbor-

hood's Asian identity and resists the cultural character of baseballing-Americana embodied in the hot dog.

60. Gary Iwamoto, "A 50-Year History of Inter*Im CDA: 1969–2019," *International Examiner* (blog), April 4, 2019, https://iexaminer.org/a-50-year-history-of-interim-cda-1969-2019/; see also "Kingdome Protest and HUD March: November, 1972—Seattle Civil Rights and Labor History Project," https://depts.washington.edu/civilr/aa_kingdome.htm, accessed January 14, 2025.

61. "Bob Santos and the Kingdome: The Fight to Preserve Seattle's Chinatown/International District," SMA, https://www.seattle.gov/cityarchives/exhibits-and-education/seattle-voices/kingdome, accessed March 7, 2023.

62. Sanders, *Seattle and the Roots of Urban Sustainability*, 70.

63. "Public Hearing, Seattle City Council" (Seattle, December 18, 1975), https://www.seattle.gov/cityarchives/exhibits-and-education/seattle-voices/kingdome.

64. "Public Hearing, Seattle City Council" (Seattle, September 9, 1975), https://www.seattle.gov/cityarchives/exhibits-and-education/seattle-voices/kingdome.

65. Robert Hodder, "Savannah's Changing Past: Historic Preservation Planning and the Social Construction of a Historic Landscape, 1955 to 1985," in *Planning the Twentieth-Century American City*, ed. Mary Corbin Sies and Christopher Silver, 361–82 (Baltimore: Johns Hopkins University Press, 1996).

66. Roberto E. Barrios, "You Found Us Doing This, This Is Our Way: Criminalizing Second Lines, Super Sunday, and Habitus in Post-Katrina New Orleans," *Identities* 17, no. 6 (2010): 586–612.

67. "Public Hearing, Seattle City Council" (Seattle, September 9, 1975), https://www.seattle.gov/cityarchives/exhibits-and-education/seattle-voices/kingdome.

68. "Public Hearing, Seattle City Council" (Seattle, September 9, 1975).

69. Mullins, *Becoming Big League*, 252–54.

70. "The Kingdome, Commemorative Magazine," 54.

71. "The Kingdome, Commemorative Magazine," 54.

72. Mullins, *Becoming Big League*, 254.

73. frankthe12thtank, "Century Link vs. the Kingdome," *R/Seahawks (Reddit)*, July 15, 2013, https://www.reddit.com/r/Seahawks/comments/1ibln3/century_link_vs_the_kingdome/.

74. LBobRife, "Century Link vs. the Kingdome," *R/Seahawks (Reddit)*, July 15, 2013, https://www.reddit.com/r/Seahawks/comments/1ibln3/century_link_vs_the_kingdome/.

75. Jayson Jenks, "Remembering the Time the NFL Tried to Silence Its Fans," *The Athletic*, December 11, 2019, https://theathletic.com/1446285/2019/12/11/remembering-the-time-the-nfl-tried-to-silence-its-fans/.

76. "King County Multipurpose Stadium," November 1974, Wesley C. Uhlman Subject Files, box 164, folder 4, SMA.

77. Division of Sales and Promotion and Bill Sears, "The Kingdome, Video Promotion Script," 1977, Stadium Administration, Series 473 Promotional Materials, box 2, folder 5, KCA.

78. "Kingdome Video Productions, Promotional Flyer" (King County Stadium, circa 1977), Stadium Administration, Series 473 Promotional Materials, box 2, folder 5, KCA.

79. "Kingdome Sports Museum," circa 1977, Stadium Administration, Series 473 Promotional Materials, box 2, folder 9, KCA.

80. "King County Multipurpose Stadium, Progress Report Newsletter" (King County Department of Community and Environmental Development, Architecture Division, and the Seattle/King County Convention and Visitors Bureau, July 1973), Stadium Administration, Series 473 Promotional Materials, box 1, folder 21, KCA.

81. Royal Brougham, "A Warm Welcome to the Big Dome," *Kingdome Commemorative Magazine*, March 1976, Stadium Administration, Series 473 Promotional Materials, box 1, folder 34, KCA. At the time, the Kingdome would be the third major domed stadium to be built, after the Astrodome in Houston and the Superdome in New Orleans.

82. Brougham, "Warm Welcome to the Big Dome," 6.

83. Bill Sears, "How the Dome Miracle Became a Reality," *Kingdome Commemorative Magazine*, March 1976, 8, Stadium Administration, Series 473 Promotional Materials, box 1, folder 34, KCA.

84. "The Stadium: All-American Monument, Stadium Impact Study," 1972, Land Use Director's Records, Model City Land Use Project: Stadium, 1971–1972, box 1, folder 9, SMA.

85. Lorraine Farrelly, *The Fundamentals of Architecture*, 2nd ed. (Lausanne, Switzerland: AVA Academia, 2012), 138.

86. Rem Koolhaas, *Delirious New York: A Retroactive Manifesto for Manhattan* (New York: Monacelli Press, 1994).

87. Farrelly, *Fundamentals of Architecture*.

88. "King County Multipurpose Stadium, Progress Report Newsletter."

89. Benjamin S. Flowers, *Sport and Architecture*, Frontiers of Sport (New York: Routledge, 2017).

90. John Owen, "Our New Dome Is Strictly Mod," *Kingdome Commemorative Magazine*, March 1976, 16, Stadium Administration, Series 473 Promotional Materials, box 1, folder 34, KCA.

91. E. J. Hobsbawm and T. O. Ranger, eds., *The Invention of Tradition*, Canto Classics (Cambridge: Cambridge University Press, 2012); Lyons, *Selling Seattle*. According to Lyons, the natural Northwest discourse emerged in the 1990s in response to historically contextual debates about nature and the urban at the time, specifically as a way to distinguish Seattle from discourses of urban decline plaguing other cities. I am suggesting here, though, that elements of that framing of the city can be seen in earlier booster efforts as well.

92. Marianna Christine Davison, "Sculpting Nature, Making Place: The Aesthetics and Ethics of Land-Shaping in Seattle," diss., Irvine: University of California, Irvine, 2022, ProQuest ID: Davison_uci_0030D_17965. Merritt ID: ark:/13030/m5q318z5. Retrieved from https://escholarship.org/uc/item/2px6toxc.

93. "King County Stadium Pamphlet, 1975–1976" (Washington Department of Commerce and Economic Development, 1976 1975), Stadium Administration Promotional Materials, Series 473, box 1, folder 2, KCA.

94. "King County Stadium Pamphlet, 1975–1976."

95. Edward W. Said, *Orientalism* (New York: Pantheon Books, 1978).

96. "King County Stadium Pamphlet, 1975–1976."

97. "Kingdome Security 'Wired for Sound,'" *The Kingdome: All-Star Edition, Promotional Pamphlet*, 1979, Stadium Administration, Series 473 Promotional Materials, box 1, folder 25, KCA.

98. "Kingdome Security 'Wired for Sound.'"

99. "Kingdome Security 'Wired for Sound.'"

100. Gibson, *Securing the Spectacular City*, 66–67.

101. Stacey Warren, "Disneyfication of The Metropolis: Popular Resistance in Seattle," *Journal of Urban Affairs* 16, no. 2 (1994): 89–107.

102. Tim Hill, Jim Clark, and Neil M. Campbell, "Kingdome Master Plan, Phase 1" (Department of Stadium Administration, 1990), Public Documents Collection, Series 1801–92, box D-777, SMA.

103. Brougham, "Warm Welcome to the Big Dome," 6.

104. meaniereddit, "21 Years Ago Today They Blew up the Kingdome. RIP," comment, *Reddit—r/Seattle*, 2021, https://www.reddit.com/r/Seattle/comments/mds53b/21_years_ago_today_they_blew_up_the_kingdome_rip/.

105. yahakum, "21 Years Ago Today They Blew up the Kingdome. RIP," comment, *Reddit—r/Seattle*, 2021, https://www.reddit.com/r/Seattle/comments/mds53b/21_years_ago_today_they_blew_up_the_kingdome_rip/.

106. throw_away_your_TV, "Century Link vs. The Kingdome," comment, *Reddit—r/Seahawks*, 2013, https://www.reddit.com/r/Seahawks/comments/1ibln3/century_link_vs_the_kingdome/.

Chapter 5. Place-Branding the Local

1. James Lyons, *Selling Seattle: Representing Contemporary Urban America* (London: Wallflower, 2004), 14–15.

2. Seattle's ubiquitous media appearance and promotion of its brand was part of a major public relations effort. City leaders hired marketing professionals to promote the city as part of the Norman Rice administration's broader revitalization and restructuring strategy. See Lyons, *Selling Seattle*.

3. Lyons, *Selling Seattle*, 8.

4. Bill Baker, *Destination Branding for Small Cities: The Essentials for Successful Place-Branding* (Portland, OR: Creative Leap Books, 2012).

5. Kevin F. Gotham and Jeannie Haubert, "Neoliberal Revitalization: Prison Building, Casinos, and Tourism in Louisiana," in *Urban Communication: Production, Text, Context*, ed. Timothy A. Gibson and Mark Douglas Lowes (Lanham, MD: Rowman and

Littlefield, 2007), 25–40; Miriam Greenberg, *Branding New York: How a City in Crisis Was Sold to the World* (New York: Routledge, 2008).

6. Greenberg, *Branding New York*.

7. Adam Arvidsson, *Brands: Meaning and Value in Media Culture* (London: Routledge, 2006).

8. Sonia Bookman and Andrew Woolford, "Policing (by) the Urban Brand: Defining Order in Winnipeg's Exchange District," *Social and Cultural Geography* 14, no. 3 (2013): 300–317, https://doi.org/10.1080/14649365.2012.762986.

9. Arvidsson, *Brands: Meaning and Value*.

10. Celia Lury, *Brands: The Logos of the Global Economy* (New York: Routledge, 2004).

11. Melissa Aronczyk and Devon Powers, *Blowing Up the Brand: Critical Perspectives on Promotional Culture* (New York: P. Lang, 2010).

12. Andy Pike, "Geographies of Brands and Branding," *Progress in Human Geography* 33, no. 5 (2009): 620, https://doi.org/10.1177/0309132508101601.

13. Timothy A. Gibson, "Selling City Living: Urban Branding Campaigns, Class Power and the Civic Good," *International Journal of Cultural Studies* 8, no. 3 (2005): 260, https://doi.org/10.1177/1367877905055678.

14. Scott Lash and Celia Lury, *Global Culture Industry: The Mediation of Things* (Cambridge: Polity, 2007), 5.

15. Sarah Banet-Weiser, *Authentic TM: The Politics and Ambivalence in a Brand Culture* (New York: NYU Press, 2012), 8.

16. Sonia Bookman, "Brands and Urban Life: Specialty Coffee, Consumers, and the Co-Creation of Urban Café Sociality," *Space and Culture* 17, no. 1 (2014): 85–99, https://doi.org/10.1177/1206331213493853.

17. On produsers and produsage, see Axel Bruns, "Towards Produsage: Futures for User-Led Content Production," in *Proceedings of the 5th International Conference on Cultural Attitudes towards Technology and Communication*, edited by C. Ess, F. Sudweeks, and H. Hrachovec, 275–84 (Australia: School of Information Technology, 2006), https://eprints.qut.edu.au/4863/. See also Henry Jenkins, *Convergence Culture: Where Old and New Media Collide* (New York: New York University Press), 2006.

18. Leslie Sklair and Laura Gherardi, "Iconic Architecture as a Hegemonic Project of the Transnational Capitalist Class," *City* 16, nos. 1–2 (2012): 60, https://doi.org/10.1080/13604813.2012.662366.

19. Emily Eakin, "The Cities and Their New Elite," *New York Times*, June 1, 2002, sec. Arts, https://www.nytimes.com/2002/06/01/arts/the-cities-and-their-new-elite.html.

20. Serin D. Houston, *Imagining Seattle: Social Values in Urban Governance, Our Sustainable Future* (Lincoln: University of Nebraska Press, 2019).

21. Costas Spirou, "Cultural Policy and the Dynamics of Stadium Development," *Sport in Society* 13, no. 10 (2010): 1423–37, https://doi.org/10.1080/17430437.2010.520934.

22. Sklair and Gherardi, "Iconic Architecture."

23. Patrick Sisson, "Amazon, New York City, and Corporate Citizenship," *Curbed-NY*, November 15, 2018, https://ny.curbed.com/2018/11/15/18097082/amazon-hq2-long-island-city-corporate-citizen.

24. "The Ballparks: T-Mobile Park," *This Great Game: The Online Book of Baseball*, https://thisgreatgame.com/ballparks-t-mobile-park/, accessed April 5, 2023.

25. Steve Friedman, "Seattle Mariners Team Ownership History," *Society for American Baseball Research* (blog), https://sabr.org/bioproj/topic/seattle-mariners-team-ownership-history/, accessed April 5, 2023.

26. Chris Scullion, "That Time When . . . Nintendo Bought a Baseball Team," *Video Games Chronicle*, January 11, 2021, https://www.videogameschronicle.com/features/that-time-when-nintendo-bought-a-baseball-team/.

27. Chris Donnelly, "Winless in Seattle: A History of the Seattle Mariners, 1977–1994," in *Seattle Sports: Play, Identity, and Pursuit in the Emerald City*, ed. Terry Anne Scott, 13–38. Sport, Culture, and Society (Fayetteville: University of Arkansas Press, 2020).

28. Murray Chass, "BASEBALL; Approval of Japanese Bid to Buy Mariners Unlikely," *New York Times*, January 24, 1992, sec. Sports, https://www.nytimes.com/1992/01/24/sports/baseball-approval-of-japanese-bid-to-buy-mariners-unlikely.html.

29. Friedman, "Seattle Mariners Team Ownership History."

30. Neil DeMause and Joanna Cagan, *Field of Schemes: How the Great Stadium Swindle Turns Public Money into Private Profit* (Lincoln: University of Nebraska Press, 2008), 110.

31. Timothy Egan, "Another Win for the Mariners: A Stadium," *Eugene (OR) Register-Guard*, October 24, 1995.

32. Elliot Almond et al., "Mariners Put Up for Sale—Owners Blame Council Members for Discussing Ballpark Delay," *Seattle Times*, December 15, 1996, https://archive.seattletimes.com/archive/?date=19961215&slug=2365157.

33. The deal included taxes on restaurants, taverns, auto rentals, admissions, lottery, and vanity plates.

34. Almond et al., "Mariners Put Up for Sale."

35. See "Washington State Ballpark Public Facilities District: Mission and History," Washington State Ballpark Public Facilities District, https://ballpark.org/mission-and-history/, accessed May 3, 2023.

36. "The Ballparks: T-Mobile Park."

37. By the time the ballpark was completed in 1999, the total cost was $517 million, with $100 million in cost overruns. The Mariners contributed approximately $126 million to the stadium, with the remainder coming from public funds. Allison Bremmeyer and Megan Ockerman, "T-Mobile Park," in *SAH Archipedia*, ed. Gabrielle Esperdy and Karen Kingsley (Charlottesville: University of Virginia Press, 2012), https://sah-archipedia.org/buildings/WA-01-033-0078.

38. Bremmeyer and Ockerman, "T-Mobile Park."

39. Kaila Lafferty, "Fans Can Skip the Line at T-Mobile Park's New Walk-Off Market," KING5, July 7, 2022, https://www.king5.com/article/sports/mlb/

mariners/seattle-mariners-t-mobile-park-walk-off-market-amazon-one/281-805a348a-e30d-4185-85f6-4ff38d030841.

40. DeMause and Cagan, *Field of Schemes*, 137.

41. Bremmeyer and Ockerman, "T-Mobile Park."

42. Naramore, Bain, Brady, and Johanson (NBBJ), "New Pacific Northwest Baseball Park, Seattle, WA," circa 1995, 2–6, 9323–02, Seattle Design Commission Project Files, box 23, folder 5, SMA.

43. "The Ballparks: T-Mobile Park."

44. "Safeco Field," MEIS architects, https://meisstudio.com/safeco-field/, accessed April 5, 2023.

45. Tim Newcomb, "Ballpark Quirks: Safeco Field Has Its Very Own Umbrella for Rainy Seattle," *Sports Illustrated*, May 30, 2014, https://www.si.com/mlb/2014/05/30/ballpark-quirks-safeco-field-seattle-mariners. Seattle is famously a rainy city; it has more than 150 days of rain on average and over forty inches of rain per year, significantly more than most other major US cities.

46. "The Ballparks: T-Mobile Park."

47. Melody McCutcheon, Hillis, Clark, Martin and Peterson Law Firm, "Letter to Scott Kemp, Department of Design, Construction and Land Use," February 20, 2001, 4603–01, Central Staff Analysts' Working Files, box 143, folder 04, SMA.

48. "Art in the Park, Seattle Mariners," MLB.com, https://www.mlb.com/mariners/ballpark/experiences/art-in-the-park/, accessed April 19, 2023.

49. "T-Mobile Park, Seattle Mariners Ballpark," Ballparks of Baseball, https://www.ballparksofbaseball.com/ballparks/t-mobile-park/, accessed April 5, 2023.

50. Author interview with Joshua Curtis, executive director of the Washington State Ballpark Public Facilities District, March 17, 2023.

51. Author interview with Joshua Curtis.

52. "North SoDo," Washington State Ballpark Public Facilities District, 2021, https://ballpark.org/north-sodo.

53. Dan Raley, *Tideflats to Tomorrow: The History of Seattle's SoDo* (Seattle: Fairgreens, 2010), 79.

54. Raley, *Tideflats to Tomorrow*, 79.

55. Raley, *Tideflats to Tomorrow*, 78.

56. When I visited SoDo, for example, there was an immersive Van Gogh experience and a *Stranger Things* immersive experience playing in the neighborhood's warehouses.

57. Freitheit and Ho Architects, "Home Plate Center: Design Review," July 2009, https://www.seattle.gov/dpd/AppDocs/GroupMeetings/DRProposal3009470Agenda ID2741.pdf.

58. J. Todd Graham, "The Six Million Dollar Mitigation," *Daily Journal of Commerce*, June 27, 2002, https://www.djc.com/news/co/11134803.html.

59. After the tiles fell from the Kingdome and voters refused a bond proposal to remodel the facility in 1995, Seahawks owner Ken Behring announced his plan to move the team to Los Angeles in February 1996. King County filed a lawsuit to keep

the team in Seattle, and the NFL threatened a $500,000 fine, halting the plan. See Clare Farnsworth, "Dark Days: 10 Years Ago, the Seahawks Nearly Moved to California," *Seattle Post-Intelligencer*, February 2, 2006, https://www.seattlepi.com/sports/seahawks/article/Dark-days-10-years-ago-the-Seahawks-nearly-1194634.php.

60. Rob Smith, "Multiple Options: Building Seahawks Stadium Was a Challenge for Architects and Engineers," *Puget Sound Business Journal*, July 21, 2002, https://www.bizjournals.com/seattle/stories/2002/07/22/focus3.html. Allen asked legislators to hold a statewide referendum on financing a new stadium. Opposition groups, including Citizens for More Important Things (which also lobbied against the Mariners Stadium) along with the groups Stop Stadium Madness and No on 48, rallied against the proposal. They argued that the city should not waste taxpayer dollars on the rich, who should put up the money themselves. But they faced a difficult battle. Allen financed the pro-stadium campaign to the tune of $2–3 million in comparison with the $20,000 budget of opposition groups. See David Schaefer, "Opposition Counts Pennies as Stadium Campaign Opens," *Seattle Times*, May 9, 1997. Further, in an unprecedented move, Allen financed the state referendum (Referendum 48) himself. As one *New York Times* article noted after the votes were tallied, "One could say that Paul Allen's money has bought him love." See Carey Goldberg, "A Decision on the Seattle Seahawks' Home," *New York Times*, May 25, 1997, sec. U.S., https://www.nytimes.com/1997/05/25/us/a-decision-on-the-seattle-seahawks-home.html. Voters approved Referendum 48 by a small margin—51.1 percent to 48.9 percent—in June 1997. Most support once again came from the suburbs. See David Schaefer, Barbara A. Serrano, and Lynne K. Varner, "Stadium Won Big in Suburbs—but Far Away, and in Seattle, Seahawk Issue Less Popular," *Seattle Times*, June 19, 1997, https://archive.seattletimes.com/archive/?date=19970619&slug=2545443.

61. Rob Smith, "Sustained Drive: Seahawks Stadium's Opening Culminates a Six-Year Effort," *Puget Sound Business Journal*, July 21, 2002, https://www.bizjournals.com/seattle/stories/2002/07/22/focus1.html. Private contributions to the stadium totaled approximately $130 million, while the public contributed up to $300 million through a lottery and taxes generated by events in the stadium/exhibition center. "Lumen Field—Stadium History and Facts," https://www.lumenfield.com/venue-info/stadium-history-facts/, accessed May 4, 2023.

62. Todd Bishop, "Rubble with a Cause," *Puget Sound Business Journal*, July 16, 2000, https://www.bizjournals.com/seattle/stories/2000/07/17/focus1.html.

63. Paul Allen, who died in 2018, played an outsized role in Seattle's development. Allen was known to some as Seattle's "Haussman." On his outsized influence, Shannon Mattern asks, "What kind of a civic vision or ideology can emerge from a development plan driven by one man's personal tastes, private fantasies, and nostalgia?" See Shannon Mattern, "Plurality in Place: Activating Public Spheres and Public Spaces in Seattle," *InVisible Culture*, no. 6 (2003), https://ivc.lib.rochester.edu/plurality-in-place-activating-public-spheres-and-public-spaces-in-seattle/.

64. Mike Sando, "Decibel Record Try Puts Mystique on Line," ESPN.com, July 9, 2013, https://www.espn.com/blog/nfcwest/post/_/id/103239/decibel-record-try-puts-mystique-on-line.

65. Smith, "Sustained Drive."

66. In 2023 the average ticket price was $127.71. See Statista, "NFL Average Ticket Price by Team 2023," https://www.statista.com/statistics/193595/average-ticket-price-in-the-nfl-by-team/, accessed January 14, 2025.

67. In a 2015 study, Washington ranked as the worst state for overburdening the poor with taxes, finding that "the poorest residents pay 16.8 percent of their income in taxes while the wealthiest sliver pays just 2.4 percent." See Patricia Cohen, "Study Finds Local Taxes Hit Lower Wage Earners Harder," *New York Times*, January 14, 2015, sec. Business, https://www.nytimes.com/2015/01/14/business/local-taxes-hit-lower-wage-earners-harder-study-finds.html.

68. Maria Saporta, "Seattle's Qwest Stadium May Guide Atlanta's Future Plans," SaportaReport, May 15, 2011, https://saportareport.com/seattles-qwest-stadium-may-guide-atlantas-plans/sections/abcarticles/maria_saporta/.

69. Ron Gans, "Designing Seattle's Newest Landmark," *Daily Journal of Commerce*, June 27, 2002, https://www.djc.com/news/co/11134759.html.

70. Gans, "Designing Seattle's Newest Landmark."

71. Regina Hackett, "Public Art Commitment Adds Passion to Stadium," *Seattle Post-Intelligencer*, July 19, 2002, https://www.seattlepi.com/news/article/Public-art-commitment-adds-passion-to-stadium-1091561.php.

72. Washington State Public Stadium Authority, "Public Art," 2021, https://stadium.org/public-benefits/public-art/.

73. Washington State Public Stadium Authority, "Public Art."

74. Traci L. Morris-Carlsten, "Trickster in Contemporary Native American Art and Thought: The Indigenous Cultural Language of Bob Haozous," *American Indian Art Magazine* (Autumn 2005): 85.

75. Adam Arvidsson, "Brands," *Journal of Consumer Culture* 5, no. 2 (2005): 235–58.

76. "Origin of the Seahawks Logo: The Story Unfolds," Burke Museum, January 27, 2015, https://www.burkemuseum.org/news/origin-seahawks-logo-story-unfolds.

77. Michael Rios, "Seahawks Logo Isn't Just Accepted by Coast Salish Tribes—It's Beloved," *Tulalip News* (blog), September 9, 2021, https://www.tulalipnews.com/wp/2021/09/09/seahawks-logo-isnt-just-accepted-by-coast-salish-tribes-its-beloved/.

78. "Lumen Field—Concessions Guide," https://www.lumenfield.com/plan-your-visit/concessions-guide/, accessed March 23, 2023.

79. Author interview with Kathleen Johnson, executive director of Historic South Downtown, March 18, 2023.

80. Quoted in Tyrah Majors, "Seahawks Unveil New Gameday Food Items for 2022 Season at Lumen Field," KIMA, September 9, 2022, https://kimatv.com/sports/seahawks-unveil-new-gameday-food-items-for-2022-season-at-lumen-field.

81. Jeffrey Hou, "'Night Market' in Seattle: Community Eventscape and the Reconstruction of Public Space," in *Insurgent Public Space: Guerrilla Urbanism and the Remaking of Contemporary Cities*, ed. Jeffrey Hou, 111–22 (New York: Routledge, 2010).

82. George Yúdice, *The Expediency of Culture: Uses of Culture in the Global Era* (Durham, NC: Duke University Press, 2003).

83. Arlene M. Dávila, *Barrio Dreams: Puerto Ricans, Latinos and the Neoliberal City* (Berkeley: University of California Press, 2004), 209.

84. Graham, "Six Million Dollar Mitigation."

85. Author interview with MaryKate Ryan, preservation planner, Historic South Downtown, March 18, 2023.

86. Author interview with Kathleen Johnson.

87. Mike Vorel, "Ten Years Later, Marshawn Lynch's 'Beast Quake' Run Continues to Send Shock Waves through Seattle," *Seattle Times*, January 15, 2021, https://www.seattletimes.com/sports/seahawks/how-marshawn-lynchs-beast-quake-which-just-turned-10-helped-prepare-scientists-for-actual-earthquakes/.

88. Gans, "Designing Seattle's Newest Landmark."

89. Sean Gregory, "The Science of Sound: How Seattle Got So Darn Loud," *Time*, September 17, 2013, https://keepingscore.blogs.time.com/2013/09/17/the-science-of-sound-how-seattle-got-so-darn-loud/#ixzz2hQBL1BVM.

90. Gregory, "Science of Sound."

91. gerg33, "Designed for Sound," *Field Gulls*, October 11, 2013, https://www.fieldgulls.com/2013/10/11/4828416/designed-for-sound.

92. Chris Ballard, "Into the Belly of Beast Mode," *Sports Illustrated Vault*, SI.com, November 11, 2013, https://vault.si.com/vault/2013/11/11/into-the-belly-of-beast-mode.

93. Ballard, "Into the Belly of Beast Mode."

94. "The 12s," Seattle Seahawks, https://www.seahawks.com/fans/the-12s/, accessed March 24, 2023.

95. At the time of writing, the world record holder for stadium noise is Kansas City's Arrowhead Stadium. See Rachel Swatman, "60 Record-Breaking Moments: When Seattle Seahawks Fans Created an Earthquake," Guinness World Records, August 20, 2015, https://www.guinnessworldrecords.com/news/2015/8/60-record-breaking-moments-when-seattle-seahawks-fans-created-an-earthquake-393205.

96. Mack Hagood and Travis Vogan, "The 12th Man: Fan Noise in the Contemporary NFL," *Popular Communication* 14, no. 1 (2016): 32, https://doi.org/10.1080/15405702.2015.1084624.

97. Greg Garber, "Toughest NFL Venues: No. 2, Built for Volume," ESPN.com, October 9, 2012, https://www.espn.com/nfl/story/_/id/8480724/nfl-hot-read-best-home-field-advantage-no-2.

98. Hagood and Vogan, "12th Man," 35.

99. Mia Hunt and Leah Pezzetti, "Which Era Was the Loudest? Scientists Analyze Seismic Activity of Taylor Swift's Seattle Concerts," king5.com, August 4, 2023, https://www.king5.com/article/news/local/swift-quake-scientists-break-down-seismic-activity-concert-lumen-field/281-c5207ddc-84ec-4712-8789-16447c57ff9e.

100. To be fair, Trump rallies tend to be held in arenas, including Madison Square Garden in New York City and PPG Paints Arena in Pittsburgh, rather than stadiums. However, he has also appeared in college football stadiums (for example, for his rally in Mobile, Alabama, at the fifty-thousand-person-capacity Ladd Peebles Stadium at the University of South Alabama in 2015). Mark Hensch, "Trump Moves Rally to 50,000-Capacity Stadium," *The Hill* (blog), August 20, 2015, https://thehill.com/blogs/ballot-box/251545-trump-moves-rally-to-50000-capacity-stadium/. Some journalists have even commented that Trump rallies feel more like sporting events than political rallies, showing how the space of the rally contributes to the sportification of politics more generally. See Adam Rogan, "From Doing the Wave to Stadium Rock Anthems, Trump Rallies Feel a Lot like Sporting Events," *Journal Times*, January 15, 2020. https://journaltimes.com/news/local/from-doing-the-wave-to-stadium-rock-anthems-trump-rallies-feel-a-lot-like-sporting/article_3b03e305-db5c-5b7f-b9c4-93c401856d2d.html.

101. In addition to US football, some European football (soccer) clubs have used the 12th Man moniker to refer to fans as well, though this tradition has not caught on in US soccer.

102. Terry Anne Scott, ed., *Seattle Sports: Play, Identity, and Pursuit in the Emerald City*, Sport, Culture, and Society (Fayetteville: University of Arkansas Press, 2020).

103. Matthew Sparke, "Excavating the Future in Cascadia: Geoeconomics and the Imagined Geographies of a Cross-Border Region," *BC Studies* 127 (Autumn 2000): 7.

104. "Independence," Cascadia Department of Bioregion, https://cascadiabioregion.org/independence-2/, accessed December 12, 2023.

105. Anna Griffin, "Far-Fetched as They Might Seem, Secession Movements Are Thriving in the NW," OPB (Oregon Public Broadcasting), March 23, 2017, https://www.opb.org/news/article/pacific-northwest-secession-state-of-jefferson-cascadia/.

106. Jake Bullinger, "Could a Cascadian Secession Actually Happen?" *Seattle Met*, May 15, 2017, https://www.seattlemet.com/news-and-city-life/2017/05/could-a-cascadian-secession-actually-be-a-thing.

107. "The Cascadia Movement," Cascadia Department of Bioregion, n.d., https://cascadiabioregion.org/the-cascadia-movement.

108. Alicia Halberg, "CascadiaNow Advocates Shift in Culture, Not Secession," CascadiaNow! July 5, 2012, https://www.cascadianow.org/articles/cascadianow-advocates-shift-in-culture-not-secession.

109. Hunter Shobe and Geoff Gibson, "Cascadia Rising: Soccer, Region, and Identity," *Soccer and Society* 18, no. 7 (2017): 953–71, https://doi.org/10.1080/14660970.2015.1067790.

110. "Cascadia News: Seattle Sounders," https://www.soundersfc.com/news/topics/cascadia/, accessed March 24, 2023.

111. Alison Hearn, "Variations on the Branded Self: Theme, Invention, Improvisation and Inventory," in *The Media and Social Theory*, ed. David Hesmondhalgh and Jason Toynbee, 194–210, Culture, Economy and the Social (New York: Routledge, 2008).

112. David Harvey, *The Condition of Postmodernity: An Enquiry into the Origins of Cultural Change* (Oxford: Blackwell, 1989), 124.

113. Scott Waalkes, "Does Soccer Explain the World or Does the World Explain Soccer? Soccer and Globalization," *Soccer and Society* 18, nos. 2–3 (2017): 166–80, https://doi.org/10.1080/14660970.2016.1166782.

114. Sparke, "Excavating the Future in Cascadia," 7.

Chapter 6. White Flight

1. George Lipsitz, *How Racism Takes Place* (Philadelphia: Temple University Press, 2011), 29.

2. Lipsitz, *How Racism Takes Place*, 6.

3. I understand white supremacy as the material practices that secure white domination while producing exclusion and premature death of people of color. See Anne Bonds and Joshua Inwood, "Beyond White Privilege: Geographies of White Supremacy and Settler Colonialism," *Progress in Human Geography* 40, no. 6 (2016): 2, https://doi.org/10.1177/0309132515613166.

4. Bonds and Inwood, "Beyond White Privilege," 6.

5. Niko Georgiades, "Minneapolis Police Murder Handcuffed Man with Neck-Kneel," Unicorn Riot, May 26, 2020, https://unicornriot.ninja/2020/minneapolis-police-murder-handcuffed-man-with-neck-kneel/.

6. Samuel L. Myers Jr., "The Minnesota Paradox," in Walter R. Jacobs et al., eds., *Sparked: George Floyd, Racism, and the Progressive Illusion* (St. Paul: Minnesota Historical Society Press, 2021), 73.

7. Jacobs et al., *Sparked*.

8. David Todd Lawrence, "Minnesota Nice White People," in Jacobs, *Sparked*, 86.

9. Chad Montrie, *Whiteness in Plain View: A History of Racial Exclusion in Minnesota* (St. Paul: Minnesota Historical Society Press, 2022), 203.

10. Kristin M. Anderson and Christopher W. Kimball, "Twin Cities Baseball Parks: Designing the National Pastime," *Minnesota History* (Fall 2003): 339–52.

11. Steven A. Riess, *City Games: The Evolution of American Urban Society and the Rise of Sports* (Urbana: University of Illinois Press, 1989).

12. Ellie McKinney, "The Short History of the Minnesota Twins' Calvin Griffith Memorial," MinnPost, September 20, 2021, https://www.minnpost.com/mnopedia/2021/09/the-short-history-of-the-minnesota-twins-calvin-griffith-memorial/.

13. Jay Weiner, Stadium Games: Fifty Years of Big League Greed and Bush League Boondoggles (Minneapolis: University of Minnesota Press, 2000), 1.

14. Weiner, *Stadium Games*, 9; Kristin M. Anderson, "The Hubert H. Humphrey Metrodome, Minneapolis, Minnesota," PhD diss., Twin Cities, University of Minnesota, 2008.

15. Montrie, *Whiteness in Plain View*, 174.

16. Anderson, "Hubert H. Humphrey Metrodome," 64.

17. Amy Klobuchar, *Uncovering the Dome: Was the Public Interest Served in Minnesota's 10-Year Political Brawl over the Metrodome?* (Prospect Heights, IL: Waveland Press, 1986), 10.

18. Weiner, *Stadium Games*, 18.
19. Klobuchar, *Uncovering the Dome*, 16.
20. Klobuchar, *Uncovering the Dome*, 17.
21. George Lipsitz, *The Possessive Investment in Whiteness: How White People Profit from Identity Politics* (Philadelphia: Temple University Press, 1998).
22. Michael Lomax, "Stadiums, Boosters, Politicians and Major League Baseball's Reluctance to Expand: An Exploration of Post–Second World War US Trends," in *The Rise of Stadiums in the Modern United States: Cathedrals of Sport*, ed. Mark Dyreson and Robert C. Trumpbour (London: Routledge, 2013), 92–109; Weiner, *Stadium Games*.
23. Klobuchar, *Uncovering the Dome*.
24. Montrie, *Whiteness in Plain View*, 189.
25. Weiner, *Stadium Games*, 74.
26. Klobuchar, *Uncovering the Dome*, 33.
27. Harvey B. Mackay, "Address to Annual Meeting of Minneapolis Chamber of Commerce," June 13, 1974, Leo Barnet Papers, box 2, folder 5, Minnesota Central Library, Minneapolis, Minnesota (hereafter, MCL).
28. Klobuchar, *Uncovering the Dome*, 41; see also Kevin J. Delaney and Rick Eckstein, *Public Dollars, Private Stadiums: The Battle over Building Sports Stadiums* (New Brunswick, NJ: Rutgers University Press, 2007).
29. Klobuchar, *Uncovering the Dome*, 20.
30. Weiner, *Stadium Games*, 77.
31. City of Minneapolis, Greater Minneapolis Chamber of Commerce, and Minneapolis Downtown Council, "Social and Economic Impact Created by a Stadium," in *A Multi-Use Sports Arena in Minneapolis*, 1977, 1–2 (Minnesota Historical Society, Gale Family Library, St. Paul, Minnesota [hereafter, MHS], GV431.M5 M52).
32. City of Minneapolis, Greater Minneapolis Chamber of Commerce, and Minneapolis Downtown Council, "Social and Economic Impact Created by a Stadium," 1–2.
33. Stadium historians debate the extent to which the stadium itself was viewed as a vehicle to urban revitalization. See Weiner, *Stadium Games*, 71; Anderson, "Hubert H. Humphrey Metrodome," 91–95; Delaney and Eckstein, *Public Dollars, Private Stadiums*, 88. On my read of the archival records, discourses of urban revitalization were key to the rationale for building and locating a new stadium in downtown Minneapolis.
34. City of Minneapolis, Greater Minneapolis Chamber of Commerce, and Minneapolis Downtown Council, "Social and Economic Impact Created by a Stadium," 4.
35. Metropolitan Council, "Stadium Locations: Metropolitan Council Comments and Recommendations," March 23, 1977, 2–3, MHS.
36. Stuart Hall, "The Whites of Their Eyes: Racist Ideologies and the Media," in *Gender, Race, and Class in Media: A Text-Reader*, ed. Gail Dines and Jean MacMahon Humez, 2nd. ed. (Thousand Oaks, CA: Sage, 2003), 91.
37. "Metrodome Visitors: The Downtown Council of Minneapolis Welcomes You to Our Community," *Minneapolis Tribune*, March 28, 1982, sec. Metrodome: A Souvenir Section, 2, MCL.

272 · Notes to Chapter 6

38. Sports Facilities Commission, "The Minneapolis Schematic Site Plan for a Single Multi-Use Sports Arena," 1977, MHS.

39. Weiner, *Stadium Games*, 72.

40. Harvey B. Mackay, "Interim Stadium Task Force Report," September 1974, Leo Bernat Papers, box 2, folder 5, MCL.

41. DeMause and Cagan, *Field of Schemes*; Roger G. Noll and Andrew S. Zimbalist, eds., *Sports, Jobs, and Taxes: The Economic Impact of Sports Teams and Stadiums* (Washington, DC: Brookings Institution Press, 1997); Weiner, *Stadium Games*.

42. Weiner, *Stadium Games*, 68.

43. Klobuchar, *Uncovering the Dome*, 100.

44. Minnesotans Against a Downtown Dome (MADD), "We Are Mad as Hell," circa 1975, Elliot Park Neighborhood Records, box 20, folder 17, MCL.

45. Senate Staff, "Critique of the Study 'Analysis of Stadium Alternatives: Twin Cities Metropolitan Area,'" March 1975, MHS.

46. Klobuchar and Guindon, *Uncovering the Dome*, 11–12.

47. "Citizen Participation and the Domed Stadium," VHS, *People and Causes* (Intermedia Arts Minnesota, circa 1974), III.37.237, MHS.

48. This sentiment is affirmed by the documents from the Stadium Task Force itself. Nowhere do they note consulting neighborhood residents or groups. See, for example, Mackay, "Interim Stadium Task Force Report."

49. Alexia Fernández Campbell, "How America's Past Shapes Native Americans' Present," *The Atlantic*, October 12, 2016, https://www.theatlantic.com/business/archive/2016/10/native-americans-minneapolis/503441/.

50. Ola Varmlanning, "A New Addition to Our Tradition, Stadium Guide," 1982, 2, 7, Elliot Park Neighborhood Records, box 20, folder 17, MCL.

51. Cedar-Riverside Project Area Committee, "Stadium in Industry Square," February 21, 1976, Leo Bernat Papers, box 2, folder 1, MCL.

52. K. B. Nowak, "Letter to Barbara Lukermann, Minnesota State Planning Agency," February 15, 1978, Elliot Park Neighborhood Records, box 20, folder 15, MCL.

53. Sasaki Associates and Minnesota State Planning Agency, "Twin Cities Metropolitan Sports Facilities: Final Environmental Impact Statements, Minneapolis, Bloomington," April 1978, MHS.

54. Elliot Park Neighborhood, Board of Directors, "Questions Regarding the Stadium Proposal," circa 1977, Elliot Park Neighborhood Records, box 20, folder 15, MCL; Elliot Park Neighborhood, "Policy Statement on Sports Stadium in Industry Square," November 7, 1977, Elliot Park Neighborhood Records, box 20, bolder 15, MCL.

55. Julian Empson, "Memo, EPNI to Stadium Organizing Committee," March 5, 1982, Elliot Park Neighborhood Records, box 20, bolder 17, MCL; "Welcome to the Neighborhood, Stadium Guide," 1982, Elliot Park Neighborhood Records, box 20, bolder 17, MCL.

56. Julie Kramer, "Neighborhoods around Stadium Face Change," *Minneapolis Tribune*, March 28, 1982, sec. Metrodome: A Souvenir Section, MCL.

57. Kramer, "Neighborhoods around Stadium Face Change."
58. Kramer, "Neighborhoods around Stadium Face Change."
59. Anderson, "Hubert H. Humphrey Metrodome," 156.
60. R. T. Rybak, "Indoors, It's a New Ballgame for the Spectator," *Minneapolis Tribune*, March 28, 1982, sec. Metrodome: A Souvenir Section, MCL.
61. Weiner, *Stadium Games*.
62. Weiner, *Stadium Games*, 98.
63. DeMause and Cagan, *Field of Schemes*, 168.
64. See, for example, Robert A. Baade and Richard F. Dye, "Sports Stadiums and Area Development: A Critical Review," *Economic Development Quarterly Economic Development Quarterly* 2, no. 3 (1988): 265–75; Noll and Zimbalist, *Sports, Jobs, and Taxes*; Mark S. Rosentraub, *Major League Losers: The Real Cost of Sports and Who's Paying for It*, rev. ed. (New York: Basic Books, 1999); Andrew S. Zimbalist, *Baseball and Billions: A Probing Look Inside the Big Business of Our National Pastime* (New York: Basic Books, 1992).
65. Delaney and Eckstein, *Public Dollars, Private Stadium*.
66. Minnesota Public Advocacy Research Team, "Squeeze Play: The Campaign for a New Twins Stadium," ed. Edward Schiappa, 1998, Minnesota Legislative Reference Library, https://www.lrl.mn.gov/docs/nonmnpub/oclc40058393.pdf.
67. Weiner, *Stadium Games*, 182.
68. Metropolitan Sports Facility Commission, "Analysis of Stadium Options," August 4, 1997, MCL.
69. Minnesota Public Advocacy Research Team, "Squeeze Play," 26.
70. Minnesota Public Advocacy Research Team, "Squeeze Play," 40–47.
71. Weiner, *Stadium Games*, 241.
72. Nolan Zavoral, "The Power of One," *Star Tribune*, July 31, 1999, Saturday, Metro Edition, sec. News; Faith and Values.
73. Minnesota Public Advocacy Research Team, "Squeeze Play," 50.
74. Committee of 17 (C-17), "C-17: New Ballpark Citizens Committee Report to the Mayor and City Council," March 2001, 3, https://www.ballparkmagic.com/_resources/c17report.pdf.
75. Author interview with Nick Koch, September 8, 2023.
76. Committee of 17 (C-17), "C-17: New Ballpark Citizens Committee Report," 12.
77. Committee of 17 (C-17), "C-17: New Ballpark Citizens Committee Report," 6.
78. Committee of 17 (C-17), "C-17: New Ballpark Citizens Committee Report," 4.
79. Metropolitan Sports Facilities Commission, "'Shape the Solution: Keep Minnesota Major League,' Stadium Issue Resource Guide," January 2002, MCL.
80. "Legislation: Minnesota Ballpark Authority," https://ballparkauthority.com/Legislation.html/, accessed January 14, 2025.
81. City of Minneapolis Planning Department, "Downtown East/North Loop Master Plan," October 2003, 15, https://minneapolis2040.com/media/1507/downtown-east-north-loop-master-plan.pdf.
82. City of Minneapolis Planning Department, "Downtown East/North Loop Master Plan," 2.

83. The North Loop was not really a neighborhood before the stadium; calling it the North Loop was a branding strategy. Author interview with Dan Kenney, Minnesota Ballpark Authority executive director, August 14, 2023.

84. Author interview with Dan Kenney.

85. Mike Ozanian, "Minneapolis City Council President Uses Bizarre Math to Push New Stadium for Vikings," *Forbes*, May 23, 2012, https://www.forbes.com/sites/mikeozanian/2012/05/23/minneapolis-city-council-president-uses-bizarre-math-to-push-new-stadium-for-vikings/.

86. Steve Berg, *U.S. Bank Stadium: The New Home of the Minnesota Vikings* (St. Paul: Minnesota Historical Society Press, in association with the Minnesota Vikings, 2016), 18.

Chapter 7. Surveillance and the Datafied Stadium

1. Christopher Thomas Gaffney, *Temples of the Earthbound Gods: Stadiums in the Cultural Landscapes of Rio de Janeiro and Buenos Aires* (Austin: University of Texas Press, 2010), 29.

2. Eduardo Bonilla-Silva, *Racism without Racists: Color-Blind Racism and the Persistence of Racial Inequality in the United States* (New York: Rowman and Littlefield, 2006).

3. Eduardo Bonilla-Silva, "The Structure of Racism in Color-Blind, 'Post-Racial' America," *American Behavioral Scientist* 59, no. 11 (2015): 1364, https://doi.org/10.1177/0002764215586826.

4. Henry A. Giroux, *The Terror of Neoliberalism* (Boulder, CO: Paradigm, 2004), 67.

5. David Theo Goldberg, *The Threat of Race: Reflections on Racial Neoliberalism* (Malden, MA: Wiley-Blackwell, 2009).

6. Sarah Banet-Weiser, "What's Your Flava? Race and Postfeminism in Media Culture," in *Interrogating Postfeminism: Gender and the Politics of Popular Culture*, ed. Yvonne Tasker and Diane Negra (Durham, NC: Duke University Press, 2007); Herman Gray, *Cultural Moves: African Americans and the Politics of Representation* (Berkeley: University of California Press, 2005).

7. This chapter, in addition to other primary research, draws on stadium design guides pitched to architects, owners, and designers to analyze stadium datafication and surveillance practices. One reason for using stadium guides is because stadium officials view surveillance and datafication as protected proprietary information central to stadium security and profitability. In addition to the guides, I also draw on press and security publications, conference programs and webinars, and published interviews with security professionals to incorporate specific examples from U.S. Bank Stadium and Target Field. The stadium guides I've consulted include Geraint John, Rod Sheard, and Ben Vickery, *Stadia: The Populous Design and Development Guide* (Abingdon, Oxon: Routledge, 2013); Martin Wimmer, Inka Humann, and Anna Martovitskaya, *Stadium Buildings*, Construction and Design Manual series (Berlin: DOM Publishers, 2016); Peter Culley and John Pascoe, eds., *Stadium and Arena Design*, 2nd ed. (N.p.:

ICE Publishing, 2015), https://doi.org/10.1680/saad.57906. Note that each of these sources considers global stadium construction and addresses other sporting spaces beyond baseball and football. As I point out in the conclusion, the evidence gleaned speaks to the broader applicability of the sportification of place globally and in other sporting spaces.

8. Rashad Shabazz, *Spatializing Blackness: Architectures of Confinement and Black Masculinity in Chicago* (Urbana: University of Illinois Press, 2015).

9. Catherine Zimmer, "Surveillance Cinema: Narrative between Technology and Politics," *Surveillance and Society* 8, no. 4 (2011): 432, https://doi.org/10.24908/ss.v8i4.4180.

10. Simone Browne, *Dark Matters: On the Surveillance of Blackness* (Durham, NC: Duke University Press, 2015), 17.

11. Mark Andrejevic, "The Big Data Divide," *International Journal of Communication* 8 (2014): 1675.

12. Jan Holnicki-Szulc, Jerzy Motylewski, and Przemysław Kołakowski, "Introduction to Smart Technologies," in *Smart Technologies for Safety Engineering*, ed. Jan Holnicki-Szulc, 1st ed. (Chichester, Eng: Wiley, 2008), 1, https://doi.org/10.1002/9780470758595.ch1.

13. Chamee Yang and C. L. Cole, "Smart Stadium as a Laboratory of Innovation: Technology, Sport, and Datafied Normalization of the Fans," *Communication & Sport*, 2020, 5. https://doi.org/10.1177/2167479520943579.

14. Scott Schlesinger, "Generative AI and Real-Time Data Transform Stadium Experiences," *RTInsights* (blog), September 27, 2023, https://www.rtinsights.com/revolutionizing-stadium-experiences-generative-ai-and-real-time-data-transformation/.

15. Pete Peranzo, "How AI Is Transforming the Sports Industry in 2023?" Imaginovation, August 6, 2023, https://imaginovation.net/blog/ai-in-sports-industry/.

16. Andrejevic, "Big Data Divide," 1676.

17. Safiya Umoja Noble, *Algorithms of Oppression: Data Discrimination in the Age of Google* (New York: NYU Press, 2018).

18. Emily M. Bender et al., "On the Dangers of Stochastic Parrots: Can Language Models Be Too Big?" in *Proceedings of the 2021 ACM Conference on Fairness, Accountability, and Transparency* (FAccT '21: 2021 ACM Conference on Fairness, Accountability, and Transparency) (Virtual Event Canada: ACM, 2021), 610–23, https://doi.org/10.1145/3442188.3445922; Jeff Raikes, "AI Can Be Racist: Let's Make Sure It Works for Everyone," *Forbes*, https://www.forbes.com/sites/jeffraikes/2023/04/21/ai-can-be-racist-lets-make-sure-it-works-for-everyone/, accessed December 27, 2023; Zachary Small, "Black Artists Say A.I. Shows Bias, with Algorithms Erasing Their History," *New York Times*, July 4, 2023, sec. Arts, https://www.nytimes.com/2023/07/04/arts/design/black-artists-bias-ai.html.

19. Hidefumi Nishiyama, "Crowd Surveillance: The (in)Securitization of the Urban Body," *Security Dialogue* 49, no. 3 (2018): 208, https://doi.org/10.1177/0967010617741436.

20. Nishiyama, "Crowd Surveillance," 209.

21. John, Sheard, and Vickery, *Stadia*, 37–38.

22. Sybille Frank and Silke Steets, "Conclusion: The Stadium—Lens and Refuge," in *Stadium Worlds: Football, Space and the Built Environment*, ed. Sybille Frank and Silke Steets (New York: Routledge, 2010), 282.

23. Nick Longworth, "Target Field Perimeter Security Approved as Part of SAFETY Act Compliance," FOX 9 Minneapolis–St. Paul, July 13, 2023, https://www.fox9.com/news/target-field-perimeter-security-approved-as-part-of-safety-act; "Beckoning Visitors Back to the Cities," *Star Tribune*, June 4, 2022, Metro edition, sec. News; Andy Mannix and Jeff Hargarten, "Downtown Minneapolis Is Back. So Is the Violent Crime," *Star Tribune*, July 31, 2022, Metro edition, sec. News.

24. Author interview with David St. Peter, Twins president, September 16, 2023.

25. Author interview with David St. Peter.

26. Andrew Sieradzski and Andrew Kelly, "Engineering Secure Stadiums," in *Stadium and Arena Design*, ed. Peter Culley and John Pascoe, 2nd ed. (London: ICE Publishing, 2015), 73, https://doi.org/10.1680/saad.57906.

27. John, Sheard, and Vickery, *Stadia*, 109.

28. Gino Spocchia, "George Floyd Protests: LA Police Use Jackie Robinson Stadium as Jail," *The Independent*, June 20, 2020, https://www.independent.co.uk/news/world/americas/us-politics/la-police-jackie-robinson-stadium-jail-george-floyd-protests-a9546911.html.

29. John Bale, "The Spatial Development of the Modern Stadium," *International Review for the Sociology of Sport* 28, nos. 2–3 (1993): 126, https://doi.org/10.1177/101269029302800204.

30. Christopher Hemming, "(28) Super Bowl LII's U.S. Bank Stadium Is Totally Tech-Tastic," LinkedIn, January 26, 2018, https://www.linkedin.com/pulse/super-bowl-liis-us-bank-stadium-totally-tech-tastic-hemming/.

31. Diane Ritchey, "2017 Security Innovation in U.S. Bank Stadium, Where Technology Is King," *Security Magazine*, January 1, 2017, https://www.securitymagazine.com/articles/87666-2017-security-innovation-in-us-bank-stadium-where-technology-is-king.

32. "Facility Management Software | 24/7 Software," 24/7 Software, https://www.247software.com/, accessed November 12, 2023.

33. "U.S. Bank Stadium Manages 750 Incidents per Game," 24/7 Software, https://www.247software.com/u-s-bank-stadium-manages-750-incidents-per-game-with-247-software/, accessed November 12, 2023.

34. "Webinar Recap: Analytics in Venue Operations and Facilities Management," 24/7 Software, October 25, 2023, https://www.247software.com/blog/webinar-recap-analytics-in-venue-operations-and-facilities-management.

35. "Webinar Recap."

36. John, Sheard, and Vickery, *Stadia*, 31.

37. Mike S. Schafer and Jochen Roose, "Emotions in Sports Stadia," in *Stadium Worlds: Football, Space and the Built Environment*, ed. Sybille Frank and Silke Steets (New York: Routledge, 2010), 236.

38. Ritchey, "2017 Security Innovation in U.S. Bank Stadium."

39. Bale, "Spatial Development of the Modern Stadium."

40. Michel Foucault, *Discipline and Punish: The Birth of the Prison* (New York: Vintage Books, 1995).

41. Bale, "Spatial Development of the Modern Stadium," 126.

42. Wimmer, Humann, and Martovitskaya, *Stadium Buildings*, 73.

43. Steve Berg, *Target Field: The New Home of the Minnesota Twins* (Minneapolis: MVP Books, 2010), 81, 89.

44. Berg, *Target Field*, 81.

45. Walter Benjamin, *The Arcades Project*, trans. Rolf. Tiedemann (Cambridge, MA: Belknap Press, 1999); Michel de Certeau, *The Practice of Everyday Life* (Berkeley: University of California Press, 1984), 93; Henri Lefebvre, *The Production of Space* (Oxford, UK: Cambridge University Press, 1991).

46. Helen Morgan Parmett, "Site-Specific Television as Urban Renewal: Or, How Portland Became *Portlandia*," *International Journal of Cultural Studies* 21, no. 1 (2018): 47, https://doi.org/10.1177/1367877917704493.

47. On Fantasy City, see John Hannigan, *Fantasy City* (London: Routledge, 1998); on the ballpark as mallpark, see Michael T. Friedman, *Mallparks: Baseball Stadiums and the Culture of Consumption* (Ithaca, NY: Cornell University Press, 2023); on creative place-making, see Ann Markusen and Anne Gadwa, "Creative Placemaking" (Markusen Economic Research Services and Metris Arts Consulting, 2010), www.nea.gov/pub/CreativePlacemaking-Paper.pdf.

48. Berg, *Target Field*, 83.

49. Author interview with Dan Kenney, Minnesota Ballpark Authority executive director, August 14, 2023.

50. Author interview with David St. Peter.

51. "Target Field Fan Guide," 2010, Minnesota Historical Society, Gale Family Library.

52. Berg, *U.S. Bank Stadium*, 167.

53. Anne Friedberg, *The Virtual Window: From Alberti to Microsoft* (Cambridge: MIT Press, 2006), 138.

54. Friedberg, *Virtual Window*, 151.

55. Friedberg, *Virtual Window*, 7.

56. Berg, *U.S. Bank Stadium*, xiv–xv.

57. John, Sheard, and Vickery, *Stadia*.

58. Gaffney, *Temples of the Earthbound Gods*, 29.

59. "Target Field Annual Suites," MLB.com, https://www.mlb.com/twins/tickets/season-tickets/suites/annual-suites/, accessed November 11, 2023.

60. "Delta Sky360° Suite," MLB.com, https://www.mlb.com/twins/tickets/season-tickets/suites/delta-sky360-suite/, accessed November 11, 2023.

61. "Delta SKY360° Club," MLB.com.

62. "Thomson Reuters Champions Club," MLB.com, https://www.mlb.com/twins/tickets/season-tickets/suites/champions-club/, accessed November 11, 2023.

63. Berg, *U.S. Bank Stadium*, 172.

64. Wimmer, Humann, and Martovitskaya, *Stadium Buildings*, 79.

65. Author interview with David St. Peter.

66. Lipsitz, *How Racism Takes Place*.

67. Frank and Steets, "Conclusion: The Stadium—Lens and Refuge," 291.

68. "Fancam," Fancam, April 21, 2021, https://www.fancam.com/.

69. "Fancam."

70. Gaffney, *Temples of the Earthbound Gods*.

71. Berg, *U.S. Bank Stadium*, 199.

72. "Thomson Reuters Champions Club," MLB.com.

73. In football, in particular, where over 70 percent of the players on the field are Black while over 80 percent of the fans in the stadium are likely to be white, these looking relations have an uncomfortable relationship with colonial practices in which "Black males were forced to perform for white audiences." See Rachel A. Griffin and Bernadette M. Calafell, "Control, Discipline, and Punish: Black Masculinity and (in)Visible Whiteness in the NBA," in *Critical Rhetorics of Race*, ed. Michael G. Lacy and Kent A. Ono (New York: NYU Press, 2011), 118. See also Thomas P. Oates, "The Erotic Gaze in the NFL Draft," *Communication and Critical/Cultural Studies* 4, no. 1 (2007): 74–90, https://doi.org/10.1080/14791420601138351; David L. Andrews, Ronald L. Mower, and Michael L. Silk, "Ghettocentrism and the Essentialized Black Male Athlete," in *Commodified and Criminalized: New Racism and African-Americans in Contemporary Sports* ed. David J. Leonard and C. Richard King, 69–94 (Lanham, MD: Rowman and Littlefield, 2010).

74. John, Sheard, and Vickery, *Stadia*, 109.

75. Adam Arvidsson, "Brands," *Journal of Consumer Culture* 5, no. 2 (2005): 235–58.

76. John, Sheard, and Vickery, *Stadia*, 24.

77. Joe Lemire, "CrowdIQ Will Make You Rethink Pretty Much Everything about Fan Behavior in the Stands," *Sports Business Journal*, June 29, 2021, https://www.sportsbusinessjournal.com/Daily/Issues/2021/06/29/Technology/crowdiq-sports-fan-behavior-sponsorships-activations.aspx.

78. "Crowd Analytics at Your Fingertips," CrowdIQ, September 9, 2019, https://crowdiq.ai/.

79. Lemire, "CrowdIQ Will Make You Rethink."

80. Lemire, "CrowdIQ Will Make You Rethink."

81. John, Sheard, and Vickery, *Stadia*, 214.

82. Michael Rand, "Club Purple at New Vikings Stadium Is 'All about the Fan Experience,'" *Minnesota Star Tribune*, February 17, 2016, https://www.startribune.com/club-purple-at-new-vikings-stadium-is-all-about-the-fan-experience/369051721.

83. "Twins Bring ARound, First Shared Augmented Reality Experience in a Live Sports Venue, to Target Field," MLB.com, https://www.mlb.com/press-release/press-release-twins-bring-around-first-shared-ar-experience-in-a-live-sports-ven/, accessed September 16, 2023; Maury Brown, "Minnesota Twins Launch First Shared AR For Live Sports App That Opens Door to Sponsorship Land Grab," *Forbes*, August 23, 2022, https://www.forbes.com/sites/maurybrown/2022/08/23/minnesota-twins-launch-first-shared-ar-for-live-sports-app-that-opens-door-to-sponsorship-land-grab/; Allison Kaplan, "Twins Bring Augmented Reality to Target Field," *Twin Cities Business* (blog), August 22, 2022, https://tcbmag.com/twins-bring-augmented-reality-to-target-field/.

84. SSB Consulting, "Case Study: For the Minnesota Vikings, SSB Central Intelligence Is a Real Game-Changer," 2019, https://affinaquest.com/wp-content/uploads/2019/05/Vikings_Case_Study.pdf.

85. Mark Andrejevic, "The Big Data Divide," *International Journal of Communication* 8 (2014): 1679.

86. Andrejevic, "Big Data Divide," 1675.

87. Natalie P. Byfield, "Race Science and Surveillance: Police as the New Race Scientists," *Social Identities* 25, no. 1 (2019): 91–106, https://doi.org/10.1080/13504630.2017.1418599.

88. "Webinar Recap."

89. 24/7 Software. "U.S. Bank Stadium Manages 750 Incidents per Game," https://www.247software.com/u-s-bank-stadium-manages-750-incidents-per-game-with-247-software/, accessed November 12, 2023.

90. See, for example, Noble, *Algorithms of Oppression*; Byfield, "Race Science and Surveillance"; Nicol Turner Lee, "Detecting Racial Bias in Algorithms and Machine Learning," *Journal of Information, Communication and Ethics in Society* 16, no. 3 (2018): 252–60, https://doi.org/10.1108/JICES-06-2018-0056.

91. Brett Hutchins and Mark Andrejevic, "Olympian Surveillance: Sports Stadiums and the Normalization of Biometric Monitoring," *International Journal of Communication* 15 (2021): 363–82.

92. Yang and Cole, "Smart Stadium as a Laboratory of Innovation."

93. Tony Webster, "Hennepin County Sheriff Circumvents State to Expand Facial Recognition Database," Tony Webster, June 3, 2016, https://tonywebster.com/journalism/hennepin-county-sheriff-circumvents-state-to-expand-facial-recognition-database.

94. Mack DeGeurin, "These 9 Stadiums Are Already Using Facial Recognition at Games," Yahoo Finance, September 5, 2023, https://finance.yahoo.com/news/9-stadiums-already-using-facial-110000157.html. Research conducted by *Slate* in 2023 suggests that twenty-one sports venues were using facial recognition. See Georgia Gee, "Here Are the Stadiums That Are Keeping Track of Your Face," *Slate*, March 14, 2023, https://slate.com/technology/2023/03/madison-square-garden-facial-recognition-stadiums-list.html.

95. "U.S. Bank Stadium Manages 750 Incidents per Game."

96. Author interview with Mercedes-Benz Stadium executive, March 28, 2022.

97. Masha Borak, "Facial Recognition-Equipped Robot Dog to Prowl US Sporting Venue," Biometric Update, September 1, 2023, https://www.biometricupdate.com/202309/facial-recognition-equipped-robot-dog-to-prowl-us-sporting-venue.

98. Author interview with Mercedes-Benz Stadium executive.

99. Frank and Steets, "Conclusion: The Stadium," 290.

100. Frank and Steets, "Conclusion: The Stadium," 290.

101. John, Sheard, and Vickery, *Stadia*, 184.

102. Gidon S. Jakar and Kiernan O. Gordon, "Dead Spaces: Sport Venues and Police Stops in a Major League, Upper Midwestern City in the United States," *Journal of Sport Management* 36, no. 4 (2022): 355–68, https://doi.org/10.1123/jsm.2021-0080.

103. Byfield, "Race Science and Surveillance."

104. Author interview with David St. Peter.

105. Stew Thornley, "Twins Highlight George Floyd and Racial Justice in Home Opener," *Society for American Baseball Research* (blog), July 28, 2020, https://sabr.org/gamesproj/game/july-28-2020-twins-highlight-george-floyd-and-racial-justice-in-home-opener/.

106. "Twins Remove Statue of Calvin Griffith from Target Field over Racist Comments," CBS News, Minnesota, June 19, 2020, https://www.cbsnews.com/minnesota/news/twins-remove-statue-of-calvin-griffith-from-target-field-over-racist-comments/.

107. Lisa Duggan, *The Twilight of Equality? Neoliberalism, Cultural Politics, and the Attack on Democracy* (Boston: Beacon, 2003).

108. Kurt Streeter, "The Talk of the Super Bowl Is Quarterbacks, Except One," *New York Times*, January 25, 2021, sec. Sports, https://www.nytimes.com/2021/01/25/sports/football/kaepernick-kneeling-protests-super-bowl.html.

109. Betsy Hefland, "Twins Owners Pledge $25 Million to Fight for Racial Justice," *Twin Cities Pioneer Press*, June 10, 2020, https://www.twincities.com/2020/06/10/twins-owners-pledge-25-million-to-fight-for-racial-justice/.

110. Author interview with Pohlad Family Foundation representative, September 6, 2023.

111. Hefland, "Twins Owners Pledge $25 Million."

112. Pohlad Family Foundation, "RACIAL JUSTICE Update 2022," 2022, https://pohladfoundation.org/wp-content/uploads/2022/08/pohlad-foundation-racial-justice-update.pdf.

113. Author interview with Pohlad Family Foundation representative.

114. Pohlad Family Foundation, "RACIAL JUSTICE Update 2022."

115. Author interview with Kristin Rortvedt, Twins Community Fund executive director, September 15, 2023.

116. "North Minneapolis," CURA Twin Cities Gentrification Project, https://gentrification.umn.edu/north-minneapolis/, accessed November 12, 2023.

117. Author interview with Kristin Rortvedt.

118. Author interview with Kristin Rortvedt.

119. Vincanne Adams, *Markets of Sorrow, Labors of Faith: New Orleans in the Wake of Katrina* (Durham, NC: Duke University Press, 2013).

Conclusion

1. Sean Gregory, "The World's Sports Stadiums Are Turning into Hospitals," *Time*, April 1, 2020, https://time.com/5813442/coronavirus-stadiums-hospitals/; Daniel Wood, "As Pandemic Deaths Add Up, Racial Disparities Persist—And in Some Cases Worsen," NPR.org, September 23, 2020, https://www.npr.org/sections/health-shots/2020/09/23/914427907/as-pandemic-deaths-add-up-racial-disparities-persist-and-in-some-cases-worsen.

2. During a 2016 NFL preseason game, San Francisco 49ers quarterback Colin Kaepernick sat and, in subsequent games, kneeled during the national anthem to protest police brutality against the Black community. NFL players across the league soon joined him in the practice. In 2018 the NFL banned kneeling during the anthem, encouraging players to stay in their locker rooms during the anthem if they intended to kneel, or risk being fined. Kaepernick became "a target for collective far-right outrage, a focal point around which commenters could explore and define their common values, grievances, and identities." See Spring-Serenity Duvall, "Too Famous to Protest: Far-Right Online Community Bonding over Collective Desecration of Colin Kaepernick, Fame, and Celebrity Activism," *Journal of Communication Inquiry* 44, no. 3 (2020): 3, https://doi.org/10.1177/0196859920911650. The movement spread to other sports leagues, including the WNBA, NBA, MLS, and MLB. Kaepernick was roundly punished by the league; he was released from the 49ers and remained unsigned by another NFL team. Take a Knee is, of course, not the first activist movement around race to use the stadium as the site of resistance. Famously, Tommie Smith and John Carlos raised their fists in a Black Power salute while the national anthem played during their 1968 Olympics medal ceremony. Like Kaepernick, they faced backlash that critiqued their "politicization" of sport. Douglas Hartmann, *Race, Culture, and the Revolt of the Black Athlete: The 1968 Olympic Protests and Their Aftermath* (Chicago: University of Chicago Press, 2003).

3. Niko Georgiades, "17 Arrested Blockading Light Rail before Super Bowl LII," *Unicorn Riot* (blog), February 5, 2018, https://unicornriot.ninja/2018/17-arrested-blockading-light-rail-super-bowl-lii/.

4. Georgiades, "17 Arrested Blockading Light Rail."

5. Jess Row, "A Safe Space for Racism," *New Republic*, November 23, 2016, https://newrepublic.com/article/138990/safe-space-racism.

6. Kent Babb and Steven Rich, "A Quietly Escalating Issue for NFL: Fan Violence and How to Contain It," *Washington Post*, October 28, 2016, https://www.washingtonpost.com/sports/redskins/a-quietly-escalating-issue-for-nfl-fan-violence-and-how-to-contain-it/2016/10/28/4ec37964-9470-11e6-bb29-bf2701dbe0a3_story.html.

7. Poe Johnson, "Playing with Lynching: Fandom Violence and the Black Athletic Body," *Television & New Media* 21, no. 2 (2020): 169–83, https://doi.org/10.1177/1527476419879913.

8. Associated Press, "NFL Fans Boo during Moment of Silence for Racial Injustice at Chiefs, Texans Game in Missouri," KTLA-5, September 11, 2020, https://ktla.com/news/nationworld/nfl-fans-boo-during-moment-of-silence-for-racial-injustice-at-chiefs-texans-game-in-missouri/.

9. Victor Mather, "'Racism Is as American as Baseball' Banner Unfurled at Fenway Park," *New York Times*, September 14, 2017, https://www.nytimes.com/2017/09/14/sports/baseball/boston-red-sox-fenway-park-racism.html.

10. Brian Murphy, "Protest Banner Disrupts Vikings–Bears Game at U.S. Bank Stadium," *Pioneer Press*, January 1, 2017, https://www.twincities.com/2017/01/01/protest-banner-disrupts-vikings-game/.

11. Georgiades, "17 Arrested Blockading Light Rail."

12. Dana Branham, "9 Freed from Jail after Arrests on Traffic Obstruction Charges during Botham Jean Protest Outside AT&T Stadium," *Dallas Morning News*, September 18, 2018, https://www.dallasnews.com/news/crime/2018/09/18/9-freed-from-jail-after-arrests-on-traffic-obstruction-charges-during-botham-jean-protest-outside-att-stadium/.

13. Samantha Liss, "Police Arrest Two Ferguson Protesters in Clash with Rams Fans," STLtoday.com, October 20, 2014, https://www.stltoday.com/news/local/police-arrest-two-ferguson-protesters-in-clash-with-rams-fans/article_dcca3100-aa78-5ea0-a55f-c8833a07a4f6.html.

14. Steve Mann, Jason Nolan, and Barry Wellman, "Sousveillance: Inventing and Using Wearable Computing Devices for Data Collection in Surveillance Environments," *Surveillance and Society* 1, no. 3 (2002): 332–33, https://doi.org/10.24908/ss.v1i3.3344.

15. Samantha N. Sheppard, *Sporting Blackness: Race, Embodiment, and Critical Muscle Memory on Screen* (Oakland: University of California Press, 2020), 15.

16. Simone Browne, *Dark Matters: On the Surveillance of Blackness* (Durham, NC: Duke University Press, 2015), 21.

17. Browne, *Dark Matters*, 21.

18. Leah Asmelash, "The Boston Red Sox Put up a Black Lives Matter Billboard over the Massachusetts Turnpike," CNN, July 23, 2020, https://www.cnn.com/2020/07/22/us/boston-red-sox-black-lives-matter-trnd/index.html; Matt Bonesteel, "Red Sox Acknowledge Racism at Fenway Park 'Is Real,' Promise Action," *Washington Post*, June 11, 2020, https://www.washingtonpost.com/sports/2020/06/11/red-sox-acknowledge-racism-fenway-park-is-real-promise-action/.

19. Sean Gregory, "Why Boston's Sports Teams Can't Escape the City's Racism," *Time*, May 2, 2017, https://time.com/4763746/boston-baltimore-orioles-adam-jones-racism/.

20. Fred Bowen, "Perspective | NFL Commissioner Says the League Should Have Listened to Players Who Took a Knee," *Washington Post*, June 10, 2020, https://www.washingtonpost.com/lifestyle/kidspost/nfl-admits-the-league-should-have-listened-to-players-who-took-a-knee/2020/06/10/4c8062da-a2f3-11ea-b5c9-570a91917d8d_story.html.

21. "Inspire Change, Super Bowl LV Commercial," 2021, https://www.youtube.com/watch?v=bu_kAMpCKME.

22. Andrew Lawrence, "Will Dr Dre's Halftime Super Bowl Show Move the NFL beyond Its Race Crisis?" *The Guardian*, February 8, 2022, sec. Sport, https://www.theguardian.com/sport/2022/feb/08/super-bowl-halftime-show-dr-dre-nfl-race-crisis.

23. Shannon Garrido and Hadera McKay, "Super Bowl Halftime Show Reflects the Black Experience, but Its Efforts Are Performative," *Berkeley Beacon* (blog), February 17, 2022, https://berkeleybeacon.com/super-bowl-halftime-show-pays-homage-to-the-black-experience-while-its-efforts-are-performative/.

24. Dave Zirin, "Was the Super Bowl Halftime Show a 'Missed Opportunity'?" *The Nation*, February 15, 2022, https://www.thenation.com/article/culture/super-bowl-halftime-show/.

25. Murray Forman, *The 'hood Comes First: Race, Space, and Place in Rap and Hip-Hop* (Middletown, CT: Wesleyan University Press, 2002).

26. Priscilla Leiva, "Super Bowl LVI Represents the Clash of Two Realities for People of Color in L.A.," *Washington Post*, February 13, 2022, https://www.washingtonpost.com/outlook/2022/02/13/super-bowl-lvi-represents-clash-two-realities-people-color-la/.

27. Hunter Shobe, "Politics, Identity, Global Branding, and the Stadium: FC Barcelona's Camp Nou," in *The Political Football Stadium: Identity Discourses and Power Struggles*, ed. Basak Alpan, Albrecht Sonntag, and Katarzyna Herd, 107–29 (Cham, Switzerland: Palgrave Macmillan, 2023), https://doi.org/10.1007/978-3-031-29144-9.

28. Sam Marsden, "Barca's Camp Nou Is Closed. Why Are They Leaving? Where Will They Go?" ESPN.com, May 30, 2023, https://www.espn.com/soccer/story/_/id/37758766/barcelonas-camp-nou-closed-plans-stadium.

29. Chris Wright and Toe Poke, "New Camp Nou: Barca's Stadium Plans to Rival Bernabeu Revealed," ESPN.com, October 20, 2021, https://www.espn.com/soccer/story/_/id/37621765/barcelona-reveal-plans-camp-nou-redevelopment-rival-real-madrid-bernabeu.

30. Doug Greenberg, "FC Barcelona Secures $1.6B Financing for Camp Nou Renovation," Front Office Sports, April 25, 2023, https://frontofficesports.com/fc-barcelona-secures-1-6b-financing-camp-nou-renovation/#.

31. Secular, *Digital NBA*.

32. Secular, *Digital NBA*, 170–71.

33. Peter Beer, "Capitalizing on the Return to Full Stadiums: Sports after Covid," https://www.picogp.com/the-picomag/capitalizing-on-return-to-stadiums/, accessed January 21, 2024; Jeré Longman, "With No Fans in the Seats, Do Sports Remain Must-Watch TV?" *New York Times*, May 20, 2020, sec. Sports, https://www.nytimes.com/2020/05/20/sports/coronavirus-sports-fans.html.

34. Toby Miller, *Greenwashing Sport* (London: Routledge, 2018), 2.

35. Mark Brown, "How Much Can Oriole Park at Camden Yards Change without Losing Its Classic Feel?" Camden Chat, December 20, 2023, https://www.camdenchat.com/2023/12/20/24009248/orioles-news-camden-yards-lease-renovations.

36. Nicole Starosielski, *The Undersea Network: Sign, Storage, Transmission* (Durham, NC: Duke University Press, 2015); Anne Kaun and Fredrik Stiernstedt, *Prison Media: Incarceration and the Infrastructures of Work and Technology*, Distribution Matters (Cambridge, MA: MIT Press, 2023).

Index

Aaron, Hank, 94
Abrams, Stacey, 95
Adams, Vincanne, 81–82
Ad Hoc Committee for the Seattle Center Stadium, 112–13
AECOM (formerly Ellerbe Becket), 51, 147
affect theory, 13–15; nature of affect and, 13–14; sports stadiums and, 16–17
African Americans: Black entrepreneurs and Atlanta Tech Village, 94; Black Power movement, 171, 225; Dirty Bird and African American expressive culture, 74–77, 95, 250–51n37; discipline and control of, 22, 58–59, 75, 190, 214–15, 223, 224; on football teams, 221–28, 278n7, 281n2; Great Migration and, 9; hip-hop and rap music, 29, 61, 73–77, 94, 95, 227–28; Jim Crow laws and, 31, 215–16; Negro Leagues, 34–35, 85, 105, 109; neighborhood displacement and, 35–37, 40–46, 48, 53–55, 77–84, 178–80; racial Otherness and, 76, 176; racist housing policies, 21–22, 35–37, 83–84, 110; and stadium surveillance and security, 43, 110, 169, 214; Take a Knee movement, 221–28, 281n2; "white flight" trend and, 9, 21–22, 89, 96–99, 110, 167–70, 180. *See also* Black Lives Matter movement; racism
Ahmed, Sara, 14
Ali, Muhammad, 40, 123
Allen, Ivan, Jr., 30–31, 35–37
Allen, Paul, 146–47, 266n263
Amazon, 103, 132, 136, 139
AMB Sports & Entertainment Group, 66
American Association of Independent Professional Baseball, 168
American League, 110, 114, 171
Anderson, Jamal, 74–75
Anderson, Kristin, 169, 182
Andrejevic, Mark, 193–94, 212, 213
Arakawa, Minoru, 137
ARound (augmented reality app), 211–12
Arrowhead Stadium (Kansas City), noise levels, 268n95
Arthur Blank Foundation, 62, 77–84, 219, 252–53n88
Arvidsson, Adam, 133–34, 152
Asian Americans: in Chinatown-International District (Seattle), 104, 115–21, 127, 142, 146, 150, 153–55, 256–57n6; displacement for Metrodome, 180; Lumen Field art installations and, 150, 153–54;

Asian Americans (*continued*): Orientalist discourse and, 127; as the Other, 127, 137
Astroturf, 21
Atlanta, 27–99; Atlanta Paradox (Sjoquist), 28–29, 61, 73–74; "Atlanta Spirit," 30–31; biracial coalition in, 28, 29–30, 31, 86; as Black Mecca, 27–30, 40, 58, 59, 61, 74–76, 94; cultural geography of, 28, 29; FIFA World Cup (2026), 60, 77, 161; Forward Atlanta advertising campaign, 31–32; Fulton County Stadium (FCS) (*see* Atlanta–Fulton County Stadium); as a global city, 27, 38–46, 48, 51, 58, 132; as a leader in human rights, 27, 31, 38–41, 48–50, 58, 76, 94; Livable Cities Initiative grant, 98; Negro League, 34–35; neighborhood revitalization and displacement, 35–37, 40–46, 48–50, 53–57, 77–84, 95, 97; Olympic Games (1996), 27, 38–56; Olympic Ring revitalization, 40–46, 49–50, 53–55; racial and income inequalities, 27–28; rap music and hip-hop, 29, 61, 73–77, 94, 95; Regional/Urban Design Assistance Team (R/UDAT), 39–40; social justice initiatives, 62, 77–84, 219; sportification of place in, 23, 38–56, 58, 59, 73–77, 79–80, 93–94, 96–99; Summerhill neighborhood, 35, 37, 40, 48, 50, 53–56, 86, 96–97; Super Bowl (2019), 48, 60, 70, 72, 74; Super Bowl bid (2014), 131, 156, 157; as a technology hub, 58, 77, 86, 89, 90, 93–94; Underground Atlanta mall revival, 29–30, 48, 77; Westside Development Initiative, 77–84, 219; "white flight" from, 89, 96–99. *See also* Centennial Olympic Stadium/Turner Field; Georgia Dome; Mercedes-Benz Stadium; Truist Park

Atlanta Braves, 46; Comcast investment in, 2, 92–93; move from Milwaukee, 30, 31–32, 110; move to Cobb County, 55–57, 59–61, 85–89, 95, 96–99; Tomahawk Chop, 94–95; Ted Turner and, 11, 30, 51, 235n2, 246n84; in the World Series (2021), 94–95. *See also* Atlanta–Fulton County Stadium; Centennial Olympic Stadium/Turner Field; Truist Park

Atlanta Center, 38
Atlanta Civic Center, 35
Atlanta Department of Planning and Development (ADPD), 38
Atlanta Falcons, 30, 40; associations with Black culture, 74–77, 95, 248n16; Dirty Bird, 74–77, 95, 250–51n57; National Football Conference championship, 74; Ticketmaster Studio, 70–71. *See also* Atlanta–Fulton County Stadium; Georgia Dome; Mercedes-Benz Stadium
Atlanta–Fulton County Stadium (FCS), 30–37; comparison with other stadiums, 48, 52, 112, 122, 123; dedication book, 34–35; demolition, 51; design and architecture, 33–34; highway system and, 33, 35, 37, 54; mediatized logic and, 33; as multipurpose stadium, 46; neighborhood revitalization and displacement, 35–37, 56, 78, 95, 97; opening (1965), 30, 32; replacements, 46–56 (*see also* Centennial Olympic Stadium/Turner Field; Georgia Dome); social class and, 34–35
Atlanta Hawks, 57–58
Atlanta Housing Trust, 83–84
Atlanta Organizing Committee (AOC), 53
Atlanta United FC, 59, 62, 70–71. *See also* Mercedes-Benz Stadium

Bale, John, 15, 18–19, 196, 198
Baltimore Orioles, 1, 22–23, 185, 232. *See also* Camden Yards
Banet-Weiser, Sarah, 134
baseball: in American culture, 6; decline of Black interest and participation in, 85; myth of American exceptionalism and, 85; Negro Leagues, 34–35, 85, 105, 109; origins of, 124–25; World Series (2021), 94–95. *See also* Major League Baseball; *and names of specific teams*
Baseball Club of Seattle (BCS), 137
basketball: National Basketball Association, 11, 231; support for Black Lives Matter movement, 223, 225–26; WNBA, 223, 225–26. *See also names of specific teams*
Bayor, Ronald, 35
Belton, Sharon Sayles, 186

Benjamin, Walter, 200
biometric technologies, 213–14
biopolitics: biopolitics of disposability (Giroux), 86, 95; biopower (Foucault) and, 58–59
BIPOC (Black, indigenous, and people of color), defined, 144. *See also* African Americans; Asian Americans; civil rights movement; Native Americans
Black Lives Matter (BLM) movement: Black Visions Collective, 221–22, 223; in Minneapolis, 166–67, 168, 194–95, 216–17, 221; stadium-based protests and, 194–96, 221–28; stadium surveillance and security measures and, 214; Take a Knee movement and, 221–28, 281n2
Blacks/African Americans. *See* African Americans
Blank, Arthur, 60, 66, 77, 78, 81, 82
Boeing, 106, 107–8, 137
Bonilla-Silva, Eduardo, 174, 191
Boston Red Sox, 226, 235n2
branding/place-branding, 132–36; Atlanta Olympic Games (1996) and, 27, 38–56; brands vs. commodities in, 134; Cascadian regional identity in Seattle, 158–61; Dirty Bird and African American expressive culture, 74–77, 95, 250–51n57; iconic stadiums and, 2, 134–36; Indigenous artworks and, 150–53; nature of, 132–33, 134; of neighborhoods near stadiums, 146; in New York City, 144; rise of, 132–34; SoDo neighborhood, 104, 136–46, 154, 256–57n6; sonic branding and the 12th Man moniker, 122, 131, 155–58, 160; in Washington, DC, 134
Browne, Simone, 192, 225

Camden Yards (Baltimore): comparison with other stadiums, 1, 51–52, 53, 89, 129, 183, 184–85; opening (1992), 1; Oriole Park in kick-off of third-generation stadiums, 22, 232; return to downtown urban core, 22–23
Carter and Associates, 98
CascadiaNOW, 159–60
Cascadian regional identity, 158–61

CCTV (closed-circuit television), 10–11, 21, 122–23, 196, 207–8
Centennial Olympic Stadium/Turner Field (Atlanta), 50–56, 230–31; Atlanta Braves move to Cobb County, 55–57, 59–61, 85–89, 95, 96–99; Braves Museum, 52; clubs and amenities, 52–53; comparison with other stadiums, 51, 53; design and architecture, 51–52; funding, 88; media infrastructure, 52–53; neighborhood displacement and revitalization, 53–55, 56, 57, 83, 95; sale to Georgia State University, 55, 97–99; site selection, 50–51; Turner Field Community Benefits Coalition, 98, 99
Central Intelligence platform, 212
CenturyLink Field. *See* Lumen Field
Citizen Action Force Group (CAF, Seattle), 117–18
Citizens Against the Stadium Hoax (CASH, Seattle), 115
civil rights movement: in Atlanta, 27, 31, 34, 38, 41, 48–50, 76, 94; in Minneapolis, 166, 171, 174, 191; in Seattle, 110, 113, 119
class. *See* social class
CNN (Cable News Network), 48, 51
Colangelo, Dave, 11
Collaborative Solutions Initiative, 218
color-blind racism, 87, 167, 191–92, 204, 206, 210–11, 214
Comcast, Atlanta Braves investment in, 2, 92–93
Committee to Save Seattle Center, 113
conceived space (Lefebvre), 18
Continental League (baseball), 171
convergence culture: media convergence and, 5–6; nature of, 5
Corporation for Olympic Development in Atlanta (CODA), 38, 44–45
COVID-19 pandemic, 71–72, 194–95, 221–22, 225–26, 231, 232–33
Cowboys Stadium (Dallas), 60, 223
creative class theory (Landry and Florida), 135
Crowd IQ platform, 210–11, 212
cultural geography: of Atlanta, 28, 29; of Minneapolis, 166–67; of Seattle, 148, 159, 161

Dakota Access Pipeline protests, 223
Dallas Cowboys, 60, 223
datafication: AI in, 143, 192–94, 211; ARound (augmented reality app), 211–12; in boundary management, 197–204; "data rich" vs. "data poor" (Andrejevic) and, 193–94; in encouraging good behavior, 209–16; facial recognition, 197, 213–14; facial recognition technology, 197, 213–14; forms of media technology in stadiums, 11, 193–94, 196–97; frictionless fan experience and, 59, 71–72, 73, 209–11, 214, 231; predictive analytics, 212–13; visual regimes of whiteness in stadiums, 207–8; zoning inside and outside stadiums, 204–7. *See also* media infrastructure
Dávila, Arlene, 154–55
Dayton, Mark, 183, 189
de Certeau, Michel, 200
Deleuze, Gilles, 13–14, 214–15
Dirty Bird (Atlanta Falcons), 74–77, 95, 250–51n57
Dome. *See* Georgia Dome
Down in Treme (Morgan Parmett), 12

Ecotopia (Callenbach), 159
Elias, Norbert, 4
Ellerbe Becket (now AECOM), 51, 147
Ennis Broadcasting, 137
entrepreneurship, 4; and The Battery Atlanta, 90–95; in Minneapolis, 181–82, 184; in Seattle, 105, 106–7, 113, 125–27
Eplan, Leon S., 34
ethnicity and race. *See* African Americans; Asian Americans; Native Americans; white spatial imaginary; white supremacy
ethopolitics (Rose), 80, 81
Evolv platform, 72, 211

facial recognition technology, 197, 213–14
Fancam platform, 207–8, 210, 213
FCS. *See* Atlanta–Fulton County Stadium
Federal Housing Act (1949), 37
Federal Housing Act (1954), 35–37
Fenway Park (Boston): Black Lives Matter and, 223; comparison with other stadiums, 1; as first-generation stadium, 1, 20, 51, 223
FIFA (Federation International de Football Association), 60, 77, 161
First and Goal, Inc., 147, 150, 153
first-generation stadiums (1870s–1950s): exclusion of African Americans, 20; Fenway Park, 1, 20, 51, 223; media infrastructure of, 20; nature of, 20; Sick's Stadium, 105, 109–10, 142–43
Flores, Brian, 227
Florida, Richard, 135
Floyd, George, 166, 194–95, 216–17, 219, 221
football (American): in American culture, 6; Black players in, 278n7; soccer vs., 160, 161; Take a Knee movement and, 221–28, 281n2. *See also* National Football League; Super Bowl; *and names of specific teams*
Foucault, Michel: on biopower, 58–59; on governmentality, 13; panopticon, 198, 214–15, 224–25; regime of truth, 17; technology of power, 19; theory of discourse, 17
frictionless fan experience discourse, 59, 71–72, 73, 209–11, 214, 231
Friedberg, Anne, 68, 202–4
Fulton County Stadium (FCS). *See* Atlanta–Fulton County Stadium
Fund Kids First, 185–87

Gates, Bill, 137
Gehry, Frank, 135
gender: Black feminists and politics of emotion and joy, 76; of fans, in night football games, 210; "In Her Hands" program, Georgia Resilience and Opportunity Fund, 84; sports and white male masculinity, 20, 85, 94–95, 129–30; stadium clubs and amenities and, 157–58; women and first-generation sports stadiums, 20
generations of sports stadiums, 18–23; first-generation (1870s–1950s) (*see* first-generation stadiums); second-generations (1950s–1990s) (*see* second-generation stadiums); third-generation

(1990s to present) (*see* third-generation stadiums); fourth-generation, 230–33
Georgia Dome (Atlanta), 46–50; clubs and amenities, 47–48; comparison with other stadiums, 47, 48, 53; described, 46–47; funding, 46, 47–48; media infrastructure, 47; neighborhood revitalization and displacement, 48–50, 56, 57, 77, 81, 95; opening (1992), 246n71; renovation (2006), 47; replacement by Mercedes-Benz Stadium, 60–62; site selection, 46, 48, 50
Georgia Stand-Up, 62
Georgia State University (GSU), 55, 97–99
Georgia World Congress Center Authority (GWCCA), 29–30, 35, 48, 60, 61–62, 78
Georgiou, Myria, 12
Giroux, Henry, 86, 95, 191
Goldberg, David Theo, 191
Goodell, Roger, 226, 227
Griffith, Calvin, 168, 171, 216
Guattari, Félix, 13–14
Guggenheim Museum (Bilbao, Spain), 135

Halegoua, Germaine R., 12
Hall, Stuart, 174
Haozous, Bob, 150–52
Hartsfield, William, 27
Harvey, David, 160–61
Heery International, 51
hip-hop/rap music, 29, 61, 73–77, 94, 95
HOK, 62, 63–64
Home Depot Backyard, 80–81
housing discrimination, 21–22, 35–37, 83–84, 110
Houston Astrodome, 21, 122
Hubert H. Humphrey Metrodome. *See* Metrodome

IBM, 69, 71, 72
indigenous people. *See* Native Americans
Industry Square Development Company (ISDC, Minneapolis), 176–77
inferential racism ("new racism"), 167, 174–75, 189, 191
Institution of Civil Engineers, 195–96

Jackie Robinson Stadium (UCLA), 195–96

Jackson, Maynard, 44
Jhally, Sut, 7–8
Johnson, Victoria, 8
jumbotrons, 2, 14, 47, 122, 210

Kaepernick, Colin, 221, 226, 227, 281n2
Kansas City Chiefs, 223
Keating, Larry, 28, 29–30, 53, 55
Kemp, Brian, 95
King, Martin Luther, Jr., 27, 96, 227–28
Kingdome (Seattle), 104, 110, 112–30; commemorative magazine, 121, 125; comparison with other stadiums, 112, 122, 123, 124–25, 129, 182; criticisms of, 135, 136–37; design and architecture, 122–25, 128–29, 156; funding, 113–14, 115, 129, 137; ground-breaking ceremonies (1972), 118–19; implosion (2000), 105, 129–30, 138, 147, 182–83; loss of ceiling tiles (1990), 129, 137, 189, 265–66n59; media infrastructure, 122–23, 127–28; as multipurpose stadium, 112, 122; museum, 122, 123, 143; neighborhood revitalization and displacement, 115–21; nostalgic form of working-class masculinity and, 129–30; opening (1976), 121; promotional materials for opening, 123–27; renovation (1988), 129; resistance and protests, 115–21; seating capacity, 122, 136–37; site selection, 112–15; Stadium Parking and Access Committee (SPARC), 119–20; surveillance and security, 127–28; 12th Man moniker and, 122, 131, 155–58, 160, 161
Klobuchar, Amy, 170–71, 172, 177
Koch, Nick, 186–88
Koolhaas, Rem, 124

Landry, Charles, 135
Lefebvre, Henri, 17–18, 200
legacy media, 2–3, 5. *See also* media infrastructure; television
Levenson, Bruce, 57–58
Liberty Media, 92
Lipsitz, George, 78, 165
lived space (Lefebvre), 18, 200
Los Angeles, sportification of place in, 227–28

Los Angeles Clippers, 228
Los Angeles Dodgers, 228
Loschky, Marquardt, and Nesholm, 147
Lumen Field (Seattle), 144, 146–61; art installations, 150–52, 153–54; clubs and amenities, 147–48, 157; comparison with other stadiums, 148; concessions, 147, 150, 153–54; design and architecture, 147–49, 156–57; funding, 146–47, 150, 266n60–61; integration of local culture, 149–55; media infrastructure, 157–58, 231; as multipurpose stadium, 158; opening (2002), 146–47, 231; renovations to integrate technologies, 146–61, 231; 12th Man moniker and, 160
Lury, Celia, 134
Lynch, Marshawn, 156

Major League Baseball (MLB): integration of, and decline of Negro Leagues, 85; new stadiums built since 1992, 2; sportification of place and, 227–28, 230
Major League Soccer, 59, 158–59
Manhattanism (Koolhaas), 124
Mann, Steve, 224
Mantle, Mickey, 107
Massey, Doreen, 16
massive media (Colangelo), 11
Massumi, Brian, 14–15
Mattern, Shannon, 11, 104
MBS. *See* Mercedes-Benz Stadium
McCarthy, Anna, 16
McQuire, Scott, 12
media infrastructure, 7–15; affect theory and, 14–17; CCTV systems, 10–11, 21, 122–23, 196, 207–8; of Centennial Olympic Stadium/Turner Field, 52–53; competition and expansion of, 2; convergence culture and, 5–6; corporate versus public service media and, 6; datafication of stadiums, 4–6, 196–97, 230; defined, 10; of first-generation sports stadiums, generally, 20; forms of technology in stadiums, 11, 193–94, 196–97; frictionless fan experience discourse and, 59, 71–72, 73, 209–11, 214, 231; of Georgia Dome, 47; green technology and, 231–32; impact on stadium development process, 3, 11; jumbotrons, 2, 14, 47, 122, 210; of Kingdome, 122–23, 127–28; legacy media in, 2–3, 5 (*see also* television); of Lumen Field, 157–58, 231; media company investments in sports teams, 2, 184, 235n2; media in building national identity, 20; mediatization of sports venues, 4–6, 10; media types and, 2–3; of Mercedes-Benz Stadium, 63, 66, 67–73, 214, 231; neoliberal city and (*see* neoliberal city); post-Hurricane Katrina rebuilding in New Orleans, 12–13, 95; of second-generation sports stadiums, generally, 21–22; sportification of place and (*see* sportification of place); sports/media complex (Jhally), 7–8; sports team investments in media companies, 2, 92–93; sports teams and, 2, 4–5, 235n2; stadiums as indicative of media convergence, 5–6; of Target Field, 1, 190–91, 194–97, 208, 211–14; theories of media city and, 11–12; of third-generation sports stadiums, generally, 22, 58; of T-Mobile Park, 138–39, 143; of Truist Park, 92–94; of U.S. Bank Stadium, 190–91, 196–98, 208, 213–14; World Wide Web and internet, 22, 40–41, 189, 232. *See also* datafication; social media; surveillance and security
mediasport (Wenner), 7–8, 191
mediasport cultural complex (Rowe), 7–8
mediating: social production of urban space through, 12; sports stadiums and, 10, 12, 59; as term, 7
mediatization: components of, 17; of sports venues, 4–6, 10; in urban branding, 133, 134. *See also* datafication; media infrastructure
mediatized: sports stadiums and, 10, 12, 59, 93–94; as term, 7
mediatizing: sports stadiums and, 10, 12, 59; as term, 7, 10
Mercedes-Benz Stadium (MBS, Atlanta), 57–84; clubs and amenities, 60, 66; comparison with other stadiums, 47, 48, 148; described, 62; design and architecture, 62–73, 77–78; Dirty Bird and African American expressive culture, 74–77,

Index • 291

95, 250–51n57; frictionless fan experience and, 59, 71–72, 73, 209–11, 214, 231; funding, 60, 62, 63, 82; Halo, 63, 65–66, 67; media infrastructure, 63, 66, 67–73, 214, 231; as multipurpose stadium, 59; neighborhood revitalization and displacement, 82–83, 97; Oculus, 63–65, 67–68; opening (2017), 62, 231; "Red" channels, 63; Westside Development Initiative, 77–84, 219; Window to the City, 63, 67–70, 148

Metrodome (Minneapolis), 171–89; comparison with other stadiums, 180–81, 182, 183, 184–85; criticism of, 183–85; design and architecture, 182, 183–84; funding, 172, 173–74, 176; highways and, 175; inferential racial logic and, 167, 174–75, 189, 191; as multipurpose stadium, 1, 183–84; neighborhood revitalization and displacement, 172–73, 177–80; opening (1982), 181–82, 183; as replacement for Metropolitan Stadium, 167, 172; roof collapse (2010), 189; site selection, 174–81, 188

Metropolitan Atlanta Olympic Games Authority, 45

Metropolitan Sports Facilities Commission (MSFC, Minneapolis), 175–77, 184–85, 187–88

Metropolitan Stadium (Bloomington, Minnesota), 167, 168–71; criticism of, 171; funding, 170–71; as multipurpose stadium, 171; opening (1956), 168, 171; site selection, 168–70

Miami Dolphins, 227

Microsoft, 77, 103, 132, 137, 146

Miller, Toby, 232

Milwaukee Braves, move to Atlanta (1966), 30, 31–32, 110

Milwaukee Brewers, 110

Minneapolis, 165–219; Black Lives Matter movement and, 166–67, 168, 194–95, 216–17, 221; Cedar-Riverside neighborhood, 178–80; central cultural district, 172; civil rights movement and, 171; comparison with other cities, 168; Dakota Access Pipeline protests, 223; Elliot Park neighborhood, 178–82; entrepreneurship and boosterism, 181–82, 184; Industry Square, 176–77, 178, 180–81; "Minnesota nice" and, 167; Minnesota paradox (Myers), 166–67; Phillips neighborhood, 178–80; social justice initiatives, 216–19; sportification of place in, 23, 200, 222; Super Bowl (2018), 213, 221–22, 223; University of Minnesota campus, 178. *See also* Metrodome; Metropolitan Stadium; Target Field; U.S. Bank Stadium; white spatial imaginary

Minneapolis Millers, 168

Minnesota Ballpark Authority, 200

Minnesota North Stars, 184, 185

Minnesotans Against a Downtown Dome (MADD), 172–73, 177

Minnesota Public Advocacy Research Team (MPART), 185–86

Minnesota Timberwolves, 184

Minnesota Twins, 1, 183–84, 235n2; formerly Washington (DC) Senators, 168, 171; mobile app, 210; social justice initiatives, 216–19. *See also* Metrodome; Metropolitan Stadium; Target Field

Minnesota Vikings, 1, 171, 183, 187–88, 189; mobile app, 209, 210, 211; social justice initiatives, 216; Super Bowl (2018), 213, 221–22, 223; technology operations management, 196–97. *See also* Metropolitan Stadium; U.S. Bank Stadium

Model Cities program (1967–1974), 108–9

Morley, David, 10

Mortenson, 201

Naramore, Bain, Brady, and Johanson (NBBJ), 122, 140, 142

National Basketball Association (NBA): COVID-19 pandemic and, 231; mediatization of sports and, 11. *See also names of specific teams*

National Football Conference (NFC) championship, 74

National Football League (NFL): "ghettocentric" aesthetics and, 9–10; new stadiums built since 1992, 2; sportification of place and, 227–28, 230; Take a Knee Movement, 221–28, 281n2; ties to the military, 6. *See also names of specific teams*

Native Americans: Atlanta Braves name and, 94; Atlanta Braves Tomahawk Chop and, 94–95; Dakota Access Pipeline protests, 223; displacement for Metrodome, 178–80; Lumen Field art installations and, 150–53; Seattle Seahawk mascot and, 153
Negro Leagues, 34–35, 85, 105, 109
neoliberal city: Atlanta as, 38–39, 53, 55, 73–77; biopolitics of disposability (Giroux) and, 86, 95; branding/place-branding and, 132–36; cultural ontology of sport and, 79–80, 81; Minneapolis as, 177, 195; racially coded signifiers of Blackness and multiculturalism in, 9, 74–77, 95; roll-back neoliberalism (Brenner and Theodore), 38; roll-out neoliberalism (Brenner and Theodore), 38–39; Seattle as, 105, 154–55; self-reliant individualism and, 4, 38, 55; sportified fans as ideal subjects, 74–77, 95, 227; waning of social welfare state and, 9
neoliberal racism, 95, 167, 191–92, 204
New England Sports Network, 235n2
New Orleans: New Orleans Superdome, 122; Tyler Perry and, 28–29; post-Hurricane Katrina rebuilding, 12–13, 95
New Orleans Saints, 74
News Corporation, 235n2
New York City: Amazon proposed urban development in, 136; Hudson Yards as model for Centennial Yards, 77; SoHo and place-branding, 144; World Trade Center terrorist attacks (2001), 6
New York Yankees, 2, 138
Nintendo of America, 132, 137–38
Nishiyama, Hidefumi, 194
North American Soccer League (NASL), 110, 158–60
NuLoop Partners, 186

OL (Olympique Lyonnais) Reign Stadium. *See* Lumen Field
Olympic Games: Atlanta (1996), 27, 38–56; International Olympic Committee, 40
Omni International (later CNN Center, Atlanta), 38

Other/Otherness: African Americans and, 76, 176; Asian Americans and, 127, 137; discipline and control, 22, 58–59, 75, 190, 214–15, 223, 224; as threat, 17, 54, 215

Pantheon (Rome), 63–64
Parks, Lisa, 10
People and Causes (1974 public access TV series), 178
perceived space (Lefebvre), 18
Perry, Tyler, 28–29
Pike, Andy, 134
PNC Park (Pittsburgh), 186
Pohlad, Bill, 217–18
Pohlad, Carl, 183–84, 185
Pohlad Foundation, 185, 217–19
Populous, 195, 197, 204, 209, 215
post-racialism, 9, 22, 167, 191, 206, 210, 211, 215–16
power dynamics: biopower (Foucault) and, 58–59; hierarchies of race, class, and gender in, 20; social space and, 18; sports stadiums and, 11–12, 16, 18, 19. *See also* racism; surveillance and security
Praeger-Kavanaugh-Waterbury, 122

Qwest Field. *See* Lumen Field

racism: color-blind, 87, 167, 191–92, 204, 206, 210–11, 214; inferential ("new racism"), 167, 174–75, 189, 191; in media infrastructure, 21–22, 194, 204–7; neoliberal, 95, 167, 191–92, 204; post-racialism and, 9, 22, 167, 191, 206, 210, 211, 215–16; social justice initiatives, 216–19; in stadium site selection process, 174–75. *See also* surveillance and security; white spatial imaginary; white supremacy
Ranier Beer Company, 109
rap music/hip-hop, 29, 61, 73–77, 94, 95
Rask, Ricky, 185
Reed, Kasim, 60–61, 97
Roc Nation, 227
Rose, Nikolas, 39, 80
Rosser International, 51
Rowe, David, 3, 7–8, 236n5
Ruano, Frank, 113, 115

Ruth, Babe, 123
Rybak, R.T., 182

Safeco Field (Seattle), 138
Santos, Bob, 119–21
Sassen, Saskia, 38
Seattle, 103–61; Asian American population, 103, 104, 106, 115–21, 127, 142, 150–55; Baseball Club of Seattle, 137; Cascadian regional identity and, 158–61; Chinatown-International District, 104, 115–21, 127, 142, 146, 150, 153–55, 256–57n6; cultural geography of, 148, 159, 161; described, 103–5; Dugsdale stadium, 109; entrepreneurship and boosterism, 105, 106–7, 113, 125–27; Forward Thrust urban renewal campaign, 106–11, 113, 118; as a global city, 103, 105, 106, 128, 132, 137–38; highways in, 109–10; historic preservation and districts, 120–21, 127, 131, 155; nature and environmental movement in, 113, 114–15, 116, 126–27, 143, 148, 150–52; Pike Place market, 118, 257n18; Pioneer Square neighborhood, 104, 115–21, 127, 131, 140, 142, 146, 149–50, 154–55, 256–57n6, 257n18; place-identity, 104–5; Seattle Center, 106, 110, 112–14, 128; SoDo neighborhood, 104, 136–46, 154, 256–57n6; sportification of place in, 23, 136–46; suburbanization and, 106; super Bowl bid (1979) and, 128; as a technology hub, 103, 105, 106, 107–8, 132, 137; white consumers and, 108; World's Fair (1962), 106, 107–8, 114–15, 157. *See also* Kingdome; Lumen Field; Sick's Stadium; T-Mobile Park
Seattle Kraken, 143–44
Seattle Mariners, 110; acquisition by Ennis Broadcasting (1989), 137; acquisition by Nintendo of America, 137–38; American League and, 138. *See also* Kingdome; T-Mobile Park
Seattle Pilots, 109–10, 114
Seattle Rainiers, 106, 109, 110, 142
Seattle Seahawks, 110; Super Bowl defeat of Denver Broncos (2014), 131, 156, 157; team mascot and Native Americans, 153;

12th Man moniker and, 122, 131, 155–58, 160, 161. *See also* Kingdome; Lumen Field
Seattle Sounders, 110, 158–60
Seattle Steelheads, 109
Seattle Supersonics, 110
second-generation stadiums (1950s–1990s), 20–23; in Atlanta (*see* Atlanta–Fulton County Stadium; Georgia Dome); highways and, 21–22; Houston Astrodome, 21, 122; inferential racism ("new racism"), 167, 174–75, 189, 191; legacy media in, 20–23; media infrastructure in, 21–22 (*see also* media infrastructure; surveillance and security); in Minneapolis area (*see* Metrodome; Metropolitan Stadium); nature of, 20–21; in Seattle (*see* Kingdome); stadium design and architecture in, 135–36; suburbanization and, 21–22
security. *See* surveillance and security
Seigworth, Greg, 14
self-reliant individualism, 4, 38, 55
Sick, Emil, 109
Sick's Stadium (Seattle), 105, 109–10, 142–43
Skidmore, Owings, and Merrill (SOM), 182
Skilling, Helle, Christiansen and Robertson, 122
Sleepless in Seattle (1993 film), 132
smart stadiums (Yang and Cole), 193
Smith, Janet Marie, 51
Smith, Tommie, 225
soccer: American football vs., 160, 161; FIFA World Cup (Atlanta, 2026), 60, 77, 161; Major League Soccer, 59, 158–59; North American Soccer League, 110, 158–60; Spotify Camp Nou (Barcelona), 229–30, 232. *See also* names of specific teams
social class: Cascadian regional identity and, 158–61; classist ideologies of urban decline and, 9; first-generation sports stadiums and, 20, 21; neighborhood revitalization and displacement in Atlanta, 35–37, 40–46, 48–50, 53–57, 77–84, 95, 97; neighborhood revitalization and displacement in Minneapolis, 172–73, 177–80; neighborhood revitalization and displacement in Seattle, 115–21;

social class (*continued*): second-generation sports stadiums and, 21; Skid Road Shelter Project (Seattle), 116, 117, 121, 127; stadium clubs and amenities and, 47–48, 52–53, 60, 66, 142–43, 147–48, 157–58, 204–6, 208, 211; 12th Man moniker and, 122, 131, 155–58, 160, 161; white masculinity and, 20, 21, 85, 94–95, 129–30; zoning inside and outside stadiums, 204–7

social media: fan performativity (Rowe) and, 3, 236n5; Mercedes-Benz Stadium (Atlanta) and, 69–70, 71; monitoring, by stadiums, 69–70; smart phone access and, 3

SoFi Stadium (Los Angeles), 227–28

SOM (Skidmore, Owings, and Merrill), 182

sonic branding, 12th Man moniker in, 122, 131, 155–58, 160

spatial triad theory (Lefebvre), 18

Spinoza, Baruch, 13

sportification of place, 3–7; in Atlanta, 23, 38–56, 58, 59, 73–77, 79–80, 93–94, 96–99; branding/place-branding and, 2, 134–36 (*see also* branding/place-branding); components of, 23; Dirty Bird (Atlanta Falcons) and, 74–77, 95, 250–51n57; globalizing, 6, 228–30; history of sportization and (Elias and Dunning), 4; in Los Angeles, 227–28; media in (*see* media infrastructure); in Minneapolis, 23, 200, 222; national identity and, 4; nature and components of, 3–4; research on extending cultural logic of sport and, 5–6; sociality in everyday sense and, 4; space vs. place and, 15–18, 79–80; sportified citizenship and government and, 200, 209–16; sports/media complex and, 7–8; stadium districts in, 77, 89, 92, 228; white masculinity and, 20, 21, 85, 94–95, 129–30. *See also* generations of sports stadiums

sportization (Elias and Dunning), 3–4

sportscape (Bale), 18–19

sports media. *See* media infrastructure

sports/media complex (Jhally), 7–8

sports stadiums (generally): affect theory and, 13–17; American vs. European, 3, 4, 6; COVID-19 and other uses of, 231; design guides, 274–75n7; economics of, 183–85; generations of (*see* generations of sports stadiums); history of, 19; media company strategies and, 2–3; media convergence and, 5–6; media market impact on development of, 3; as media-sport-spaces, 7–15; mediatization of sports venues, 4–6, 10; power dynamics and, 11–12, 16, 18, 19; protests against racial injustice, 194–96, 221–28; role in city and regional identity, 2; Roman, 63–64, 123; as sacred spaces, 65–66; site-specificity and, 16; social media and, 3 (*see also* social media); space vs. place and, 15–18; state and local incentives for, 2; urban governance and, 3; urban media infrastructure and, 7–15. *See also* sportification of place; *and names of specific stadiums*

Spotify Camp Nou (Barcelona), 229–30, 232

SSB Consulting, 212

stadiums. *See* generations of sports stadiums; sports stadiums; *and names of specific stadiums*

starchitects, 136

Steinbrueck, Victor, 118

St. Paul Saints, 168

St. Peter, David, 195, 201, 206, 216–17

suburbanization, 21–22, 90–95, 106; highway systems and, 21–22, 33, 35, 37, 54, 109–10, 175; "white flight" trend and, 9, 21–22, 89, 96–99, 110, 167–70, 180. *See also* Metropolitan Stadium; Truist Park

Super Bowl: Atlanta (2019), 48, 60, 70, 72, 74; Los Angeles (2022), 227–28; Minneapolis (2018), 213, 221–22, 223; Seattle bid for (1979), 128; Seattle Seahawks defeat of Denver Broncos (2014), 131, 156, 157; Tampa (2021), 226

surveillance and security, 190–219; African Americans and, 43, 110, 169, 214; artificial intelligence in, 143, 192–94, 211; athletes and, 208; biometric technologies, 213–14; boundary management in, 197–204; CCTV systems, 10–11, 21, 122–23, 196, 207–8; crowd control and risk management in, 194–207; data analytics and, 165, 192–94, 197, 209–16; encouraging good behavior through, 209–16; facial recognition, 197, 213–14; at Kingdome, 127–28; at Mercedes-Benz Stadium, 68, 72–73, 214; panopticon (Foucault) and, 198, 214–15, 224–25; policing in, 215; predictive analytics, 212–13; racism in, 21–22, 194, 204–7; role in racial ordering, 192–94; in second-generation stadiums, 21–22; sousveillance (surveillance from below) and, 224–25, 228; at Target Field, 1.190–91, 194–97, 204–6, 208, 211–14; at U.S. Bank Stadium, 190–91, 196–98, 208, 213–14; zoning within and outside the stadium and, 204–7

Swift, Taylor, 158

Take a Knee movement, 221–28, 281n2
Target Field (Minneapolis), 167, 168, 183–89; ARound (augmented reality app), 211–12; boundary management, 197, 198–99, 204–6; clubs and amenities, 204–6, 208; commemorative souvenir book, 189, 199–200; Committee of 17 (C-17), 186–89; community cohesion and, 200–201, 204; comparisons with other stadiums, 1, 186; concessions, 201; design and architecture, 194–96, 201, 204–6; funding, 185–89; localism in construction and operation, 1, 201; media infrastructure, 1, 190–91, 194–97, 208, 211–14; opening (2010), 1, 216; proponents of, 183–85; seating, 204–5; site selection, 188–89; views of city, 199–200, 202; zoning inside and outside, 204–6
television: analog vs. digital engagement with sports and, 5; CCTV systems, 10–11, 21, 122–23, 196, 207–8; CNN, 48, 51; Comcast/NBC Universal, 2, 92–93; in-person attendance vs., 2–3; revenue from live sports, 5; in second-generation sports stadiums, 21; WTBS cable station, 30, 51, 235n2
Texas A&M University, 122
third-generation stadiums (1990s to present): in Atlanta (*see* Centennial Olympic Stadium; Mercedes-Benz Stadium; Truist Park); color-blind racism and, 87, 167, 191–92, 204, 206, 210–11, 214; in Minne-apolis area (*see* Metrodome; Target Field; U.S. Bank Stadium); nature of, 22–23; neoliberal racism and, 95, 167, 191–92, 204; Oriole Park in kickoff of, 232; in Seattle (*see* Lumen Field; T-Mobile Park); stadium debate and, 183–89; stadium design and architecture and, 135–36, 232; surveillance and security, 190–219

T-Mobile Park (Seattle), 136–46; art installations, 150–52; clubs and amenities, 142–43; comparison with other stadiums, 186; concessions, 139; design and architecture, 138–42, 143; funding, 138, 264n37; Home Plate Center development, 146; media infrastructure, 138–39, 143; museum, 142–43; naming rights, 138; rail access and, 141; Washington State Major League Baseball Stadium Public Facilities Board (PFD), 138–40, 143–44

Tomahawk Chop (Atlanta Braves), 94–95
topophilia (Bale): Dirty Bird (Atlanta Falcons) and, 75, 77; nature of, 15; sonic effects at music concerts and, 158; Tuan on, 15–16
Truist Park (Cobb County, Georgia), 85–99; The Battery Atlanta, 90–95; comparison with other stadiums, 48, 89; design and architecture, 90–92; funding, 90; media infrastructure, 92–94; as mixed-use development/stadium district, 89, 90–95; opposition to Braves move to, 96–99; role in urbanizing the suburban, 90–95; site selection, 86–89
Trump, Donald, 94, 158, 224, 269n100
Tuan, Yi-Fu, 15–16
Turner, Ted: Atlanta Braves and, 11, 30, 51, 235n2, 246n84; CNN and, 51; WTBS cable station, 30, 51, 235n2
Turner Field. *See* Centennial Olympic Stadium/Turner Field
12th Man moniker, 122, 131, 155–58, 160
24/7 Software, 196–97
Twin Cities, defined, 166. *See also* Minneapolis
Twins Community Fund (TCF), 217, 218–19

UBS. *See* U.S. Bank Stadium
Uhlman, Wesley C., 113, 119

University District Improvement Association (UDIA, Minneapolis), 178
University of Washington Huskies, 104–5, 147, 161
urban governance: citizenship and identity as ideals, 8–9, 23, 79–80; media market and sports stadium development, 3; sportification of place and (*see* sportification of place)
U.S. Bank Stadium (UBS, Minneapolis): boundary management, 197–99, 201–4, 205–6; clubs and amenities, 205–6, 208, 211; commemorative souvenir book, 189, 201; Crowd IQ platform, 210–11, 212; design and architecture, 201–4, 205–6; frictionless fan experience and, 209, 210–11; media infrastructure, 190–91, 196–98, 208, 213–14; as multipurpose stadium, 197–98; opening (2016), 216; site selection, 188; Super Bowl (2018), 213, 221–22; views of city, 199–200, 201–4; zoning inside and outside stadium, 205–6

Vick, Michael, 61
virtually mobile gaze (Friedberg), 68

War on Poverty, 108–9
Washington, D.C.: urban branding in, 134; Washington Senators move to Minnesota, 168, 171
Washington State Public Stadium Authority (PSA), 146, 147, 153–54
Washington State Stadium Commission, 112–14
West, Cornel, 227
West Coast Negro Baseball Association, 109
Western Management Consultants, 112–14
Westside Tax Allocation District Community Improvement Fund (Atlanta), 62
white spatial imaginary (Lipsitz), 168, 171–72, 175–78, 182, 190–92, 194, 196; boundary management in, 197–204; color-blind racism and, 87, 167, 191–92, 204, 206, 210, 214; inferential ("new racism") and, 167, 174–75, 189, 191; Lipsitz on, 165, 207; nature of, 165–67; neoliberal racism and, 95, 167, 191–92, 204; stadium as white space and, 222–23; visual regimes of whiteness, 207–8; zoning inside and outside stadiums and, 204–7
white supremacy: Dirty Bird and African American expressive culture, 74–77, 95, 250–51n57; nature of, 270n3; "white flight" trend and, 9, 21–22, 89, 96–99, 110, 167–70, 180; white homogeneity and, 170–71. *See also* white spatial imaginary
Williams, Jeannette, 118
Williams-Russell and Johnson, 51
WNBA (Women's National Basketball Association), 223, 225–26
World Series (2021), 94–95
World Trade Center terrorist attacks (2001), 6
Wrigley Field (Chicago), 51
WTBS cable station (Atlanta), 30, 51, 235n2

Yamauchi, Hiroshi, 137
YES network, New York Yankees investment in, 2
Yreka Rebellion (1941), 159

HELEN MORGAN PARMETT is the Edwin W. Lawrence Professor of Forensics and an associate professor of English and Film and Television studies at the University of Vermont. She is the author of *Down in Treme: Race, Place, and New Orleans on Television*.

The University of Illinois Press
is a founding member of the
Association of University Presses.

Composed in 10.25/13 Marat Pro
with Trade Gothic LT Std display
by Lisa Connery
at the University of Illinois Press

University of Illinois Press
1325 South Oak Street
Champaign, IL 61820-6903
www.press.uillinois.edu